Contents

About the Contributors

John H. Westerhoff III is Professor of Religion and Education at the Divinity School of Duke University.

O. C. Edwards, Jr., is President and Dean of Seabury-Western Theological Seminary. Formerly he taught New Testament and Patristics at Nashotah House.

Leonel L. Mitchell is Professor of Liturgics at Seabury-Western Theological Seminary.

Milton McC. Gatch is Academic Dean and Professor of Church History at Union Theological Seminary.

William P. Haugaard is Professor of Church History at Seabury-Western Theological Seminary.

Fredrica Harris Thompsett is Executive Director of the Episcopal Church's Board for Theological Education and Adjunct Professor of Church History at The General Theological Seminary. Formerly she taught Church History at Seabury-Western Theological Seminary.

Sister Mary Charles Bryce, O.S.B., is Associate Professor of Religion and Religious Education in the School of Religious Studies of The Catholic University of America.

Constance J. Tarasar, Lecturer in Religious Education at St. Vladimir's Orthodox Theological Seminary, was formerly Executive Secretary both of the Department of Religious Education of the Orthodox Church of America and of the Orthodox Christian Education Commission.

John E. Booty is Professor of Church History at Episcopal Divinity School.

Foreword

This book grew out of a conversation. O. C. Edwards told John Westerhoff that he believed that Westerhoff's efforts to help contemporary Christians move from a school model of Christian formation to a fuller catechesis could be aided by a historical argument. A survey of the history of catechesis would show that the school model, taken for granted by many, is actually a relative late-comer on the scene of socialization into the church. With the transience of this model demonstrated, those involved in catechetical responsibility might be enabled to question its adequacy and to become open to wider and deeper possibilities.

Westerhoff agreed and was excited about the idea, but felt that the history should be written by specialists in the various periods rather than by one person. Together the two began to compile a list of the colleagues who could be most helpful in the task and to solicit their collaboration. A look at the list of contributors will show how successful they were in their efforts to find the best.

The shape of the book as assembled is rather like that of a hero sandwich. A number of slices of historical research are fitted between two hunks of Westerhoff's reflections on the catechetical task. The first of these, which deals with the challenge of catechesis, seeks to define the catechetical task in its wholeness so that we will be less willing to be satisfied with any reductionist approaches to the task. This presentation also serves to prepare the reader for the variety of catechetical methods that will be encountered in the historical chapters. The second contribution of Westerhoff is the final chapter of the book, which looks to the future of Christian formation. It begins with a critique of the current norm in catechesis, the Sunday School, sketches in the components of a full catechetical program, and concludes with Westerhoff's vision of a life-long pilgrimage in faith that has seven stages, each with its catechetical and liturgical component. The relation of Westerhoff's normative and methodological bread to the historical meat, cheese, lettuce, tomatoes, and onions is implicit rather than explicit, but the flavor and the dietary adequacy of either would be diminished considerably without the other.

This history of catechesis could not have been written without the efforts of many co-laborers. First and foremost are the scholars who wrote the history. A number had already done considerable research on catechesis during their periods. Others engaged in work that was new for them and, we believe, trailblazing for the scholarship of their periods. For their enthusiasm, cooperativeness, and erudition, we are grateful. Several persons contributed much to the editorial task. Among these, Mrs. Eleanor Petersen of Seabury-Western, Mrs. Anne Kellam of Duke, and Mr. Daniel Sullivan of Morehouse-Barlow are especially to be thanked.

Our only regret is that the editor under whom the work was begun did not live to see it completed. Robert Gilday had edited books by both authors before and, in the course of doing so, had befriended them in innumerable ways as he had many other authors before and after them. This book was offered to Morehouse-Barlow because he was there, and the original intention, of which he was never informed, was that it would be dedicated to him. Now it can only be offered in his memory. We are consoled, though, by the thought that somewhere among the choirs of angels and archangels, Bob sits with a puckish grin over all this fuss and continues to intercede with higher powers for us as he has done so often in the past.

The Present Situation

Chapter 1
The Challenge: Understanding the Problem of Faithfulness

John H. Westerhoff III

This book is about catechesis, the process by which persons are initiated into the Christian community and its faith, revelation, and vocation; the process by which persons throughout their lifetimes are continually converted and nurtured, transformed and formed, by and in its living tradition.

It needs to be acknowledged, however, that the words *catechetics, catechesis, catechist,* and *catechumen* typically have not been used by Protestants. Further, among Roman Catholics these words have become associated in the modern period with the ecclesiastical establishment and with conservative efforts at doctrinal indoctrination. Nevertheless these words have surfaced very recently in parts of the Protestant world outside the United States and also are being reaffirmed and reformed within the Roman Catholic Church.

Catechesis in the early church, while associated with a pedagogical strategy (verbal transmission), had a broader and deeper meaning functionally. To be either literalistic or restrictive in the use of language prevents meaningful discourse over time. The archaic character of the word "catechesis" provides a sense of continuity with the past in a day when our efforts are shallow because we are singularly enamored with the new and with the ways of our scientific, post-enlightenment, modern age. The fact that "catechesis" is a word with no commonly agreed upon meaning can make it a most helpful symbol in a day when people are erroneously looking for impossible absolutes and certainties. Every age must be open to new insights; every age must adjust to given social conditions. A term which can bridge history and provide a basis for new understandings gives us an openness to the future which is just as essential as our rootage in the past. Further, in an ecumenical era it is good to have a word whose use goes back to a time when the church was united. It is my contention that we need to re-establish and re-define the word "catechesis." One way to do that is to describe it phenomenologically and then to examine the phenomenon as it appears in its various forms and with its diverse aims throughout the history of the church.

The word "catechesis" is derived from a Greek word which means *to resound or echo, to celebrate or imitate, to repeat another's words and deeds.* When first used by the church it referred to the activity of instruction by oral repetition. That is, persons were taught by having them sing out the answers to posed questions. Nevertheless, while that was the way the word was used at first, we always need to be careful not to confuse a phenomenon with its particular cultural or historical expression. The meaning of catechesis, as we propose to use it, is much richer than its original use.

By catechesis we mean every activity used by the church to celebrate and imitate the word or actions of God. Through catechesis the community of faith proclaims its faith in word and deed and calls itself to a more living, conscious, and active faith. As such catechesis includes *kerygma* and *didache. Kerygma* points to the proclamation or announcement of the Gospel—the action of God in Jesus Christ; it is a call to new perceptions, experiences, and actions; it is "preaching" through deeds and words for the transformation of human life, personal and social; its aim is conversion or new beginnings and the internalization of the Gospel. *Didache* points to the illumination or the making sense of our experiences, to the interpretation and the application of faith; it is teaching for the formation of a Christian life style; its aim is nurture or growing-up in the faith. As such, catechesis involves all those actions within a community of faith that enhance and enliven faith, that make divine revelation known, and that aid persons and the community in realizing their vocation.

Catechesis is best understood as the process content of the Christian faith. It answers three "how" (not "what") questions: (1) How is faith (understood as perception) acquired, enhanced, and enlivened, or how do we come to know God and Salvation? (2) How is divine revelation (understood as experience of God and Salvation) made known, or how do we live in relationship to God?

and (3) How is vocation (understood as reflective action) realized, or how do we act with God in history on behalf of salvation?

Catechesis is the symbolic, interactive, dialectical process (not technique) of enculturation and acculturation. Catechesis is addressed within a living, learning, worshipping, witnessing community of faith. To catechize is to participate with others in the life-long pilgrimage of catechesis. To be a catechumen is to be a pilgrim; to be a catechist is to be a compassionate companion and guide to pilgrims.

Catechetics and catechesis designate ways or means of believing, being, and behaving in community, and not any particular context such as school or family, or end such as particular ideas a person "acquires" or "receives." Rather, catechesis, understood as process, is best defined as deliberate, systematic and sustained interpersonal helping relationships of acknowledged value which aid persons and their communities to know God, to live in relationship to God, and to act with God in the world.

Catechesis is not simply accidental, but implies intentional, mindful, responsible, faithful activities; is not only for children, but implies life-long sustained efforts; is not indoctrination, but implies the necessity of open, mutually helpful interpersonal relationships and interactions of persons within a community; is not concerned with just one aspect of life, but with all of life—the political, the social, and the economic. Catechesis implies the presence of something we can only call "wholeness", that is, it involves the entire person, the totality of his or her life, and it affects all of that person's relationships—with God, self, neighbor, and the natural world.

Catechesis aims to provide persons with a context for experiencing the converting and nurturing presence of Christ, day by day as they gather in the Lord's name with other baptized persons to be confronted by God's Word and Gospel, to respond to the gift of faith, to pray for the world and church, to share God's peace, to present the offerings and oblations of their life and labor, to make thanksgiving for God's grace, break bread and share the gifts of God, and thereby be nourished to love and serve the Lord. Catechesis aims to provide persons with a context for falling in love with Christ, so that, having their eyes and ears opened, they might perceive and experience personally the Gospel of God's kingdom come. It further aims to provide a context for persons to live in a growing and developing relationship with Christ, so that they might be a sign of God's kingdom come.

Finally, it aims to provide a context for persons to reflect and act with Christ on behalf of God's kingdom.

The church is the family of God—a visible, historical, human community called to convert and nurture people in the Gospel tradition so that they might live under its merciful judgment and inspiration, to the end that God's will is done and God's kingdom (community or government) comes. The church is the body of Christ—a hidden, prophetic creature of God's spirit, an instrument of God's transforming power, and a witness to God's continuing revelation in history.

It is one church, a paradox to the mind: sinful yet holy; immanent yet transcendent; divided yet one; continuously in need of reform yet the bearer of God's transforming eternal Word; a human institution and a holy community; a disparate assembly of baptized sinners living, sometimes unconsciously, by grace yet also an intentional, obedient, steadfast, faithful company of converted, visible saints; a mystery even to itself but aware, in often incomprehensible ways, that it has a mission in the world and a ministry, both to those who by birth or decision find themselves, not entirely by choice, within that family which bears the name Christian, and to all people.

The church's mission, like Christ's, is to live in and for the Gospel, to witness *to* and to be a sign *of* God's coming kingdom. That is, to become what it already is (only more so): the incarnate body of Christ.

The church is a pilgrim community of memory and vision. The vocation of the church is to hear God speak, to see God act, and to witness in word and deed to these experiences. Christianity from the beginning has been essentially a missionary community: the Gospel has been committed to the community. The responsibility of being a living sign of and a witness to that Gospel is the vocation of every Christian. Christians, as ambassadors of Christ and the Gospel, are to be of service to all people so that individual and corporate life might be more truly human and enriching.

Catechesis implies the need for (1) a knowledge and understanding of the Church's living tradition and the reflective cognitive abilities to use that tradition in responsible decision-making, (2) a deepened authentic piety that unifies attitudes, sensibilities, motivations, commitments and values into an exemplary style of life in community, and (3) a clear vision of God's will for individual and corporate human life with concomitant skills for its realization.

Thereby are believing, being (becoming), and behaving united in the lives of persons who in community have a relationship to Christ and a commitment to the Gospel.

Catechesis is a pastoral ministry. It is a ministry of the Word, in which the faith is proclaimed and interpreted in verbal and nonverbal ways for the formation and transformation of persons and the community whose end is a lived love-relationship with God and neighbor. It is a ministry of the Word in which persons are both converted and initiated into, and nurtured and nourished in, an understanding and way of life. Catechesis occurs within a community of faith where persons strive to be Christian together. Catechesis aims to enable the faith community to live under the judgment and inspiration of the Gospel to the end that God's will is done and God's community comes. It unites all deliberate, systematic and sustained efforts to discover the vision and will of God, to evaluate the community's interior and exterior life, and to equip and stimulate the community for greater faithfulness.

Not only do people need to understand and affirm catechesis, they need to be helped to envision its actualization within parish life and to plan, develop, and actualize those sorts of communal activities which will contribute to its realization in the lives of persons and the community.

Catechesis, as a pastoral activity of intentional socialization, includes every aspect of the church's life intended to incorporate persons into the life of an ever-changing (reforming), tradition-bearing (catholic) community of Christian faith. It is a process intended both to recall and to reconstruct the church's tradition so that it might become conscious and active in the lives of maturing persons and communities. It is the process by which persons learn to know, internalize, and apply the Christian revelation in daily individual and corporate life. As such, catechesis aims to enable the faithful to meet the two-fold responsibility which Christian faith asks of them: community with God and neighbor. Catechesis, therefore, is a life's work shared by all those who participate in the mission and ministry of the Christian Church. It values the interaction of faithing souls in community, striving to be faithful in-but-not-of the world. The fundamental question which catechesis asks is this: What is it to be Christian together in community and in the world? To answer this question is to understand the means by which we *become* Christian within a community of faith. Catechesis, therefore, intends to aid us to understand the implications of Christian faith for life and our lives, to evaluate critically every aspect of our individual and corporate understandings and ways, and to become equipped and inspired for faithful activity in church and society.

Importantly, catechesis acknowledges that we are enculturated or socialized within a community of memory and vision. Baptism incorporates us into a family with a story, a living tradition. This adoption into a new community creates a change intrinsic to the self. We are historical beings, implicitly and explicitly influenced and formed by the communities in which we live and grow. Catechesis acknowledges this influence and challenges all persons to be morally responsible both for the ways in which they live in community and for the ways by which they influence the lives of others. While catechesis affirms that persons are both determined and free, the product of nurture and the agent of nurture, it makes it incumbent upon the community of faith to accept responsibility for disciplined, intentional, faithful, obedient life together. Still, we cannot afford to believe that nurture alone provides an adequate understanding of the educational ministry of the church. Without evangelization and conversion, nurture is inadequate.

Until we acknowledge the place of evangelization as an aspect of catechesis, nurture will remain impotent. Evangelization refers to the process by which the Christian community of faith, through the proclamation of the Gospel in word and deed, leads persons inside and outside the church to radical reorientations in their perceptions, experiences, and lives. Evangelization testifies, through transformed lives, to the acts of God both within and without the community of faith. When we evangelize we witness through word-in-deed to the acts of God in Jesus Christ. Without this witness to the Lordship of Christ, to the good news of God's new possibility, and to the Gospel's prophetic protest against all false religiousness, the church loses its soul and becomes an institution of cultural continuity maintaining the status quo, rather than an institution of cultural change living in and for God's kingdom. Evangelization as one aspect of catechesis (the other being assimilation) is best understood, therefore, as the means by which the church continually transforms its life and the lives of its people into a body of committed believers, willing to give anything and everything to the cause of mediating historically God's reconciling love in the world.

Christian faith runs counter to many ordinary understandings and ways of life. It is hardly possible for anything less than a converted, disciplined body to be the historical agent of God's work in the world. Conversions are a necessary aspect of ever-developing mature Christian faith whether or not one grows up in the church. The church can no longer surrender to the illusion that child nurture, in and of itself, can or will rekindle the fire of Christian faith either in persons or in the church. We have expected too much of nurture. We can nurture persons into institutional religion, but not into mature Christian faith. The Christian faith by its very nature demands conversions. We do not gradually educate persons to be Christian. To be Christian is to be baptized into the community of the faithful, but to be a mature Christian is to be continually converted and nurtured in the Gospel tradition within a living community of Christian faith.

Authentic Christian life is personal and social life lived on behalf of God's reign in the political, social, economic world. One cannot be nurtured into such life—not in this world. Every culture (and institution, including the church) strives to socialize persons to live in harmony with life as it is. The culture calls upon its religious institutions to bless the status quo, and it calls upon religion's educational institutions to nurture persons into an acceptance of life as it is.

But God calls his/her people to be signs of Shalom, the vanguard of God's kingdom, a community of cultural change. To live in the conviction that such countercultural life is our Christian vocation in-but-not-of the world necessitates conversion as well as nurture.

Who but the converted can adequately nurture? And who but the nurtured can be adequately prepared for the radicalness of transformed life? Without the witness of Word-in-deed, which is the evangelical act, conversion cannot occur. Without nurture, the converted cannot adequately bear witness in the world. Unless conversion and nurture both occur, the church will have difficulty being the Church of Jesus Christ, the bearer of the Gospel in the world. Evangelization and socialization both must be acknowledged as aspects of a faithful catechesis.

Nurture focuses on spiritual formation and the growth of persons within a community of faith. Evangelization focuses on spiritual transformation and the conversion of persons within a community of faith. Evangelization proclaims and explains the Gospel so that faith might be aroused. Nurture makes possible the growth and development of faith. Catechesis as intentional socialization includes both in a pastoral ministry of continual change and assimilation, reform and growth.

The fact that there is some question today about what constitutes the educational ministry of the church needs no documentation. If once the church had some clear commitments, understandings, and ways, now it appears to be confused. At the same time an awareness of need for a renewed commitment, a serious search for new understandings, and a plethora of new efforts have emerged. Still, we lack a comprehensive theory and practice adequate to our times.

The "proclamation" (*kerygma*) and the "incorporation" (*didache*) of the Christian Gospel tradition have been central to the church's pastoral ministry since the beginning of the Christian era. Yet, over the centuries these related efforts (which together comprise catechesis) have changed—most dramatically in the fourth, eleventh, and sixteenth centuries. Today we face a similar crisis. Suggestions for adequate responses abound. Some turn for insight to theology, some to the social sciences, some to education. A host of programs are advocated. Some emphasize our intellects, some our affections, and some our life styles. Still most look a great deal like efforts in our most recent past. It appears as if our memories and imaginations are limited; we seem to be unaware that the twentieth century presents us with a radical turning point in the church's history, a turning point which calls for a radical catechetical response.

The church in each age needs to be faithful to both the Christian tradition and its historic situation. An understanding of our foreparents' attempts to be faithful is essential if we are to do likewise.

I once attended a party where I was called upon to introduce all the guests. I knew everyone, so that was not an unreasonable request. I went around the circle of guests easily calling off the names. Then I noticed from the corner of my eye a woman sitting by the fireplace. Suddenly I panicked. I could not remember her name. There were five guests to go. Four, three, two, and at last in frustration and shame, I had to ask her to introduce herself. My lapse of memory meant that I could no longer function effectively in the present.

I thought at the time what an awful thing it must be to lose one's memory completely. People who have lost their memories no longer remember who they are. That means that they can no longer function effectively in the present and that they have no secure plans for the future. They have lost their past and that has emptied their present of meaning and clouded their future. We must have contact with the past if only for the sake of the present and the future.

The church could, I suppose, lose its memory as well. It is certainly tempted to do so often enough. But a church which has lost its memory of the past can only wander about aimlessly in the present and despair of its future. The church needs the past, if only for the sake of the present and the future.

We who live in the United States are not as a matter of course oriented toward the past. As an immigrant people we typically have longed to make a fresh start, untrammeled by the past. That does not mean that we have lived altogether without a sense of history, but the past has tended to play a lesser role than the present and the future.

The plain fact, however, is that the church cannot escape the past no matter how much it may wish to do so. It cannot escape the past because of the nature of the Christian faith. The Christian faith is not an appeal to philosophy, ethics, or personal experience, but an appeal to history. Christianity is founded upon a historicist perspective.

The more comprehensive our knowledge of the past, the less likely we are to imagine we need to begin the quest for understanding from scratch, to take one aspect of our remembered past overseriously, or to romanticize the present, forgetting that the world is more than we who are alive today.

The invitation to study the history of catechesis is not an irrelevant call to forsake the pastoral mission of the church and to lose oneself in a past no longer recoverable. It is rather a call to abandon peripheral matters, to put an end to aimless meanderings and nervous activism so that we might respond faithfully to the present and imagine responsibly the future. Human life is not possible without memory.

In every time and in every place in the history of the Christian Church, the community of faith has attempted to develop a faithful catechesis. Today we are confronted by the same responsibility. Nevertheless, to do so we need to know both how our ancestors addressed this continuing challenge and how they succeeded and failed in their efforts. Informed and encouraged by their attempts to be faithful, we can respond better to our shared tradition and to our own unique historical situation, and we can envision an alternative faithful future.

The New Testament Church

Chapter 2
From Jesus to the Apologists

O. C. Edwards, Jr.

What have been taken as early histories of Christian education have usually been about something else. This can be seen from a review of some of the major works. The most careful study of educational systems in Israelite and Greco-Roman history written for Christian educators is *Educational Ideals in the Ancient World* by William Barclay (Barclay, 1959). This work gives excellent, detailed descriptions of the education of children among the Jews, Spartans, Athenians, and Romans. Yet in none of these systems would a child have received Christian education, but rather the contrary. When the author comes to speak of the Christian attitude toward pagan culture and the child in the early church, he deals with a period later than that covered in this chapter.

Undoubtedly the most important effort to write about the early history of Christian education is Lewis Joseph Sherrill's *The Rise of Christian Education*, which begins with the Old Testament and goes through the Middle Ages (Sherrill, 1944). There is much in the book that still repays careful study. There are good descriptions of Hebrew and Jewish education (and the distinction between them is important). What is said about Jesus' teaching, though, has far more to do with content than pedagogical method, and while it was rather enlightened for the time in which it was written, it lacked the insight into its subject that the use of form criticism and redaction criticism has produced in the last thirty-five years. What is said about "Education in Primitive Christianity" makes the same confusion of content with method and thus sounds like New Testament theology rather than a history of Christian pedagogy. There is some effort to reconstruct the context in which instruction was given, but it involves more conjecture than sociological analysis. The rest of the book deals with periods later than ours.

In *Education in the New Testament,* Ian A. Muirhead attempts to rescue the concept of Christian education from the disrepute into which it had fallen because of the dichotomy between *kerygma* and *didache* made in the movement dedicated to the study of "biblical theology." Muirhead's rescue efforts were made largely by the word-study method that few biblical scholars would employ now. He also makes critical assumptions that would be hard to justify today. What results is much more of an effort to say that teaching is a good thing than any description of how it was done in the New Testament church. The argument is that *kerygma* and teaching were never actually separated in practice and that there is an inevitable christological aspect to teaching. Further, what was taught was not merely informational, but a total way of life. Finally, the teaching process was animated and motivated by the presence of the Holy Spirit in the church. While the defense is sound and the justification is true, we are still left without a history of pedagogy in the early church (Muirhead, 1965).*

The reason that we do not have a history of Christian education for the first century and a half of our era is that explicit evidence is lacking for the construction of such a history. As Barclay said, the New Testament has practically nothing to say about the education of children (Barclay, 1959, p. 253). It also has very little to say about how non-Christians were persuaded to accept a Christian view of reality, what preparation persons received for Christian initiation, how those who had been initiated continued to deepen their understanding of Christian faith, or how anyone was trained to accept special responsibilities in the community.

During the entire period under investigation, Christianity existed as a counterculture. It was an optional understanding of reality available to those who were prepared to dissent from the majority culture. The methodological problem is to devise a way to study how the Christian faith, as an alternative system for understanding reality, could be propagated, inculcated, and legitimated. Since we lack direct information on these questions, the only option is to infer as much as possible from what is known

---

*After writing this chapter I learned of the existence of Joseph A. Grassi, *The Teacher in the Primitive Church,* but have not been able to procure a copy for examination, so I cannot say to what extent it succeeds where others have failed (Grassi, 1973).

about how the Christian group in a particular place at a particular time related to the society in which it existed, how it was organized socially, what patterns of family life existed within it, what structures of reality were integral to the theological phase it represented, and how its "rites, rituals, symbols, expressions of beliefs, attitudes, and values, organizational patterns, and activities" (Westerhoff and Neville, 1974, p. 41) combined to socialize its members.

This task of reconstructing catechesis in earliest Christianity, indirectly and by inference, is dependent upon the constructive use of five kinds of data:

(1) The chronology of early Christian documents,

(2) The developmental history of Christian institutions such as ministry, sacraments, and canon,

(3) The chronology of phases of theological development within the biblical literature rendered accessible through the application of form and redaction criticism,

(4) The sociological investigation of earliest Christianity, as in the work of Theissen, Holmberg, Kee, Gager, and Malherbe, and

(5) The insight that the sociology of knowledge, as represented by Peter Berger, gives to any effort to construct and maintain views of reality.

Such an effort at reconstruction could be very frustrating for readers whose interest is in the history of catechesis rather than in the method and sources for sociological interpretation of earliest Christianity. To them the only justification for what follows is that (a) more direct methods have failed to produce the knowledge they seek, and (b) confidence in results is in proportion to the reliability and therefore the explicitness of method.

THE MINISTRY OF JESUS

No phase to be studied in this chapter reveals the methodological difficulties of this period so well as its initial one. While scholars are coming more and more to agree that the basic teaching of Jesus was to proclaim that the control of the forces of evil over history was being broken and that God's reign was being inaugurated in and by his ministry, very little is known about the duration and scene of that ministry and even less is known about the extent to which a social group that accepted his proclamation came into existence during his lifetime. As is well known, Mark and his synoptic imitators present a very different chronology and geography for the ministry of Jesus from that presented in the Fourth Gospel. Since harvest occurs in the spring in Palestine, the story of the disciples plucking grain on the Sabbath (Mark 2:23-28) is the only datum in the synoptics that requires the ministry of Jesus to have lasted longer than one year. John, on the other hand, depicts Jesus going to the Passover celebration in Jerusalem several times, implying a ministry of at least four years. Since these were not the only occasions on which Jesus went to the city in the Fourth Gospel, a very different impression is given of the locale of Jesus' ministry from that which emerges in the synoptics, where, with the exception of the Lucan account of Jesus in the Temple at the age of twelve, he only goes to Jerusalem to die. In the synoptics the ministry of Jesus is confined to the region around the Lake of Galilee and the gentile territory to the north.

This uncertainty about the length and geographical distribution of Jesus' ministry makes even harder the already difficult question of whether one can speak of anything like an organization of his followers. The gospels tell of his addressing large crowds and, at times, of their having come long distances to hear him. Ignoring the question of theological motivation for any such statements, it remains true that nothing is said about whether members of his audience heard him often or only once or twice. Luke tells of a group of witnesses assembled during the Galilean ministry, but, as Conzelmann has shown, they have a special role in his scheme of how the gospel is proclaimed and it is difficult to say what degree of historical recollection is involved (Conzelmann, 1960, p. 194; cf. Acts 1:21ff.). All of the gospels place women followers as well as members of the Twelve at Jesus' tomb, so he must have had at least that many followers who went with him from Galilee to Jerusalem, even if the crowds of Palm Sunday had turned against him by Good Friday. (No judgment is intended here of how much time elapsed between Jesus' entry into Jerusalem and his execution.)

The picture that Theissen gives of the Jesus movement in Palestine from the Resurrection to the end of the Jewish War in 70 A.D. furnishes insight into the ministry of Jesus both directly and by inference from what he says about the later period (Theissen,

1978). He sees the Jesus movement as one of the reform movements that developed during the time of Roman rule in Palestine. Other such movements include the people of Qumran and the Zealots. These movements reflected the oppressive economic situation that included both a Roman and a religious system of taxation, a division of interest between Jerusalem and the country areas, unstable, divided, and ineffective government, and an identity crisis for Judaism that led to various schemes to intensify standards of Jewish behavior. Theissen sees the work of Jesus' disciples after his disappearance as that of wandering charismatics who led a life deprived of home, family, possessions, and protection as they moved around the country spreading Jesus' reforms in the period before Christianity was recognized to be a separate religion from Judaism. In time they built up local communities of followers, but even though these accepted the proclamation of the charismatics as true, they continued to live in the world and indeed were barely distinguishable from their neighbors who were attached to other reform movements or none. They did, however, furnish the economic support that the wandering charismatics needed and accepted the authority of these charismatics as normative for their belief and behavior. This, of course, means that these local communities were very loosely structured. The attachment of the local communities to the movement was loose enough for them to be described by so unspecific a word as "sympathizers." Membership was determined locally, though, since the wandering charismatics did not baptize nor did they administer the discipline of the exclusion of "sinners."

Theissen intended his study to depict the situation of the Jesus movement between 30 and 70 A.D. There is reason, as will be seen below, to consider this picture inadequately nuanced for that period. Nevertheless, it does offer what are probably some genuine insights into the Jesus movement during the lifetime of Jesus. His relations to the great majority of his followers could hardly have been closer than that of the wandering charismatics to the communities of their local sympathizers that Theissen describes.

If the communities of the Jesus movement were organized in this way during his ministry, what may we legitimately project about socialization within those communities? Obviously, these communities fitted closely into the society from which they sprang, and not many differences would have been discernible between the members and their neighbors. They would tend to display a higher righteousness both in terms of living out the love command- ment and in terms of the more exacting standard of behavior that it implies. Undoubtedly, they would discuss with their neighbors the relative merits of their reform movement over its competitors and invite them to hear Jesus or one of his followers when oppor- tunity was given with the hope that they would wish to become members of the movement. Much controversy exists about the institution of baptism, but two points seem overwhelmingly likely: (1) that it was practiced during the ministry of Jesus, and (2) that it was not associated with death and resurrection in Jesus until after he died and rose. Thus it probably was, like the baptism of John, associated with imminent eschatological expectation, with the difference that it was preparation for the glorious reign of God rather than for the dreadful Day of the Lord. This means that the life of the community was characterized by anticipation of the breaking in of the kingdom. People were baptized into the community who became convinced that God's reign was being inaugurated by Jesus.

Meetings of the community would thus be for the purpose of discussing the evidence that this was so, including miracles that were happening within the community as well as at the hands of Jesus and the Twelve. There would also be times of prayer for the kingdom to come. The overwhelming eschatological tone of the Lord's Prayer would chime in perfectly. Fellowship meals would be regarded as an anticipation of the messianic banquet. In such a situation, organization would be very loose and all authority would belong to Jesus and his immediate representatives. The imminent expectation of the end would militate against the development of complex liturgies, doctrines, or standards of behavior.

PALESTINIAN CHRISTIANITY

While much of Theissen's description of the Jesus movement as a mutual support system of wandering charismatics and local communities applies to the time between the death of Jesus and the end of the Jewish War (the period for which he intended it) as well as it does to the time of Jesus' ministry, form and redaction criticism provide a view of more diversity within the movement than his description suggests. Chiefly, a distinction is made between the community in Jerusalem and that outside the city. A part of the total picture, though, is a third group, the Hellenistic Jews who had migrated to Jerusalem, become Christians there, and were a part of the Jerusalem Christian community until their relaxed attitudes toward the law brought down on them the persecution of the Temple authorities as well as the ire of their more observant fellow Christians in Jerusalem. This persecution, referred to in Acts 8:1, appears to have been exclusively against the Hellenistic Jewish Christians and, despite what Acts says at this point, did not touch the Palestinian Jewish Christians. As a result of this persecution, Hellenistic Jewish Christians fled to gentile territory and thus began the gentile mission in such places as Cyprus and Antioch, to be discussed in a later chapter.

Our knowledge of this period comes to us indirectly and by inference. No Christian writings from this period have been preserved, if indeed there were any. Rather, this is the time during which the traditions about Jesus were passed down orally. Form criticism was developed to study this oral transmission. When K. L. Schmidt discovered that individual stories or sayings of Jesus, rather than connected narrative sequences, were the units in which the tradition about Jesus was handed down, he inaugurated a new epoch of gospel study (Schmidt, 1919). It was on his foundation that Martin Dibelius and Rudolf Bultmann built. For our purposes there is an important distinction between the approaches of these two fathers of form criticism. As Bultmann said:

> When M. Dibelius pursues his "Constructive Method," i.e.; when he reconstructs the history of the synoptic tradition from a study of the community and its needs; and when, contrariwise, I proceed from the analysis of the particular elements of the tradition, we are not opposed to each other, but rather engage in mutually complementary and corrective work (Bultmann, 1963, p. 5).

This is to say that Dibelius understood his work to be to ask why the early church preserved certain traditions about Jesus and not others. He performed it by asking to what use each kind of story or saying would have been put. In what life situation (*Sitz im Leben*) would the needs of the church be met by relating this information about Jesus? He found three main situations in which it would be appropriate to relay these traditions: missionary preaching, worship, and catechesis (Dibelius, 1935, pp. 1-36).

The program of Dibelius has not yet been carried much beyond his tentative beginnings. As John Gager has said, "Despite all their talk about the need to determine the *Sitz im Leben* of a given passage . . . students of early Christianity have given remarkably little attention to the social dimensions of these communities" (Gager, 1975, p. 10). As a matter of fact, it took the development of redaction criticism to make such attention possible, as will appear below. Gager, himself, however, has pointed to one social dynamic that would have been common to Jewish Christianity both in Jerusalem and in Palestine at large, that of dealing with the death of the Jesus and therefore with the apparent failure of God's reign to be inaugurated by his proclamation of it. Drawing on the work that L. Festinger and others have done on the behavior of contemporary millenarian movements when the end of the world does not occur on the schedule they had announced (Festinger *et al.*, 1956), Gager has suggested that the situation of the Jesus movement at time of the death of Jesus was one of "cognitive dissonance," i.e., "a condition of distress and doubt stemming from the disconfirmation of an important belief" (Gager, 1975, p. 39). In groups formed recently enough for their own life as a group not to be in itself an adequate reason to continue to exist, such as the early church, the first response to the disconfirmation of an important belief is to begin to proselytize others. Ridicule of the group over the failure of its prophecy is a powerful impetus to such missionary activity. The group's ability to deal with further disconfirmation (such as the delay of the second coming) depends on how much identification with the group has become an adequate reason for continuation of the group.

The ability of the group with a disconfirmed belief to engage in proselytism depends on the capacity of its members to rationalize the non-occurrence of the expected event and to show how its occurrence has only been delayed, to maintain that the time of its coming had only been miscalculated slightly, or to transpose the expected experience into another category so that fulfillment of the prophecy takes an entirely different manifestation from that originally predicted. In treating this point, however, Gager overlooks an element that should be the key to understanding the early church's resolution of its cognitive dissonance over the death of the Messiah Jesus. When he says that "even the event of the resurrection . . . seems not to have eradicated these doubts" (Gager, 1975, p. 43), he fails to distinguish between the followers of Jesus who remained loyal to him and those outside the Christian movement. The resurrection was convincing to the followers; it only failed to convince those who were not witnesses of it and did not believe in it. Even if a modern interpreter doubts that Jesus rose or that there was even an undefined "Easter event" (as liberal theologians may call it), she or he can see that a hallucination of the risen Christ would be a most effective psychic resolution of the cognitive dissonance occasioned by the death of a messianic claimant. What more concrete form could reinterpretation of the original prophecy take? What more powerful impetus to renewed proselytizing zeal? And, of course, orthodox Christians have always believed that the church's missionary imperative grew out of the vision of the risen Christ.

Source critics had long believed that Q, the source used by Matthew and Luke in addition to Mark, was a collection of material about Jesus, largely sayings, that had been assembled in or near Palestine by 50 A.D. Form critics have shown that the narratives also had been passed down by word of mouth with individual stories as the unit of tradition. It is the accomplishment of recent scholarship to note that the two kinds of material were originated and preserved in different milieus: the church at Jerusalem preserved narratives that showed Jesus as an interpreter of the Torah, and the church in the rest of Palestine preserved the "sayings" material that we identify as Q. These differences in the kind of tradition about Jesus created and preserved by the communities inside and outside Jerusalem are related to characteristic differences of structure and interest between the two communities. (It should be noted that reference to the "creation" of a tradition about Jesus by-passes the question of whether the tradition was based on a historical reminiscence, even though it is assumed that many of the traditions owe their origin more to theology than to memory.)

Although there are many reasons to question the overall reliability of the reconstruction in Acts of the earliest Christian community in Jerusalem, Paul's brief words in Galatians 1-2 reinforce the assumptions that Peter was the first leader of the Jerusalem community, that he was succeeded by James, the Lord's brother, and that the attitude of this Palestinian Jewish Christian community toward the Torah was much more conservative than that of the Hellenistic Jewish Christian group that was forced by persecution to leave Jerusalem. It is to be assumed, then, that the Jerusalem Christians, still distinguished from the rest of Judaism only by their belief that the crucified and risen Jesus was the Messiah, engaged in controversy with the Pharisees and others over the interpretation of the Torah. Norman Perrin, from whom our chronology of theological development in the New Testament is largely drawn, correctly points to the story of Jesus' teaching about divorce in Mark 10:2-12 as an example of the stories arising from this environment (Perrin, 1974, pp. 43f.). It was in this setting, too, that there originated an apologetic for the messiahship of one who had been put to the accursed death of crucifixion, based largely on an interpretation of the crucifixion as a fulfillment of prophecies in Psalms 22 and 69 and in Isaiah 53 (although it no longer seems appropriate to speak of anything like a complete pre-Marcan passion narrative; cf. Kelber ed., 1976).

Until recently it was the custom of exegetes to say that while the narrative material of the synoptics communicates *kerygma*— the proclamation of salvation through Jesus—the sayings material in Q is concerned with *didache*—ethical instruction growing out of that proclamation. However, since H. E. Tödt (Tödt, 1965) studied references to the Son of Man in Q, it has been recognized that the community producing this collection of sayings was very eschatological in its interests and had its own characteristic form of christological proclamation. The discussion has been advanced since then in three articles by Ernst Käsemann. In the first of these (Käsemann, 1969, pp. 66-81), he examines a group of sayings appearing in various parts of the canon that exemplify a form of the rule of "an eye for an eye." He calls these sayings "sentences of holy law." They state that the response a person makes to some aspect of early Christianity will be the response that person will meet at the time of judgment. Käsemann suggests that such sayings originated in the Palestinian Christian community shortly after the resurrection. In an atmosphere of expectation of an imminent return of Jesus, this community felt that it was guided by the Holy Spirit speaking through prophets within the group. By such sayings the prophets set limits for behavior within the community as it awaited what it expected to be the rapid coming of the Son of Man. This is to say that the Palestinian Christian community outside Jerusalem lived in an atmosphere of enthusiastic apocalypticism, guided by Spirit-filled prophets rather than by the legal-minded Disciples in Jerusalem, as Käsemann points out in his second essay (Käsemann, 1969, pp. 82-107). It is this community that lies behind Q. The teaching of that community has been set forth systematically by Richard A. Edwards (R. Edwards, 1976).

In some ways, this recognition of two different streams of Christianity within Palestine during the years between Easter and the Fall of Jerusalem raises as many questions as it answers. We have virtually no information, for instance, about how these two communities related to each other. What is known, however, is enough to make it clear that earlier attempts to reconstruct the life of the church during this period are usually accurate (to the extent that they are accurate at all) for only one of these two communities (e.g., Bultmann, 1951, I, 27-42, 53-62). Factors affecting socialization in the community in Jerusalem must therefore be distinguished from those in the rest of Palestine.

It seems likely, for instance, that Christians in Jerusalem would not have seemed so radically different from their non-Christian-but-fellow-Jewish neighbors as the Palestinian Christians would have. Their regular participation in the worship of the Temple would have been something they shared with the rest of the population. Their very disputes about the Torah would have appeared at home among the disputes between other parties and reform movements: Sadducees, Pharisees, Zealots, and Essenes. In the characteristic utterances of the community that produced Q, on the other hand, the "either/or" quality of the sentences of holy law, while addressed primarily to their own members, must have had some strong implication of exclusiveness to those who did not accept their proclamation of the coming Son of Man. Perhaps an analogy to the relation of the Q community to Palestinian society in general can be found in the place that a millenialist sectarian congregation such as Jehovah's Witnesses has in the society of a contemporary Southern town, where almost everyone accepts some form of evangelical Christianity. The stronger the millenial expectations, the better the analogy.

The community in Jerusalem was structured around the Twelve, especially Peter as the first witness of the resurrection and later James as the brother of the Lord. The number "twelve" symbolized the hope for the reconstitution of the twelve tribes of Israel. The authority of the Twelve and the importance of the Jerusalem church to the rest of Christianity was recognized to a degree even by Paul (Galatians 2:1-2; cf. 2:7-8, which recognizes Peter's authority to preach to the circumcised, and 2:11, in which the support of the poor at Jerusalem is promised by Paul). The Twelve led both in the controversy with non-Christian Jews over the interpretation of the Torah and also in the search for Old Testament prophecies of the Messiah who died and rose again. It would be going too far, though, to compare them to the supreme sanhedrin as the Christian court of last resort for settling questions about the interpretation of the Torah (Gerhardsson, 1961, pp. 245-61).

The Palestinian community behind Q, on the other hand, shows itself to have been charismatic and to have placed emphasis on communications from the Holy Spirit through the medium of Christian prophets. While some prophets may have looked after chains of tiny congregations, other prophets were resident in individual congregations (Käsemann, 1969, p. 92). The enthusiastic quality of the life of the community suggests that some *charisma* was shared by most of the members, which in turn suggests a more cohesive and exclusivistic corporate life for these congregations than Theissen postulated. All the members of the families that made up these congregations must have had a deeper sense of being different from the society at large than members of the Jerusalem community had.

Each of these Jewish Christian communities had its characteristic form of christological expression. Jerusalem thought of Jesus as the crucified Messiah who had risen; his role had called on him to perfect the interpretation of the Torah. His Spirit was at work in the community and enabled it to continue his work of Torah interpretation. The Palestinian community, on the other hand, spoke of Jesus chiefly as the Son of Man who would soon return in glory to judge the world.

THE HELLENISTIC CHRISTIANITY OF PAUL'S LETTERS

In Perrin's schema of the phases of New Testament Christianity that we have been following, the next two stages are "Hellenistic Jewish Mission Christianity" (Perrin, 1974, pp. 47-50) and "Gentile Christianity Apart from Paul" (pp. 50-54). While it is certain that there were such stages, the reconstruction of those is even more conjectural than that of others since they produced no documents and the only literary traces of such movements that remain are scattered in Acts, which came from a much later period and has polemical interests of its own that distort its picture of those stages. It will be sufficient to say that Hellenistic Jewish Mission Christianity was the effort of Greek-speaking Jewish Christians, driven from Jerusalem to such places as Antioch, and their successors to spread Christianity in the Hellenistic world by beginning missions in synagogues. There converts to Christianity were received from the Jewish Diaspora and from the "God-fearing" gentiles who had become attracted to the synagogues in the Hellenistic cities. The synagogues affected would be polarized by this missionary activity until the converts went into schism and formed Christian synagogues. Acts, with apparent accuracy, treats this as Paul's missionary method as well. These communities appropriated from the pagan vocabulary the terms "Son of God" and "Lord" as the words that would most adequately suggest to their hearers the Christian understanding of the importance of Jesus. In these circles, too, the interpretation of the Septuagint in a Christian sense, the adaptation of synagogue organization and liturgy, the development of special Christian liturgical formulae, and emphasis on the resurrection were characteristic phenomena. In work begun directly among the gentiles unconnected with the synagogue, though, the similarity of Christianity to "mystery cults" and of Jesus and his representatives to "divine men" furnished potential converts with categories for understanding this new movement, even if the missionaries themselves were not flattered by the association. In this early Greek Christianity the concept by which the work of Christ was understood was that of the descending/ascending Redeemer; this theological work is expressed in a number of christological hymns, such as Philippians 2:6-11, Colossians 1:15ff., etc.

Any effort to study socialization in the early church, though, must have more abundant materials from which to build. The letters of Paul furnish such materials, and by far the most successful effort to date to use sociology as a tool for understanding the early church has dealt with this material. Bengt Holmberg has made use of the same study of charismatic leadership by Weber that Theissen and indeed most of the other pioneers in the sociological interpretation of the early church have used, but he has done so in a much more thorough-going and illuminating way than any of them (Holmberg, 1978).

According to Weber, any legitimate leadership (*Herrschaft*) must have one of three kinds of validity: traditional, rational/legal, or charismatic. A charismatic leader is one who is accorded his position because of exceptional sanctity, heroism, or exemplariness of character. The charismatic feels called by God, but his call has to be recognized by followers for him to become a leader. This leader always understands his vocation to be to restore the religious tradition to its pristine state. Because of this goal of restoration, the technique often appears revolutionary, but the intention is always to establish a new status quo, or, as advocates would say, to restore the old one. Such leaders acquire both a staff of close disciples and a wider circle of followers. The staff is completely dependent upon the leader, having been called by him, having its tasks assigned by him, and having no rank or status independently of him. This staff lives with the leader on a communal basis and they are supported by the wider circle of followers. Since the sole authority is the revelation to the leader, there is no administrative organization nor is there a set of rules.

The appropriateness of this as a description of Jesus and his followers is obvious, but the significant contribution of Holmberg has been to go on and see how what Weber has to say about later stages in the history of charismatic movements applies both to the Jerusalem church and to Paul. Weber had talked about the "routinization" of charismatic movements that occurs especially when the original leader dies and his staff moves into leadership of the ongoing movement. (Incidentally, the exclusively masculine pronouns are taken over from Holmberg's references to the early church and imply no suggestion that women are less likely to be charismatic leaders than men.) As may be detected from the use of the word "routinization," Weber tended to denigrate this stage in the history of a movement by the attribution of unworthy motives to staff members as their reasons for keeping the movement going. Holmberg, however, draws on the insights of Berger and Luckmann to criticize Weber from the point of view of the sociology of knowledge. In doing so he removes the value-negative charging implied in the statement that what was charismatic and inspired has degenerated into mere routine. Rather, he says, the intention of the charismatic leader has been realized in the institutionalization of his reforms. Since charismatic leaders always understand their mission to be to restore the ideal conditions of the past, institutionalizing those conditions is intrinsic to the mission of all charismatic movements.

An early stage of institutionalization can begin within the life of the charismatic leader, but the process is not completed until his death or disappearance. At that time the staff becomes the group elite who have all the qualities of charismatic authority except that of having that authority rest on themselves; for them it is an authority derived from the original leader and in their time it can only be approached through such mediating channels as representatives, offices, traditions, and rites. The preliminary stage within the life of the charismatic leader is called primary institutionalization, and the stage when the staff inherits is called secondary institutionalization.

Holmberg's revision of Weber has two values. The first and most important is undoubtedly the antidote that it gives to all romanticism lamenting the debasement of a charismatic movement into an institution by showing the institutional goal of the original charismatic intention. The value most relevant to this study, though, is its illumination of the activity of the Jerusalem church and Paul by the concept of secondary institutionalization. Since the Twelve were appointed by the Lord himself, they were the seed from which all legitimate growth occurred. The basic creed, sacraments, christology, cult, and—to a degree—organization of all other churches had to be derived from them. Paul himself could never overcome this dependence, and the main significance of the collection he took for the Jerusalem church was undoubtedly its recognition of the right of the Twelve to be supported as leaders of the charismatic movement. Paul's own status as an apostle was neither that of a member of the Twelve nor that of the plenipotentiary agent (*shaliach*) of a congregation such as Antioch, but was something in between that gave him the special status accorded at the Jerusalem council, a status that was never given unambiguous public validation by the Jerusalem church.

In relation to the churches that he founded, though, Paul had a very different status. He was the minor founder of groups of which Jesus had to be regarded as the major founder. Thus Paul may not have been the originator, but he was the transmitter—and in being so he was a charismatic entrepreneur. He was the authority par excellence for his converts under the limitations of his status as minor founder. His own term for this relation was that he was their "father," a self-limiting term that still gave him the right to intervene in the smallest details of their life, whether by direct action when he was present with them or indirectly through his own staff or letters when he was not. His authority was indeed so great that only incipient offices developed during the time of his ministry among them. In Corinth, at any rate, he did not really distinguish between pneumatic displays and offices as gifts of the Holy Spirit (*charismata*, 1 Corinthians 12-14).

Since his work in a particular place depended upon having access to a home large enough for assemblies, the conversion of the owner of such a home was crucial to his strategy. The leisure, administrative skills, education, and affluence (all to be distinguished sharply from mere social status) of such persons gave them enormous advantages for becoming the local, indigenous leaders in the congregations that Paul founded. Certainly Paul made it quite clear that such practical abilities seemed more important to him in the life of the church than ecstatic phenomena. Yet Paul retained so much authority over his congregations even while he was away that it is doubtful that even these capable persons had much authority in his absence. Paul himself seems to have taken no initiative in developing offices in his congregations, but rather freely legitimated what arose spontaneously. Up to this point I have followed Holmberg, but I see no reason myself for doubting that, since most of Paul's congregations were developed from synagogue members and admirers, his own congregations understood themselves reflexively as synagogues acknowledging the messiahship of Jesus and thus automatically took on the organization of synagogues, including elders on whom hands had been laid.

Another recent study that could cast light on the socialization of Christians in the congregations founded by St. Paul is Ronald Hock's book on *The Social Context of Paul's Ministry: Tentmaking and Apostleship* (Hock, 1980). A student of Abraham J. Malherbe (of whom more later), Hock set out to question every aspect of the prevailing consensus about Paul's occupation as a tentmaker. (Although this work is entirely historical and scholarly, it nevertheless should furnish some good perspective on current non-stipendiary or "tentmaking" ministries.) The prevailing view has been that Paul practiced a trade because doing so was expected in the calling of a rabbi, that his attitude toward work was very positive, and that this attitude was typically Jewish and at odds with contemporary Greco-Roman views. Hock offers arguments to bring each of those points into serious question and he ranges over a vast selection of classical literature to give detailed information about the life of an artisan in the ancient world: his training, social status, travels, and relation to intellectual activity.

The principal obstacle to using Hock's work in the current project is manifested in the following quotation:

> Paul's affirmation of freedom is thus an unmistakable indication
> that he understood the issue of apostolic support in terms of the
> debate among intellectuals generally over the appropriate means of
> support (Hock, 1980, p. 61).

While it is certainly true that at the time there was a debate between
philosophers and sophists over whether they should be supported
by (a) charging fees, (b) becoming members of the households of
the wealthy, (c) begging, or (d) working, it is not at all clear that
Paul regarded his apostleship as belonging to the same category of
"intellectual work"—to use Hock's term—as the vocations of the
other groups. His sense of direct call from God to a particular
work in a unique eschatological situation belongs exclusively to
the milieu of early Jewish Christianity and it is unlikely in the
extreme that any Greco-Roman models played any conscious part
in the formation of his sense of identity as an apostle. While it is
true that his converts would have been familiar with these pagan
analogies, their own acceptance of the Christian construction of
reality within the charismatic community of the Pauline congregation would have militated strongly against their drawing
comparisons between Paul's role and that of other itinerant en-
trepreneurs of world views in their society.

Hock's emphasis on the amount of time that Paul would have
needed to work to support himself and the opportunities that the
shop gave for evangelization, though, are points well taken.
Paul's unwillingness to accept support also needs to be understood
in terms of what Holmberg has to say about the right of the charismatic leader to be supported; as a father who transmitted a
gospel that he did not originate, Paul's transmission of it was the
only thing that was his own to give and thus he could boast in that
one weak offering (1 Corinthians 9:15-18).

While in *Social Aspects of Early Christianity* Malherbe makes
the mistake of his pupil Hock in understanding Paul too much in
analogy to wandering Greco-Roman philosophers and sophists,
he does perform the useful service of offering a number of kinds of
evidence to show that the social class of Paul's converts covered
the whole spectrum of Hellenistic society, thus refuting the common opinion that all early Christians were slaves and outcasts
(Malherbe, 1977). He also calls attention to the social significance
of the house church, as does also Michael Green (Green, 1970).
One of the most successful efforts to apply sociological insight to
the history of the early church, though, is that of Howard Clark

Kee in his book *Christian Origins in a Sociological Perspective* (Kee, 1980). He, too, calls attention to the diversity of social class represented in Paul's missionary congregations:

> The church set for itself the problem of blending into one society members whose backgrounds were as diverse as village hand crafts-men, women of wealth and prestigious families, minor Roman officers, social and moral outcasts, persons with rhetorical and philosophical training, some reared in strict Jewish legal environ-ments, and others who were "ordinary men of no education" (Kee, 1980, p. 98).

Most of these, as noted above, were either Jews of the Diaspora or Greco-Roman "God-fearers" (persons attracted to Judaism who were not full proselytes because of the ritual and, therefore, the social separation from their own culture that would have been required) who were converted to Christianity.

The question arises of why Gentiles from the Mediterranean coast of what is modern Turkey and from the Aegean coastline would have been attracted to a Semitic religion and its upstart daughter. The answer usually made recognizes the appeal that monotheism and high ethical standards had to contemporary philosophy. To these Kee adds the sense of divine destiny of God's covenant people and efforts to deal with the problem of evil. He also counts the status of women in the church:

> Ironically, Paul has been accused of holding antifeminine views, as his placing women in a position of seeming subservience to their husbands (1 Corinthians 11:3). But in relation to the culture of the Roman world, Christian women seem to have been given wider opportunities and to have been accorded a position far closer to equality with men than was the case in any other human associations of the time (Kee, 1980, p. 89).

Also important in the formation of these Christian groups was the kind of marginality that Theissen saw as important in the formation of reform movements within Palestinian Judaism during the ministry of Jesus. Kee quotes Hans Mol in defining marginal groups as those "that stand on the boundary of larger groups or societies, neither completely belonging nor suffering outright rejection" (Kee, 1980, p. 55; cf. Ramsey MacMullen, 1966). Another factor was the lack of personal involvement that most religions in the Greco-Roman world required of their practitioners.

The official religion was either a matter of state or a matter of family and did not involve the ordinary citizen deeply. For that reason, oriental religions that involved impressive initiatory rites were being imported in quantity to satisfy needs for personal religion (Kee, 1980, pp. 82-85; E. R. Dodds, 1965; A. von Harnack, 1908, pp. 432f.). While Christianity was often placed in that category by many pagans of the time, it succeeded in winning the world because of its deep differences from them.

This extensive study of efforts to interpret the work of Paul sociologically now puts us in position to ask the questions about how persons were socialized into his Christian communities that we have asked of others. The first has to do with the relation of the Christian community to the larger society. That obviously has changed greatly because the previous situations studied were always of Christians functioning as Jewish reform movements within Palestine. Now the scene has shifted dramatically to the alien world of Greco-Roman society in which Jews were a powerful minority (often estimated at one-seventh of the population of the Roman empire) that was generally hated and, to a degree, persecuted, but which attracted admirers and hangers-on from high-minded and alienated members of pagan society. Choosing to cast one's lot with the Christians, then, was to make a decisive break with the majority culture and to cast one's lot with a minority culture. This step itself was so radical as to involve a deep shift of identity; any socialization into the Christian community was radical. When that was reinforced by expectation of the imminent end of the world, one can see how deep the formation of even the least aligned Christian must have been.

The social organization was impressive, too. Bringing together people who could never have met together as peers under any other circumstances must have given these Hellenistic Christians a sense of doing something so radical that their identity was further strengthened, no matter what strains this diversity must have placed on their common life, as we see in the problems caused by the rich at the eucharist (1 Corinthians 11:20-22; Malherbe, 1977, pp. 82-84). The most distinctive feature of their social organization, though, was their leadership, as Holmberg points out. That leadership consisted exclusively of Paul himself. True, he acknowledged dependence on the Jerusalem church and sometimes had to contend with rival missionaries. True, some practical and pneumatic offices were in a nascent state. Nevertheless, one of the strongest socializing forces in the Pauline congregations was the fact that Christian belief and Christian behavior—down to extraordinary details—were what Paul said they were. His construction of reality in a Christian way was conveyed to them first and foremost by his presence among them, secondarily through his staff, which has been reckoned by Malherbe to number forty on the basis of a count of persons listed in the epistles (Malherbe, 1977, p. 47), and only tertiarily by the letters that we know to be so powerful.

The effect on family life was deep, even if the baptism of a whole household may not have involved the baptism of infants (a debate that may be prescinded here). Households apparently could be evangelized by husbands, wives, children, or slaves. While it may be that the lists of duties of members of a household (*Haustafeln*) all belong to later literature attributed to Paul but not written by him, they have antecedents enough in the genuine Pauline literature to make us well aware that he was concerned about, and felt free to levy judgments concerning, the responsibilities of husbands and wives to one another, the reciprocal duties of parents and children, and of slaves and masters. He also spoke of the duties of citizens (Romans 13:1-7). Paul, then, made very explicit connections between Christian identity and particular patterns of family life (Kee, 1980, pp. 95f.; Malherbe, 1977, pp. 50-53).

In dealing with what we have called "the structures of reality integral to the theological phase" of a stage in the development of early Christianity, Kee makes good use of the important work on the sociology of religion by Hans J. Mol (Kee, 1980, p. 101; Mol, 1976). Mol's primary concern is the way that a sense of sacred identity is developed by either an individual or a group. He says that four mechanisms are required to accomplish this process that he calls sacralization. The first is the construction of a sacred world view, a way of understanding reality from the perspective of the religious belief; Mol calls this *objectification*, since the view is not understood merely as a point of view, but is identified with the nature of objective reality. The second mechanism involved in sacralization is called *commitment* by Mol and refers to acceptance of the religious community's construction of reality as the truth about the world. The response of Paul's converts to his preaching was this kind of commitment. The other two mechanisms listed by Mol are myth and ritual.

To an extent, we have already seen how objectification and commitment occurred in the Pauline congregations. We need now to see the way that myth and ritual functioned in them. Kee, following G. S. Kirk, distinguishes between three kinds of myths. Some are narratives that tell of the eponymous ancestors of a group and thus communicate ethnic history. The stories of the patriarchs in Genesis fall into this category. Other myths are related to ritual and are recited to give continuity to the community or even to the cosmos itself. The institution narrative at the eucharist and the responses to questions at the Passover seder are examples. The third kind of myth functions to wrestle with the fundamental problems of the universe, such as suffering and death. The story of the Fall in Genesis 3 is such a speculative and explanatory myth.

This distinction between three kinds of myths casts light on the christology of the descending/ascending Redeemer that Paul and his churches inherited from early Greek Christianity. This christology, related ultimately to the Wisdom christology of the Hellenistic Jewish mission church, is, in Kirk's terminology, speculative rather than narrative. This makes it different from the christology of the Palestinian church, which was essentially narrative in its presentation of the significance of Christ, stating that significance in the vocabulary of Jewish apocalypticism's doctrine of two ages. Thus it was natural for Palestinian Christianity (except for the community that produced Q) to express its faith in stories about Jesus. On the other hand, the redeemer revealer with whom one dies and will rise, of whom Paul speaks, needs very little narrative presentation, and indeed we find very little information about the life of Jesus in the writings of Paul.

The social function, then, of this speculative sort of myth is to enable Paul's hearers to deal with the fundamental problems of life and death. Thus the salvation preached by Paul has characteristically different emphases from those of apocalyptic Palestinian Christianity. This may also be seen in the rites that are used in the sacralization process of the Pauline churches. Baptism is going down with Christ into death in order that one may rise with him at the last day. The Pauline understanding of the eucharist is also related to the death of Christ and a sacrilegious communion is a failure to discern the body of Christ. Both sacraments, therefore, deal with the incorporation of the Christian into the Body of Christ and into his saving death (Romans 6:3, 1 Corinthians 11:29). The rites thus enact the myths.

THE COMMUNITIES THAT PRODUCED THE GOSPELS
AND OTHER COMMUNITIES

Although less than half the literature that makes up the New Testament has been considered so far, what follows will be presented in a much more sketchy fashion than the preceding sections. One reason is that New Testament scholars have been slower to apply sociological analysis to what remains of the canon. Yet some of the material, especially the gospels, presents special difficulty for this kind of study. The gospels and Acts are presented as records of past events, and while it is assumed that interests of the church contemporary with their writing shaped their presentations of the past, it is not always easy to tell what comes from historical and what comes from contemporary interests. As Raymond Brown has recently pointed out:

> *Primarily*, the Gospels tell us how an evangelist conceived of and presented Jesus to a Christian community in the last third of the first century, a presentation that indirectly gives us an insight into that community's life at the time when the Gospel was written. *Secondarily*, through source analysis, the Gospels reveal something about the pre-Gospel history of the evangelists' christological views; indirectly, they also reveal something about the community's history earlier in the century . . . *Thirdly*, the Gospels offer limited means for reconstructing the ministry and message of the historical Jesus. (Brown, 1979, p. 17).

To safeguard from distortion his own efforts at reconstructing the interests of the community behind the Johannine literature, Brown placed himself under the limitations of (1) basing his theory on the gospel as it now exists rather than on his efforts to reconstruct sources for the gospel, (2) paying closest attention to those passages in John that seem less likely to be historically accurate than the corresponding passages in the Synoptics, and (3) arguing from silence only when the silence is on matters that could hardly have been omitted accidentally (Brown, 1979, pp. 20f.). When such limitations are observed, one can be much less confident about making detailed reconstructions of the interests of the communities that produced the various gospels.

There seems to be little doubt, for instance, that Mark is conditioned mightily by an expectation that Jesus would soon return, an expectation that was undoubtedly related to the Jewish revolt against the Romans, whether before the actual outbreak of hostilities, during the war, or after the destruction of the Temple. Such an expectation gives a very distinct coloration to the community that holds it; the life and behavior of the community is controlled by it. The explanation of Jewish terms and institutions and the use of Latin loan words also suggests that the gospel was written in a Greco-Roman rather than a Semitic locale, which would also shape the life of the group. Also plausible is the contention of Theodore Weeden and Norman Perrin and his students that Mark was written to refute a Semitic christology of the royal warrior Messiah and a Hellenistic christology of a "divine man" or "wonder worker," reinterpreting these in the light of a "Son of Man" christology that saw Jesus as one who, while he had authority on earth during his lifetime and would have even more at the final judgment, would nevertheless live out his messianic role mainly through messianic suffering (Perrin, 1974, pp. 161f.; Weeden, 1971; Kelber, 1974, ed. 1976, 1979). Again, both the community's own characteristic belief and its relation to other early Christian groups holding to other interpretations of the significance of Jesus would have had important implications for the plausibility structure of the community from which the gospel emerged. As Brown has pointed out, though, the scholars mentioned probably push the evidence too far when they assume that Mark's calling attention to the misunderstanding of the disciples during Jesus' lifetime suggests that his community was at enmity with Peter and the Twelve for the way they preached after the resurrection. "A presentation of some misunderstanding on the part of the Twelve during Jesus' ministry is not irreconcilable with a great respect for the Twelve in the church" (Brown, 1979, p. 19).

Such impressionistic treatment of the community that produced one of the gospels cannot examine (and does not even have the data for such an examination) the various structures that are used to legitimate that community's construction of reality. It does, however, proceed from Berger's presupposition that:

> the reality of the Christian world depends upon the presence of social structures within which this reality is taken for granted and within which successive generations of individuals are socialized in such a way that this world will be real *to them* (Berger, 1969, p. 46).

All that can be done with reference to the communities that produced the gospels is to point out what some of those structures were.

Although Matthew used Mark and Q as sources, the gospel as we have it either comes from a community that is engaged in controversy with Pharisaic Judaism or incorporates material that originated in such a controversy. (While the majority of scholars hold to the former interpretation, others point with good reason to the presence within the gospel of material that suggests a dialogue with gentiles.) The provenance of this gospel thus appears to be some place on the boundary between the Semitic and Greco-Roman worlds, such as Antioch, in the closing years of the first century. The controversy with the Pharisees gives to this gospel its most distinctive features: formula quotations from the Old Testament with a christological interpretation (K. Stendahl, 1968; B. Lindars, 1961), the use of Jesus' "law of love" as the hermeneutical key to interpreting the Torah (Bornkamm, Barth, Held, 1963), and the use of extensive catechetical material that explicitly contrasts Christian moral and ritual standards with those of the Pharisees by the use of such a formula as "You have heard that it has been said (i.e., by Moses) . . . but I say to you . . ." (Kee, 1980, pp. 140-43).

This catechetical material probably comes closer than anything else in the New Testament to resembling the kind of material that will be discussed in most of the other chapters of this book, and it has its direct descendants in works to be discussed later in this chapter—the *Didache* and the so-called *Epistle of Barnabas*. Much of it occurs in the Sermon on the Mount where Christian righteousness is contrasted with the standards of the Pharisees on such topics as murder and anger (5:21-26), adultery and lust (5:27-30), divorce (5:31-32), swearing and oaths (5:33-37), retaliation (5:38-42), love of enemies (5:43-48), and alms, prayer, and fasting (6:1-18). Matthew 18:15-35 also deals with the inter-relation of members of the Christian community and progressive steps for dealing with recalcitrant members, steps which culminate in excommunication. It is obvious that the Matthean congregation's ongoing debate with the synagogue did more than anything else to reinforce in its members their sense of what it meant to be Christians.

Luke and Acts are from a very different milieu than that of Matthew, although they appear to come from nearly the same time. The main purposes of this two-volume work, purposes that are inter-related, are to console the church on the delay of the *parousia* (Conzelmann, 1960) and to account for the mission to the gentiles (Haenchen, 1971). The argument in each volume is historical, with the gospel telling of the life of Jesus and Acts recounting the triumphant spread of the church to the center of the Greco-Roman world, Rome itself.

Acts, then, has as its subject the time of Paul, and with the exception of certain anachronisms and some smoothing of the obstacles in the path of the expanding church, the situation depicted is that of Paul as studied above. The unity between Paul and Jerusalem is probably exaggerated, the differences between the gospel and Judaism are understated, the acceptability of Christianity to civil authorities is overestimated, and the degree of organization of the local congregation probably anticipates a later stage of development. Conditions that shape the life of the community are despair over the tardiness of Jesus' return and the Hellenistic environment in which the life of the church is being lived out. The details of this latter impact have been well articulated by Kee:

> The book was written not only as a source of information and inspiration for Christians but also as a skillful propaganda document with the aim of showing that the Christian movement was apolitical, promoting peace, inclusive across social and ethnic, and religious lines, culturally aware, and under divine control. As such it may even have been addressed to a secondary audience—to literate middle-class pagans. In any event, it would help Christians prepare for responding to social and political opprobrium or to the attempt to dismiss them as ignoramuses or illiterates (Kee, 1980, p. 149).

While a number of efforts have been made to study the community that lies behind the Johannine literature (*see especially* Käsemann, 1968, and Martyn, 1968, rev. 1979), the effort most convincing to me is that of Raymond Brown (1979). He sees the community as originating with an ordinary group of early Christians in or near Palestine, a group that included someone who was not a member of the Twelve who was to be known eventually as the Beloved Disciple. The conversion of a group of Samaritans to that group shifted it away from the Temple piety that the Twelve persisted in for some time and from a Son of David christology toward one that stressed the pre-existent, divine status of Jesus. The addition of a group of gentile converts to this community caused not only a break with the synagogue and with Jewish Christians who had a low christology, but even meant some real differences of emphasis (within a relation of open communications) between the Johannine community and the communities that centered around the Twelve. It was at this stage that the Fourth Gospel was written and it may have been at this time that the community moved into gentile territory, possibly Ephesus.

The struggle with Judaism caused some members of the group so to emphasize Jesus' pre-existence that they came to doubt the significance of his humanity. Their opinion caused schism within the community, with a loyalist group that considered itself faithful to the Beloved Disciple writing the three epistles against the secessionists. Eventually, the secessionists were absorbed into the Gnostic movements of the second century and the adherents of the author of the epistles became reconciled to the Great Church, persuading that church of its high christology and accepting from that church a ministerial and teaching hierarchy that it had been formerly reluctant to acquire. Almost every aspect of this historical reconstruction of the community that produced the Johannine literature would repay analysis in terms of the implied plausibility structures, but space is lacking and the reader is undoubtedly able to project most of the implications.

In addition to the gospels there are three other documents in the New Testament that show clearly that the ways that the communities producing them constructed reality in a Christian manner were directly related to the social contexts in which those communities were located. These documents are Hebrews, James, and the Revelation. Again, space is lacking to specify their plausibility structures in any detail. We can only point to the social situations that caused them to develop their structures the way they did.

Hebrews comes from a community of Christians who were converts from the sort of Platonizing Hellenistic Judaism that developed in Alexandria and is best represented in the writings of Philo. Many of the members seemed in danger of relapsing into the religious community from which they had been recruited, and the epistle is an effort to dissuade them that is couched in the theological and exegetical categories common to the two communities. James, for all its claim to be written by a brother of the Lord, would be a typically Hellenistic Jewish writing (though not Alexandrian) were it not for a couple of references to Jesus and a polemic against a debased Paulinism. What appear to be a number of allusions to sayings of Jesus may be merely references to moral commonplaces of contemporary Judaism that either Jesus or the evangelists also took up. While the thought is thoroughly Jewish in its background, the writing, which includes puns and rhetorical devices, shows that the writer had a good Greek education. Thus even Jewish Christianity spoke with a Greek accent when it flourished in a Hellenistic environment.

A very different situation is represented in the Revelation, which came from Christian communities on the Aegean coast of what is modern Turkey from the period of the emperor Domitian when worship of the Roman emperor was becoming a legal requirement in that vicinity. In these utterly Hellenistic cities, Christians who felt that their very lives were being threatened reverted to the completely Jewish literary genre of apocalyptic in a very ungrammatical if clear and powerful Greek. (For related but not identical presentations, *see* Kee, 1980, pp. 139-40, 149-51. For a psychotherapeutic view of the value of the Revelation to its original audience, *see* Gager, 1975, pp. 49-57).

THE INSTITUTIONALIZATION OF CHARISMA IN EMERGING CATHOLICISM

Up until now we have dealt with the implications for socialization within the church of the church's existence in alien societies, whether Jewish or Greco-Roman pagan. However, the next stage to be considered, that which produced the Pastoral and Catholic epistles and the writings of the Apostolic Fathers, was a time not so much of conflict with an external group that was antagonistic to Christianity as of conflict within the church over who were the representatives of authentic Christianity. The dynamics of this inner-church conflict gave their own characteristic pattern to the structures that created and legitimated Christian identity. The period over which this conflict was occurring is known to scholars as early or emerging catholicism. Lewis Coser has said that there are two basic forms of conflict, "in-group" and "out-group." The emerging catholic period, then, is a time of in-group conflict, but the social functions of both kinds of conflict are essentially the same: conflict is a form of socialization and is an essential element in the formation and persistence of groups.

The process that Weber called routinization and Holmberg corrected to institutionalization (see above, p. 23) during this

period has been analyzed well by Gager. To begin with, he points
to the necessity of the process:

> If we accept as a fundamental law the transformation from no rules
> to new rules, we may not at the same time lament the routinization
> of the primitive enthusiasm that characterizes all charismatic or
> millenarian groups in their second generation and sometimes even
> earlier (Gager, 1975, p. 67).

Thus he is able to conclude that "a good deal of nonsense has been
written about the *decline* of primitive Christianity into 'early
Catholicism' " (*Loc. cit.*; italics mine). As he points out, though,
the process is not limited to the two stages of charismatic beginnings
and consolidation (reaction), but includes also "a secondary
action, or reaction, which is normally based on an idealized
image of the original action" and a fourth stage which is the
starting over of the whole cycle.

Emerging catholicism was a third generation Christian phenomenon, coming after the original charismatic leadership of
Jesus and the replacement of him after his death by members of
his staff (the Twelve) and witnesses (in one sense or another) of his
resurrection (like Paul). During even the secondary period the
leadership was still charismatic in everything except having its
vision and authority originate with itself. While the leaders of the
third generation continued to display some charisma, by then
their authority depended on having legal and/or traditional status
as well. Thus they came to combine the three kinds of leadership
Weber describes: charismatic, legal/rational, and traditional. In
post-apostolic Christianity, therefore, it was necessary to develop
authoritative patterns of leadership in succession to Jesus and the
Twelve. This, obviously, was the development of the orders of
ministry that exercised by law and tradition the authority that
Jesus and his staff had exercised by charisma. Thus one of the
most important structures for socialization and legitimation in
the post-apostolic church was the three-fold ministry of bishops,
presbyters, and deacons, which has been described too often to
merit repetition here (e.g., Edwards, 1973, pp. 121-33). Even
this, though, was not without its resistance and reaction, as in the
Johannine epistles (see above, p. 35) and later in Montanism and
monasticism.

The Johannine epistles, incidentally, come from this period of
in-group conflict within the church and, as shown by Brown's

analysis reported above, represented a struggle between two groups that both claimed to be the inheritors of the true nature of the original group. Each side tried to prove its claims to represent the authentic tradition by appeals to the Fourth Gospel, the charter document of the group. Such appeals to writings came in time to be made by both sides in all such disputes and thus the need arose for both a canon, an authoritative list of inspired Christian writings, and rules for the interpretation of Scripture. Most of this activity lies beyond the period under discussion, but the directions that this dispute would take were already visible in remarks of the author of 2 Peter:

> First of all you must understand this, that no prophecy of scripture is a matter of one's own interpretation, because no prophecy ever came by the impulse of man, but men moved by the Holy Spirit spoke from God (1:20, 21).

> So also our beloved brother Paul wrote to you according to the wisdom given him, speaking of this as he does in all his letters. There are some things in them hard to understand, which the ignorant and unstable twist to their own destruction, as they do the other scriptures (3:15, 16).

Eventually the problem of how Scriptures were to be interpreted correctly would be solved by appeal to an authoritative summary of the biblical faith, such as that which Tertullian was to call "the rule of faith." These summaries were to take on a credal shape. Authoritative teaching was also one of the most important duties of the clergy, especially the bishops, in later days. But even Paul had to take on the problems of in-group conflict. He resolved it usually by an effort to refute the positions of his opponents with overwhelming theological arguments. In the emerging catholic period of the New Testament, though, the attitude of Tertullian was already being anticipated by references to "the faith once delivered to the saints" (Jude 3) and "the pattern of sound words" (2 Timothy 1:13, 14). In this we see the process that led to the development of creeds as important tools in the socialization of Christians into the church and in the legitimation of the faith that members professed. Needless to say, nothing so sharpens the sense of belonging to one's own group as the necessity to distinguish the group's beliefs clearly from those of another group which appear very similar but which would threaten the values most dear to one's own group. Thus even heresy contributed to the creation of a sense of Christian identity among the orthodox.

The fourth constituent of the reality-building structure of the emerging catholic church was the sacraments of baptism and eucharist. These, of course, had existed in the church from the beginning, but during this period their importance came to be explained in a stronger way. As Holmberg pointed out, when the charismatic leader dies, charismatic authority (the leader's access to the sacred) is not communicated directly, but is mediated through representatives, offices, traditions, and rites (Holmberg, 1980, pp. 180-81). The danger feared from this transition by some German scholars (e.g., Conzelmann, 1969, pp. 303-07) is that the church will come to be regarded as a "salvation-conferring institution" (*Heilsanstalt*) that has power to dispense the grace of salvation independently of the believer's faith in Christ.

While the effect of much of this chapter has been to argue that the institutionalization of the church was necessary, inevitable, and implicit to Jesus' original intention to reform Judaism, and while I do not believe that the emerging catholic church ever became a *Heilsanstalt*, the author in whom the movement is thought to have most closely approached the danger zone was Ignatius of Antioch (Conzelmann, 1973, p. 20). This danger was seen in his insistence that all in the church be done in connection with the bishop, and his use of, among others, the metaphor of "medicine of immortality" to describe the eucharist (Ephesians 20:2). Robert Grant is undoubtedly correct, though, in reminding us both that Paul (1 Corinthians 11:30) and John (6:57) related eternal life to the eucharist and that "medicine of immortality" is not to be taken more literally here than "deadly drug" is in a description of heresy in Trallians 6:2 (Grant, 1966, pp. 2, 53).

Also important in the plausibility structure of emerging catholicism is its explicit machinery for socialization, its program of direct preparation for Christian initiation, i.e., catechesis in the strict sense. In spite of the claim of Archbishop Carrington to have discovered evidence of a pattern of catechesis used as baptismal preparation from very early times in the church in material common to Colossians, Ephesians, 1 Peter, James, and other New Testament documents (Carrington, 1940), and our already having detected catechetical patterns to Matthew 5, 6, and 18, the first fully developed picture we get of such catechesis is in the *Didache*. This document developed over quite a long period and thus it is never possible to say that all of its provisions were observed at any one time. Nevertheless, Robert Kraft has been able to reconstruct this general picture of community practices: pre-baptismal ethical instruction and fasting, baptism in the three-fold name (administered in one of several ways) followed immediately by anointing and the eucharist, fasting twice a week, Sunday corporate worship, the use of the Lord's Prayer, and other matters (Kraft, 1965, p. 66).

Much of the material of the catechesis as such in the *Didache* is a teaching about "two ways," the ways of virtue and vice. This material closely parallels a section of the *Epistle of Barnabas*, so the two are thought to depend on a common tradition. The "summary of the law," ten commandments, sayings attributed to Jesus in the gospels, and other Old and New Testament ethical paranesis are the basis of this instruction. While there are hints of catechetical programs in other literature coming from this period (Grant, 1976, pp. 32-49), the next extensive and clear evidence belongs to the following chapter.

THE APOLOGISTS

In the middle of the second century a group of Christian writers began to appear who tried to address the Greco-Roman world in its own vocabulary and concepts. The ostensible reason for this aggressive literary behavior was that Christians were being persecuted. There was no empire-wide effort to destroy Christianity yet, but local mob violence could erupt under a screen of imperial permission to do great damage to the church, as may be seen from the deaths of Ignatius and Polycarp. (Incidentally, the witness of the martyrs was itself a powerful structure for spreading and reinforcing Christian belief.) The earliest of the apologies, then, and some of the later ones were addressed to Roman emperors to defend Christians against such charges as atheism, incest, and cannibalism. Included in this group are the apologies of Quadratus, Aristides, Justin Martyr, Melito of Sardis, and Athenagoras.

The charge of atheism did not mean, of course, that the Christians believed in no gods, but only that they did not participate in the official cult, a charge which had implications of treason. The name given to the incest of which the Christians were accused was Oedipean intercourse, after the sin of Oedipus Rex, who unknowingly killed his father and married his mother. The cannibalism was referred to as Thyestean banquets in allusion to Thyestes, whose children were served to him as a meat dish after he raped the wife of his brother Atreus. Possibly the latter two charges result from misunderstandings of the Christian ideal of brotherly love and of the eucharist, or possibly they were just stock charges against secret religious groups. At any rate, Athenagoras offers a fair sample of the Christian response:

> They bring three charges against us: athesim, Thyestean banquets, and Oedipean unions. If these are true, spare no class among us, prosecute our crimes, destroy us root and branch, including our women and children—if indeed *any* human being could be found living like wild animals in that way! . . . But if these charges are fabrications and empty slanders owing their existence to the fact that by a natural principle evil opposes virtue and that by divine law opposites war against each other, and if you yourselves are our witnesses that we are not guilty of any of these crimes since you merely command us not to confess, then it is only right that you examine our conduct, our teachings, and our zeal and obedience to you, your house, and the empire. In so doing, you will at length grant us a favor equal to that enjoyed by our persecutors (Athenagoras, *Legatio* 3:1, 2, trans. Schoedel).

By showing that they were persecuted solely for being Christians rather than for any crimes, the Apologists hoped to have the legal risks of being Christians removed. The legal form of such petitions was that of a *libellus* addressed to the emperor; if he granted the request by signing the petition, the signed document (rescript) would have the force of law (Grant, 1970, pp. 86-93, 101-19). There has been much scholarly debate about how much any of these writers expected their apologies to be read by the emperors and, since others, such as Tatian and Theophilus of Antioch, addressed their works explicitly to cultured pagans in an effort to convert them to Christianity, the suggestion has also been made that the basic purpose of these writers was missionary (Daniélou, 1973, pp. 7-37).

Certainly their works contain much criticism of Greco-Roman mythology, morals, cults, and culture in general. This is especially true of the apology of Tatian, who seemed more interested in heaping vituperation on the Greeks than he did in recommending anything Christian:

> Has anything worthwhile come from your philosophy? Which of your most serious men has been without hypocrisy? . . . While Plato was philosophizing, he was sold by Dionysius on account of his greedy stomach. And Aristotle, who stupidly set a limit to Providence and restricted happiness to the things which give pleasure, very

boorishly flattered Alexander, forgetting that he was a boy. . . . I
should laugh at those who still accept Aristotle's teachings, those
who say that sublunar affairs are not directed by Providence, but
are closer to the earth than the moon is and are lower than its course,
and therefore themselves provide providence for the things that lack
it. Also, according to Aristotle, those who do not have beauty,
wealth, bodily strength, and good birth, do not have happiness. Let
such men philosophize! (Tatian, *Oratio* 2:1, 2, trans. Grant and
Edwards).

Others, though, understood the reason (*logos*) responsible for
Greek philosophy to have been the divine Word (*logos*) that was
active in the creation of the world and that became incarnate in
Jesus. On this basis, Justin Martyr was able to regard Heraclitus
and Plato as "Christians before Christ" (Justin, *1 Apologia* 46)
and thus to see the doctrine of creation in Genesis as being essentially the same as that of Plato in the *Timaeus* (*Ibid.*, 59).

Obviously, the Apologists represent a vast change from anything that had appeared before in Christian literature. Instead of
producing a literature of conflict—whether with Jews, gentiles,
or heretical fellow Christians, these writers try to show that
Christian faith is consonant with all of the highest values their
pagan neighbors already have. It seems unlikely, though, that
even this missionary purpose exhausts the goals of the Apologists.
The needs of Christians at the time have been compared with
those of educated Jews in Egypt at the time of Philo who "found it
easier to cling to Judaism so long as they knew that Judaism stood
on an equal level with Hellenism" (V. Tcherikover, quoted by
Gager, 1975, p. 86). When the church reached the point where it
was not content to be an alien sub-culture within the Greco-Roman
world but wanted to see itself as belonging to the wider society as
well, it had to show that what it believed was the perfection of all
that the wider society yearned for in its best moments:

Their latent function was not so much to change the pagan image of
Christians as to prevent that image from being internalized by
Christians themselves (Gager, 1975, p. 87).

CONCLUSION

Thus ends our effort to try to study how the Christian alternative
system of reality was propagated, inculcated, and legitimated in
the earliest days of the church through a study of how the Christian

group in a particular place at a particular time related to the society in which it existed, how it was organized socially, what patterns of family life existed within it, what structures of reality were integral to the theological phase it represented, and how its "rites, rituals, symbols, expressions of beliefs, attitudes, and values, organizational patterns, and activities" combined to socialize the members of the group (above, p. 12). Four main phases have been depicted: the church in conflict with Judaism, the church in conflict with Greco-Roman Hellenism, the church in conflict with itself, and the church in dialogue with Greco-Roman Hellenism.

The earlier sections made extensive use of recent studies in the sociological analysis of the New Testament while the later ones had to be content to sketch the picture in with broad strokes both because sociological study has not been done in such detail for the later periods and because of limitations of space. It could seem to the casual reader that little has been learned about the way that a sense of identity as a Christian was communicated during the first century and a half of our era. We began, after all, by admitting that the New Testament has virtually nothing to say about the way that Christian children were educated in the faith, how nonbelievers were converted, how persons were prepared to receive Christian initiation, how the initiated continued and deepened their formation as Christians, or how anyone was trained for special responsibility in the church.

In the mass of exegetical and sociological detail that has constituted the bulk of this chapter, however, there has appeared a good bit about ways in which Christian identity was built and reinforced. When these ways are lifted out of the context of the arguments in which they are presented and listed together, it can be seen that we know much about how Christian identity was formed in the New Testament period and immediately afterwards even if we know nothing about Christian education in the narrow sense during that time. The most powerful influence in this process was probably the relation of the Christian community to the society among which it lived; Christians understood themselves over against the larger group and the contrast between themselves and all the others did much to sharpen their sense of being members of a group. This is to imply what is in fact true, that conflict is a powerful force in building identity. Early Jerusalem Christianity, the church in Palestine outside Jerusalem, the membership of

Paul's churches, and the communities that produced the gospels all understood themselves to be in one degree of conflict or another with the surrounding social order. Emerging catholicism existed at a time when the conflict was within the Christian community. Only during the time of the Apologists was there an effort to move from an adversary relation to one of dialogue.

Another powerful socializing force in the early church was its leadership. This began with the charismatic leadership of Jesus and moved on to the secondary charismatic authority of the Twelve, the prophets in the Palestinian churches, and Paul. By the time of emerging catholicism charismatic authority was being supplemented with legal/rational and traditional authority as orders of ministry began to develop and to offer mediated channels of access to the sacred.

Certainly the thought systems of New Testament Christians contributed much to their sense of identity. A case in point is expectation of an imminent second coming. It has also been noted that each of the stages of New Testament Christianity we have examined has had its own characteristic ways of stating its beliefs about the significance of Jesus. Other theological differences that have enabled Christians to distinguish themselves from others have had to do with arguments between themselves and the Jews, especially those concerning the interpretation of the Torah both in terms of behavior and christologically. Then, too, when early Christians read what we call the Old Testament and saw what they considered to be prophecy after prophecy that had been fulfilled in their own times, that also strengthened their faith.

We saw that there was some teaching activity in the New Testament period and afterwards and discovered catechetical patterns in Matthew, the *Didache*, and the *Epistle of Barnabas*, at least. This system of belief was not only taught, it also had to be defended against disagreements and appearances of disconfirmation, so there was a considerable activity of legitimation taking place as well. Furthermore, early Christians were engaged in sharing their faith with others, and evangelization of others has always been one of the surest ways of strengthening one's own belief; one has heard it said that Latter-day Saints send out their young people as missionaries more to strengthen their own belief than to persuade others to share it. Efforts to resist heresy and schism had a similar effect, as did the defense of Christians against false charges made against them by outsiders. The witness of the martyrs was indeed the seed of the church through the impression it made on others, as Tertullian pointed out. On the other hand, one's own successful endurance under threat of persecution both showed the faith that was already there and deepened it.

Then, too, there were the specifically religious forces contributing to a sense of Christian identity. The sacraments of baptism and the eucharist gave those who received them their initiation into the community and the renewal of their participation in it. By the same token, when someone was excommunicated, those who remained within the fellowship were made much more conscious of their membership. The group experience of corporate worship was also identity-building. Familiar hymns and liturgical formulas reiterated and strengthened beliefs. Devotional practices such as prayer and fasting increased one's awareness of being Christian. On the other hand, abstaining from practices in which outsiders engaged heightened the sense of being different. When miracles were reported in the group, faith was strengthened again. Religious experiences were also a factor that contributed to a sense of Christian identity, especially, though not exclusively, visions of the risen Christ or inspiration by the Holy Spirit as when one spoke in tongues.

Social and economic factors had their own part to play in the Christian formation of persons. Contributing financially to the Christian enterprise both showed and intensified belief. Meeting in the homes of the wealthy may have increased the confidence of humbler Christians in the truth of their religion. Certainly the way that the church embraced all social classes as no other institution in antiquity did was considered by many to be a proof of the truth of the gospel. Since many of those who responded to Christian preaching were previously included in the vast numbers who lived in socially marginal situations, that resolution of their marginality was a reason to be grateful for their conversion. Then, too, Christianity was a family affair that saw important obligations for every member of the household and also attributed dignity and respect to the less powerful members of households: women, slaves, and children.

Without knowing, then, how the earliest church performed its technically educational tasks, we can nevertheless be aware of a vast array of structures that existed to inculcate and reinforce a sense of Christian identity.

SELECTED BIBLIOGRAPHY

Barclay, William, *Educational Ideals in the Ancient World.* Grand Rapids: Baker Book House, 1974. A reprint of the 1959 edition.

Berger, Peter L., *The Sacred Canopy: Elements of a Sociological Theory of Religion.* Anchor Books. Garden City: Doubleday & Co., 1967.

Bornkamm, Günther; Barth, Gerhard; and Held, H. J., *Tradition and Interpretation in Matthew.* Translated by Percy Scott. New Testament Library. Philadelphia: Westminster Press, 1965.

Brown, Raymond E., *The Community of the Beloved Disciple.* New York: Paulist Press, 1979.

Bultmann, Rudolf, *The History of the Synoptic Tradition.* Translated by John Marsh. Oxford: Basil Blackwell, 1963.

————, *Theology of the New Testament,* Vol. I. Translated by Kendrick Grobel. New York: Charles Scribner's Sons, 1951.

Conzelmann, Hans, *The History of Primitive Christianity.* Translated by John E. Steely. Nashville: Abingdon, 1973.

————, *An Outline of the Theology of the New Testament.* Translated by John Bowden. New York: Harper & Row, 1969.

————, *The Theology of St. Luke.* Translated by Geoffrey Buswell. New York: Harper & Row, 1960.

Daniélou, Jean, *A History of Early Christian Doctrine Before the Council of Nicaea;* Vol. II: *Gospel Message and Hellenistic Culture.* Translated by John Austin Baker. Philadelphia: Westminster Press, 1973.

Dibelius, Martin, *From Tradition to Gospel.* Translated by Bertram Lee Woolf. New York: Charles Scribner's Sons, 1935.

Dodds, E. R., *Pagan and Christian in an Age of Anxiety.* Cambridge: The University Press, 1965.

Edwards, O. C., Jr., *How It All Began: Origins of the Christian Church.* New York: Seabury Press, 1973.

Edwards, Richard A., *A Theology of Q: Eschatology, Prophecy, and Wisdom.* Philadelphia: Fortress Press, 1976.

Festinger, L.; Riecken, H. W.; and Schachter, S., *When Prophecy Fails.* New York: Harper & Row, 1956.

Gager, John, *Kingdom and Community: The Social World of Earliest Christianity.* Englewood Cliffs, N.J.: Prentice-Hall, Inc., 1975.

Gerhardsson, Birger, *Memory and Manuscript: Oral Tradition and Written Transmission in Rabbinic Judaism and Early Christianity.* Acta Seminarii Neotestamentici Upsaliensis, Vol. XXII. Lund: C.W.K. Gleerup, 1961.

Grant, Robert M., *The Apostolic Fathers: A Translation and Commentary;* Vol. I: *Ignatius of Antioch.* Camden, N.J.: Thomas Nelson & Sons, 1966.

_____, *Augustus to Constantine: The Thrust of the Christian Movement into the Roman World.* New York: Harper & Row, 1970.

_____, "Development of the Christian Catechumenate," *Made, Not Born: New Perspectives on Christian Initiation and the Catechumenate.* Murphy Center for Liturgical Research. Notre Dame: University of Notre Dame Press, 1976.

Green, Michael, *Evangelism in the Early Church.* Grand Rapids: William B. Eerdmans Publishing Co., 1970.

Hänchen, Ernst, *The Acts of the Apostles: A Commentary.* Translated by R. McL. Wilson *et al.* Philadelphia: Westminster Press, 1971.

Hock, Roland F., *The Social Context of Paul's Ministry: Tentmaking and Apostleship.* Philadelphia: Fortress Press, 1980.

Holmberg, Bengt, *Paul and Power: The Structure of Authority in the Primitive Church as Reflected in the Pauline Epistles.* Coniectanea Biblica, New Testament Series, Vol. II. Lund: C.W.K. Gleerup, 1978. Reprinted with different page numbers, Philadelphia: Fortress Press, 1980.

Käsemann, Ernst, *New Testament Questions of Today.* Translated by W. J. Montague. Philadelphia: Fortress Press, 1969.

_____, *The Testament of Jesus: A Study of the Gospel of John in the Light of Chapter 17.* Translated by Gerhard Krodel. Philadelphia: Fortress Press, 1968.

Kee, Howard Clark, *Christian Origins in Sociological Perspective: Methods and Resources.* Philadelphia: Westminster Press, 1980.

Kelber, Werner H., *The Kingdom in Mark.* Philadelphia: Fortress Press, 1974.

_____, *Mark's Story of Jesus.* Philadelphia: Fortress Press, 1979.

_____, ed., *The Passion in Mark.* Philadelphia: Fortress Press, 1976.

Lindars, Barnabas, *New Testament Apologetic.* New Testament Library. Philadelphia: Westminster Press, 1961.

MacMullen, Ramsay, *Enemies of the Roman Order.* Cambridge, MA: Harvard University Press, 1966.

Malherbe, Abraham J., *Social Aspects of Early Christianity.* Baton Rouge: Louisiana State University Press, 1977.

Martyn, J. Louis, *History and Theology in the Fourth Gospel*, rev. ed. Nashville: Abingdon, 1979.

Mol, Hans J., *Identity and the Sacred*. New York: The Free Press, 1976.

Muirhead, Ian A., *Education in the New Testament*. Monographs in Christian Education, No. 2. New York: Association Press, 1965.

Perrin, Norman, *The New Testament: An Introduction*. New York: Harcourt Brace Jovanovich, Inc., 1974.

Schmidt, K. L., *Der Rahmen der Geschichte Jesu*. Berlin: Trowitsch, 1919.

Sherrill, Lewis Joseph, *The Rise of Christian Education*. New York: Macmillan & Co., 1944.

Stendahl, Krister, *The School of St. Matthew and Its Use of the Old Testament*, new ed. Philadelphia: Fortress Press, 1968.

Theissen, Gerd, *The First Followers of Jesus: A Sociological Analysis of the Earliest Christianity*. Translated by John Bowden. London: SCM Press, 1978.

Tödt, H. E., *The Son of Man in the Synoptic Tradition*. Translated by Dorothea M. Barton. New Testament Library. Philadelphia: Westminster Press, 1965.

von Harnack, Adolf, *The Mission and Expansion of Christianity in the First Three Centuries*. Translated and edited by James Moffatt. New York: G.P. Putnam's Sons, 1908.

Weeden, Theodore J., *Mark: Traditions in Conflict*. Philadelphia: Fortress Press, 1971.

Westerhoff, John H., III, and Neville, Gwen Kennedy, *Generation to Generation*. Philadelphia: United Church Press, 1974.

The Ancient Church

Chapter 3
The Development of Catechesis
in the Third and Fourth Centuries:
From Hippolytus to Augustine

Leonel L. Mitchell

Hints provided in earlier authors of a catechumenal instruction of adult candidates for baptism are developed and flower into a full catechetical system in the writers of the third and fourth centuries. The catechetical work of Ambrose in the West, and of Cyril of Jerusalem, Theodore of Mopsuestia, and John Chrysostom in the East remain the classics in the field, and the work of Cyril in particular became a model for such instruction. The necessity of producing behavioral and cultural change in those converted in increasing numbers from paganism demanded more than an intellectual exposition. It required an environment suitable for conversion and growth into Christ.

HIPPOLYTUS: "THE APOSTOLIC TRADITION"

The Apostolic Tradition of Hippolytus, usually dated about 215, is frequently put forward justifiably as a model of the liturgy of the ancient church. The late Burton S. Easton, professor of New Testament at General Theological Seminary and an early editor of the text, said of it:

> They represent the normal practices at Rome in Hippolytus's younger days, and he is quite sincere in believing that they are truly apostolic and therefore unalterable. And that they actually are rules of real antiquity is shown by the corroboration they receive from other early Christian writers, among whom Tertullian in particular describes usages extraordinarily like those expounded by his Roman

> contemporary. *The Apostolic Tradition*, consequently, is more than
> a source for Roman customs at the beginning of the third century; it
> may with equal safety be invoked for the practices of even fifty years
> earlier (Easton, 1934, p. 25).

The study of this work, nevertheless, is a labyrinth of pitfalls
for the unwary, since neither the text nor the context is secure.
Only a few fragments of the original Greek text survive, none of
which deal with the catechumenate. The most reliable witness is
a single sixth-century manuscript containing a Latin translation
of the major part of the work. The second best witness is an eleventh-
century manuscript of a Coptic (Egyptian) translation, also
incomplete. The reconstruction and identification of the text has
been a sort of scholarly jigsaw puzzle and is the work of the present
century. One scholar has even raised the possibility that the work
represents nothing but the author's "ideal" church, and reflects
actual practice nowhere.

Even with these reservations, the work is too important to
ignore, and even if it could be proved, which is far from the case,
that it does not represent late second-century Roman usage, it still
describes something very like what must lie behind third- and
fourth-century practice.

The principal section on catechumens, chapters 15 to 20 in the
edition of Dom Bernard Botte, is missing in the Latin and therefore
depends on the Coptic. Newcomers to the faith, it tells us, are
brought to the teachers before the people arrive and are examined
as to their manner of life. Are they married? Are they slaves? If
they are the slaves of Christians, do their masters recommend
them? The primary considerations seem to be ethical:

> If his master is a heathen, teach him to please his master, that there
> be no scandal. If any man has a wife, or a woman a husband, they
> shall be taught to be contented, the man with his wife and the
> woman with her husband. But if any man is not living with a wife,
> he shall be instructed not to fornicate, but to take a wife lawfully or
> remain as he is (Cuming, 1976, p. 15).

There is also an initial inquiry about trades and professions,
and those engaged in occupations considered unsuitable for Christians are told to desist. Most forbidden occupations are those
considered immoral or which involve any sort of participation in
formal pagan worship, such as the making of statues of the pagan
gods, or the teaching of classical literature (!).

The expectation is that catechumens will spend three years as hearers of the word, but it is not *kronos* (time) but *tropos* (conduct) which is to be judged. During this time they receive instruction and pray, not yet with the faithful but by themselves. They are also forbidden to exchange the peace or to eat with the faithful *in cena dominica*, which probably means at the *agape* since there would have been no question of their participation in the eucharist. They are not given blessed bread as the faithful are, but exorcized bread and an individual cup.

No description is given of the instruction which the catechumens receive, but the teacher, at the end of the instruction, lays hands upon them, prays for them, and dismisses them. Finally the catechumens are told that they need not fear arrest, for if they make their witness before the magistrate, they are considered as baptized in their own blood.

The picture which emerges from *Apostolic Tradition* is of catechumens forming a separate class in the church, distinct from the baptized faithful. They are Christians *in fieri*. Their participation in the life of the community, although restricted, is not optional. They are treated much the way contemporary fraternities treat "pledges." They are excluded from the privileges of membership as uninitiated, but to those in the outside world they are members with a real place in the life and concern of the church.

At the end of the three-year catechumenate, those who are to receive baptism are chosen. This group of *electi* (chosen) are called by later Latin authors *competentes* (seekers), as opposed to the simple *audientes* (hearers). In Greek they are called *photizomenoi* (those being enlightened). In the fourth century the seekers are those actually preparing for baptism, in contrast to those who remain catechumens for some time, like Augustine, or until the approach of death, like Constantine.

Apostolic Tradition asks of the seekers:

> Have they lived good lives when they were catechumens? Have they honored the widows? Have they visited the sick? Have they done every kind of good work? (Cuming, 1976, p. 17).

If their sponsors bear witness that they have, they are admitted "to hear the Gospel." It is not certain what that means, and there are a number of scholarly theories which need not detain us. What is clear is that the examination is on the manner of life of

the candidates. No questions are asked concerning their understanding of Christian doctrine, or even of their acceptance of
Jesus Christ, although presumably some form of rudimentary
belief must have been responsible for their initial approach to the
church. This confirms our view that the instruction which they
received was primarily in Christian living and was to enable them
to adopt what we would call a Christian lifestyle, not to make
them theologians.

The period of actual preparation for baptism is marked by daily
imposition of hands and exorcism, and presumably by instruction
as well, although nothing is said of that. If they have "heard the
word in faith" it will be manifest in the purity of their lives.

References to instruction in the baptismal rites themselves are
few but significant. Immediately before the reception of communion by the newly-baptized, "The bishop shall give a reason
for all these things to those who receive," and at the end of the
rites:

> We have handed over to you in brief these things about holy baptism
> and the holy offering, for you have already been instructed about
> the resurrection of the flesh and the other things as it is written. But
> if there is anything else which ought to be said, the bishop shall say it
> privately to those who have received baptism. Unbelievers must not
> get to know it, unless they first receive baptism (Cuming, 1976, p.
> 22).

Sacramental instruction, at least according to the Coptic translator, was not to be given to the unbaptized, but the bishop was
to explain the meaning of what was done to the newly-baptized,
and if there were more to be imparted, it was to be done privately
later. On the other hand, Scriptural instruction as far at least as it
concerns the resurrection had already been given, apparently as a
part of the catechumenate.

In *Apostolic Tradition* we find the three stages of catechesis at
least in outline. There is general instruction in Christian living for
those who come to hear the word. "Hearing the word" also implies
some biblical instruction. There is more intensive instruction,
described as hearing the Gospel, in the period of immediate baptismal preparation. Finally, at the time of baptism, and immediately
thereafter, there is sacramental instruction, or mystagogy. This is
the same pattern we find in the classic writers of the fourth century.

THE CATECHETICAL SCHOOL OF ALEXANDRIA

The work of the catechetical school of Alexandria and its famous masters, Clement and Origen, is, strangely enough, only peripherally related to our study. Although we are told by Eusebius that Origen engaged in the instruction of catechumens, the Christian school at Alexandria was really a type of higher education on the model of the pagan philosophical schools. Its object was to provide for orthodox Christianity the sort of intellectual respectability which Greek philosophy or Gnostic speculation provided. It was to lead the Christian Gnostic to true knowledge and initiation into the holy mystery of God and Christ. As Clement rhapsodizes:

> Then thou shalt have the vision of my God, and shalt be initiated into those holy mysteries, and shalt taste the joys that are hidden away in heaven, preserved for me "which neither ear hath heard, nor have they entered into the heart" of any man (Butterworth, 1960, p. 253).

Yet when, in the opening chapter of his *Paedagogus* (Instructor), he expounds what we might call his educational theory, it sounds much like the traditional Christian catechetical system. His first phase of instruction he calls exhortation. His work by that title, *Protrepticus*, is, for the circumstances of its composition, a work of evangelism. It seeks to draw the educated student of Greek philosophy to Christ. The *Paedagogus*, his second volume, is what he considered as elementary instruction. It is largely of a moral nature. *Didascalicus* (Teacher) should properly have been the third section of Clement's work, since he considered intellectual education to be the third stage of the education of the Christian Gnostic, but, from what he says in the opening chapter of *Stromateis* (Miscellanies), he chose instead to write in riddles, making his meaning clear only to those who understood. The parallel to the *disciplina arcani*, the concealing of the rites of church from the unbaptized, is too strong to be ignored. Intellectual education, Clement believes, is not for everyone, but only for those who were not content with what Origen calls an "unreasoned and common faith."

Clement's school was apparently a personal enterprise which was destroyed in the persecution of 202. When it was restored by Origen, it was with the support of the bishop. In 215 Origen divided the school curriculum, bringing in a new teacher to instruct the beginners, while he himself taught the more advanced students.

With the work of Origen we have moved well beyond the instruction of catechumens to the establishment of a theological academy, which has none the less taken the basic plan of catechetical instruction as the outline of its curriculum, as many of Origen's exegetical and theological works clearly reflect. He wrote in the *Peri Archon:*

> The holy apostles, when preaching the faith of Christ, took certain doctrines, those namely which they believed to be necessary ones, and delivered them in plainest terms to all believers, even to such as appeared to be somewhat dull in the investigation of divine knowledge. The grounds of their statements they left to be investigated by such as should merit the higher gifts of the Spirit . . . There were other doctrines, however, about which the apostles simply said that things were so, keeping silence as to how or why; their intention undoubtedly being to supply the more diligent of those who came after them, such as should prove to be lovers of wisdom (i.e. Philosophers) with an exercise to display the fruit of their ability (Stevenson, 1968, p. 212).

Origen himself was obviously concerned with the Christian philosophers who had received the gifts of language, wisdom, and knowledge, but he does provide us with a somewhat idiosyncratic listing of the doctrine which the apostles taught in plain terms. Presumably these are the doctrines which were to be imparted to all Christians, while the other, more advanced material, was for the lovers of wisdom.

The first such doctrine is the unity of God, "who created and set in order all things, and who, when nothing existed, caused the universe to be." In next place comes the doctrine of Christ:

> He who came to earth, was begotten of the Father before every created thing. And after he had ministered to the Father in the foundation of all things, for all things were made through him. In these last times he emptied himself and was made man, was made flesh, although he was God; and being made man, he still remained what he was, namely God. He took to himself a body like our body, differing in this alone, that it was born of a virgin and of the Holy Spirit. And this Jesus Christ was born and suffered in truth and not merely in appearance, and truly died our common death. Moreover he truly rose from the dead, and after the resurrection companied with his disciples and was taken up into heaven (Stevenson, 1968, pp. 212-3).

Certainly, Origen here is rehearsing the preaching of the apostolic church, the *kerygma,* which he says is preserved unaltered and handed down in unbroken succession from the apostles to the churches of his own day. It must have been something like this which Origen taught his catechumens, some of whom, Eusebius tells us, went to martyrdom.

The third doctrine Origen mentions is "that the Holy Spirit is united in honor and dignity to the Father and the Son," and inspired the saints, prophets, and apostles.

He also states as apostolic doctrine the temporal creation of the world and therefore the necessity of its end, the reward and punishment of the human soul after death, the resurrection of the body, the freedom of the human will and the reality of the moral struggle, and the existence of good angels and of the devil and his angels.

This, of course, reflects Origen's own interests and the controversies in which he was engaged, but it does give a clue to the content of basic catechetical education. I think we can also assume that much of the instruction was biblically based, and that its goal was to produce a holy person, not a theologian.

CATECHESIS IN JERUSALEM

A more fertile field for our investigation of catechesis in the ancient church is fourth-century Jerusalem. We are fortunate in possessing two major overlapping sources for the practice of the Jerusalem church in this period. The first is the complete set of catechetical lectures thought to have been delivered by Cyril of Jerusalem in 348, along with a complete set of mystagogical lectures given to the newly baptized. The mystagogical lectures were not given in the same year as the pre-baptismal lectures and are thought by many scholars to be the work of John, Cyril's successor as bishop of Jerusalem. This question of authorship is not of great importance for our purposes, since the lectures do represent the Jerusalem church, and in any case they must have been quite similar from year to year. It is, in fact, likely that Cyril's lectures were substantially copied for over a century. The second source we possess is the journal of the pilgrim Egeria, or Etheria, usually described as a Spanish nun, who visited Jerusalem in the 380's.

Fourth-century Jerusalem was a place of pilgrimage. The new buildings of Constantine on Golgotha and other sacred spots, and the opportunity to walk in the holy places where the Savior taught and died and rose again, were a powerful magnet for pilgrims, or perhaps simply for tourists. Piety after the conversion of Constantine was more historical and less eschatological than it had been in earlier centuries, and there was an increased desire to celebrate sacred anniversaries, to visit sacred sites, and to venerate the relics of the martyrs. The *Martyrium* in Jerusalem, the great church Constantine had built on the site of the death of the King of Martyrs, with the adjacent shrine of the *Anastasis*, or Resurrection, containing the empty tomb, was the natural focus of this piety. Fourth-century Jerusalem was no longer the obscure city of *Aelia Capitolina*; it was now the Holy City. What was done in Jerusalem was reported and copied throughout the Christian world.

There is no mention in our sources of the long period of "hearing the word" which *Apostolic Tradition* describes, except for Cyril's instruction that his hearers are not to divulge what is taught them to catechumens. Apparently there were still many catechumens who were not candidates for baptism. By the middle of the fourth century there were probably a substantial number who had identified themselves with Christianity, not necessarily for political advantage, but who were not yet ready to "take the plunge" in the baptismal waters.

The time set apart for the catechizing of those preparing to be baptized at Easter was *quadragesima*, our 40 day Lent. Egeria tells us that Lent in Jerusalem was eight weeks, since they did not fast on Saturday or Sunday (except on Holy Saturday), and that they called it *Heortae* (The Feasts). Before Lent the names of those wishing to be baptized were turned in and written down by a presbyter. At the beginning of Lent a solemn ceremony took place, which she describes in detail.

The bishop's throne is set up in the great nave of the *Martyrium*. The presbyters sit in chairs with him on either side, with the deacons and other clergy standing behind. The effect is certainly that of a formal act of the hierarchically ordered church. Those seeking baptism (*competentes*) are brought up with their sponsors and questioned by the bishop. The questions concern the manner of life of the candidate. Neighbors as well as sponsors are asked to respond, and Egeria says, "It is not too easy for a visitor to come to baptism if he has no witnesses who are acquainted with him."

Those who are well reported are enrolled by the bishop, and others are told to amend their ways before coming to the font. Each male candidate was accompanied by a godfather and each female candidate by a godmother. After their enrollment they were seated in a semi-circle facing the bishop and clergy, all together forming a complete circle. The sponsors and such other of the faithful as wished were permitted to attend the lectures, but the ordinary catechumens were excluded.

The Procatechesis, the address delivered on this occasion, is the first of the lectures of Cyril that is preserved. It gives us a picture of what sort of thing was said.

The candidates are addressed as *photizomenoi* (those who have come to be enlightened) who have been enrolled for baptism. Then two negative examples are given them: that of Simon Magus, who "while his body went under the water, his heart let not in the light of the Spirit," and that of the man who came to the feast without a wedding garment. Cyril's comment is, "There has been nothing to stop you coming here with your soul covered in the mire of your sins." He tells them that they have forty days in which to put off the covering of sin and clothe themselves in the proper wedding garment, otherwise, he warns them, they will receive only the water and not the Holy Spirit. Clearly conversion, not theological education, is the goal. Even, he suggests to his audience, if you have come from an ulterior motive,

> now you are inside the ecclesiastical fishnets. Let yourself be taken. Jesus is angling for you, not to make you die, but by his having died, to make you live (Telfer, 1955, p. 68).

Cyril goes on to urge the candidate to participate eagerly in the preparations for baptism. "Let your feet hasten to these times of instruction. Submit yourself to be exorcized with all eagerness." They are urged to persevere through these catechizings, to learn the things they are taught, and to hide them from catechumens. Cyril's reason for this concealment is that the catechumen cannot comprehend the material. This is the *disciplina arcani* to which we have already made reference. Although the reason given here is sufficient, we must realize that the practice of concealing the "mysteries" from those not yet initiated was common in the pagan mystery cults to which many of the converts to Christianity had formerly belonged. To some extent the revelation of hidden mysteries was a part of their expectations, and the catechists appear to have built upon these expectations.

According to Egeria the daily exorcism of the *competentes* took place first thing in the morning, after what we would call Morning Prayer. Although exorcism is not congenial to most twentieth-century American Christians, it was an integral part of the ancient preparation for baptism. The comment of William Telfer is most significant:

> The most important thing about the pre-baptismal exorcism was that, in those days of increased numbers, it supplied the surviving element of individual and personal ministry in the preparation for the candidates (Telfer, 1955, p. 33).

His point is that no great intellectual demands were made of the exorcist, only piety and the ability to say the exorcisms. It was therefore possible to have a large corps of exorcists, so that each candidate might be in the charge of an individual exorcist. This was certainly true in Jerusalem, if anywhere, as the *Martyrium*, where the catechesis took place, was particularly mentioned by Jerome as a place of exorcism.

Following the exorcisms, the candidates sat in a circle in the nave of the *Martyrium*, where the bishop's chair had again been placed, while the bishop gave his instructions. According to Egeria, the instructions took three hours and were held every day for seven weeks. Contrary to the custom of other churches, there were no instructions in Jerusalem during what we call Holy Week. This was presumably because of the special observances connected with that week in Jerusalem, which Cyril is believed to have introduced. The instructions were attended by the sponsors, and by as many of the faithful as wished, but were closed to catechumens. Egeria's description of the content of the lectures is instructive:

> His subject is God's Law: during the forty days he goes through the whole Bible, beginning with Genesis, and first relating the literal meaning of each passage, then interpreting its spiritual meaning. He also teaches them at this time all about the resurrection and the faith. And this is called *Catechesis*. After five weeks' teaching they receive the Creed, whose content he explains article by article in the same way as he explained the Scriptures, first literally and then spiritually (Wilkinson, 1971, p. 144).

Cyril, in his Procatechesis, said that as catechumens they had heard the Scriptures without understanding, but now that the Holy Spirit was fashioning their minds into mansions for God, when they heard the Scripture in the future they would understand its mysteries. Egeria was, in fact, impressed by the ability of the people to follow the Scripture in Jerusalem, an ability which she ascribed to the three hours of daily instruction during Lent.

If we turn from Egeria to Cyril's lectures, we shall see that they follow the general pattern which the Western pilgrim expounded. There is, however, one significant problem. All the evidence indicates that the instructions were held daily, but there are only twenty lectures, counting the Procatechesis. This is apparently not simply a peculiarity of the set of lectures we happen to possess, but the way it was normally done. Perhaps the best explanation is Telfer's suggestion that in the bilingual church of Jerusalem twenty lectures were given in cultured Greek, the ones we possess, while twenty more were given in the vernacular *Syriste* (Palestinian Aramaic), but this cannot be considered more than a convenient hypothesis.

Cyril, in the Procatechesis, mentions the reading of Scripture as a part of the instruction of the candidates, and in the lectures Scriptural texts are given for all but the Procatechesis. These texts correspond to the citations given in two Armenian lectionaries which reflect fifth-century Jerusalem usage. Nineteen readings are assigned by the Armenian lectionary to pre-baptismal instruction and four to post-baptismal lectures (Wilkinson, 1971, pp. 276-7). There are, in fact, only eighteen lectures in the surviving series, but the eighteenth is a double lecture broken by the *redditio symboli*, the recitation of the creed by the candidates for baptism, and the passage assigned by the Armenian lectionary for lecture 19 is quoted twice in the second part of Cyril's final lecture.

It appears that a standard series of catechetical lectures was given each year on fixed Scriptural texts, and that having missed one for some reason in the year from which the lectures are preserved, Cyril combined the final two, like many other lecturers before and since. We may assume, then, that the topics of Cyril's catechetical lectures were traditional for over a century, at least in the Jerusalem church.

The outline of Cyril's lectures is clearly the baptismal creed of the Jerusalem church, which is taught to the candidates in the *traditio symboli* in the fifth lecture.

The first two lectures, on Isaiah 1:16 and Ezekiel 18:20, deal
with the need for moral integrity, and for repentance and confession
of sins in preparation for baptism. Lecture three, on Romans 6:3,
deals with the meaning of baptism. The three together might be
taken as dealing with "one baptism of repentance unto the remission
of sins," although the creedal statement has not yet been introduced.
The rites themselves are not discussed until the mystagogical
lectures, and by comparing lecture three with them we can see
the different type of sacramental instruction which Cyril felt it
appropriate to give to those preparing for baptism and to those
already baptized.

The approach here is through biblical narrative, recounting
the preaching of John and the baptism of Christ, thereby tying
baptism to the call to repentance and confession in the first two
lectures. Cyril tells the candidates that Jesus by his own baptism
has broken the heads of the dragons who dwell in the water and
bound them so that the baptized have "power to tread upon
serpents and scorpions."

> For you descend into the water laden with your sins. But the invoca-
> tion of the grace causes your soul to receive the seal, and after that it
> does not let you be swallowed up by the dread dragon. You go down
> "dead indeed in sin," and you come up "alive unto righteousness"
> (Telfer, 1955, p. 96).

The reference is, of course, to Romans 6, the appointed lesson.
Cyril's sacramental premise is simple: "The water washes the
body and the Spirit seals the soul." The emphasis is on the joint
action of water and Spirit to raise us to newness of life. "The seal
of the Spirit" is what we would call the inward part of the sacrament, while the water is the outward part.

In lecture four Cyril turns to doctrine, for he tells his *photizomenoi* that the way to godliness lies in both good works and
pious dogmas. He then gives what he calls a brief recapitulation
of the indispensable dogmas. He implies that this recapitulation
will be the basis of the remainder of his lectures, but, in fact, they
follow the outline of the baptismal creed which he presents in the
next lecture. This arrangement of the material appears to be
Cyril's own, probably based on that in Origen's *Peri Archon*. The
lecture is entitled "The Ten Doctrines" in the manuscript, but it is
not clear exactly what the ten are. The text is Colossians 2:8f,
which certainly lends itself to the kind of exposition Cyril gives,

combining Platonic philosophy with a concern for practical moral action by the candidates. It includes a section on Holy Scriptures which spells out which books are canonical and warns against others. The sermon contains a sort of apology to "the more advanced" of his hearers for giving them instruction more fitting for children and spoonfeeding them. His listing of doctrines includes the "monarchy" of God, Christology, the Virgin birth, crucifixion, burial, resurrection, ascension, the coming judgment, Holy Spirit, soul, body, and our resurrection. This may well have been Cyril's preferred organization of material, but, as we have said, he follows the traditional outline of the creed, which is introduced in lecture five.

For Cyril the *traditio symboli,* the teaching of the text of the creed to the candidates, is the moment when they pass from being catechumens to believers. The basis of this homily is Hebrews 11, and it deals with faith. Cyril, following tradition, is quite specific:

> Now the one and only faith that you are to take and preserve in the way of learning and professing it is that which is now being committed to you by the Church as confirmed throughout the Scriptures. . . . This doctrine I want you to commit to memory word for word and say it over to one another as much as you can, not writing it on paper but using memory to engrave it on your heart (Telfer, 1955, pp. 123-4).

The text of the creed was repeated phrase-by-phrase for them to commit to memory. They were warned not to let any catechumen overhear them repeating it, but to memorize it as a guarantee of fidelity to the Gospel, for "this creed embraces in a few phrases all the religious knowledge contained in the Old and New Testaments together." The creed is the real core of his instructions and the homilies which follow are a phrase-by-phrase commentary on it. Cyril calls the creed *Pistis* (Faith) and tells the *photizomenoi* that they are to preserve and maintain the Faith which he has delivered to them.

The creed itself is to be memorized, both for what it is in itself as a summary of Scriptural teaching and the profession which will be made at baptism, and also, clearly, because it is the outline of the instruction, and its repetition will call to mind the entire content of the instruction given on it. The creed was not recited in worship in the early church, except in connection with baptism, and it is from this use that the creeds developed.

The actual topics covered by the remaining lectures are (6) the unity of God, (7) the Fatherhood of God, (8) the Omnipotence of God, (9) God the Creator, (10) one Lord, Jesus Christ, (11) "the only begotten Son of God, born of the Father before all ages, True God, through whom all things were made," (12) the Incarnation, (13) the Crucifixion and Burial of Christ, (14) the Resurrection of Christ, his Ascension, and his Sitting at the right hand of the Father, (15) "And he will come in glory to judge the living and the dead, whose kingdom shall have no end" and the Anti-Christ, (16 and 17) Holy Spirit, and (18) the resurrection of the flesh, the Catholic Church, and eternal life. The reconstructed text of the Jerusalem creed (which, of course, is not printed out in the manuscripts) is this:

> We believe in one God the Father Almighty, Maker of heaven and earth, and of all things visible and invisible. And in one Lord Jesus Christ, the only-begotten Son of God, true God begotten of the Father before all worlds, by whom all things were made; who was made flesh and was incarnate, crucified and entombed, who rose again on the third day and ascended into the heavens, and sat down on the right hand of the Father; who is coming in glory to judge the living and the dead, whose kingdom shall have no end. And in one Holy Spirit, the Paraclete, that spake in the prophets. And in one baptism of repentance for the remission of sins, and in one holy catholic Church, and in the resurrection of the flesh and the life of the world to come (Telfer, 1958, pp. 124-5).

In the middle of the last lecture Cyril refers again to the creed, repeating it once again and urging the candidates for baptism to repeat it with him. He then gives the candidates an opportunity to recite the creed individually, a ceremony called the *redditio symboli*.

Egeria says that it took place on the Saturday before the beginning of Holy Week. The bishop's chair, she says, was placed at the back of the apse behind the altar, and the candidates went up to him one by one and recited the creed, after which the bishop addressed them:

> During these seven weeks you have received instruction in the whole biblical Law. You have heard about the faith and the resurrection of the body. You have also learned all you can as catechumens of the content of the Creed. But the teaching about baptism itself is a deeper mystery, and you have not the right to hear it while you remain catechumens. Do not think it will never be explained; you

will hear it all during the eight days of Easter after you have been baptized. But so long as you are catechumens you cannot be told God's deep mysteries (Wilkinson, 1971, p. 145).

Cyril, at the conclusion of his final lecture, describes his purpose as preparing their souls to receive the heavenly gifts. He says that he has given them as many lectures as possible during the forty days "concerning the holy and apostolic faith it was given to you to profess," and that further lectures concerning the meaning of baptism and the spiritual and heavenly mysteries of the altar will be given them after Easter in the *Anastasis*, the holy place of the resurrection:

> In these you will be instructed again in the reasons for each of the things that took place. You will be given proofs from the Old and New Testaments, first, of course, for the things that were done before your baptism, and next how you have been made clean from your sins by the Lord with the washing of water by the Word, then how that you have entered into the right to be called "Christ" in virtue of your "priesthood," then how you have been given the "sealing" of fellowship with the Holy Spirit, then about the mysteries of the altar of the new covenant . . . and finally, how for the rest of your life you must walk worthily of the grace you have received . . . (Telfer, 1955, pp. 193-4).

There are, of course, minor differences between the two accounts, but the overall picture of what was done in the Jerusalem church is clear enough. The Lenten instructions were doctrinal and practical, heavily laced with references to the Bible. Cyril certainly does not, in the lectures we have, undertake a systematic exegesis of the Old and New Testaments, as Egeria implies was customary, but the pattern of instruction on the creed is sufficiently clear. Detailed sacramental instruction was postponed until after baptism. Cyril suggests that the candidates received only basic instruction in what to do before the event itself.

THE JERUSALEM MYSTAGOGUE

The scholarly debate over the authorship of the post-baptismal lectures, or mystagogical catecheses, need not concern us, since the lectures are certainly from Jerusalem in the fourth century, whether they were written by Cyril or his successor John (Yarnhold, 1978). As we have seen, Egeria and Cyril agree that these lectures were given in the week after Easter in the *Anastasis* itself, the site of the empty tomb:

> The newly-baptized come into the Anastasis, and any of the faithful who wish to hear the Mysteries; but, while the bishop is teaching, no catechumen comes in, and the doors are kept shut in case any try to enter. The bishop relates what has been done, and interprets it, and, as he does so, the applause is so loud that it can be heard outside the church (Wilkinson, 1971, p. 145).

The bishop of Jerusalem has, indeed, almost the ideal setting for impressing his hearers. Coming as the mystagogy does at the climax of the intensive period of catechesis and following hard on the administration of the rites themselves in the night of the Easter Vigil, the imparting of this knowledge, which had previously been withheld at, so to speak, the very place where their redemption was accomplished, must have moved the neophytes deeply.

Both Egeria and Cyril, in the final catechetical lecture, speak of lectures every day in the Easter week, but the series we possess has only five lectures, and the Armenian lectionary provides for only four. Current scholarly opinion is that the lectures were given only when the bishop could be present at the *Anastasis.*

The first lecture is on the rites before baptism, chiefly the renunciation of the devil. The text is 1 Peter 5:8-14, and the lecture is an explanation in straightforward terms of the meaning of what is said and done. The anointing of the door-posts of the ancient Hebrews with the blood of the paschal lamb against the angel of death is put forward as a type of our salvation from the tyranny of Satan by the blood of the unblemished Lamb Jesus Christ.

The second lecture, on Romans 6:3-14, discusses the rites of baptism itself, and Cyril explains his sacramental theology:

> We did not really die, we were not really buried, we were not really crucified and raised again, but our imitation was in a figure, while our salvation is in reality (Cross, 1960, p. 60).

By our celebration of the rites, we perform in a figure (or icon) those things which Christ suffered in reality, and by this imitation we obtain salvation, not in a figure but in truth.

√ The third lecture is on the holy chrism. Its text is 1 John 2:20-8. "As He was anointed with the spiritual oil of gladness, the Holy Ghost . . . so ye were anointed with ointment (*myron*), having been made partakers and fellows with Christ." Cyril's theme is that we are imitators of Christ, being anointed as he was, and from this anointing (*chrism*) we are called Christians. These things, he says, happened to the priests of the Old Testament figuratively, "but to you not in a figure; because ye were truly anointed by the Holy Ghost" (Cross, 1960, p. 66). Cyril's sacramental understanding of the anointing is clear:

> While thy body is anointed with visible ointment (*myron*), thy soul
> is sanctified by the Holy and life-giving Spirit (Cross 1960, p. 65).

The fourth lecture is on the eucharist, with the text 1 Corinthians 11:23ff. Here Cyril departs from his pattern of the first three lectures and discusses not the rite but the theology of the eucharist. On the analogy of the changing of water into wine at the wedding in Cana, he asks:

> Since then He Himself has declared and said of the Bread, *This is my
> Body*, who shall dare to doubt any longer? (Cross 1960, p. 68).

The lecture makes clear that the neophytes go directly from the anointing described in the previous lecture to the eucharist dressed in white baptismal robes, indicating that baptism, chrismation, and first communion were integrally the rites administered to the candidates at the Easter Vigil.

Lecture five, on 1 Peter 2:1ff, deals again with the eucharist, and this time returns to the pattern of exegeting the rite:

> We call upon the merciful God to send forth His Holy Spirit upon
> the gifts lying before Him; that He may make the Bread the Body of
> Christ, and the Wine the Blood of Christ; for whatsoever the Holy
> Ghost has touched, is sanctified and changed (Cross, 1960, p. 74).

This corresponds to his statement in lecture three:

> For as the Bread of the Eucharist, after the invocation of the Holy
> Ghost, is mere bread no longer, but the Body of Christ, so also this
> holy ointment (*myron*) is no more simple ointment, nor (so to say)
> common, after the invocation, but the gift of Christ; and by the
> presence of His Godhead, it causes in us the Holy Ghost (Cross,
> 1960, p. 65).

Our intention is not to examine the sacramental theology of the Jerusalem mystagogue in detail, but rather to see how he presents that theology to those who have just been baptized. As the creed was the framework of his exposition to the candidates for baptism, so the text of the rite itself is the framework for his explanation of the sacraments. The neophytes are reminded of what was done, and the theological explanation is then given. There is, of course, a certain artificiality in this, since the tendency of the mystagogue is to attribute one effect to each ritual act and to avoid ambiguity in the interests of clarity of presentation.

Cyril does not seem to have been able to follow his own method in lecture four, and instead speaks directly from the Pauline account of the Last Supper of the meaning of the eucharistic food, but the tendency in both the mystagogical and catechetical lectures is to be practical and to tell the new Christians what they need to know and believe in order to live as Christians. It is not surprising, then, that the final lecture contains a phrase-by-phrase commentary on the Lord's Prayer. Other catechists provide a *traditio* of the Lord's Prayer as well as the creed in the final lectures before baptism, but Cyril includes it here, in its place in the eucharistic liturgy. In either case the use of the Lord's Prayer with an understanding of its meaning is expected to be a part of the new life of the baptized.

The combination of our sources provides us with a detailed picture of the catechetical instruction given in fourth-century Jerusalem. The candidates were given first biblical and then credal instruction, with a heavy emphasis on practical morality, and after baptism instruction in the meaning of the sacraments and the Lord's Prayer was given, with the goal of enabling the new Christians to live the life in Christ.

ST. JOHN CHRYSOSTOM

This same emphasis on practical morality is found in the baptismal instructions of St. John Chrysostom. We do not have a complete course of instruction from John Chrysostom, but we do have what we might call the key addresses from two series of instructions given in Antioch, probably in the years 388 and 390. The more extensive series contains a sermon on the occasion of the enrollment of the candidates for baptism, another at the conclusion of their instructions describing what will happen to them in the baptismal rites (a sermon apparently delivered at the Easter Vigil itself), and his sermons to the newly baptized during Easter week. These last are not about the meaning of the rites but are moral exhortations to them to live the Christian life. These homilies were discovered in 1955 by Fr. Antoine Wenger, A.A., in a manuscript in the Stavronikita monastery on Mt. Athos (Wenger, 1957).

Wenger's discovery called attention to the other series of homilies, those thought to have been preached in 388, which had been published in 1909 as part of an obscure volume from the University of St. Petersburg (Papadopoulos-Kerameus, 1909). This contained four homilies: one given thirty days before Easter to the candidates, one given ten days later, one preached on Maundy Thursday describing the rites, and the same Easter sermon found in the other series. It has been suggested, not unreasonably, that these sermons were preached in the same year as Chrysostom's homilies on Genesis and his Easter week sermons on Acts (Harkins, 1963, pp. 17-8).

Chrysostom was a priest of the Church of Antioch and not its bishop when these homilies were given, and his role may have been somewhat different from that of Cyril in Jerusalem. These series appear to be complete and interrelated, and presumably represent Chrysostom's contribution to the preparation of the candidates. They are in many ways typical of the sermons of Chrysostom and show his activities as a catechist and mystagogue. Chrysostom greets those enrolling for Easter baptism as being betrothed for spiritual marriage and enlisted for military service in spiritual warfare. The catechumens, in their sinfulness, are described as "deformed and ugly, thoroughly and shamefully sordid." Seeing his bride in such as state, the heavenly Bridegroom has come to her,

> that by his own blood He might sanctify her; that, having cleansed her by the bath of baptism, He might present her to Himself a Church in all her glory. To this end He poured forth His blood and endured the cross that through this He might freely give sanctification to us too, and might cleanse us through the bath of regeneration, and might present to Himself those who before were in dishonor and unable to speak with confidence, but now are glorious without spot or wrinkle, or any such thing (Harkins, 1963, pp. 29-30).

The force of Chrysostom's argument is somewhat lost on us in our different cultural context, but he likens baptism to the coming of the bridegroom at night to claim his bride. He takes the girl, who had sometimes never even seen him before, from her father's house and brings her to his own, producing an instantaneous change in both environment and lifestyle. The change expected in the catechumens at baptism is, Chrysostom tells them, this dramatic. The marriage contract is simply to renounce their former life of service to the Evil One and to accept the service of Christ. This involves right belief in the Trinity and a new life in the power of Christ:

> Even if one is a fornicator, or an adulterer, or effeminate, or unnatural in his lust, or has consorted with prostitutes, or is a thief, or has defrauded others, or is a drunkard, or an idolater, the power of the gift and the love of the Master are great enough to make all these sins disappear and to make the sinner shine more brightly than the rays of the sun, if he will only give evidence of good resolution (Harkins, 1963, pp. 32f.).

Chrysostom likens the training of the catechumenate to the practice sessions of a wrestling school. They are not fraught with spiritual danger for the candidate, but after baptism, he warns them, the real contest against the power of Evil One begins:

> Let us learn, during this time of training, the grips he uses, the source of his wickedness, and how he can easily hurt us. Then, when the contest comes, we will not be caught unaware nor be frightened, as we would be if we were to see new wrestling tricks; because we have practiced among ourselves and have learned all his artifices, we will confidently join grips with him in combat (Harkins, 1963, p. 141).

Chrysostom couples this teaching with practical warnings: against expensive clothes, omens, oaths, performances in hippodrome and theater, and especially against sins of speech. We may take these as typical of Chrysostom's moral concerns and a commentary on his own culture.

In the lecture which he gave to the candidates who had begun their preparation ten days previously, Chrysostom reiterated his moral exhortations, but also talked about the significance of the season of Christ's triumph over death and the devil as the time of baptism. Exegeting Romans 6, he explains that,

> in baptism there are both burial and resurrection together at the same time. He who is baptized puts off the old man, takes up the new, and rises up, just as Christ has arisen through the glory of the Father (Harkins, 1963, p. 152).

He describes the catechumens as taken captive by Christ in his victory over the devil, but captives being transformed from slaves into free citizens. He refers all of this to the exorcism which the catechumens must undergo, at which they stand naked and barefoot "to remind you by your appearance that the devil held sway over you." His picture of what is happening is most striking:

> The catechumen is a sheep without a seal; he is a deserted inn and a hostel without a door, which lies open to all without distinction; he is a lair for robbers, a refuge for wild beasts, a dwelling place for demons. Yet, our Master decreed that through His loving-kindness this deserted, doorless inn, this robbers' refuge should become a royal palace. On this account He sent us, your teachers, and those exorcists to prepare the inn beforehand. And by our instruction, we who teach you are making strong and secure the walls of the inn which were weak and unsound (Harkins, 1963, p. 195).

The importance of the catechetical task in preparing candidates to receive the baptismal gifts has seldom been so forcefully stated.

The final pre-baptismal address in both series is chiefly devoted to a description of the baptismal rites. This differs from the practice of Jerusalem, and other fourth-century evidence, where this information was delayed until the post-baptismal lectures.

Chrysostom explains that the true actor in the sacraments is not the priest, but the Triune God.

> [The priest] is only the minister of grace and merely offers his hand because he has been ordained to this end by the Spirit. The one fulfilling all things is the Father and the Son and the Holy Spirit, the undivided Trinity. It is faith in this Trinity which gives the grace of remission from sin; it is this confession which gives to us the gift of filial adoption (Harkins, 1963, p. 53).

Chrysostom explains that he has described these events before they take place so that when the candidates come to the event itself they may set their minds on things above and "see the objects of bodily sight more clearly with the eyes of the spirit."

His Easter sermon commends the example of St. Paul to the neophytes. Chrysostom's attitude is well summarized in this passage:

> Since we have become Christ's and have put him on, since we are judged deserving of His spiritual food and drink, let us train ourselves to live as men who have nothing in common with the affairs of this present life. For we have been enrolled as citizens of another state, the heavenly Jerusalem. Therefore, let us show forth works worthy of that state . . . (Harkins, 1963, p. 77).

In a real sense Chrysostom's post-baptismal instruction is not catechesis but moral exhortation, the purpose of which is to assure that the lessons of the catechumenate and the rites of initiation are not forgotten by the neophytes. The final sermon, preached not only to those baptized in the city but to those who have come in from the countryside for the final day of the Easter octave, concludes:

> And especially do I exhort you who have recently put on Christ and received the descent of the Spirit. Each day look to the luster of your garment, that it may never receive any spot or wrinkle, either by untimely words, or idle listening, or by evil thoughts, or by eyes which rush foolishly and without reason to see whatever goes on. Let us build a rampart about ourselves on every side and keep constantly before our minds that dread day, so that we may abide in our shining brightness, keep our garment of immortality unspotted and unstained and deserve those ineffable gifts (Harkins, 1963, p. 130).

In many ways, Chrysostom's catecheses are too personal and too culturally conditioned to be helpful models for the present. I believe their chief value is to show us one of the great Christian preachers fulfilling this role and speaking to the adult converts of his day about real issues in their lives and about the power of Christ to change those lives through the sacraments of baptism and eucharist.

THEODORE OF MOPSUESTIA

Theodore was a friend and contemporary of Chrysostom. His baptismal homilies, written in Greek, are preserved only in Syriac. It is believed that they were at one time used as a textbook for catechesis in the Church of Antioch. In their Syriac form they became classics of the Syriac-speaking Nestorian Church, centered in Edessa and later in the Persian Empire.

Theodore's addresses are much more traditional in structure than Chrysostom's. There are ten homilies on the creed, one on the Lord's Prayer, and five on baptism and the eucharist. It appears that, like Chrysostom, Theodore explained baptism before the candidates received the sacrament, but his last three lectures on the eucharist appear to have been given after baptism. His style is exceedingly diffuse and repetitive, and his homilies are more often quarried for information about the rites than read as sermons. If Chrysostom is moralistic, Theodore is doctrinal.

Theodore tells those preparing for Easter baptism that his topic is "the New Testament which God established for the human race through the Economy of our Lord Jesus Christ, when he abolished all old things and showed new things in their place."

> Because of this covenant we receive the knowledge of these mysteries so that we should put off the old man and put on the new man who is renewed after the image of Him who created him where there is neither Jew nor Greek, bond nor free, but Christ is all and in all. This will take place in reality in the next world when we shall have become immortal and incorruptible . . . While still on earth we have been inscribed in that awe-inspiring glory of the future world through these mysteries (Mingana, 1932, pp. 19-20).

This participation, Theodore assures his listeners, requires faith, and faith is expressed in the "profession of faith which we make before Christ the Lord at the time of our baptism." The first ten lectures consist of a careful exposition of Trinitarian faith expounded in the creed. In the tenth lecture, having completed his discussion of the doctrine of the Holy Spirit, Theodore returns to the Matthean commission to baptize in the name of the Trinity and explains that baptism into the name of the Father, Son, and Holy Spirit follows upon the doctrinal exposition of the catechumenate. He then moves from that to the One Catholic Church into which we are baptized.

> He [Christ] calls the Church all the congregation of the faithful who worship God in the right way and those who after the coming of Christ believed in Him from all countries till the end of the world and the second coming of our Savior from heaven, which we are expecting (Mingana, 1932, p. 112).

The lecture concludes with a discussion of the notes of the church and the resurrection of the body.

The sermon on the Lord's Prayer was given the day after the final sermon on the creed. Theodore explains that after commanding the apostles to baptize, the Lord said, "And teach them to observe all things I have commanded you." Therefore "the doctrine of religion," right knowledge, and life in accordance with the commandments are required of the baptized. "They added," he tells them, "to the words of the Creed the prayer which our Lord taught in short words to His disciples, *because it contains the teaching for good works in sufficient manner*"

(Mingana, 1933, p. 1). The homily expounds the prayer line-by-line and at the end restates its importance as a guide for good life and good works, to accompany the right belief taught in the creed.

At the beginning of his next lecture, the first on baptism, Theodore defines a sacrament as "a representation of unseen and unspeakable things through signs and emblems," and therefore "words are needed to explain the power of signs and mysteries" (Mingana, 1933, p. 17).

The remainder of the lectures are almost completely devoted to a description of the rites of baptism and eucharist and a theological interpretation of these rites. The final lecture, however, concludes with a warning against unworthy communion and an exhortation to use the "medicine of repentance" administered in God's name by the priests as "physicians of sins."

Theodore's style is not congenial to us, his theology has been condemned as leading to Nestorianism, and his interpretation of the liturgy is rejected by modern commentators. He was, nevertheless, a teacher of wide influence and high repute among his contemporaries, and the formal structure of his presentations (creed, Lord's Prayer, and sacraments) still commends itself.

AMBROSE OF MILAN

The works of Ambrose of Milan provide clear Western parallels to the great Eastern catechists. Three writings of Ambrose, *Explanatio symboli*, *de Sacramentis*, and *de Mysteriis*, are specifically catechetical.

Ambrose tells us that he gave daily instruction to the catechumens *de moralibus* during Lent at the time when the lives of the Patriarchs and the precepts of Proverbs were being read. References in his homilies *de Abraham* indicate that they were preached to those preparing for baptism at the time. Book I of these homilies does deal with right conduct, while Book II follows Philo in treating the mystical sense of the narrative. It certainly appears that other exegetical homilies of Ambrose on the books read during Lent were of the same character; this leads us to believe that this instruction was the occasion for many of the patristic biblical homilies. Egeria, you may remember, included biblical exegesis among the matters presented to the candidates for baptism.

Ambrose says that the enrollment of the *competentes*, or seekers of baptism, took place on Epiphany, on which day he extended an invitation to the catechumens to enroll. The creed was taught to the *competentes* (*traditio symboli*) on Palm Sunday. The *explanatio symboli* is a transcript of the ceremony as Ambrose conducted it. He speaks of this as following the scrutinies and exorcisms of the candidates. Clearly it is a high point in the preparation, which follows not only instruction and exorcism but public examination. Ambrose repeats the text three times in the homily, and tells them to memorize it, not to write it down. It will be easier to remember, he tells them, if they do not write it but keep it in mind for the *redditio*.

We shall probably be less willing than Ambrose to assure catechumens that the twelve apostles wrote the creed, which is therefore in twelve articles, but we can admire the simplicity and directness with which he teaches the meaning of the twelve articles of the creed.

He begins his post-baptismal lectures by saying that it would not have been right to give a reasoned account of the sacraments earlier because faith must precede reason. Baptism is the sacrament of conversion, and the purpose of catechesis before baptism is to bring the candidates to faith—thus instruction is joined to exorcism and scrutinies,

> in order that trained and instructed thereby, you might become accustomed to walk in the paths of our elders and to tread in their steps, and to obey the divine oracles; to the end that you might, after being renewed by baptism, continue to practice the life which befitted the regenerate (Srawley, 1950, p. 122).

He mentions the *disciplina arcani* which would have prevented him from speaking of the sacraments to the uninitiated even if he had wished, but concludes,

> it were better that the light of the mysteries should reveal itself unasked and unexpected than be preceded by some discourse (Srawley 1950, p. 123).

All of our mystagogues, even those who describe the baptismal rites (but not the eucharist) in their final pre-baptismal lecture, speak of this discipline which conceals from catechumens the mysteries of the sacraments, but there seems here to be a conviction that it is *better* to wait until after the sacraments have been received to explain their meaning. They are first to be seen with the eyes of faith, and only then can they be examined in the light of reason.

Those being taught to conform their lives to the gospel are given moral instruction. Instruction in the sacraments is reserved for those living the sacramental life.

Ambrose's method of exposition is to describe the rites in detail, and then to explain their meaning by means of a number of Old Testament typologies. In fact, Ambrose's mystagogical work is significant for its mystical interpretation of Song of Songs. In addition to the exposition of the rites of baptism and eucharist in such detail that *de Sacramentis* is a major source for our knowledge of early Latin liturgy, Ambrose expounds the Lord's Prayer and recommends the Psalter to the new Christians as a source for their own prayers.

It is difficult not to compare the work of Ambrose to that of Cyril of Jerusalem. There are differences of theological emphasis between them, but the pattern of their work is so similar that it is reasonable to assume that both are following an established pattern of Christian catechesis, which the Antiochines, exemplified by Chrysostom and Theodore, had varied slightly.

Candidates for baptism are instructed in Christian living, in the Bible, and in the creed. The Lord's Prayer is expounded, either to the newly-baptized or to those about to be baptized, not only as a prayer to be memorized and recited, but as a model for their own prayer. And in the days immediately following baptism, instruction is given in the meaning of the sacraments for their new life in the risen Christ.

ST. AUGUSTINE

Although Augustine wrote several treatises on the theology of baptism and took part himself in the catechesis of candidates, he wrote neither a treatise on the rites of Christian initiation nor a complete course of catechetical instruction. F. van der Meer, in his book *Augustine the Bishop*, has collected from various primary and secondary sources most of what Augustine tells us about the preparation of candidates for baptism (van der Meer, 1961, pp. 353-61), but it tells us little or nothing new about such preparation.

Augustine did make one unique contribution, however, his treatise *de catechizandis rudibus*, which might be translated *Instruction for Beginners*. It is not a course of catechetics, but an explanation of what to say to an inquirer to move him or her to enroll as a catechumen. The treatise consists of an explanation of what to do, followed by two examples, a shorter and a longer one. This is not formal liturgical catechesis, but what I would call evangelism—a first approach to the uninitiated who come asking questions.

Augustine considers whether the catechist is dealing with a single inquirer, with whom a conversation is appropriate, or with a group which must be addressed in a sort of sermon. He also considers the varied educational backgrounds from which inquirers may come. He then deals with reasons why the catechist may be unhappy about his task. What he actually says, although interesting, is not as important as is the clear understanding that what is taught is conditioned by the person of both teacher and pupil. The catechist needs to be in tune with the gospel which he is proclaiming, if the message is to be heard.

The content of this preliminary instruction is, Augustine says, a story, a *narratio*, of the mighty acts of God from creation to the present. Theories are not to be propounded but the story, the *kerygma*, proclaimed. God acted in history; he did not expound propositions. The appeal of the story should be that God loved the world, so that the hearer is moved by the love of God. As a spur to the will, he would conclude with teaching about the Last Things and the punishment of the wicked, and provide some warnings against heretics. This is not essentially different from the Apostolic preaching in Acts, although his model instruction is more extensive.

We must remember that this is not the catechesis itself, but only the opening instruction which will encourage inquirers to enroll and begin the course of instruction which will lead to the *traditio symboli*, the teaching of the creed, and to biblical, moral, and sacramental teaching. Its purpose is not so much to instruct as to convert, and Augustine is quite concerned that it be tailored to the individual inquirer.

The picture which emerges then is of a highly specific beginning, which motivates the convert to enroll as a catechumen and begin the more formal instruction, leading to the sacramental life in Christ.

CONCLUSION

The method followed in this essay has been to build up piece-by-piece from the examination of early Christian authors a picture of the process of becoming a Christian in the third, fourth, and fifth centuries.

The initial contact is made by the inquirer. Augustine addressed his treatise to the Carthaginian deacon Deogratias whose ministry this was, so we may assume that normally some minister of the church was the person who interviewed inquirers and sought to convince them to enter the catechumenate. Earlier Hippolytus described sponsors bringing inquirers to the bishop.

After initial admission to the catechumenate they began a period of religious and cultural readjustment to a Christian lifestyle as hearers of the Word. When they were ready, and the church was prepared to accept them as seekers of baptism, they moved into an intensive period of preparation marked by daily instruction, exorcism, and other liturgical acts. It is to this period that the formal catechetical lectures on Scripture and creed belong. The creed was solemnly delivered to the candidates for baptism and formed the basis for their moral and doctrinal formation. Instruction in the Lord's Prayer, and by extension in the life of Christian prayer, was given either immediately before baptism or as part of the post-baptismal mystagogy.

Some of the classical mystagogues explained the baptismal ceremonies in the final instruction before baptism, but more often this was deferred until after baptism, when sacramental instruction was combined with moral exhortation for the living of the new life in the risen Christ.

This classical pattern apparently developed in the second and third century and continued on even beyond the end of the adult catechumenate in the early middle ages.

ANNOTATED BIBLIOGRAPHY

Botte, Bernard, ed., Ambroise de Milan, *Des Sacrements, Des Mystères, Explication du Symbole*. Paris: Editions du Cerf, 1961. The best Latin text of these three treatises with a French translation and introduction by a leading liturgical scholar.

Butterworth, C. W., *Clement of Alexandria*. Loeb Classical Library. Cambridge: Harvard University Press, 1960. A standard edition of the Greek with an English translation.

Cross, Frank F., *St. Cyril of Jerusalem's Lectures on the Christian Sacraments*. London: S.P.C.K., 1960. A convenient edition and translation of the Mystagogical Catecheses with a helpful introduction.

Cuming, Geoffrey, J., *Hippolytus: A Text for Students*. Grove Liturgical Study 8. Bramcotte, Notts: Grove Books, 1976. An English translation of Apostolic Tradition with a simple introduction, based on the work of Dix and Botte.

Easton, Burton S., *The Apostolic Tradition of Hippolytus*. Cambridge: The University Press, 1934, reprint Archon Books, 1962. The earliest edition of Hippolytus, with a preface by the late professor of New Testament of General Theological Seminary, readily available in paperback.

Harkins, Paul W., translator, St. John Chrysostom, *Baptismal Instructions*, Ancient Christian Writers. Westminster, Md.: Newman Press, 1963. An English translation of all of the catechetical homilies of Chrysostom with an extensive introduction and notes.

McCauley, Leo P. and Stephenson, Anthony A., *The Works of St. Cyril of Jerusalem*, 2 vols. Washington: Catholic University Press, 1969-70. The best English translation of the complete series of Cyril's pre- and post-baptismal homilies.

Mingana, A., *Woodbrooke Studies*, Vol. 5. Cambridge: W. Heffer and Son, 1932. Edition and translation of Theodore of Mopsuestia's lectures on the creed.

_____, *Woodbrooke Studies*, Vol 6. Cambridge: W. Heffer and Son, 1933. Edition and translation of Theodore of Mopsuestia's lectures on the Lord's Prayer, baptism, and eucharist.

Popadopoulos-Keremous, A., *Varia Graeca Sacra*, pp. 154-183. St. Petersburg: 1909. An extremely obscure Russian publication of the Greek text of one series of Chrysostom's homilies translated by Harkins (*see above*).

Paulin, Antoine, *Saint Cyrille de Jérusalem Catéchète*. Lex Orandi 29. Paris: Cerf, 1959. Study of Cyril's catechesis in French.

Srawley, J. H., *St. Ambrose on the Sacraments*. London: S.P.C.K., 1950. English translation of *de Sacramentis* and *de Mysteriis* with an extensive introduction by a distinguished scholar of early liturgy.

Stevenson, J., *A New Eusebius*. London: S.P.C.K., 1968. A source book for early church history, containing translated selections from ancient writers, cited for its translation of passages from Origen.

Telfer, William, *Cyril of Jerusalem and Nemesis of Emesa*. Library of the Christian Classics 4. Philadelphia: Westminster, 1955. Excellent translation of selected lectures from Cyril's catechetical lectures, with a brilliant introduction.

van der Meer, F., *Augustine the Bishop*. London and New York: Sheed and Ward, 1961. Summarizes Augustine's information on Christian initiation in one chapter and discusses *de catechizandis rudibus* in another.

Wenger, Antoine, Jean Chrysostome, *Huit Catéchèses Baptismales*. Sources Chrétiennes 5. Paris: Cerf, 1957. The original publication with French translations of the newly discovered series of baptismal homilies by Chrysostom. English translation by Harkins (*see above*).

Wilkinson, John, *Egeria's Travels*. London: S.P.C.K., 1971. The best English translation of Egeria's diary containing her descriptions of the Church of Jerusalem, with introduction, maps, and many aids to understanding the material.

Yarnhold, Edward, "The Authorship of the Mystagogic Catecheses attributed to Cyril of Jerusalem," *Heythrop Journal* 19 (1978), pp. 143-161. The latest discussion of authorship. Its notes refer the interested reader to earlier discussion. Yarnhold argues that Cyril did write the lectures.

The Medieval Church

Chapter 4
Basic Christian Education from the Decline of Catechesis to the Rise of the Catechisms

Milton McC. Gatch

It is one of the greater historical ironies that the period of the church's greatest and most sustained importance as the central institution of Western culture is usually regarded as one that does not, on the whole, provide us with useful models or norms for Christian instruction, or catechesis, especially if catechesis is regarded as an activity associated with the rites of initiation. As Josef Jungmann has observed, the catechumenate as a class and catechesis as a method of educating Christian initiands and initiates passed out of existence in the Middle Ages. No system of training for children or adults arose to replace what had been lost, and simultaneously the liturgy became less and less comprehensible to a majority of the people. Thus it is a "puzzle" that the age saw a great "flowering of Christianity" (Jungmann, 1962, p. 11).

The preceding essay in this volume has treated the ancient church and especially the development of catechetical instruction as it appears, fully developed, in the fourth century. This instruction apparently included catechetical instruction in the strict sense of training given in the weeks just preceding baptism and also "mystagogic" instruction on the most sacred mysteries of the faith, which was delivered in the days immediately following baptism at Easter. Perhaps no scene in the history of Christian education is more moving than that described by the pilgrim Egeria in Jerusalem itself in the 380's. Having gone through the catechesis in Lent and been instructed by the bishop in Holy Week, the Jerusalem catechumens were baptized. Although they had received the *symbolum*, or Creed, however, they underwent baptism before its mysteries had been explained, and only during the octave of Easter was it made clear to them what had happened to them at their baptism. After the daily morning services, they gathered in Easter week at the *Anastasis*, or Holy Sepulchre, where the resurrection itself was believed to have occurred. The doors were shut to all who had not received baptism:

> The bishop stands leaning against the inner screen in the cave of the Anastasis, and interprets all that takes place in Baptism, . . . and, as he does so, the applause is so loud that it can be heard outside the church. Indeed the way he expounds the mysteries and interprets them cannot fail to move his hearers (Wilkinson, 1971, pp. 145-6).

The very success of the church in the late Roman Empire made inevitable the decline of the catechumenate as a class of adults preparing for initiation, however, and quite as necessarily presaged the decline of catechesis as a system of instruction for initiands and recent initiates. From the sixth century or thereabouts, when that decline began, through the fifteenth century, no conscious or consistent adjustment was made to accommodate to this fact. Nevertheless, instruction in the basic concepts of Christianity continued to be given and to be a primary concern of the leaders of the church.

This essay attempts to outline the history of such instruction in a cursory way and to introduce a number of typical and exemplary documents of basic Christian education in the fundamentals of faith throughout the Middle Ages. Most of the documents to be discussed are of English origin; but it can be argued that, on the whole, they are typical of what is to be found throughout Europe in the period. To prevent this study from becoming a superficial survey of the history of medieval education or of medieval piety, its focus has been kept very narrow. The history of schools, of the universities, and of theology is excluded, as also are the history of ascetic or mystical discipline for the education of the soul and the history of devotional literature. Our subject is instruction in the faith available to all women, men, and children at several points in the Middle Ages. Our question is, What took the place in the Middle Ages of the ancient catechesis with its handing over (*traditio*) of the credal affirmation to the initiands? Or, posed differently, this inquiry asks whether there was any continuity in basic Christian instruction between the ancient catechesis as practiced in the fourth century and the charge to godparents in the baptismal office of the First Prayer Book of Edward VI (1549) that,

> ye shall call upon [your Godchildren] to heare sermons, and chiefly you shal prouide that thei may learne the Crede, the Lordes prayer, and the ten commaundementes, in thenglish tounge: and all other thinges which a christian manne ought to knowe and beleve to his soules health (Gibson, 1910, p. 241).

To answer these queries, one may first review the relationship of basic education to the rites of Christian initiation and then examine samples of general ecclesiastical teaching addressed to lay audiences in the Middle Ages.

THE SEPARATION OF CATECHESIS AND INITIATION

Peter Göbl (1880) in the standard history of medieval catechesis referred in his title to the early part of the period as the time of the *Verfall des Katechumenats*—the "decadence" or "decline of the catechumenate." This "decline"—almost disappearance—of the catechumenate and (with it) of catechetical instruction can be traced to a number of correlative causes. Chief among them, functionally, was the fact that, as the populace of the Roman Empire became christianized, the class of catechumens or candidates for initiation virtually disappeared. No longer were those seeking baptism adults, except on the frontiers where mass baptisms of defeated and converted Germanic and Slavic tribes occurred. Rather, the custom of infant baptism constantly gained ground throughout Europe, and it came increasingly to be believed and taught that infants ought to be baptized as soon as possible after birth. For a considerable time and varying according to place, it remained the general custom (especially for families living a reasonable distance from the seat of a bishop) for baptism to be reserved to the vigils of Easter and of Pentecost, the full rite of initiation under the presidency of the bishop being preserved. By the fifteenth century, it was virtually the universal custom that baptism was performed by presbyters within the octave of an infant's birth. It might be performed earlier (and by a lay person, if need be) if the newborn child appeared to be in imminent danger of death (Fisher, 1965, esp. ch. vii).

It is not to our purpose here to trace in all its ramifications the effects of this development upon the liturgy; nor can one pause to detail at leisure the consequent lengthening of the interval between baptism, which became a rite performed by presbyters, and confirmation, which in the West remained a rite reserved to the episcopate (*Ibid.*, ch. viii). Nevertheless, it is necessary to outline briefly the rite of initiation as it was celebrated in the early and in the later periods of the Middle Ages in order to introduce the difficulties which arose for the catechetical system as a consequence of the liturgical development.

The history of baptismal liturgies in the early Middle Ages is a complex one, involving ultimately the virtual disappearance of the regional rites of baptism and confirmation in favor of rites known as Roman, which were, in fact, composite liturgies based upon not only Roman use but also the customs of other areas of Western Europe (Jones *et al.*, 1978, esp. pp. 110-17; Fisher, 1965, esp. chs. i, iv). Two documents can serve here as a base for a description of the liturgy of initiation as it was disseminated under the aegis of Charlemagne and his advisers and their successors in the eighth century and later. The first of these is the so-called Gelasian Sacramentary, an eighth-century collection based on Roman formularies but with Gallican contributions, at least in the arrangement of elements of the rite. The manuscript of the *Gelasianum*—which has no direct connection with Pope Gelasius (492-496)—is now in Rome (Vatican, Reginensis 316) but was written in France, probably near Paris, shortly before the reforms of Charlemagne (H. A. Wilson, ed., 1894; Whitaker, 1960, pp. 156-86). The second document is known as *Ordo Romanus XI*. It has its origin in the Roman baptismal rite of the sixth century, but is based upon manuscripts produced in France no earlier than the ninth century (Andrieu, 1948, pp. 417-47; Whitaker, 1960, pp. 186-94). Both documents reflect the reverence of northern European Christians for Roman liturgical customs, and both show the Roman rite of initiation as adapted in the North at a time when the transition from adult to infant initiates had clearly been made and the language and rubrics of the liturgy adjusted to this fact.

In the *Gelasian Sacramentary* the portions relevant to the rites of initiation begin at the Third Sunday in Lent, where "the Mass is celebrated for the scrutinies of the elect" (Whitaker, 1960, p. 156). The scrutinies had originally included both exorcisms and examinations of the catechumens on their knowledge of the faith and on the conduct of their lives or their knowledge of Christian moral teaching. The elect were those catechumens who, having already undergone considerable instruction, had been enrolled in Lent as candidates for initiation at the coming Paschal season. At the Mass on the Third Sunday in Lent the names of the sponsors ("the men and women who are to receive the infants from the font") and of the elect are read during the Canon (p.157). The propers for the two following Sundays also are "for the Scrutiny" but do not call for the reading of the list of persons enrolled for baptism or of their sponsors.

The scrutiny itself seems to have been conducted on a weekday determined by local convenience. A public announcement, delivered first on the Monday of the third week of Lent, declared that the scrutiny is a process "when the elect are instructed in divine things" (p. 159). Nevertheless, a rubric and the petitions of the canon make it clear that the elect undergoing the scrutiny are "infants." Not simply those newborn in Christ after baptism, but the newborn in terms of chronological age, they were probably children who had been born since the preceding Easter or Pentecost when the rite of baptism was administered. Called into the church in the order in which their names had been given in, the infant catechumens were arranged with the males (and their sponsors) on the right and the females on the left and were admitted by prayer and signing with the cross to the status of the elect (pp. 159f.). Salt was given to each as a sign of both medical purgation and of wisdom. Finally there came exorcisms delivered by the acolytes—three each for males and for females—to rid the candidates of possession by the "accursed devil" (pp. 160ff.). In the *Gelasianum* the essential meaning of the term 'catechize' has changed from examination on faith and morals to exorcizing as a means of purifying those who are not of sufficient age to be examined on their knowledge and behavior, as a rubric for Holy Saturday (p. 173) finally makes clear.

The rest of the ceremonies of the scrutiny in the *Gelasian Sacramentary* have, as one scholar has said, "an air of unreality" (Fisher, 1965, p. 9). They involve the *traditio* of handing over of the teaching of scripture, of the creed, and of the Lord's Prayer. It is possible that each of these was the focus of the scrutiny for one week, the exorcisms being essentially repeated. In the introduction of Scripture (pp. 162ff.), the four Gospels were borne to corners of the altar with candles and incense. A priest explained the meaning of the word "gospel" and introduced the four evangelists and their signs: Matthew (man), Mark (lion), Luke (ox), and John (eagle), citing Ezekiel 1:10 as the source of this typology. Then, in succession, a few verses were read from the beginning of each of the four books by the deacons. The priest followed each of these with a brief exposition, relating the appropriateness of the evangelists' signs. (The lion is suitable to Mark, for example, because of the wilderness references of Mark 1:3.) The introduction concludes with an apt if strained metaphor:

> And so now the Church, being pregnant by your conception, glories that amidst her festal worship she labours to bring forth new lives subject to the Christian law: so that when the day of the venerable Pascha shall come, being reborn in the laver of baptism, ye shall be found worthy like all the saints to receive the promised gift of infancy through Christ our Lord (p. 164).

The *traditio* of the creed is likewise fanciful, if one recalls that the recipients are infants, "mewling and puking" (to adopt Shakespeare's phrase). They are to receive the symbol, writing it "not on any corruptible material but on the pages of your heart" (p. 165). An acolyte takes one of the baby boys "and holding him in his left arm places his hand upon his head." The creed is received first in Greek (perhaps a reflection that Greek was the original liturgical language of the Roman church but more likely recalling the period of Byzantine control of Rome in the sixth century [Fisher, 1965, p. 10]). The creed used is the Nicene, not the Apostles' Creed, which was the ancient Roman baptismal creed, and the Greek text is transliterated to the Latin alphabet for the benefit of the clergy. It is repeated in Latin, and the priest provides a brief exposition. The final section of the scrutiny is similar in form. The deacon introduces the subject of prayer, and the *Pater noster* is handed over with brief comments on the initial address to God as father and on each the seven major petitions of the prayer.

The preparation is completed with the *redditio symboli* or return of the creed on Holy Saturday (pp. 173ff.). After another exorcism, the ceremony of the *effeta*, or the opening of the nostrils and ears with spittle (a ceremony that may also have been used in the *Gelasianum* in the exposition of the Gospels), an anointing with exorcised oils, and the renunciation of Satan, the creed is then returned. But it must be recited for the catechumens by the archdeacon, who then dismisses them until the time of the baptism proper. The baptism itself follows the vigil and its lessons. Afterwards the bishop seals the infants and they receive the sevenfold gifts of the Spirit. The rubrics note that essentially the same order may be used on the eve of Pentecost, and there are appended a number of other prayers useful at baptism, especially in circumstances of sickness (pp. 180ff.).

The Gelasian rites for Lent and Easter seem not to be the papal rites but those of a titular church in Rome. They assume the unity of the rites and the availability of a suffragan bishop to perform the crismation (or confirmation) with its gift of the sevenfold Spirit (Fisher, 1965, pp. 24f.). Above all, the *Gelasianum* is witness to continuity with the initiatory rites of the fourth and fifth century: of catechesis as the central business of Lent culminating with the great vigil, baptism, and mass of Easter—all of which have centrally in mind the reception of the new-born *infantes*, the catechumens who, having become elect, are now made full members participating in the eucharist. However, these central figures at the pivotal feast of the Christian year have now become infants indeed, and surrogates must not only respond for them but also act out an elaborate charade of their pre-initiatory training.

The situation presupposed in the *Ordo Romanus XI* is essentially similar, except that in the *Ordo* we see the paschal rites as performed in the presence of the bishop of Rome himself. Here it must suffice to comment on several pertinent departures from the order of the *Gelasianum*. The days of the scrutiny, which seem to vary in the *Gelasian Sacramentary*, are fixed in *Ordo XI* on the *quarta feria* or Wednesday (Whitaker, 1960, p. 186). It is immediately more clear that the candidates are infants, and there is greater detail about the arrangement of their places in church as they are called to the scrutiny. It is specified that the catechumens or elect are to be taken from the church during mass and returned at the end for the scrutiny. The number of performances of the scrutiny, including that of Holy Saturday, is seven in *Ordo XI*, which corresponds to "the sevenfold grace of the Spirit" (p. 192). It is stressed that the crismation, or confirmation, by the pope is the completion of the integral initiatory action (p.194). Indeed, like older catechumens, the infants are communicated at the Easter mass, care having been taken to insure that they have not eaten or been suckled between baptism and communion. They are also to be communicated and to make oblations daily throughout the octave of Easter, perhaps in parallel with the obligation of

attending the concluding, or mystagogic, catecheses in earlier
times (p. 194).

The practice of initiation remained, at least in Rome, essentially
stable into the twelfth century (Fisher, 1965, pp. 25-29; an *ordo*
ed. Andrieu, 1938, pp. 238-49). That is to say, it remained a rite
in which the bishop was the principal minister, and it retained as
much of the magnificence of the classical Paschal liturgy as was
possible, given the radical alteration of the catechumenate itself.
Nevertheless, away from Rome the mere size of dioceses and the
consequent inaccessibility of bishops made it difficult to maintain
the unity of the rite with the bishop as the pivotal figure, and the
fear of early death often led to the performance of baptism sooner
after birth than restriction of the rite to Easter or to Easter and
Pentecost permitted (Fisher, 1965, pp. 27f.). This was particularly
so in Anglo-Saxon and Anglo-Norman Britain (*Ibid.*, ch. iv).

Later, two further developments, the separation of first communion from baptism and the lengthening of the period between
baptism and confirmation (*ibid.*, chs. vi-vii), created a gap during
which the educational obligations of the godparents and the
educational opportunities for the church might be developed. By
no means, however, does the need of training for participation in
Christian society or the sense that an educational crisis was caused
by the eclipse of the educative function of the catechumenate
seem to have motivated these developments. They came to pass
largely because of other, purely fortuitous, contingencies: on the
one hand, the remoteness of bishops (enhanced by their increasingly political functions) and, on the other, an increased reverence
for the sacrament, which made it risky (given the digestive capacities of infants) to communicate the very young. Baptism thus lost
its association with both Easter and the first reception of communion. The catechetically-based scrutiny was also largely lost,
and training (as a responsibility of godparents or sponsors) became
a matter to be considered in the years following baptism, if at all
(*Ibid.*, pp. 116f.).

Developments in the initiatory rites from the thirteenth century
onwards cannot be detailed here, but it is necessary to pause to
review the state of affairs at the end of the Middle Ages. A convenient text is that of the *Sarum Manual* as printed in 1543 on the
eve of the introduction of the Book of Common Prayer. It is
typical of both English and European initiatory rites at the end of
the Middle Ages (Collins, 1960; Fisher, 1965, pp. 158-81). At this

stage, as we shall see, there had been a radical reordering in the relationship between initiation and instruction in the basic aspects of faith and morals.

The rites of initiation begin with an order "for the making of a catechumen," which descends from the scrutiny (Fisher, 1965, pp. 158-65). It begins at "the doors of the church," to which it assumes infants have been brought by "the midwife." It is also assumed that infants may also "have been baptized at home"— usually when they seemed sickly at birth—by a lay person or priest. After a number of prayers and the exorcism and administration of salt, multiple exorcisms follow with the prayers appropriate to males or females. A gospel suitable to the presentation of infants is read, and the *effeta* is followed by the *traditio*, which now consists of the recitation of the Lord's Prayer, the *Ave Maria*, and the creed. A blessing follows, and the child—now a catechumen —is brought into church, where the font is elaborately blessed (*Ibid.*, pp. 165-72). A rubric at the end of the blessing of the font shows the ancient connection with the rite to Easter and Pentecost: on the vigils of those feasts the rite is not to proceed further or the oil and chrism added to the water unless there are candidates for baptism present. These feasts have seemingly become simply days when the font is blessed and the water can be reserved for baptisms as need arises within the coming season. In other rubrics (*ibid.*, p. 177) it seems clear that only healthy children born within the octave before Easter or Pentecost are baptized at the vigils of those feasts.

The child is brought to the font by the godparents. The baptismal office proper (*ibid.*, pp. 173-79) begins with renunciations and a truncated *redditio*. After the baptism there are two gospel lections (Mark 9:17-29 and John 1:1-14). A long rubric at this juncture gives instruction for administration of baptism in necessity and describes the rites that must be performed in church over a child so baptized. Most important, however, are the strictures given for godparents:

> Men and women who receive children [from the font] at baptism are appointed their sureties before God, and therefore must frequently admonish them when they are grown or capable of discipline, that they guard their chastity, love justice, hold to charity, and above all things are bound to teach them the Lord's Prayer and angelic salutation ["Hail Mary"], the symbol of the faith and how to sign themselves with the sign of the cross.

Wherefore persons are not to be received nor admitted as godparents except those who know the aforesaid things, because godparents must instruct their spiritual children in the faith, which they cannot do unless they themselves have first been instructed in the faith (*Ibid.*, pp. 177-8).

Godparents must also, the rubric continues, take responsibility to present children to the bishop for confirmation. The *Manual* (*ibid.*, p. 178) seems to lay it down that the reception of communion will be delayed until after confirmation unless a person is in danger of death—a recognition (perhaps peculiarly English at this time) that confirmation had originally been unitive with baptism and was thus prerequisite to reception of communion.

The *Manual* is a priest's book, and one might not expect to find the liturgy for confirmation in it, for, in the Western churches, that rite had remained an episcopal office. Confirmation is, however, found in the *Sarum Manual*—widely separated from baptism—among a group of episcopal blessings (*Ibid.*, pp. 180-81). The service is short and without reference to the preparation of the confirmands. A slightly later Roman pontifical, however, presumes confirmation at a rather younger age and enjoins instruction of the confirmands upon their godparents (*Ibid.*, pp. 182-85). At any rate, the rite had almost universally become separated from the other ceremonies of initiation, and the way was clear for the Reformers' attempt to restore catechesis to connection with confirmation or with baptism deferred to the age of discretion.

By the ninth century, the ancient catechesis had already given way before the practice of baptizing infants, and no provision had been made for the training of these infants in the fundamentals of the faith after their baptism. Their sponsors and the clergy acted for them in the *traditio* and *redditio* of the creed and other basic formularies. By the twelfth century it was assumed that godparents had accepted the responsibility for teaching children the basic formularies: the creed and Lord's Prayer and (later) the *Ave Maria*, which became an increasingly common form of devotion from the twelfth century. It seems that godparents also had the duty of inculcating the young with essential moral teachings of the church. Thus, in a sense, catechesis, or the basic education of Christians, in the Middle Ages was derived from the liturgy of initiation: from the scrutiny, *traditio*, and *redditio*, which were conceived as containing the minimal outline of faith and morals.

The reformers would agree with this basic conception of the fundamentals of faith, the "thinges which a christian manne ought to knowe and beleue to his soules health." The difference was that the reformers devised catechisms as a formal means of handing over basic formularies and examining candidates for initiation on their meaning, and they made catechizing a prerequisite to initiation or (where infant baptism was retained) to the completion of initiation.

There is a very real sense in which catechesis in the Middle Ages was the responsibility of parents and godparents. As a domestic responsibility, often probably inseparable from vocational training, it took place behind doors that are usually closed to the historian. Our major glimpses of the process come from the rubrics in liturgical texts dealing with initiation about what godparents and parents were supposed to do for their charges and from a few late texts that treat domestic education. It is clear, however, that both the pietists of the fifteenth century and the reformers felt that the church itself should assume a larger role in the educative process. The new catechisms were, at very least, a kind of ecclesiastical final examination on the portion of an infant's training that was entrusted to the sponsors and family. It must also be stressed that the domestic educational obligations were not without other strong reinforcements. These included regular participation in liturgical worship, the sacrament of penance, (which was a major means of moral instruction), and the Christian assumptions of the community (Jungmann, 1962, pp. 13-19). The reasons for the feeling of many persons in the late Middle Ages (the reformers among them) that the system was inadequate probably had more to do with historical and social change than with the intrinsic inadequacies of the accommodations made in catechesis at the beginning of the medieval centuries. Were this not so, it is difficult to imagine that the flowering of Christian culture in the Middle Ages could have occurred.

Because modern observers, including the present writer, can rarely avoid incredulity at what appears to us to be a charade of catechesis as it persisted in the scrutiny and *traditio* of baptism throughout the Middle Ages, it should be noted here that the educational assumptions of these ecclesiastical practices are not at all out of step with general medieval assumptions about the nature of education. The decline of the catechetical system, in the first instance, coincided with the decline of the classical system of education. Although it is too easy to denigrate the learning of those who kept studies alive, education changed radically after the sixth century (Riché, 1976, *passim*). What continued to be taught was, first, what minimally needed to be known and, second, what had been inherited from the tradition of the church. It is not at all surprising that the program of catechetical instruction was greatly reduced or that the handing on of such basic formularies as the creed and Lord's Prayer was sufficient for the formation of lay Christians; indeed, the mere fact that this was done was perhaps a major achievement of which twentieth-century Christians can properly stand in awe.

Furthermore, although it is a difficult fact to appreciate now at what some regard as the end of the age of literacy, learning throughout the Middle Ages was, above all, oral learning. The notion of the grading of subject matter so that one began with the elementary and proceeded to the complex and sophisticated was only coming to be appreciated at the end of the medieval period (Ariès, 1962, pp. 142f., 145-50). To add to the distance of medieval ideas of education from our own, the very concept of childhood was unknown to the early Middle Ages. The child was depicted as a small adult; he was dressed according to social station rather than age; he took his place in the world of work as soon as infancy had ended, which event often coincided with weaning "at about the age of seven" (*Ibid.*, esp. pp. 33, 50, 128, 411). An important shift in ideas about the nature of the family and the rise of the notion of childhood coincides with the Reformation and the beginning of the modern period (*ibid.*, esp. pp. 365ff., 411f.), and these changes account in large part for the feeling that the practice of catechesis between the decline of the catechumenate and the introduction of catechism was inadequate:

> The great event . . . was the revival, at the beginning of modern times, of an interest in education. This affected a certain number of churchmen, lawyers and scholars, few in number in the fifteenth century, but increasingly numerous and influential in the sixteenth and seventeenth centuries when they merged with the advocates of religious reform. . . .

> Henceforth it was recognized that the child was not ready for life, and that he had to be subjected to a special treatment, a sort of quarantine, before he was allowed to join the adults (*Ibid.*, p. 412).

In the course of the Middle Ages the ancient catechumenate

virtually disappeared and with it went catechesis as it had been practiced in the fourth and fifth centuries. Although no new, formal system arose to provide for the educational loss thus suffered, the new role of the sponsors at baptism and other community supports seem to have sufficed to provide children with at least a minimal knowledge of the fundamentals of Christian faith and practice.

GENERAL INSTRUCTION FOR CHRISTIANS

The fact that catechesis as instruction related to the process of initiation was essentially handed over to sponsors during the Middle Ages is not, by any means, to be taken as indicating that the church institutionally abdicated its educative role, and a few of the many documents that reveal the church functioning conscientiously as educator of the people in other ways (also clearly derived from the tradition of catechesis and the ancient practice of initiation) must now be examined. It may be helpful to recall that the faithful could and did attend the catechetical and mystogogic instructions with the catechumens in the fourth and fifth centuries. On this practice a tradition of continuing education or of continuing instruction in the fundamentals of faith and the Christian life is founded.*

Charlemagne and his ecclesiastical advisers had the general instruction of the people and the provision of the clergy with materials for the performance of this duty high on their agenda. The Emperor's *Admonitio Generalis* of 789 and the canons and general summary of a series of synods convoked by Charles in 813 provide the most important evidence of this major concern (Gatch, 1978, pp. 47f.; McKitterick, 1977, pp. 12-14). The *Admonitio* and the canons insist upon the importance of the teaching role of

---

*I must largely ignore the catechesis given newly converted peoples before baptism. Mass baptisms of converted or defeated peoples were common, especially in the early Middle Ages. Sometimes preparation was cursory or even non-existent, although the Anglo-Saxon missionaries were exemplary in their educational efforts and greatly influenced the Carolingian educational revival (which was, in a sense, a side-product of this concern). For the most part, however, the christianization of converts was a result of their gradual acculturation. On this subject, see Schmidlin, 1933, pp. 186ff., and general histories of the Anglo-Saxon and Carolingian churches.

the clergy, especially of the bishops. Canon xvii of the Synod of Tours in 813 is the most instructive:

> It is our unanimous opinion that each bishop should have homilies containing needful admonitions by which his subjects may be taught, that is, concerning the catholic faith, in order that they may be able to embrace it, concerning the perpetual retribution of the good and the eternal damnation of the evil, concerning the coming general resurrection and last judgment and by what works one may merit eternal life and by what works be excluded from it. And that each should be diligent to translate clearly the same homilies into the rustic Romance language or German, in which all may the more easily be able to understand the things that are said (Gatch, 1977, pp. 34, 194-5).

Despite the use of the word "homilies" (normally restricted to expository preaching, usually on the biblical lection for the day) to describe the sources bishops are to use in teaching the people, it is clear in the Carolingian legislative documents that the discourses bishops are to deliver are general ones that can be called catechetical in that they are to expound, first, the basic texts handed over to the elect before baptism and, second, common moral precepts. Outlines of the content of this sort of teaching are closely parallel to instructions to bishops on the content of catechesis in the baptismal context (e.g., the text printed by McKitterick, 1977, p. 41). Basic texts for catechesis—the creed, Lord's Prayer, and a few brief commentaries on them—survive in German from the period (*ibid.*, pp. 192-96; Gatch, 1978, pp. 48-51), but little trace of the preachers' expositions of them in the people's language survives. This is probably because the bishops translated *ad libitum* from Latin. Yet it is significant testimony to the church's obedience to the catechetical task in the early Middle Ages that catechetical texts like the creed and Lord's Prayer are almost invariably among the oldest surviving samples of writing in the newer European languages.

It is from Anglo-Saxon England in the late tenth and early eleventh centuries that there is the clearest and earliest evidence of how the church went about this aspect of its magisterial or teaching office. There is a large body of sermons and other materials in Old English useful to preachers from this period. It seems clear that these texts were prepared as aids to catechetical teaching. Probably they were used in a vernacular office which might be introduced in the Latin mass just after the reading of the Gospel or, occasionally, used in extra-liturgical settings. Called the Prone in later times, this office might include a translation or paraphrase of the Gospel, occasionally with some explanation, teaching based on the great catechetical texts (the creed and "Our Father"), moral instruction, and prayer (Gatch, 1977, pp. 37f.).

It seems to have been thought desirable to have such preaching at least every other week, but it also seems clear that it was most common in Lent and Easter. It is an English peculiarity that there was an extraordinary concentration of such material for the three Rogation Days just before Ascension. This may be because the Rogation Days were used for the scrutiny in preparation for baptism at the vigil of Pentecost, just as the concentration of frequent preaching in Lent and Easter reflected the ancient delivery of catechetical instruction at those seasons. It may have been the case in Saxon England that baptism had come to be almost exclusively associated with Pentecost. A monastic text, the *Regularis Concordia*, which contains the most complete description of the paschal rites in England at the time, does not mention baptism in its description of the rites of the Eve of Easter, although it alludes to the blessing of the font. The *Concordia* does, however, introduce other ceremonies on Good Friday and Easter morning which dramatically emphasize contemplation on the passion and resurrection and help to maintain the magnificence of the ancient paschal observances (Symons, 1953).

Among the anonymous sermons in Old English, there survive a remarkable number assigned to the days of Rogation (*In Letania Maiore*—a specially English designation for Rogationtide). A recent catalogue lists at least fifteen such texts, some of which occur in more than one manuscript; other sermons belonging originally to this group have probably lost their calendrical designations (Cameron, 1973, pp. 98-100). A number of these sermons are hortatory in tone, and they tend to emphasize the coming Last Judgment as the sanction for moral behavior in a manner consistent with the injunctions to catechetical preaching in the canons of the Synod of Tours and in similar Carolingian documents.

It was perhaps to bring teaching in Rogationtide into line with an understanding of the content of catechesis that was at once both more orthodox and more complete that Ælfric, the greatest of the Anglo-Saxon sermon writers, selected materials for his Rogation sermons. Ælfric, a monk of Cerne Abbas and later Abbot of Eynsham, worked chiefly in the last decade of the tenth and first decade of the eleventh century. His great achievement was the preparation of a large body of sermons for delivery to the laity, probably in a setting not unlike that of the Prone. Many of these sermons are exegetical; and the body of most of the texts, following an English paraphrase of the gospel pericope, was frequently adapted from the homilies of the Latin church fathers, which Ælfric found anthologized in homiliaries (collections of homilies arranged for reading in the night office on Sundays and major feasts). Ælfric's sermons, even those treating almost exclusively exegetical materials, are, I believe, catechetical in purpose (Gatch, 1977, pp. 47-59, esp. p. 51). Because Ælfric is an excellent representative of the best teaching of his own times, and also because the documentation of the sermon materials he prepared for use by other preachers is unusually complete, he will be treated here at some length. It may also be argued, moreover, in justification of rather detailed treatment of some of Ælfric's most specifically catechetical writing, that the homiletical form found in his work and the catechetical themes he develops are characteristic of catechetical teaching throughout the Middle Ages.

A number of the sermons of Ælfric are clearly catechetical. Often such sermons are marked for a given season in the liturgical calendar or for use whenever the preacher finds it convenient to use them: *vel quando volueris* (*Ibid.*, pp. 50f.). Another designation for such generally useful sermons in the anonymous collections and occasionally in Ælfric's work is *Sermo ad populum*. In addition to sermons for unspecified occasions, Ælfric included seven clearly catechetical pieces for Rogation or the Greater Litany—some of them composite or multiple sermons—in his two series of *Sermones catholicae* and his *Lives of Saints* (*see* the canon list in Pope, 1967, pp. 139, 141, and 141 n. 2). A review of the two full sets of Rogation-day sermons in the two series of *Sermones* will serve for a review of Ælfric's notion of the proper scope and content of catechesis. Since the arrangement of Ælfric's two series implies the notion that it was adequate to preach roughly every other week, the provision of two full sets of Rogation sermons for use in alternate years so that the congregation will not be bored by repetition indicates the importance attached to such preaching by the Anglo-Saxon Church in the period following the great tenth-century monastic reform. True to his own principles, Ælfric managed to devise the six sermons so that no text would be treated twice and no subject examined more than once.

The first sermon of the group in the First Series is headed generally *In Letania Maiore*, but is clearly intended for Monday, the first of the three Rogation Days. It begins with an explanation of these "prayer days," which were established by Mamertus, bishop of Vienne, in the fifth century during an earthquake. Mamertus' rites imitated the penance of Nineveh in response to Jonah's preaching. Like the people of Vienne, Ælfric's congregation is expected to offer prayers and to participate in processions behind the relics of their churches (Thorpe, I, 1844, 244-6). After this introduction, he turns to his chief matter and expounds the Gospel of the day (Luke 11:5-13), following St. Augustine, whose exegesis of the text was found in some versions of the great Homiliary of Paul the Deacon (Smetana, 1959, p. 189). This piece follows essentially the form of Ælfric, usual exegetical Sunday sermons with paraphrase and explication of the Gospel.

The first of the more strictly catechetical sermons for Rogationtide is the Tuesday sermon, which expounds the Lord's Prayer. Ælfric introduces the prayer as it is presented in Luke 11:1-4 and proceeds to speak of the fatherhood of God and the consequent brotherhood of all humanity, both rich and poor. He goes through the prayer, giving the Latin and a translation and explanation of each of its seven petitions. Ever aware of the multiple meanings of Scripture, he explains, for example, that the "bread" of the fourth petition has three senses: it is food for the physical body of man in his worldly life; it is also spiritual sustenance or food of the soul, which the Christian receives in the church; and it is the food of the eucharistic meal (pp. 264-6). Ælfric also explains that the first three petitions pertain both to the present and to the eternal life, although the final four refer only to the present life since the need for food and forgiveness and for protection from transgressions and temptations are all transitory human needs (p. 270).

The last sermon of the Rogation set in the First Series concerns the faith and is explicitly linked to the creed, which with the Lord's Prayer is a basic text which "every Christian man ought to know" (p. 274). Rather than explain the creed phrase-by-phrase, however, Ælfric adapts the *De Trinitate* of Augustine, including such famous notions as Augustine's teaching that the soul, in its faculties of memory, understanding, and will, is like the nature of the godhead itself (p. 288).

The Rogation sermons of the Second Series are quite different and yet fully in accord with the general guidelines for catechetical teaching. The first, or Monday, sermon is a general discourse on Christian moral law, which begins with the comment that "Laymen require that teachers should impart to them the evangelical lore, which they have learned in books, that men should not err through ignorance" (Thorpe, II, 1846, 314). Beginning with Jesus' summary of the law as loving God and loving one's neighbor as oneself, Ælfric explores the nature of Christian love and stresses that love of Christ issues in acts of charity. He applies this teaching to various classes in the church and general society and states that one's obedience in his station in life will determine his eternal reward or punishment. "Let us," he concludes, "merit the everlasting life with God, by cessation from evil and performance of good" (*Ibid.*, p. 332).

The Tuesday sermon is a composite one which provides in its three sections materials that might be arranged or combined by the preacher (Godden, 1973, p. 212) in order to fulfill the injunction that catechetical teaching ought to include reflection on the Last Things. The anonymous homilists were fond of vivid, apocalyptic sources that gave dramatic depictions of the afterlife. Ælfric was almost unique among his contemporaries for his critical sense that uncanonical texts of this sort ought to be used with great caution. At the outset, he refers to the apocryphal *Vision of Paul*, which was a source for several Old English sermons (Gatch, 1964). Ælfric points out that Paul himself said that he could not communicate the content of visions, and thus it is wrong to rely on a "false composition" that purports to relate what Paul had said "no earthly man may speak" (Thorpe, II, 1846, 332). As a substitute for such teaching, Ælfric adapts in English the account of the vision of a priest named Fursey, which circulated in a separate document (Ælfric's probable source) and which was also recounted by Bede in the *Ecclesiastical History*. In spirit and form this visionary exemplum is itself very close to the *Vision of Paul*. Fursey was once ill and when he was at the point of death, angels prematurely took his soul to heaven. The angels were ordered to return the soul to the body, although Fursey did not want to return. Restored to life, Fursey died again three days later. This time the angelic guides of his departed spirit were challenged by devils, and in the course of an elaborate vision of the afterlife, Fursey was first slightly burned by the fire of purgation for a minor transgression and then in heaven met two old friends and heard the heavenly host singing. Ordered to return once more to earthly life, Fursey passed again through the penal fire before his soul and body were reunited. He resumed preaching for about twelve years before there was a final separation of body and soul.

The second section (*alia visio*) of the materials for Rogation Tuesday preaching in the Second Series is a similar vision involving one Drihthelm, which Ælfric adapts from Bede's *History* (*Ibid.*, pp. 348ff.) Drihthelm, a layman, apparently died one evening but arose the next morning. Then, dividing his property among his wife and children and the poor, he retired to the abbey at Melrose. There he revealed to King Aldfrith and others the vision he had received during his brief period of apparent lifelessness. He, like Fursey, had made a tour of the cosmos of the afterlife. Drihthelm's vision was concentrated on judgment and punishment, but at the end he saw the light, smelled the fragrance, and heard the melodies of heaven and was promised that if he would amend his life, he might abide in that "winsome dwelling" (*Ibid.*, p. 354). Ælfric concludes his account of Drihthelm with a reference to the *Dialogues* of Gregory the Great as a collection of similar visions. "Great is God's mercy over mankind, to those who are benevolent," he declares finally:

> We in this life may help the departed that are in torment, and we may, among ourselves in life, aid each other to the life above, if we observe this; and those who were perfect, and have attained to the kingdom of God, may aid both us and the departed that are in torment, if they are not totally condemned (*Ibid.*, p. 356).

Ælfric's materials for Rogation Tuesday conclude with a "Hortatory Sermon on the Efficacy of the Holy Mass" (*Ibid.*, pp. 356ff.). This piece, too, is derived from Bede and involves a thane, Ymma, who was captured in battle and made a slave. Ymma's brother, a priest named Tuna, said mass daily for Ymma, and daily Ymma's slave's bonds burst. As Ymma remarks, "If . . . I were now in the other world, then were my soul released from torments through the holy masses" (*Ibid.*, p. 358). Ælfric observes that Gregory has corroborative tales in his *Dialogues*, which were available in an Old English translation.

The Rogation Wednesday sermon in the Second Series is an exegetical piece on the pericope for the vigil of the Feast of the Ascension and, at least in part, is based on writings of Augustine anthologized in the homiliary (Smetana, 1959, p. 198). The Gospel, John 17:1-11, deals with Christ's prayer that he might be glorified and is thus thematically suited to the Ascension. Ælfric concludes his explication with advice to his hearers and readers that they should set their hopes on the glorified Christ and stresses that they must be attentive to the teachers who are able to unfold for them the mysteries and doctrines enshrined in the Latin texts of Scripture and commentary. In view of the coming judgment "ye need so much the more the comfort of books, that, through their precepts, ye may turn your minds from this life of exile to the eternal one of which we are speaking" (Thorpe, II, 1846, 370). Thus, although he has turned from general catechetical teaching to exposition of Scripture, Ælfric still has very much in mind the teaching themes of the Rogation Days. Later additions made for this sermon by Ælfric tend to stress man's hope of heaven and Christ's continuing concern for mankind in ways that also undergird the catechetical themes of Rogationtide.

It should be stressed that, whereas the First Series of *Sermones catholicae* collects sermons that are for the most part to be read straightforwardly to the people, the Second Series gives more choice to the preacher to select from the variety of materials Ælfric has prepared for them. This is especially true of the visionary matter for Rogation Tuesday. Another evidence for this principle of allowing the preacher some discretion in the use of material is the appendix at the end of the Second Series in some manuscripts. It collects specifically catechetical texts in English translation: the Our Father, the Apostles' and Nicene Creeds, other prayers, and a treatise labeled "On Penitence" but covering the catechetical subjects (*Ibid.*, pp. 596-608). Ælfric may stand as a paradigm for the effort in the early Middle Ages to catechize the people. He is conscientious, conservative, orthodox, and clear in his teaching. His considerable body of work is all catechetical in intent, but his six items for the Rogation Days in the *Sermones catholicae* are consciously catechetical, especially in their intent to touch upon the major themes of catechesis derived both from the liturgy of initiation and from the efforts of the Carolingian legislators and reformers to revive the general teaching office of the church. The topics Ælfric treated in his Rogation sermons— the creed, the Lord's Prayer, Christian ethics or moral law, and the Last Things or vision of judgment, which ought to inspire all Christians to fulfillment of the law—are the standard materials of medieval catechetical teaching.

To document the fact that Ælfric's teaching in the catechetical

Rogationtide sermons was not unlike the best of catechetical preaching throughout the Middle Ages, it is enough to point out that Thomas Aquinas delivered catechetical sermons in Italian at Naples shortly before his final illness during Lent in 1273. The course of sermons was more rigorous than Ælfric's, however, and it reflected the more elaborate systematization of Christian thought that had been developed by Thomas's time. Thomas preached daily from Septuagesima Sunday, the beginning of the pre-Lenten season, until Easter. His topics for his fifty-seven or fifty-nine sermons were the "two precepts of charity, the ten precepts of the law, the Apostles' Creed, the Our Father, and possibly the Hail Mary" (Weisheipl, 1974, p. 319). This scheme retains stress on the creed and Lord's Prayer as essential texts. The *Ave Maria* (as noted above) had become a common devotional addition to these texts. The sermons on charity (the commandments on loving God and one's neighbor, which are central to Ælfric's sermon for Rogation Monday in his Second Series) and those on the law systematized the moral teaching of catechesis; eschatological teaching had apparently become a less central topic. Unfortunately, Thomas's catechetical sermons now survive only in the form of Latin notes made while he was preaching and later revised by another hand. When Thomas was canonized, it was frequently testified that the sermons were moving and that they had been heard by "almost the whole population of Naples . . . every day" (*Ibid.*, p. 319; on the Latin summaries, *see* pp. 401-403, nos. 86-89).

Of more central interest here, however, must be a literature too vast to be surveyed in a short space: the catechetical guides or handbooks for preachers that were prepared in England in the thirteenth century and after. The foundational document for all later medieval English legislation and handbooks on the subject of catechetical instruction is the canon *Ignorantia sacerdotum* promulgated at a council at Lambeth in 1281 by John Pecham, archbishop of Canterbury (Douie, 1952, pp. 134f.; Owst, 1926, p. 282). Pecham was a Franciscan, and it is important to remember that both of the mendicant orders—the Franciscans, or "Friars Minor," and the Dominicans, or "Friars Preachers," among whom Thomas Aquinas is to be counted—came into existence in response to the need for a ministry to the growing urban population of medieval Europe and so both stressed popular preaching. Pecham's "Constitutions," in a section entitled *De informatione simplicium* ("On the instruction of simple folk"), stresses the need to teach the fundamentals of faith in the vernacular at least four times annually (text reprinted as "P" in Simmons and Nolloth, 1901). The contents of this teaching are not dissimilar to the materials covered by Thomas in the Lenten sermons at Naples a few years earlier. The Lord's Prayer and Hail Mary are omitted, however, and the teaching on the sacraments is expanded (Pantin, 1955, pp. 193-4; Douie, 1952, p. 135).

In the fourteenth century, John Thoresby, archbishop of York from 1351 to 1373, issued an expanded set of instructions for catechists in Latin, which was based on Archbishop Pecham's Lambeth canon of 1281 ("C" in Simmons and Nolloth). An expansion in English verse was also prepared at Thoresby's behest ("T" in *ibid.*) by John Gaytrige (or de Taystek), a Benedictine monk in York. Still later an even longer English versification of the instructions for catechists was made by a Lollard writer who retained the name of Thoresby as author to certify the orthodoxy of his work. This version restored teaching on the Lord's Prayer and other traditional points of catechesis omitted by Pecham and Thoresby (Pantin, 1955, p. 212; text "L" in Simmons and Nolloth). Pecham's work and its derivatives were the basic sources of a host of catechetical manuals for priests and for the growing number of literate laypeople throughout the fourteenth and fifteenth centuries (Douie, 1952, pp. 138-42; Pecham, 1934, pp. 83ff.).

Gaytrige's version of the catechetical manual begins with a summary of the creation and fall of man. Because of sin, man no longer has knowledge of God by natural gift but must learn about salvation in the church. The present, widespread ignorance is laid to the clergy. Therefore, Archbishop Thoresby has ordained,

> That ilkane [i.e. every priest] that vndir him has kepynge
>   of saules,
> Openly on Inglis opon sononndaies
> Teche and preche thaim, that thai haue cure of (ll. 48-50).

The teaching of the clergy is to cover six topics, all of which have a specified number of subdivisions: the fourteen points (or articles) of faith, the ten commandments, the seven ecclesiastical sacraments, the seven acts of mercy, the seven virtues, and the seven deadly sins. All of these are to be learned by the laity and passed on to their children, if they have any. The people are to be examined upon the six topics when they make their Lenten confessions and are to be subjected to penances if their knowledge is inadequate (*Ibid.*, ll. 51-76). The points in the body of the work are set forth clearly and simply. They cannot be outlined in detail here, but it may be worth noting that, in treating the sacraments of baptism and confirmation, neither Thoresby's Latin nor Gaytrige's English verse mentions catechesis as an aspect of initiation (*Ibid.*, ll. 275-305). The work concludes with the statement that the Archbishop offers forty days' indulgence to all who know the six articles of catechesis. Through them, one knows God, whom to know (as St. John says) "It is endeles life and lastand blisse" (*Ibid.*, l. 575).

Correlative with the development of these handbooks designed as guides for the preacher as catechist (works that are clear forerunners of the catechisms of the Reformers) are the numerous, more general handbooks for preachers that were produced in the later Middle Ages, the genre of the *ars praedicandi*, the rhetorical guide to "the art of preaching." The *artes praedicandi*, traditionally associated in the earliest known examples with preaching upon a theme or text in the universities in the thirteenth century, perfected the form of the sermon as a tightly organized text with carefully constructed and articulated parts. The typical scheme "specifies a subject matter and then lays out a plan of arrangement for sermons, with *protheme* or *antetheme* followed by a *prayer* and then statement of *theme* (scriptural quotation) with *division* and *subdivision* of that quotation *amplified* through a variety of modes" and occasionally leading to a conclusion (Murphy, 1974, pp. 310ff.; quotations at p. 331). The *artes* may not have arisen in and been confined in their use to the universities, but they certainly reflect, in their quest for persuasive articulation of catechetical or homiletical argumentation, the more logically-oriented sensibility of later medieval churchmen. They attempted to teach the preacher to make a fine art of handing over to the people the fundamental aspects of the faith. They are, in other words, both "scholastic" (in the sense in which the word came later to be derisive) and pastoral in their effort to present the faith in a clear and orderly way.

The lengths to which writers went to serve the needs of the catechetical preacher by providing him with useful and theologically appropriate material are truly impressive. An example is a handbook written in Latin for English preachers in the fourteenth century, the *Fasciculus morum*. The work is constructed to provide treatments of the seven deadly sins and their correlative virtues.

The centrality of the vices and virtues in the *Fasciculus morum* reflects the fact that, from the twelfth and thirteenth centuries onwards, the vices and virtues became more and more conventionally the basic framework for teaching Christian morality. Other, more traditionally catechetical, topics (the creed, the Lord's Prayer and the like) were also treated, as were still other, more contemporary themes (Wenzel, 1978, pp. 9-13). The *Fasciculus morum*, although written in Latin, contains an impressive number of short poems in English, which testify to the fact that it was intended for use by preachers whose audience and language for preaching were English. The work was intended as a reference work for preachers who would take upon themselves responsibility for organizing their own sermons. A number of manuscripts include a remarkable apparatus which contains forty-two outlines of sermons for Sundays and major feasts. The outlines have cross references to appropriate exemplary materials in the seven divisions of the main body of the *Fasciculus*. The utility of the work is further enhanced in these manuscripts by an alphabetical index of their contents. Clear division of the parts of the work and marginal indications of subject matter also served this end (*Ibid.*, pp. 47-50). Thus *Fasciculus morum*, ostensibly a treatise on the seven deadly sins, was made at the same time a compendium of "catechetical matters" and a guide to the catechist or preacher (Wenzel, 1976, p. 29).

The vernacular poems that are found in preachers' manuals like the *Fasciculus morum* and in commonplace books like that of Friar John of Grimestone are evidence of the efforts of the preacher to command the attention of his audience (Wenzel, 1978, pp. 89ff.). The poems in thirteenth- and fourteenth-century manuscripts are often meditative in tone and reflect the increasingly affective piety of Christians in the later Middle Ages. John of Grimestone includes, for example, lyrics in which Christ speaks to the audience, asking mankind to participate imaginatively in his suffering:

> Sinful man, bethink and see
> What pain I suffer for love of thee
>   (Luria and Hoffman, 1974, no. 215; *see also* nos. 216-17).

John also includes poems that borrow from the traditions of amorous verse and probably reflect as well the traditional interpretations of the Song of Songs to speak of the suffering that is involved in true, "adventurous" love—a suffering akin to that of Christ for the world and of true Christians for their faith (*Ibid.*, no. 18). Occasionally the quest of preachers for popularity and vividness evidently went too far. Narrative illustrations of gluttony and lechery in treatments of the seven deadly sins were particularly susceptible to excesses of rhetorical colorfulness. The friars were regarded as the preachers most prone to going too far to captivate and amuse their congregations by popularizing their matter. They and other preachers became, thus, the objects of a large satirical literature. Chaucer's Pardoner in *The Canterbury Tales*, for example, has only one theme in his preaching—that avarice is the root of all evil—which he uses in the service of his own avarice to fleece those who hear him.

On the whole, however, churchmen labored long and hard in pursuit of their duty to instruct the folk in the basic truths of the faith. The literature of preaching throughout the Middle Ages testifies to the persistence of leaders of the church in pursuit of the catechetical ideal. The persistence of complaints about both lay and clerical ignorance, which culminated with the sixteenth-century Reform, may be evidence either that the bishops and other clergy worked inadequately on the church's teaching mission in the Middle Ages or that salvation and sound public morals do not come from teaching and preaching alone.

CONCLUSION

The history of catechesis, or the teaching to the laity of the fundamentals of Christian belief and morality, from the decline of the ancient catechumenate to the introduction of catechisms by the reformers is a twofold history. There is, first, the story of the church's failure to adjust the rites of initiation to a changed situation in which the initiates were not adults assenting in faith to a demanding new religion but infants being accepted in God's family by their faithful parents and sponsors. On this side, the history is one in which the great sacrament of Christian initiation lost its coherence and became two sacraments, baptism and confirmation. This was a development in which Christian initiation virtually lost its original educative function. The dilemma raised by the decline of the catechumenate remains a perplexing problem for modern Christianity. On the other hand, there was a tradition of teaching the fundamentals of the faith that derived from the ancient initiatory rites with their emphasis upon handing over the contents of the faith and inculcating the form of Christian life. This tradition was at the very core of the medieval under-standing of the nature of the teaching ministry of the church. It was shaped in the legislation of the Carolingian reformers and was embodied in teachers like Ælfric of Eynsham; it was nourished and developed throughout the Middle Ages by bishops and writers of guides for ministers and by the preachers themselves. It is from the joining in the late-fifteenth and early-sixteenth centuries of this strand of medieval catechetical theory and practice with a belief that education in the faith and initiation into the church ought to be inseparable that the modern history of catechesis takes root.

BIBLIOGRAPHY

Andrieu, Michel, *Le Pontifical Romain au Moyen-Âge.* Vol. 1. Le Pontifical Romain du XIIᵉ Siècle. Studi e Testi, 86. Vatican: Biblioteca apostolica Vaticana, 1938.

————, *Les* Ordines Romani *du Haut Moyen Âge.* Spicilegium Sacrum Lovaniense, Études et Documents, 11(1931) and 23(1948). Louvain: Université Catholique.

Ariès, Philippe, *Centuries of Childhood: A Social History of Family Life.* (1960) Translated by Robert Baldick. New York: Vintage Books (Random House), 1962. Contains observations of great insight on medieval educational assumptions.

Cameron, Angus, "A List of Old English Texts," *A Plan for the Dictionary of Old English.* Edited by Roberta Frank and Angus Cameron. Toronto: University of Toronto Press, 1973. pp. 25-306.

Collins, Arthur Jeffries, ed., *Manuale ad usum precleribus ecclesiae Sarisburiensis.* Henry Bradshaw Society, Publications, 91. Chichester: Moore and Tillyer. 1960.

Cross, F. L., *The Oxford Dictionary of the Christian Church*, 2nd ed. by F. L. Cross and E. A. Livingstone, 1974. Oxford: The University Press, 1977. Useful short articles and bibliographies on almost all the subjects of this article.

Douie, Decima, *Archbishop Pecham.* Oxford: Clarendon Press, 1952. A standard scholarly biography.

Fisher, J. D. C., *Christian Initiation: Baptism in the Medieval West, A Study in the Disintegration of the Primitive Rite of Initiation.* Alcuin Club Collections, 47. London: SPCK, 1965. The definitive recent study of baptism and confirmation in the Middle Ages.

————, *Christian Initiation, The Reformation Period: Some Early Reformed Rites of Baptism and Confirmation and Other Contemporary Documents.* Alcuin Club Collections, No. 51. London: SPCK, 1970.

Gatch, Milton McC., "The Achievement of Ælfric and His Colleagues in European Perspective," *The Old English Homily and its Backgrounds.* Edited by Paul E. Szarmach and Bernard F. Huppé. Albany: State University of New York, 1978. pp. 43-73. A survey of early prose writing in the vernacular.

————, *Preaching and Theology in Anglo-Saxon England: Ælfric and Wulfstan.* Toronto: University of Toronto Press, 1977. Part II discusses the Old English sermons as catechetical documents.

————, "Two Uses of Apocrypha in Old English Homilies," *Church History*, 33(1964), 379-91.

Gibson, E. C. S., ed., *The First and Second Prayer Books of Edward VI.* Everyman's Library, 448. London: J. M. Dent & Sons Ltd., 1910. Reprinted 1957.

Göbl, Peter, *Geschichte der Katechese im Abendlande vom Verfalle des Katechumenats bis zum Ende des Mittelalters.* Kempten: Jos: Kösel'schen Buchhandlung, 1880. The standard study, still extremely useful.

Godden, Malcolm, ed., *Ælfric's Catholic Homilies, the Second Series: Text.* Early English Text Society, S.S.5. London: Oxford University Press, 1979.

————, "The Development of Ælfric's Second Series of *Catholic Homilies,*" *English Studies,* 54(1973), 209-16.

Hézard, M. le Chanoine, *Histoire du Catéchisme depuis la Naissance de l'Église jusqu'à nos Jours.* Paris: Victor-Retaux, 1900.

Jones, Cheslyn; Wainwright, Geoffrey; and Yarnold, Edward, eds., *The Study of Liturgy.* London: SPCK and New York: Oxford, 1978. A scholarly textbook with extensive and helpful bibliography. Because of the variety of its authors, the work is uneven.

Jungmann, Josef Andreas, *Handing on the Faith: A Manual of Catechetics.* Revised translation by A. N. Fuerst based on 2nd German ed., 1955. New York: Herder & Herder, 1962. A useful, brief history. Relies heavily on Göbl's work.

Luria, Maxwell S. and Hoffman, Richard L., *Middle English Lyrics. . . .* New York: W. W. Norton & Company, 1974. Reference to poems is by number.

McKitterick, Rosamond, *The Frankish Church and the Carolingian Reforms, 789-895.* London: Royal Historical Society, 1977. A useful survey of the evidence, although the documents are sometimes overinterpreted to give an unduly optimistic view of the state of Carolingian pastoral care and education.

McNeill, John T., *A History of the Cure of Souls.* New York: Harper & Brothers, 1951.

Murphy, James J., *Rhetoric in the Middle Ages: A History of Rhetorical Theory from Saint Augustine to the Renaissance.* Berkeley: University of California Press, 1974. Murphy's chapter 6 on "The Art of Preaching" is the most recent and authoritative general essay.

Owst, G. R., *Literature and Pulpit in Medieval England. . . .* 1933, 2nd revised ed., Oxford: Basil Blackwell, 1961, 1966.

————, *Preaching in Medieval England: An Introduction to Sermon Manuscripts of the Period* c. *1350-1450.* Cambridge Studies in Medieval Life and Thought. Edited by G. G. Coulton. Cambridge: The University Press, 1926. Owst's two works remain the standard studies of English preaching in the Middle Ages.

Pantin, W. A., *The English Church in the Fourteenth Century*. Cambridge: The University Press, 1955. Useful survey of preachers' manuals.

Peckham, John Laimbeer, *Archbishop Peckham as a Religious Educator*. Yale Studies in Religion, 7. Scottdale, Pennsylvania: Mennonite Publishing House, 1934. A useful, though not historically rigorous, introduction.

Pope, John C., ed., *Homilies of Ælfric: A Supplementary Collection*, 2 volumes. Early English Text Society, nos. 259 and 260. London: Oxford University Press, 1967 and 1968.

Reu, M., *Catechetics or Theory and Practise of Religious Instruction*. Chicago: Wartburg Publishing House, 1918. A Lutheran textbook with good bibliography and fairly good historical survey.

Riché, Pierre, *Education and Culture in the Barbarian West: Sixth Through Eighth Centuries*, 3rd ed., 1962. Translated by John J. Contreni. Columbia, South Carolina: University of South Carolina Press, 1976. Surveys the decline of classical education and the rise of ecclesiastical education.

Schmidlin, Joseph, *Catholic Mission History*. Translated by Matthias Braun. Techny, Illinois: Mission Press, S.V.D., 1933.

Schneyer, Johannes Baptist, *Geschichte der katholischen Predigt*. Freiburg: Seelsorge Verlag, 1969. The most reliable recent study.

Simmons, Thomas Frederick, and Nolloth, Henry Edward, eds., *The Lay Folks' Catechism, or the English and Latin Versions of Archbishop Thoresby's Instruction for the People*. . . . Early English Text Society, Original Series, 118. London: Kegan Paul, Trench, Trübner & Co., 1901. Reprinted, Millwood, New York: Kraus Reprint Co., 1975.

Smetana, Cyril L., "Ælfric and the Early Medieval Homiliary," *Traditio*, 15(1959), 163-204.

Symons, Thomas, ed., *Regularis Concordia Anglicae Nationis Monachorum Sanctimonialumque: The Monastic Agreement of the Monks and Nuns of the English Nation*. Medieval Classics. London: Thomas Nelson & Sons Ltd., 1953.

Thorpe, Benjamin, ed., *The Homilies of the Anglo-Saxon Church. The First Part Containing the* Sermones Catholicae *or Homilies of Ælfric*, 2 volumes. London: for the Ælfric Society, 1844, 1846. For the Second Series, Thorpe is now superseded by Godden, 1979. I have, however, cited Thorpe, whose translation may be useful to readers of this essay.

Weisheipl, James A., *Friar Thomas d'Aquino: His Life, Thought, and Work*. Garden City, New York: Doubleday & Company, Inc., 1974. The basic scholarly account in English of the career of Thomas.

Wenzel, Siegfried, *Verses in Sermons*: Fasciculus Morum *and Its Middle English Poems*. The Mediæval Academy of America, Publication No. 87. Cambridge, Massachusetts: The Mediæval Academy of America, 1978. Contains references to literature and much useful information on medieval preaching, especially in England.

————, "Virtues, Vices, and Popular Preaching," *Medieval and Renaissance Studies: Proceedings of the Southeastern Institute of Medieval and Renaissance Studies, Summer, 1974*. Edited by Dale B. J. Randall. Durham, N. C.: Duke University Press, 1976. pp. 28-54. Wenzel's study is primarily literary but is the best recent work on preaching in England in the later Middle Ages.

Whitaker, E. C., *Documents of the Baptismal Liturgy*. Alcuin Club Collections, No. 42. London: SPCK, 1960.

Wilkinson, John, *Egeria's Travels*. London: SPCK, 1971.

The Reformation—I

Chapter 5
The Continental Reformation of the Sixteenth Century

William P. Haugaard

REFORMATION EMPHASES SIGNIFICANT
FOR CATECHESIS

Catechesis is a key to understanding the church life which emerged from the magisterial and radical reformations in sixteenth-century Europe. Students may dispute the degrees of effectiveness of the intentional efforts to evoke and to nurture Christian faith in various communities on the continent, but no one can seriously doubt that the reformers considered catechesis a primary responsibility of ecclesiastical organization and leadership. No group of church leaders in any age of the Christian era has placed so great an emphasis on the command to "teach" (*didaskō*) in the Matthean injunction to make disciples and to baptize (28:19-20). Portuguese and Spanish missionaries in the sixteenth century traveled to far-flung corners of the earth, baptizing millions whose forbears had never heard of Jesus Christ. The continental reformers, by contrast, confined their efforts to territories in the very heartland of Christendom where universal baptism prevailed, but where, in Luther's view, a seamstress might teach her daughter the trade but "now even the great learned prelates and bishops themselves do not know the Gospel" (1883, VI, 461; 1955, XLIV, 206). To make the Gospel known and understood, as the reformers had perceived it, became the principal thrust of their reforms in doctrine, liturgy, and discipline.

Three aspects of the continental Reformation are of prime importance in assessing catechesis from a twentieth-century perspective. The reforming bodies all shared (1) an intense concern for the personal apprehension of Christian faith, (2) a concentrated focus on the Holy Scriptures, and (3) the presupposition of a Christian society that partook of many elements of the medieval *corpus christianorum*.

Personal Apprehension of Christian Faith

The reformers judged that the church in which they had been raised required no more than conformity to her rites and regulations; she failed to nurture the personal relationship between God and his people. Accordingly, they unanimously accepted Martin Luther's dictum that each man and woman must do his or her own believing. Christ must be preached, the Wittenberg reformer insisted, that he may not only be Christ, "but Christ for you and for me" (1883, VII, 58; 1955, XXXI, 357). A pamphleteer in the first decade of Lutheran polemics devised a dialogue between an unlearned but intelligent father and his son newly returned from studies at Wittenberg; with evangelical fervor, the son proclaims that God himself asks the sinner,

> "Do you believe that I can help you?" If he believes, he is helped already, and thus God awakens him by His grace, which is promised him in the Gospel, which he has received. Thereupon follows the right faith, that he believes God, who will help him (Meyer, 1967, p. 97).

"Right faith" required personal trust evoked among the baptized only as they perceived and grasped the character of the deity. In Johann Brenz' larger catechism of 1528, the catechist repeatedly asks, "What benefit do you derive," or "What is the value to you" of clauses of the Apostles' Creed ("*was Nutz?*"; "*quid utilitatis?*" or "*quid commoditatis?*"; Cohrs, 1900, XXII, 159-176; Wills, 1955, pp. 116-123). The reformers insisted that such a trust *in* God, arising out of a knowledge *of* him, must lead the believer *to* respond *to* him. John Calvin declared the highest heavenly wisdom to be

> that people, fixed on God by a sincere faith, call upon him, and, so that they may nourish their confidence, exercise themselves in meditating upon his benefits; and that then they entirely give themselves in submission to him. Moreover we learn from this that right reverence to God begins with faith (on Psalm 78:7; 1863, XXXI, 724; 1847, X, 233; DeJong, 1967, p. 167).

A. R. Brouwer has aptly noted that Christian education in Calvin's understanding is "not to be conceived as a mere imparting of doctrines and shaping of conduct. It is first, last, and always, the nurturing of a life—a life which God has granted to the covenant child" (1965, p. 27). Although Anabaptist leaders asked obedience to New Testament laws as they understood them, they linked their regenerate life closely to a personal relationship with God in Christ. Pilgram Marpeck, for example, wrote,

> This is the covenant (*Verpundt*) in baptism, that we, through the knowledge of the Lord and Savior Jesus Christ, put off and flee the filth of the world and bind (*verpinden*) ourselves with Christ unto a new life, so that, just as Christ was raised from the dead, we too, as newborn from the dead, may enter into a new way of life (quoted in Armour, 1966, p. 119).

Although the flowering of Spanish mysticism abundantly demonstrates that a personal relationship with God in Christ was in no way an exclusively protestant concern in the sixteenth century, the reformers, who devised new structures of pastoral, liturgical, and organizational life, attempted to shape these so that believers might be challenged and enabled to enter upon such a relationship with their deity.

To avoid misunderstanding this element of protestant religion in the sixteenth century, we are well warned by T. F. Torrence that in much preaching after the mid-seventeenth century, attention was turned "inward upon the self," concentrating upon the personal experience of Christ, the appropriation of his benefits and the internal working out of sanctification, whereas

> at the Reformation preaching was concerned with presenting Christ and His graces and focussing the attention of the people upon Him, while in the application of the Gospel the people were directed towards their neighbours in Christian love and charity (1959, p. xlviii).

The subjective apprehension of Christian truth, which made possible a personal relation with God, rested upon the objectivity of that truth. The character of that objective truth, however, would not allow it to be limited to a set of facts, for, as Torrence writes, proper instruction in the reformation tradition must always

> reckon with an event of communication which is also an event of reconciliation, and with the transcendent operation of the Holy

Spirit who enables man to receive truth beyond his natural powers and so to be lifted up above himself in communion with God (1959, pp. xxii-xxiii).

Peter DeJong, although writing specifically of Calvin, describes the educational concerns of any of the continental reformers:

Catechesis . . . might never be allowed to degenerate into mere impartation of information about God and his mighty works; it had to be a call to personal involvement with and response to the God of the covenant who spoke directly and decisively through the words which faithful pastors taught (1967, p. 193).

Only as catechesis in the Christian community made it possible for each man and woman who comprised it to know the central claims of God's revelation could they have the necessary data by which they might respond. Only as the data itself underlined the personal outreach of God to each person could catechesis effectively undergird the call to communion with God in Christ.

Focus on Holy Scripture

Although the reformers' teaching on the Bible as the authoritative Word of God rested on traditional Christian doctrine, their study of Holy Scriptures led them to new insights into the ways of God with man and provided a platform from which they protested much current teaching supported by the papal magisterium. The roots of Luther's distinctive doctrine lie in the early university lectures that he offered at Wittenberg in which he deeply probed into the texts of the Psalms and New Testament epistles. When Ulrich Zwingli began his reforming ministry as People's Pastor in Zurich, he placed the Gospel of St. Matthew on the pulpit desk and proceeded chapter after chapter to share his interpretations with the congregation, later proceeding to Acts, various epistles, the other gospels, and finally parts of the Old Testament.

When the reformers insisted that the Holy Scriptures belonged to the whole membership of the church, they were following a path already laid down by the humanists. Even after writing against Luther, Erasmus scornfully replied to an attack on his biblical work, citing an epigram,

"If the people be allowed to treat of the holy scriptures, there is a danger that, coming into places of little respectability, they will be handled by hands anointed with leather and grease." O weighty reasons! As if the holy scriptures are not considered worthy of common use if they are not amidst silken garments and are not to be handled by hands unless these have been anointed with balsam! (1706, IX, 786C).

Erasmus' differences with the reformer of Wittenberg did not dilute the zeal which they shared for putting the scriptural books in the hands of the people. With the growing resistance of many Roman Catholic authorities to vernacular Bibles, it was left largely to the protestant communities to promote translations. The fruits of the prodigious efforts of translators, publishers, and revisers are demonstrated by Luther's great work, a formative landmark in the modern German language (1522-34), the Zurich Bible in which all but the prophets and apocrypha are based on Luther (1530), Olivetan's Neuchâtel Bible in French (1535), the various Dutch Bibles including the Biestkens Bible of the Mennonites (1558), the Italian (Venice, 1532 and Geneva, 1562) and Spanish (Basle, 1569), Bibles sponsored by exile communities, and the complete Bibles which appeared before the end of the century in Swedish (1541), Danish (1550), Polish (1563), Czech (1579-93), and Hungarian (1590) (Greenslade, 1963, pp. 94-140). In the year following the appearance of Luther's New Testament, a pamphleteer described a university student advising his father, who read German and could speak a little Latin, to buy himself a Bible, "since it has now been put into German by Martin" (Meyer, 1967, p. 90). The vernacular Bibles were available to be read in liturgical worship, to be quoted in sermons and lectures, and, among the literate minority of the population, to become the first treasured volume in many a family library.

To the reformers, the Bible was far more than an authoritative norm for teaching; through its writings God reached out continuously to initiate, to expand, and to correct the believer's understanding and his response, which formed part of the process of biblical communication. Luther wrote,

Many people hear God's Word (which is nothing but the wisdom of God), and yet learn nothing from it, because they regard it as a word, but not as the Word of God. Then they allow themselves to think that they understand it as soon as they have heard it. But if they regarded it as the undoubted Word of God, they would surely think: "Well then, God is greater than you and will say something great. So rather let us listen with seriousness and awe, as one ought to listen to a god." Behold, then the heart is beginning to become wise; for it desires to listen with seriousness to God's Word. . . . Whoever seriously regards God's Word as God's Word well knows that he will forever remain its student and disciple (on Psalm 111:20; 1883, XXXI, part 1, 425-426; 1955, XIII, 385-386).

Although theologians of the Reformed school agreed with Lutherans on the unique role of the Scriptures in nurturing faith and on the importance of faithful listening, they judged obedience, as well as faith, to be essential for effective communication. John Calvin, insisting on man's inability to know God apart from revelation, wrote in the *Institutes*:

In order that true religion may shine upon us, we ought to hold that it must take its beginning from heavenly doctrine and that no one can get even the slightest taste of right and sound doctrine unless he be a pupil of Scripture. Hence there also emerges the beginning of true understanding when we reverently embrace what it pleases God there to witness to himself. But not only faith, perfect and in every way complete, but all right knowledge of God is born of obedience (1.6.2; 1960, I, 72; 1863, XXX, 54).

Zwingli, urging Dominican nuns in Zurich to seek God directly through Scripture, appealed to his own experience:

The doctrine of God is never formed more clearly than when it is done by God himself and in the words of God. Indeed I make bold to say that those who make themselves, that is men, the arbiters of Scripture, make a mockery of trust in the Spirit of God by their design and pretension, seeking to wrest or force the Scriptures according to their own folly. . . . When you say that an arbiter is needed to decide the issue and to compel those who are defeated I deny it: for even the most learned of men are fallible except in so far as they are led by God. . . . I know for certain that God teaches me, because I have experienced the fact of it. . . . When I was younger, I gave myself overmuch to human teaching. . . . But eventually I came to the point where led by the Scriptures and Word of God I saw the need to set aside all these things and to learn the doctrine of God direct from his own Word. Then I began to ask God for light and the Scriptures became far clearer to me . . . than if I had studied many commentators and expositors (1940, I, 111-113; Bromiley, 1953, pp. 89-91).

Within two years some of Zwingli's disciples concluded, in opposition to their teacher, that the Bible did not condone infant baptism. One of their leaders, Conrad Grebel, writing to Thomas

Müntzer, whom he thought to be a possible kindred spirit in Germany, urged him "to esteem as good and right only that which can be found in fairly clear and unambiguous scripture" (von Muralt, 1952, p. 14; Williams, 1957, p. 75). The Bible became as central to the life and faith of the Anabaptists as to Lutherans and Reformed. Michael Sattler rested his case before his execution with a defense reminiscent of that of Luther at Worms; asking for scholars and the Bible, he challenged the court:

> If they prove to us with the Holy Scriptures that we err and are in the wrong, we will gladly desist and recant; . . . but if no error is proven to us, I hope to God that you will be converted and receive instruction (Williams, 1957, pp. 141-2; Köhler, 1908, pp. 329-330).

Disagreements over scriptural interpretations divided radical from magisterial reformers, and Lutheran from Reformed theologians, and, indeed, they frequently marred the unity of individual churches. Yet with the common conviction that God had given the Scriptures as a primary means of touching human minds and hearts, the Bible provided both the ground and much of the content for catechesis in all these churches.

Medieval Society Writ Small

From the time of Constantine through the sixteenth century, the vision of a truly Christian society on earth dominated understandings of human community. Medieval equivalents of sociological and political theory presupposed the *respublica christiana*. Adherents of imperial and papal authority might debate the best means to approximate an ideal society. The rediscovery of Aristotle might allow *homo naturalis* to be distinguished from *homo christianus*. The Renaissance might awaken men and women to the contributions of classical civilization and to the integrity of human life on earth. Yet, whatever their differences over goals and values in organized community, citizens of the western world in 1500 deemed the Christian faith to be as much a part of their societal organization as their political obligations and their family relationships. Catechesis, whether effective or not, was woven into the warp and woof of the entire complex mesh of their community life.

Although the Reformation shattered the religious unity of the *corpus christianorum*, the reformers remained largely wedded to the medieval understandings of religion in the community. The major milestones of religious detente, the 1555 Peace of Augsburg and the 1598 Edict of Nantes, both reflected the momentum of the old understandings: the principle of *cuius regio, eius religio* in the Empire, acknowledging the prince's right to determine the religion of his subjects, and Protestant rights in France, establishing a second religion beside the first. To a large degree, the older notion of the universal Christian commonwealth was now reduced to the confines of a nation, a principality, or a city-state.

Religious divisions reflected national and regional loyalties that had traditionally divided medieval society. Martin Luther's reliance on the Saxon Elector to implement religious reform and his appeal to the German nobility against Roman exactions have been judged cynical uses of non-religious instruments and loyalties to achieve his religious goals. Similar judgments have been applied to reformers in cities who brought about religious change through the increasingly influential bourgeois councils that sought freedom from lay and clerical feudal lords. To make such judgments is to forget the *respublica christiana*. Reformers turned to the civil magistrates and the princes because they held God-given authority within the one society of baptized Christians. They appealed to local conditions and employed civil geographical divisions because these were given realities in the life of the *Christian* community. The city council of Basle concluded the introduction to its church order of 1529 with these words:

> Therefore, we have made the following order to the praise of God and for the good of ourselves and others, in the name of the holy Trinity whose servants we are, for the establishment of a Christian, honorable, and peaceful life, not respecting the fact that the duty to advance such things more justly belongs to the spiritual superiors who are supposed to be concerned for the salvation of our souls (Richter, 1846, I, 120).

Those properly charged with responsibilities for religious reform were not carrying them out, and so the councilors exercised their authority to set standards on matters ranging from doctrine and sacraments to the proper manner of dress. The medieval concept of a unified society continued to reign through the new forms of the reformation churches.

The reformers were vividly aware of the difference between the vast majority of men and women who took their religion relatively lightly and those more fervent souls or "earnest Christians" whose faith dominated the many aspects of their lives. Luther, in the introduction to the German Mass, toyed with the notion that, in addition to the Latin and German orders of service, he might prepare a third "truly evanglical order" for "those who want to be Christians in earnest and who profess the gospel with hand and mouth." In the face of practical realities, however, he wrote that he neither was able nor desired "to begin such a congregation or assembly or to make rules for it" (1955, LIII, 63-64; 1883, XIX, 75). Martin Bucer more seriously, although equally unsuccessfully, proposed the formation in Strasbourg of voluntary fellowships (*Gemeinschaften*) of Christians willing to submit to more intensive instruction and discipline than the bulk of the population (Pauck, 1961, p. 121).

Only the Anabaptists defined their religious community in opposition to the larger society in which they lived; the 1527 Schleitheim Confession declared:

> truly all creatures are in but two classes, good and bad, believing and unbelieving, darkness and light, the world and those who [have come] out of the world, God's temple and idols, Christ and Belial; and none can have part with the other (Wenger, 1950, p. 71; Köhler, 1908, p. 309).

In a 1538 debate at Berne, after acknowledging a debt to Luther, Zwingli, and other magisterial reformers, an Anabaptist continued, "yet we recognized a great lack as regards repentance, conversion, and the true Christian life" (Hershberger, 1957, p. 39). Anabaptists did not totally deny the medieval vision of society, but reduced it in size, not just to the geographical divisions of the magisterial reformers, but to the narrower confines of the separated withdrawn community. Harold Bender has succinctly summed up the Anabaptist vision of society: since, for the believer,

> no compromise dare be made with evil, the Christian may in no circumstance participate in any conduct in the existing social order which is contrary to the spirit and teaching of Christ and the apostolic practice. He must consequently withdraw from the worldly system and create a Christian social order within the fellowship of the church brotherhood. Extension of this Christian order by the conversion of individuals and their transfer out of the world into the church is the only way by which progress can be made in Christianizing the social order (Hershberger, 1957, p. 53).

Anabaptists did not attempt to redefine the relationship between civil and ecclesiastical authorities, but rather to build a society that had as few links as possible to organized society outside of the church. The self-sufficient agricultural communities of the Hutterites, with their principles of common ownership, illustrate most vividly the Anabaptist understanding of Christian society. More than a trace of the vision of the medieval *corpus christianorum* remained embedded in the Anabaptist ideal.

The proclamation and the nurturing of Christian faith was a primary responsibility of the whole body of baptized Christians. The family, and, except in Anabaptist churches, civil authorities shared with ordained ministers the responsibility for catechesis. In the teaching and practice of the continental reformers in the sixteenth century, catechesis derived its distinctive characteristics both from their theological emphases on personal apprehension of religious faith and on the centrality of the Scriptures and from their ingrained presuppositions about Christian society.

THE WRITTEN CATECHISM AS LITERARY GENRE AND CATECHETICAL TOOL

The sixteenth century was the golden age of "the catechism," for, in spite of some precedents in earlier centuries, the written catechism, as we know it, was born among the Lutheran and Reformed, taken up by their associates in England, adopted by Jesuits for counter-reformation use, and employed much more sparingly by Anabaptists. Today we employ the Greek form "catechesis" for the whole educational process, but at the beginning of the Reformation, the Latin *catechismus* and its derived words in the vernacular languages also designated that process, not a written work. It had also designated "the form of examination by the priest with answers by parents and godparents at a baptism and the examination of a child at his first confession" (Küther, 1963, p. 164). Martin Bucer, describing an ideal earthly kingdom of God, laid down as a first rule the obligation to make known to children "the Church's catechism" (*ad Ecclesiae eos catechismum*) and to lay a solid foundation "through the catechism of Christ" (*per Christi catechismum*; 1955, p. 114; Pauck, 1969, p. 280). "Teaching of the Church" conveys to twentieth century minds the primary connotations of Bucer's use of "catechism." M. Reu identified Luther's 1525 use of "*catechismus puerorum*" (children's catechism) as its first explicit designation of a writing (Reu, 1916, p. 240, but September, not February; *see* Luther, 1930, III, 431 and 582; cf. Cohrs, 1900, XX, 169-170 and XXIII, 248).

Reforming zeal and the printing press combined to make the type of catechism we know today. "Catechisms" were produced in such bulk and with so great an impact upon the literate European population that by the end of the century the primary meaning of *catechismus* and its vernacular derivatives had shifted to designate a particular literary genre which could even be applied to a question-and-answer style writing that might not concern religion at all.

Antecedents for sixteenth-century catechisms are found in medieval episcopal orders requiring clergy to teach the principal points of the Christian faith, in material suggesting how priests might fulfill teaching responsibilities, and in a very few manuals intended for children and adolescents to memorize (DTC, 1903, X, part 2, 1896-1906; Reu, 1915). Some of these proposed the Apostle's Creed, the Decalogue, and the Lord's Prayer and *Ave Maria* as key guides of doctrine, morality, and devotion—usually, however, along with other items deemed worthy of memorization and meditation. John Gerson's *A B C des simples gens*, for example, also included the sets of seven virtues, gifts of the Holy Spirit, beatitudes, bodily and spiritual acts of mercy, sacraments, consecrations, and gifts of the blessed (Reu, 1915, p. 575). Luther drew on tradition when he declared that he could not base his own catechesis

> better or more plainly than has been done from the beginning of Christendom and retained till now, i.e., in these three parts, the Ten Commandments, the Creed, and the Our Father. These three plainly and briefly contain exactly everything that a Christian needs to know (1955, LIII, 64-65; 1883, XIX, 76).

In style, German reformers were influenced by the *Kinderfragen* (Children's Interrogatory) of the Bohemian Brethren whose Czech form went back at least to 1502, and whose German translations began appearing by 1522 (Cohrs, 1900, XX, 9-11; Müller, 1887, pp. 3-5 and 29-39; *compare* Sodergren, 1946, p. 133). Although the *Kinderfragen* did not include the Lord's Prayer, the style of its questions and answers is much closer to reformation forms than are other antecedents. Stressing personal response, it begins, "What are you? . . . A rational and mortal creature of God" (Müller, 1887, pp. 11-28).

The concentration on the Creed, Decalogue, and Lord's Prayer is pointedly underlined in the 1525 printing of a Catechetical Poster (*Katechismus-Tafel*) in Zwingli's Zurich (Cohrs, 1900, XX, 126-127). Containing the Ten Commandments, a few scriptural texts concerning the law, the Our Father, the *Ave Maria*, and the Creed, the poster measured about fifteen by twelve inches. It could be used at home, in a school room, or in newly white-washed churches to provide a focus for devotional meditation in the absence of the recently removed images.

Cohr lists more than fifty items in his collection of German evangelical catechetical works published before Luther's Short Catechism of 1529 (1900, *passim* and XXXIX, xiii-xv). Some of these are very brief, a number are not in a form we would identify as a "catechism," and some form parts of other works, but the sudden flow of this instructional material testifies to the impact of the reformers and to the catechetical concerns of the people and pastors who provided a market for the printers' new products. Among these productions in nascent Lutheran and Reformed communities are Wolfgang Capito's *Kinderbericht* (Instruction for Children) of 1526 in Latin and German in Strasbourg; the "Questions and Answers for the Examination of Children," produced possibly as early as 1525 by Oecolampadius in Basle; the first book to be entitled *Catechism*, prepared by Andreas Althamer of Ansbach, published in Nuremberg in 1528; and, in the same year, the smaller and larger catechisms of Johann Brenz, destined to have a long life due to their later official authorization in Württemberg (Cohrs, 1900, XXI, 85-201, XXIII, 5-19, XXII, 3-39 and 129-185; Wills, 1947, pp. 271-280, and 1955, pp. 114-127). As these works were being published, Martin Luther's burning concern for effective catechesis was stimulating some of his most influential writings.

Martin Luther and Lutheran Catechisms

Historians have long marked the year 1520 for the publication of Luther's call to reform in the *Appeal to the German Nobility*, his scholarly sacramental theology in the *Babylonian Captivity*, and his discussion of faith in the *Freedom of a Christian*. The year ought to be noted as well for his *Brief Form of the Ten Commandments, of the Creed, and of the Lord's Prayer*. Intended for his Wittenberg congregation, the *Brief Form* expressed Luther's pastoral insistence on Christian nurture. Reu points out that

Luther introduced three significant innovations in traditional catechetics (1916, pp. 237-239). In the preface Luther explained his concentration on the three documents to be expounded in the book:

> These three contain fully and completely everything that is in the Scriptures and that ever should be preached and everything that a Christian needs to know, all put so briefly and so plainly that no one can make complaint or excuse, saying that what he needs for his salvation is too long or too hard to remember (1883, VII, 204; 1915, II, 354).

Secondly, he deliberately put them in an order which would emphasize his understanding of the process of salvation:

> Three things a man needs to know in order to be saved. First, he must know what he ought to do and what he ought not to do. Second, when he finds that by his own strength he can neither do the things he ought, nor leave undone the things he ought not to do, he must know where to seek and find and get the strength he needs. Third he must know how to seek and find and get this strength . . . the Commandments teach a man to know his illness, so that he feels and sees what he can do and what he cannot do, and what he can and what he cannot leave undone, and thus knows himself to be a sinner and a wicked man. After that the Creed shows him and teaches him where he may find the remedy—the grace which helps him become a good man and to keep the Commandments; it shows him God and the mercy which He has revealed and offered in Christ. In the third place, the Lord's Prayer teaches him how to ask for this grace, get it, and take it to himself (1915, II, 354-355; 1883, VII, 204-205).

Finally, instead of the customary manner of considering the Apostles' Creed in twelve articles, he divided it into three, "for the Trinity is the chief thing in the Creed, on which everything else depends" (1915, II, 368; 1883, VII, 214). By this division, which he reasserted in his 1529 catechisms, Luther concentrated on the principal thrusts of each section, creation, redemption, and sanctification (Tappert, 1959, pp. 344-345; Luther, 1883, XXX, part 1, 362-368; *see* Reu, 1904b, pp. 442-446). Luther included the *Brief Form* in the Prayer Book (*Betbuchlein*) published in 1522 which went through thirty-five German and two Latin editions in the following twenty-five years.

In the preface to the 1525 German Mass Luther urged a question-and-answer style of teaching for sound learning. It was not enough to learn by rote; children and servants must "be questioned point by point and give answer what each part means and how they understand it." Giving some examples of how the questioning might proceed, Luther adds,

> One may take these questions from our *Betbuchlein* where the three parts are briefly explained, or make others, until the heart may grasp the whole sum of Christian truth under two headings or, as it were, pouches, namely, faith and love (1955, LIII, 65-66; 1883, XIX, 76-77).

After urging others to prepare comprehensive sets of questions and answers, Luther turned to the task himself. In despair at the ignorance of the people and the incompetence of pastors he began to complete the *Small Catechism* in January 1529, publishing it in parts on posters, like the Zurich catechetical poster, so that it might immediately begin to be used in churches, schools, and homes. The first edition of the initial posters, including the Ten Commandments, the Creed, and the Lord's Prayer, sold out within a month, and by March the sections on Baptism, Confession, and the Sacrament of the Altar were out, to be followed shortly by forms of morning and evening prayers, table graces, and a final scriptural "table of duties." The *Small Catechism* rapidly appeared in Latin and Low German, and although Reu ignores the Reformed catechisms in declaring that Luther's work pushed out all other catechisms except for those of Brenz, his dictum remains true for the Lutheran bodies. Before the century was out, the *Small Catechism* was available in Bohemian, Danish, Dutch, English, Estonian, Finnish, French, Icelandic, Italian, Lettish, Greek, Polish, Old-Prussian, Slovenish, Spanish, Swedish, and Wendish. The relative brevity, the crisp clarity, and the direct, rather than polemical style of the work have all contributed to its record as the catechism of the continental Reformation used most extensively through four succeeding centuries (Reu, 1904b, p. 436; 1916, pp. 239-249; Grimm, 1960, pp. 124-127).

While working on the *Small Catechism*, Luther also refined catechetical material from sermons which emerged as the *Large* or *German Catechism*. The initial edition discussed Decalogue, Creed, Lord's Prayer, Baptism, and Sacrament of the Altar, and a section on confession was soon added. The style strikes a modern reader as curious, for Luther interjects comments about *why* or *how* certain things should be taught into the midst of his expository explanations. The preface of the first edition in 1529 urged heads of household to use it in fulfilling their responsibility to examine "children and servants at least once a week and ascertain what they have learned of it, and if they do not know it, to keep them faithfully at it." As second preface, added to, rather than substituted for, the earlier one, appeared in the following year; Luther berated pastors who neglected their catechetical duties, "lazybellies and presumptuous saints" who think themselves "learned and great doctors." He urged all Christians, but especially pastors,

> not to try to be doctors prematurely and to imagine that they know everything. Vain imaginations, like new cloth, suffer shrinkage! Let all Christians exercise themselves in the Catechism daily, and constantly put it into practice, guarding themselves with the greatest care and diligence against the poisonous infection of such security or vanity. Let them continue to read and *teach*, to learn and meditate and ponder (Tappert, 1959, pp. 362, 359, 361; Luther, 1883, XXX, part 1, 129, 126, 128-129; *italics mine*).

Luther uses the word "catechism" here in the sense of basic teaching. Tactfully, he witnesses to his own practice "every morning, and whenever else I have time" to recite the "Lord's Prayer, the Ten Commandments, the Creed, the Psalms, etc." since "I cannot master it as I wish, but must remain a child and pupil of the Catechism" daily (Tappert, 1959, p. 359; Luther, 1883, XXX, part 1, 126). Luther is not merely commending a salutary devotional practice; rather he is urging inadequately instructed and insufficiently motivated priests to use this and similar materials to inform their own grasp of theology and to guide them in teaching others. The distinctive thrusts of the two prefaces are directed at parents and pastors, who share catechetical responsibilities.

The two catechisms of Luther illustrate a perennial problem of Christian education. Concerned persons may begin to focus on children and youth as the "future of the church," but sooner or later in the preparation of material aids, the focus must be broadened to include the various categories of responsible adults who require nurture, not only in the possible techniques of teaching, but in the content of the catechesis which they are expected to impart. The church's education of the young is inextricably bound up with adult education.

Luther set great store by the catechisms. As Grimm has pointed out, he carefully avoided designating them "textbooks in theology," always describing them as "summaries of Christian Faith" (1960, p. 138). He once commented that "the catechism is the Bible of the laity, wherein is comprehended the whole sense of Christian teaching which every Christian needs to know for eternal bliss" (1912, V, 581 [#6288]). In 1539, seeing heresies emerging on the horizon, he commented,

> We indeed have the catechism [*i.e.* teaching] from the pulpit which has not been so in a thousand years. For you cannot gather so much out of all the books of the fathers as is taught by the grace of God today in the little catechism [*i.e.* printed form] (1912, IV, 434 [#4692]).

In a decade "cathechism" had come to denote, with varying shades of emphasis, both the process of nurture in the faith and particular written instruments designed to communicate that faith.

Catechisms in the Reformed Churches

By 1529 the division between Luther and Swiss reformers had begun to harden. Lutheran affirmations, even in the simple forms of the catechisms, grated on theological understandings in Switzerland and the upper Rhine, and, consequently, churches in these areas produced catechetical material which would distinguish their teaching from that of Lutherans as well as Roman Catholics. Leo Jud at Zurich produced a larger and smaller catechism in 1534 and 1535, and Henry Bullinger wrote a lengthy exposition of the Decalogue, Creed, Our Father, and the sacraments in 1556 (Reu, 1904a, I, part 3, division 2, 993-1060 and division 1, 701*-705*; Staedtke, 1972, p. 136f [#'s 283, 291, and 297]; Lang, 1907, pp. 54-116). Unhappiness at Strasbourg with Capito's earlier *Kinderbericht* stimulated Bucer to prepare *The Larger Catechism* in 1534, and when this turned out to be too lengthy for children, to write *The Shorter Catechism* in 1537. Bucer advised in the preparation of a reforming church-order in Kassel in Hesse in 1539 in which his catechism was adopted and appeared in at least six editions within the decade. Modified to avoid Bucer's leanings towards Luther, the catechism was adopted at Berne and later used in French translations as well (Stupperich, 1952, pp. 52-53 [#'s 48 and 56]; Eells, 1931, pp. 154-155; Hubert, 1900, pp. 401-404; Reu, 1904a, I, part 1, 23-90; Sehling, 1902, VIII, part 1, 131-142; DTC, 1903, X, part 2, 1909). These and other Reformed catechisms found some limited acceptance, but it was John Calvin in Geneva and the Heidelberg reformers in the Palatinate who prepared the catechisms which, like that of Luther, found international acceptance and use.

The theological guide of Reformed Christianity, Calvin's *Institutes of the Christian Religion*, was born of the reformer's concern for simple catechesis. In the letter to Francis I which prefaces the initial 1536 edition, Calvin declared:

> When I first set myself to writing this present book, Sire, nothing was farther from my thought than writing things that would be presented to your Majesty. My intention was only to teach some rudiments by which those touched by any good affection to God might be instructed in true piety.

After observing the persecutory policies of high French officials, he decided to direct the work both to those for whom he had originally intended it and, as well, to the king as a "confession of faith" by which he might better judge the wisdom of using "fire and sword" against such teachings (Calvin, 1863, XXX, 9; 1960, I, 9; Wendel, 1963, pp. 144-147). If Calvin's original intention was partially obscured in the first edition as he shaped it into a fuller doctrinal statement, it was obliterated in his final 1559 edition, five times as large as the original. The line distinguishing simple catechesis from theological exposition and norms of doctrinal orthodoxy is never easily defined.

Calvin must have realized the inadequacy of the *Institutes* for his original purpose, for his *Instruction in Faith* appeared in 1537 as a straightforward exposition of the principal tenets of Christianity. As in the *Institutes*, Calvin began with the problem of our knowledge of God—a knowledge for which we are created and found only in Scriptures where God's works are described "not by the perversity of our judgment, but by the rule of eternal truth" (1863, L, 33, 35; 1949, pp. 17, 20). Calvin proceeded to the Decalogue, Creed, and Lord's Prayer, expanding on their expositions to include points of law, Christian doctrine, and prayer which they do not explicitly discuss. He then treated sacraments and human traditions, as well as ministry, discipline, and the magistrate, these last three reflecting Reformed, in contrast to Lutheran, convictions that Scripture prescribed an order in these matters to which believers ought to conform.

Calvin produced a question-and-answer catechism in French after his return to Geneva in 1541; two decades later, in his final words to the Genevan ministers, he declared that,

> On my return from Strasbourg I hastily made the Catechism, for I would never have accepted the ministry if they had not sworn to these two points: to be trained in maintaining the Catechism and the discipline; and as I wrote it, they came fetching pieces of paper the size of a hand and carried them to the printer.

He hinted that, had he had the leisure, he might have revised it, but he conservatively urged them to leave it for "all changes are dangerous and sometimes are harmful" (1863, XXXVII, 894). Calvin may have been influenced by the dialogue style he observed in Strasbourg, but the content follows the 1537 *Instruction*, with the opening exchange: "What is the chief end of human life? . . . To know God" (Torrance, 1959, p. 5; Calvin, 1863, XXXIV, 9-10). In contrast to the *Instruction*, however, Calvin departed from Luther's order of Decalogue before the Creed; reversing the order, he suggested the law primarily served as a guide for Christian living rather than principally as a schoolmaster to bring us to Christ. Occasionally it is not the child but the catechist who offers instructive material to which the child merely replies, "I understand so," "That is so." DeJong points out that for Calvin, catechesis

> was intrinsically a dialogue between minister and catechumen in the presence of the living God of the covenant who through his Word of grace and salvation actively engages in molding the hearts and lives of his people to his praise. . . . The total involvement of both human parties is required in this spiritual dialogue (1967, p. 183).

Catechesis presupposed a personal relationship which provided the context for imparting information.

The lengthy *Genevan Catechism* could not meet all the catechetical needs of the city. The preface to a 1562 Genevan manual for family use entitled *Instruction of Christians* described the situation:

> The doctrine of the honor and service which almighty God requires of us is so perfectly inferred and laid out in the Catechism dedicated to all the Churches of Jesus Christ . . . that there was really no need to make an additional treatise or book. But . . . we are so weak that we are immediately discouraged if we are not helped. For this

reason, several, wanting to overcome such weakness, have made some summaries and instructions to serve as reminders for those who are not capable of understanding and retaining what is taught at greater length elsewhere, and for greater ease, they have included in the said instructions only the prayer of our Lord Jesus Christ which is the pattern of all other prayers, the summary of our Christian faith, and the Ten Commandments of the Law of God where we learn what his Majesty commands and forbids to us (Peter, 1965, pp. 11-12).

Beginning in 1545, primers designed to introduce a child to both learning and piety had appeared in Geneva with identical or similar texts for "A little treatise necessary for those who wish to receive the holy Supper of our Lord," and "The manner of questioning children to be received at the Supper." It is to such *abécédaires* that the 1562 preface refers, and Peter has convincingly argued that Calvin himself provided the actual texts for these simple instructions, intending them to serve alongside the *Genevan Catechism* with its fuller theological discussions (1965, pp. 14-20).

When Calvin wrote the Lord Protector of England in 1548 advising him on religious reformation, he suggested these two levels of catechetical instruction:

> First, there ought to be an agreed summary of doctrine that all ought to preach, which all prelates and curates swear to follow, and no one ought to receive any ecclesiastical charge who does not promise to keep such an agreement. Next, there ought to be a common formula of instruction for little children and ignorant people that serves to make them familiar with sound doctrine so that they may discern it amidst the lies and corruptions which may be introduced to the contrary. Believe me, Monseigneur, the Church of God will never be preserved without catechesis [*sans Cathechisme; catechesi carero*] (1863, XLI, 71-72, 84; 1857, II, 177).

Although these two levels do not correspond exactly to Luther's two catechisms, they reflect the same concerns for authorized instructional materials designed for differing human capabilities. The *Institutes*, the *Genevan Catechism*, and the simpler instructions form a chain of works reflecting Calvin's vision of the church as a great school of religion.

The apex of Reformed catechisms was reached in 1563 at Heidelberg when the faculty of theology, led by Zacharias Ursinus and Caspar Olevianus, produced a catechism which Elector Frederick III formally authorized for the Palatinate (Thompson, 1963, pp.

15-27, 78-81). Even so vigorous a defender of Calvin's educational contributions as DeJong contrasts the *Genevan Catechism* with "the striking balance and beauty for which the *Heidelberg Catechism* has won a warm place in the churches for centuries" (1967, p. 183). Although its treatment of the Ascension precluded agreement with Lutherans on eucharistic presence, the catechism embodied the positive teachings of Bucer and Calvin on the Supper rather than the minimizing doctrines characteristic of Zurich. As for predestination, the catechism's omission of any development of the doctrine brings it in closer line with Zurich—and the relatively early *Genevan Catechism*—than with Genevan teaching in the later years of Calvin. This irenic, if "undeniably Reformed," character to the Heidelberg's teaching of "the faith commonly held by Reformed Catholicism" undoubtedly accounts in part for its continued attraction for nineteenth and twentieth century theologians and pastors (Thompson, 1963, pp. 29-31 and 53-92, 124-256 and 158-179).

Berkhof describes the Heidelberg's reordering of topics as "the real reformation of the catechetical tradition," a pattern Ursinus had already introduced in his 1561 *Minor Catechism*:

"What does the word of God teach? . . . First it shows us our misery; then, by what means we may be freed from it; and what gratitude is to be shown to God for this liberation (Lang, 1907, p. 200; Thompson, 1963, pp. 86 and 78).

A similar answer appeared in the Heidelberg itself, and both catechisms were ordered accordingly (Lang, 1907, pp. 4-5; Reu, 1904a, I, part 1, 243; Torrance, 1959, p. 69). By dividing consideration of the "law" between discussion of "our misery" and "gratitude," it takes a middle ground between the catechetical orders of Luther and Calvin, recognizing the law equally as preparation for, and response to, God's saving work in Christ. Creed, sacraments, ministry, and discipline all fall under the means of redemption, and the Decalogue and the Lord's Prayer under the human gratitude due to the Almighty.

The Heidelberg emphasizes personal involvement. Commentators have noted the "personal, experiential manner," "existential" mood, and its design, not "for the conversion of those outside, but for the upbuilding of those within the redeemed community." The first question declares one's comfort to be "that I, with body and soul, both in life and in death, am not my own, but belong to my faithful Saviour Jesus Christ" (Miller, 1963, p. 538; Thompson, 1963, p. 172; Torrance, 1959, p. 69; Lang, 1907, p. 4; Reu, 1904a, I, part 1, 242). The only Reformed catechism to come close to rivaling the continued popularity of Luther's *Small Catechism* ends as it had begun:

> *Amen* means: That is indeed true and certain. For my prayer is much more certainly heard of God than I feel in my heart that I desire such things of Him (Torrance, 1959, p. 96; Lang, 1907, p. 52; Reu, 1904a, I, part 1, 263).

The *Heidelberg Catechism*, like the Genevan, required a relatively mature mind, and in 1585, a summary version appeared following the same topical order (Thompson, 1963, p. 88; Reu, 1904a, I, part 1, 268-273). Catechetical work in Heidelberg as elsewhere required tools designed for the specific human materials with whom they were to be used.

Anabaptist Catechisms

Sixteenth-century Anabaptists, with two exceptions, did not take up the new catechetical written forms. Catechisms gradually penetrated Anabaptist communities only in succeeding centuries. The exceptions, both in Moravia, were Balthasar Hubmaier's congregation in Nikolsburg and the Hutterite Brethren (ME, 1955, I, 527-530). Hubmaier in 1526 prepared *A Christian Lehrtafel ["teaching table"] which Everyone Ought to Know Before He is Baptized in Water*, embodying a dialogue between two members of the noble Nikolsburg family who supported the brief, unique Anabaptist conversion of an established parish. No evidence suggests that the *Lehrtafel* continued in use after the demise of the Anabaptist predominance in Nikolsburg (Hubmaier, 1962, pp. 306-326).

The Hutterite *Bruderhofs* in Moravia used an authoritative catechism whose set forms are reflected in recorded testimony of heresy trials. Although the earliest dated copy is from 1584, the author seems to have been Peter Riedemann who died twenty-eight years earlier, a man known to have been familiar with the teachings of Hubmaier (ME, 1955, I, 529; II, 149, and 833-834; Friedmann, 1966, p. 21; Wiswedel, 1940, p. 42). Built around the Decalogue, Creed, and Our Father, the three texts, however, are nowhere included. Brief sections on creation, the fall, punishment for sin and the exodus precede the Ten Commandments; baptism and the Supper follow the Our Father. Wiswedel, commenting on the treatment of the Creed, notes that although the order of the apostolic symbol is followed, the content demonstrates the Anabaptist concern "to put its own patterns in the place of the symbols" (1940, p. 42). The description of the church follows the Anabaptist understanding so thoroughly implemented in Hutterite life and practice:

> It is a congregation of all true believers who are separated from the uncleanness of the world by the pure teaching of Christ, gathered and united through a godly life on the true rock of Christ, his Apostles and Prophets, adorned with all Christian virtues, and are illumined with the Word of God, wherein they become a spiritual sacrifice offered with pure hearts, pleasing to God through Christ (Wiswedel, 1940, p. 54).

The catechisms of the continental Reformation, evidenced by the denotation of a distinct literary genre, provided new tools for the church's age-old mission of catechesis. Conceived in response to the needs of the young and the "simple," the catechisms quickly were directed not only to those who would be taught, but also to those who would instruct them. Two classes of catechisms, with undefinable gradations of degrees of difficulty among them, were produced in Latin and the vernacular languages. As both Lutheran and Reformed became concerned for right doctrine in relation to one another, the catechisms came to serve as litmus-paper tests of doctrinal orthodoxy. Luther's two catechisms joined the confessions of faith in the 1580 *Book of Concord*, and Calvin, in dedicating the Latin edition of the *Genevan Catechism*, wrote that "the agreement which our churches have in doctrine cannot be seen with clearer evidence than from catechisms, . . . all the faithful holding them as their common symbol of Christian communion" (1863, XXXIV, 7-8; 1849, II, 35). The line between the more substantial catechisms and the confessions of faith became as blurred as that between classes of catechisms. Philip Schaff in his *Creeds of Christendom* indiscriminately includes Luther's *Short Catechism*, the *Heidelberg Catechism*, and, by title, the *Genevan Catechism* (1877, III, 74-92, 232, and 307-355). Berkhof describes the threefold purpose of the Heidelberg "as a catechism for youth, as a guide for preaching, and as a credal statement" (Thompson, 1963, p. 81). Calvin might declare a catechism to be a symbol of

Christian communion, and Lutherans might entitle their symbolic tome a *Book of Concord*, but the catechisms serve as well as symbols of Christian division and instruments of discord.

Catechisms continued to play a significant role in the lives of the churches of the continental Reformation. The Reformation provided a tool, that, with all of its problems of application, has proven extraordinarily useful in the post-Gutenberg world.

STRUCTURES OF REFORMATION SOCIETY FOR CATECHESIS

Catechesis in practice takes place through particular institutions, individuals, groups, and activities. In the sixteenth-century reformation parishes, family, schools, ordained ministers, liturgical worship, initiation, and discipline all served catechetical purposes, and it is to these that we turn.

The Family

Within the *respublica christiana*, sixteenth-century reformers looked to the family, as the basic building-block of human society, to provide the initial locus of Christian catechesis—not, however, the nuclear family of the twentieth century, but a socio-economic unit that might include parents, children, a variety of blood relatives, and, depending on the status of the family, a smaller or larger number of servants. In the sixteenth century, the word *familia* meant "household," a working social body, and only secondarily denoted its core related by blood and marriage. Aristotle had described the origin of the state from the adhesions of villages to one another, which, in turn, were constituted by the mutual drawing together of families. The family arose out of two relationships: man and woman *and* master and slave, for Aristotle approved the words of Hesiod, " 'First house and wife and an ox for the plough,' for the ox is the poor man's slave" (*Politics*, 1.1.6; 1252b.10). The Bible reinforced this understanding, for as Calvin remarked in commenting on Genesis 17:4, "it is sufficiently evident that different nations had their origins from the holy patriarch [Abraham]" (1863, LI, 236; 1847, I, 446). Renaissance westerners could, without making too many adjustments, identify their own households with those of both the tribal nations described in the Old Testament and of the city-states of Greece.

Erasmus, like other Christian humanists, turned to parents for the initial religious nurture of their children. After first principles were inculcated at the mother's knee, Erasmus encouraged continuing education at home, ideally by the father, more practically by a tutor. Fathers who neglected their children's religion were warned:

> Does he not act absurdly who adorns the hat, while there is a neglected, uncombed, and mangy head underneath? And is it not much more absurd to devote a fitting solicitude to the mortal body while taking no account of the immortal soul (*De Pueris*; 1969, I, part 2, 27).

Erasmus sought to evoke a clear-headed intellectual grasp of Christian faith in his many educational endeavors; the home, he believed, laid down the initial and critical foundation (Woodward, 1906, pp. 116-126).

In Luther's view the *pater familias* was, ideally, a principal catechist of the church. The prefaces to the German Mass and to the small and large catechisms insist upon the religious responsibility of fathers to children and servants. Headings in German editions of the *Small Catechism* designated the household head as inquisitor and leader of prayers (Luther, 1883, XXX, part 1, 241; Reu, 1916, p. 247). In a 1525 sermon Luther emphasized the importance of firm benevolent paternal rule:

> We see a city to be nothing more than an aggregate of households, and so a kingdom is an aggregate of cities and villages. Where the household is well ruled, so will the whole realm and its government (1883, XVI, 500-501).

Not only do children owe obedience to their parents, but parents, as "bishops and kings" in their own homes, are responsible for their children's spiritual and material well-being (XVI, 504; cf. Grimm, 1960, p. 103). As he described catechesis in the society he knew, Luther remarked that "if parents and guardians won't take the trouble to do this, either themselves or through others, there will never be a catechism [i.e., catechesis]" (1955, LIII, 65; 1883, XIX, 76). In the preface to pastors in the *Small Catechism*, he admonished them to urge parents, as well as governing officials, to rule wisely and educate their children, for if they do not, they are guilty of damnable sin,

> for by such neglect they undermine and lay waste both the kingdom of God and the kingdom of the world and are the worst enemies of

God and man. . . . Tell them that God will inflict awful punishments
on them for these sins.

Accordingly in his example of the mode of confession,

> a master or mistress may say: "In particular I confess in your presence
> that I have not been faithful in training my children, servants, and
> wife to the glory of God" (Tappert, 1959, pp. 340, 350; 1883, XXX,
> part 1, 276-277, 386 [1531 ed.]).

Luther once remarked,

> Instruction in church does not edify the adolescent, but testing in the
> home, explanations of the catechism, and testing in confession, these
> are worth much more (1912, III, 679 [#3875]).

Lutheran churches reflected this emphasis, as parents or sponsors
often determined when their children were to be presented to the
pastor to be examined for admission to their first communion
(Repp, 1964, p. 24).

Martin Bucer, deeply concerned for the social order, regarded
marriage as a *res politica* requiring careful ordering,

> for unless that first and most sacred union of man and woman is
> established in a holy way, so that household discipline flourishes
> among the spouses according to God's precept, how can we expect a
> race of good men? (Pauck, 1969, p. 316; Bucer, 1955, p. 153).

Bucer, like Luther considering parents as catechists, urged that
laws be made to order

> parents to educate and establish their children in Christ's faith and
> obedience with great care, and with a just penalty appointed for
> those who themselves infect their children with either false doctrine
> or bad morals or permit them to be infected by others. . . . Those
> who neglect this when it is in their control snatch back the children
> whom they have consecrated to the Lord and hand them over to the
> dominion of Satan (Pauck, 1969, p. 280; Bucer, 1955, p. 114).

Reflecting social differences of Rhineland cities from Saxon
communities, as well as different personal perceptions of the roles
of the sexes, Bucer's discussions suggest a more significant role for
the mother than do those of Luther's composition. Similar mixes
of sociological and personal differences may lie behind Bucer's
omission of references to responsibility for servants.

When John Knox inquired of Calvin whether illegitimate children or those with Roman Catholic or excommunicate parents ought to be admitted to baptism, Calvin, after consulting with his fellow Genevan pastors, replied with a resounding "yes"—provided there be assurance of genuine Christian nurture, if not by parents, then by sponsors who were assumed to be of the family. Only if this is impossible is the church to refuse baptism,

> for nothing is more preposterous than to insert into the body of Christ those for whom we have no hope that they will become his disciples. Whereby, if none of his relatives appear to pledge his faith to the church, and especially undertake the care of teaching the child, the act is a mockery and the baptism defiled (1863, XLV, 667 [#3128]; *see* Knox to Calvin, XLV, 619 [#3106]).

The Genevan church assumed parental responsibility, and in default of such parental concern, they looked to godparents to provide it—much as Lutherans who sometimes associated baptismal sponsors with parents in responsibility for catechesis. At the beginning of Calvin's involvement in the Genevan Reformation in 1537, Articles of Organization proposed that parents teach children "a brief and simple summary of the Christian faith"— presumably the *Instruction in Faith* of that year. "At certain seasons" parents were to bring children to be examined by the ministers "until they have been proved sufficiently instructed" (Calvin, 1954, p. 54; 1863, XXXVIII, part 1, 13). Following Calvin's return, the 1541 Ordinances tightened regulations by which parents were to bring children to Sunday noon catechism, and, by implication, to encourage learning of "the sum" of what the *Catechism* contained: parents neglecting their duties were to be called to account (Calvin, 1954, p. 69; 1863, XXXVIII, part 1, 28). As Thompson has described the process,

> the elders came round to each house to see if little Jacques knew what was the chief end of man. If his answer was other than God, the father of the household might well expect to be disciplined (1963, p. 33).

The Reformed, like the Lutherans, held parents responsible for Christian catechesis, and, in addition, attempted to introduce discipline to ensure that they fulfilled their responsibilities.

Since children did not become members of Anabaptist churches, concern for catechesis by parents was not often reflected in theological writings or official church documents. Anabaptist parents in the sixteenth century, however, lived under the shadow of persecution, and a concern to nurture their children in so precious a faith was seldom absent. A printer's servant from Cologne, shortly before his execution in 1558, wrote his wife from prison in a letter heavily sprinkled with biblical quotations:

> Be of good courage, and bring up your children in good manners, and in the fear of God, that their natural propensities may be mortified; and take an example from yourself, how you bring them up in their weakness, with great labor and trouble, and give the breast to them to whom the Lord has commanded milk to be given. You are also to give them the rod, according to the command of the Lord, when they transgress and are obstinate. . . . Remember the words of Sirach where he says (7:26): "Shew not thyself cheerful to thy daughter, nor laugh with her, lest she become bold against thee . . ." But teach her the law of our God, that she may put her hope in the Almighty and Most High, and may never forget the benefits bestowed upon us through Christ (van Bracht, 1886, p. 559; *see* Williams, 1962, pp. 800-801).

Only among the Hutterites were parents not given responsibility for the religious upbringing of their own children, for in the disciplined community life of the *Bruderhofs*, material and spiritual nurture was a responsibility shared by all church members.

The reformers, in general, held believing parents responsible for their children's catechesis. Luther expressly charged the heads of households with care for servants as well. Christian faith was to be nurtured in the home, not only by parental love and example, but also by explicit and systematic examination and exposition.

The Schools

It has been recently observed that "if the thirteenth century was the age of the universities, the sixteenth deserves to be known as the age of the grammar schools" (Bolgar, 1968, p. 431). Renaissance concerns for revitalized education for life and reformation concerns for effective catechesis reinforced each other. Humanist and reformer agreed on the unity of education and religion. A modern reader may be startled to pick up a sixteenth-century book entitled "Primer" and discover it to be a book of prayers.

The humanists who most profoundly influenced western education aimed at the reinvigoration of religion. Marjorie Boyle sums up the theological foundation of Erasmus' union of piety and grammar:

> The same Christ who confers sonship on man, bidding him by grace to express this filiation in true religion, is the *Logos* who confers intelligibility on man, bidding him to express with grace his understanding in true eloquence. Piety and humanism, religion and eloquence, mutually serve and interpret (1977, pp. 69-70).

Woodward commented that for Juan Luis Vives, "in the training of the young, *pietas* and *eruditio* are a consistent unity" (1906, p. 189). Even those reformers such as Luther who were in some sense anti-humanist were profoundly influenced by the linguistic and educational emphases of the Renaissance, and their common concerns were channeled into the refurbishment of old schools and the establishment of new institutions.

Before the Reformation the elementary vernacular schools and the Latin grammar schools were attached to monasteries, to cathedral and collegiate churches, to chantries, and occasionally to a town or borough government. In the fifteenth century in the low countries and Germany, the Brethren of the Common Life had introduced significant innovations in school organization and teaching methods. Age levels and curriculum of universities and grammar schools overlapped, and reformers and their opponents sought to control both, but as Bolgar points out,

> the grammar schools with their smaller and less eminent staffs, drawing their pupils from a limited area and securely under the thumb of the local administration, proved much more convenient instruments (1968, p. 431).

Although an admirer of Luther may overstate the case when he declares him "the greatest, not only of religious, but of educational reformers," another stands on firmer ground when he declares him the first educator in modern times "to make the state aware of its great obligations to society" in education and to see "the need for universal, compulsory education" (Painter, 1889, p. 168; Grimm, 1960, pp. 79 and 84; *see* Eby, 1952, pp. 67-79). Luther argued for more adequate educational preparation for the needs of government, law, and other professions, but, above all, he stressed the importance of effective Christian nurture in the schools and the preparation of effective pastors and schoolmasters to catechize the larger society. In 1524 Luther wrote an open letter to the councilors of the German cities urging them to restore the schools "everywhere being left to go to wrack and ruin" and to establish libraries "that the good books may be preserved and not lost, together with the arts and languages which we now have by the grace of God" (1955, XLV, 348 and 373; 1883, XV, 28 and 49). Why should councilors concern themselves with such matters? Because parents may fail to do their duty.

> Even if parents had the ability and desire to do it themselves, they have neither the time nor the opportunity for it, what with their other duties and the care of the household. Necessity compels us, therefore, to engage public schoolteachers for the children—unless each one were willing to engage his own private tutor. But that would be too heavy a burden for the common man, and many a promising boy would again be neglected on account of poverty. . . . It therefore behooves the council and the authorities to devote the greatest care and attention to the young. . . . The welfare of a city does not consist solely in accumulating vast treasures, building mighty walls and magnificent buildings. . . . A city's best and greatest welfare, safety, and strength consist rather in its having many able, learned, wise, honorable, and well-educated citizens (1955, XLV, 355-356; 1883, XV, 33-34).

Arguing here for the Latin grammar schools, Luther was concerned that they produce able and useful citizens, as well as those

> who can dig into Scripture, expound it, and carry on disputations. A saintly life and right doctrine are not enough. Hence, languages are absolutely and altogether necessary in the Christian church (1955, XLV, 363; 1883, XV, 40).

In this vigorous appeal to the civil authorities, Luther urged an appropriate and flexible program for both boys and girls; for some, an hour a day would suffice while they learn a trade or work at home, whereas the most able would devote full time to study (1955, XLV, 368-371; 1883, XV, 44-48).

Six years later, in a treatise urging parents to keep their children in school, Luther suggested a whole range of catechetical tasks for which he believed schools could fit men and women. All boys ought to study,

> even those of lesser ability. They ought at least to read, write, and understand Latin, for we need not only highly learned doctors and

masters of Holy Scripture but also ordinary pastors who will teach the gospel and the catechism to the young and ignorant, and baptize and administer the sacrament. That they may be incapable of doing battle with heretics is unimportant. . . . In like manner we must also have sacristans and other persons who serve and help in relation to the office of preaching and the word of God. Even though a boy who has studied Latin should afterward . . . become a craftsman, he still stands as a ready reserve in case he should be needed as a pastor or in some other service of the word. . . . It is especially easy in our day to train persons for teaching the gospel and the catechism because not only Holy Scripture but also knowledge of all kinds is so abundant. . . . Even women and children can now learn from German books and sermons more about God and Christ—I am telling the truth!— than all the universities, foundations, monasteries, the whole papacy, and all the world used to know. Ordinary pastors, however, must be able to use Latin. They cannot do without it any more than scholars can do without Greek and Hebrew (1955, XLVI, 231-232; 1883, XXX, part 2, 545-547).

Luther demonstrated the importance he assigned to schools,

If I could leave the preaching office and my other duties, or had to do so, there is no other office I would rather have than that of schoolmaster; . . . for I know that next to that of preaching, this is the best, greatest, and most useful office there is. Indeed, I scarcely know which of the two is the better. For it is hard to make old dogs obedient and old rascals pious. . . . Young saplings are more easily bent and trained, even though some may break in the process. It surely has to be one of the supreme virtues on earth faithfully to train other people's children; for there are very few people, in fact, almost none, who will do this for their own (1955, XLVI, 253; 1883, XXX, part 2, 579-580).

Although Luther explicitly related the catechetical importance of schools to the preparation of catechists at various levels of competence, implicit throughout was the belief that they would also provide basic Christian nurture.

School programs which evolved under Luther's influence provided fundamental catechesis. In the preface to the German Mass, he described Wittenberg schoolboys attending daily Matins and Vespers, chanting psalms to keep them "well versed in the Latin Bible" and taking turns reading the lessons in Latin and German from the Bible or the catechism (1955, LIII, 68-69; 1883, XIX, 79-80). Philip Melanchthon enthusiastically implemented educational policies urged by Luther, his humanist loyalties fortifying his reformation convictions. Counselor to princes, cities, and pastors, Melanchthon through his work in reforming and organizing universities and schools won the title of *Praeceptor Germaniae* (Woodward, 1906, pp. 211-243; Eby, 1952, pp. 81-84). With Luther's advice and full approval, Melanchthon devised the 1528 *Instructions for Visitors of Parish Pastors* in Saxony with its detailed ordering of the schools. Catechesis was specified both for children learning grammar and for those more advanced who read Virgil and Cicero. The primer for the youngest included the Creed, Our Father, and other prayers along with the alphabet. Catechesis should include, but not be confined to Scripture. Pupils were to memorize psalm verses and the three basic documents of the catechisms, and the master was to explain these latter, not touching on "points of dissension." Such books as Matthew, 1 and 2 Timothy, 1 John, and Proverbs could be grammatically expounded, but masters were warned against Isaiah and Romans, "for it is fruitless to burden the youth with hard and deep books" (1955, XL, 314-320; 1883, XXVI, 236-240). The Saxon schools were to offer children basic catechesis to compensate for negligent parents and to supplement the efforts of faithful ones. When Luther's *Short Catechism* appeared in Latin, *Paedagogi* ["instructors"] replaced *Vater* ["father"] as the indicated leader (1883, XXX, part 1, 283-345, 4th column). Most Latin catechisms were similarly designed for the schools, and even some vernacular catechisms, as the one Urban Rhegius prepared for East Friesland, indicated a dialogue between "master" and "pupil" (Reu, 1904a, I, part 3, division 2, 1200-1227; Latin examples, pp. 594f, 823f, and 1386f). Brenz's *Larger Catechism* was prescribed for Württemberg vernacular elementary schools in 1559 (Wills, 1955, p. 115).

Johann Bugenhagen advised a number of governments in northeastern Germany and Denmark, and Eby has judged his services to popular education "greater in practical results than those of either Luther or Melanchthon" (Eby, 1931, p. 192). In the 1528 Brunswick church ordinance, Bugenhagen declared the first of three steps for reformation, "good schools for children," listing it ahead of preachers of the "pure word of God" and the "common money chest" for charity (Richter, 1846, I, 107; Eby, 1952, p. 80). In the Latin schools, as in Saxony, children were to

> learn the Ten Commandments, the Creed, the Lord's Prayer, the Christian Sacraments, with as much explanation as is suitable for children, also learn to sing the psalms in Latin and read passages every day from the Latin scriptures (Eby, 1931, p. 193; Richter, 1846, I, 108; Koldewey, 1886, p. 27).

Unlike Saxony, vernacular schools were also supported with the
city providing two masters for the catechesis of boys and school-
mistresses "grounded in the gospel and of good report" for girls'
schools (Eby, 1931, pp. 204-205; Koldewey, 1886, pp. 36-37).
Bugenhagen, like Luther, required schoolchildren to attend daily
church services, and on Sundays, they were to recite the three
basic catechetical documents and scriptural verses concerning the
sacraments (Koldewey, 1886, pp. 38-46).

Reformed churches, more thoroughly permeated by humanism
than Lutheran communities, emphasized schools even more
strongly as a locus for catechesis. The Strasbourg catechisms of
Bucer and Zell describe the interrogator as an *Underrichter*,
Le[h]rer, or *Meister* ["instructor", "teacher", "master"] (Reu,
1904a, I, part 1, 25, 68, 90, and 106; Sehling, 1902, VIII, part 1,
131). Bucer urged that schools be established to allow all boys and
girls to attend so that they might "learn the writings and catechism
of our faith." In addition to discouraging the "godless idleness" of
youth, schools would enable them to read Holy Scripture diligently
which "contributes more than anything else to the restoration of
the image of God" (1955, p. 239; Pauck, 1969, p. 336). Bucer
offered this advice to the English Edward VI, but it reflected his
Strasbourg experience where John Sturm founded his celebrated
academy in 1538. A modern commentator remarks that without
Bucer's "preliminary work, the establishment of the Protestant
gymnasium and the subsequent realization of the ideas of John
Sturm would never have been possible" (Kohls, 1960, p. 405). In
Bucer's own time an Augsburg visitor declared that if Bucer had
done nothing more than found the school, "his work would be
noble and blessed, for schools like them I have never seen before
in my life" (Gilbert, 1919, p. 328).

Although Sturm borrowed from the schools of the Brethren of
the Common Life where he had been educated and from humanist
schools in France where he had taught, the "phenomenal" success
was his, and Bolgar judges that Sturm's adaptation of the humanist
tradition "made the grammar school into an educational instrument
perfectly suited to the needs of the religious struggle of the time"
(1968, p. 431; *compare* Eby, 1952, pp. 92-93; Henkel, 1962, pp.
44-45). With pupils, colleagues, and friends from both Lutheran
and Reformed churches, Sturm provided Protestant and humanist
education remarkably free from the confessional battles that
marred his own residence in Strasbourg.

The Renaissance school colloquy combined linguistic exercises with moral, and, sometimes, religious teaching. No colloquy touched the popularity of that of Maturin Cordier, which appeared in more than 150 editions in Latin and vernacular languages, the latest in 1904. A French humanist who accepted Calvin's invitation to Geneva in 1536, Cordier taught and administered schools in Geneva, Neuchâtel and Lausanne. The dialogues, set within the schoolchild's world, both reflected and reinforced attitudes which Cordier wished his schools to incorporate and inculcate. A recent study of "the most popular schoolbook outside the middle ages" describes its religious flavor:

> The strongest impression of the pervasive religious exposure in the school comes not so much from the dialogues whose purpose was to teach a particular lesson as from the omnipresent references to God's aid, God's will, or God's blessings, which appear as no more than passing remarks in nearly every dialogue. . . . In nearly every one of the over two hundred dialogues we see the idea driven home of the boy's spiritual dependence on the will of God and his responsibility to aid his brother's spiritual development whenever possible (Hudson, 1978, p. 73; Bolgar, 1968, p. 435; *see also* Woodward 1906, pp. 154-179).

The colloquies depict a style of Christian nurture available and natural in the reformation era, but impossible to reproduce today.

Calvin expressed concern for schools in Geneva in the first year after his arrival. The 1541 draft *Ordinances*, in describing the ministerial order of "doctor" or "order of schools" called for two theological doctors in the Old and New Testaments. The *Ordinances* also proposed a college to prepare children "for the ministry as well as for civil government," and also to prepare an audience apt to understand since no one can profit from theological lectures unless he is first "instructed in the languages and the humanities" (Calvin, 1954, pp. 62-63; 1863, XXXVIII, part 1, 21). The desire to establish a grammar school to prepare pastors and other professionals resembles Luther's concerns, but, Calvin furthermore suggests that the whole citizenry could benefit from theological education requiring the linguistic skills of the schools. The *Ordinances* specifically suggest that the school accommodate not only children but also "others who would like to profit" (1883, XXXVIII, part 1, 21). Christian nurture in the Reformed tradition has often incorporated biblical and theological sophistication challenging the mental capacities of its lay as well as ministerial members.

In 1559 Calvin finally succeeded in founding the Genevan Academy, partly on Sturm's model, with Theodore Beza as its first rector. Reid has summed up the assumptions on which Calvin built his ideas of education:

> Holding that man could not, because of his sinfulness, come by any human means to a true knowledge of God, and so of the universe which God had created . . . he insisted that the only hope for man was "regeneration" whereby he could grasp the meaning of God's revelation in the Scriptures. Until God touched man's heart, even a "head" knowledge of the Scriptures was really useless. But when God did take action, man then came to faith, seeing all things *sub specie aeternitatis*.

Calvin required students to sign a Confession of Faith, for "what point would there be in teaching men who were unbelievers, and so could never have a true knowledge?" (Reid, 1955, p. 20). First-year students used the *Genevan Catechism* in Latin and French to accustom them to using and pronouncing Latin. Students were required to sit together in their own parish churches for sermons on Wednesday, for two sermons and for catechism on Sunday. On Saturdays, younger pupils discussed the section of the *Catechism* to be expounded the following day, while the top two classes read parts of the New Testament in Greek. Students took their turns reading prayers to open and close classes, practiced singing the metrical psalms daily, and at the day's end, three of them would recite in French the Lord's Prayer, the Creed, and the Ten Commandments (Reid, 1955, pp. 24-28; Calvin, 1863, XXXVIII, part 1, 71-79). The school, as designed and implemented, provided a key element for the Christian nurture of the city's youth.

Except for the Hutterites, the scattered groups of the radical reformation did not organize their own schools in the sixteenth century. In the close community life of the *Bruderhofs*, common responsibilities of parenting were assigned to schools, and, centuries before kindergartens became known in the west, the "Little Schools" of the Hutterites took charge of children from two to six. The "Big Schools" carried the children up to the age of twelve, providing them with a thorough knowledge of the Bible and their distinctive catechism together with basic skills of vernacular language. The school was really a community home. A detailed "School Order" of 1578, after discussing details of discipline, sanitation, and meals, concludes:

> let each one deal with the children by day and by night as if they

were his own, whether in the matter of giving them to eat and drink or taking up or laying down, or leading about or carrying, or cleaning or washing, whatever is necessary, so that each one may be able to give an account before God (Bender, p. 240).

Christian nurture consisted principally of building the characters Hutterites believed to be commanded by God which would fit them for community responsibilities in the tightly-knit *Bruderhofs* (Bender, 1931 and Wiswedel, 1940, *passim*; ME, 1965, II, 149-151).

Schools for magisterial reformers and for Hutterites were not institutions to be set alongside of the "church." The school was a social structure of the church in which catechesis could take place by explicit teaching of religious fundamentals and by enabling children to read vernacular Bibles and catechisms. The Latin education of the grammar schools ensured a supply of persons able to undertake various catechetical roles; especially among the Reformed, leaders hoped that schools might also develop a theologically sophisticated laity.

The Ministry: Authoritative Leaders and Catechists

Much of the life of the reformation churches revolved around the ordained ministry. Although reformers repudiated the hierarchical structure and the sacramental character of holy orders, they vigorously retained the ministerial office with its liturgical role in worship. In describing the office, both magisterial and radical reformers emphasized preaching and teaching, both fundamental elements of Christian catechesis. Luther condemned past practices in the *Babylonian Captivity*:

> Whoever does not preach the Word, though he was called by the church to do this very thing, is no priest at all, and . . . the sacrament of ordination can be nothing else than a certain rite by which preachers are chosen in the Church. . . . They are also called pastors because they ought to pastor, that is, to teach. . . . See how far the glory of the church has departed! The whole earth is filled with priests, bishops, cardinals, and clergy; yet not one of them preaches so far as his official duty is concerned, unless he is called to do so by a different call over and above his sacramental ordination (1883, VI, 564-566; 1955, XXXVI, 112-113).

Most of the 1528 instructions for Saxon visitors do not concern institutional regulations so much as they lay down what the pastors are to teach in such matters as justification, the commandments, prayer, and the sacraments (Luther, 1955, XL, 274-306; 1883, XXVI, 202-229).

Bucer observed that the presiding elder of a church ought "to have the ability to teach others and be endowed with prudence and zeal to govern and watch for backsliders" (1955, p. 60; Pauck, 1969, p. 231). John Calvin distinguished between pastors and doctors but maintained the teaching responsibility of pastors:

> Teaching is, no doubt, the duty of all pastors; but to maintain sound doctrine requires a talent for interpreting Scripture, and a man may be a *teacher* [*doctor*] who is not qualified to preach. *Pastors*, in my opinion, are those who have the charge of a particular flock; though I have no objection to their receiving the name of *teachers* [*doctorum*], if it be understood that there is a distinct class of teachers [*doctorum*], who preside both in the education of pastors and in the instruction of the whole church (on Ephesians 4:11; 1847, XLI, 280; 1863, LXXIX, 197-198).

Few theologians have exalted the minister's authority more than the Genevan reformer:

> We must allow ourselves to be ruled and taught by men. This is the universal rule, which extends equally to the highest and to the lowest. The church is the common mother of all the godly, which bears, nourishes, and brings up children to God, kings and peasants alike; and this is done *by the ministry*. Those who neglect or despise this order choose to be wiser than Christ (on Ephesians 4:12; 1847, XLI, 282; 1863, LXXIX, 199).

The Genevan city authorities partially conceded Calvin's proposal for complete ministerial control of the schools, that preaching elders and doctors might keep a tight hold on all catechesis, whether it be explicit or mixed in with the teaching of grammar and rhetoric (Reid, 1955, p. 11; Calvin, 1954, LXIII, 63 and 63n; 1863, XXXVIII, part 1, 21-22, 21n). The teaching role of the minister held a primary place for Calvin, who described the church as a school [*schola*] from which "our weakness does not allow us to be dismissed until we have been pupils for the whole course of our lives" (*Institutes*, 4.1.4; 1863, XXX, 749; 1960, II, 1016).

Although Anabaptists did not view the ministry as a profession for which long schooling was required, or even desirable, teaching stood high among the functions they assigned to the pastoral office. The 1527 Schleitheim Confession included as duties of the pastors [*Hirten*]:

> to read, to admonish and teach, to warn, to discipline, to ban in the

church, to lead out in prayer, . . . to lift up the bread, . . . and in all things to see to the care of the body of Christ (Wenger, 1950, p. 72; Köhler, p. 310).

Pastors of reformation churches took responsibility for the catechetical instruction of youth and systematic teaching of the whole congregation. Luther arranged for the office of catechist in Wittenberg in 1521 (Reu, 1916, p. 239). Luther described early morning services on Monday and Tuesday at which "we have a German lesson on the Ten Commandments, the Creed, Lord's Prayer, baptism, and sacrament, so that these two days preserve and deepen the understanding of the catechism" (1955, LIII, 68; 1883, XIX, 79). He envisioned that daily services would draw at least "the priests and pupils, and especially those who, one hopes, will become good preachers and pastors" (1955, LIII, 13; 1883, XII, 36). Luther and Melanchthon recommended to Saxon visitors that, since servants and young people attend vespers Sunday afternoon, there ought to be "constant repetition, through preaching and exposition of the Ten Commandments, the articles of the Creed, and the Lord's Prayer" as well as "marriage and the sacraments of baptism and of the altar"; these were invariably to be accompanied by word-for-word recitation of the three basic documents "for the sake of the children and other simple unschooled folk" (1955, XL, 308; 1883, XXVI, 230-231).

Elector John at the 1530 Diet of Augsburg received this judgment from Luther on pastoral catechesis:

> For surely Your Electoral Grace's territory has more excellent pastors and preachers than any other territory in the whole world, and their faithful, pure, and fine teaching helps to preserve peace. As a consequence, the young people, both boys and girls, grow up so well instructed in the Catechism and the Scriptures that I am deeply moved when I see that young boys and girls can pray, believe, and speak more of God and Christ than they ever could in the monasteries, convents, and schools of bygone days, or even of our own day (1930, IV, 325-326; 1955, XLIX, 307).

Lutheran churches generally stipulated that all pastors were to preach on catechetical fundamentals regularly during the course of a year (Repp, 1964, p. 23).

Bucer urged pastors to use catechisms for the unlearned "whether they are children in age or in the amount of sense they have." Like any good teacher, a minister must:

examine his students on what he has explained or shared in an effort
to get them to learn better, questioning them to see how each has
understood the matter and giving them an opportunity to ask him
about anything that has not been well enough understood (Pauck,
1969, p. 234; Bucer, 1955, p. 64).

In criticizing English practices, Bucer insisted that the catechism
ought "to be taught and explained on every festal day," noting
that "in Germany there are not a few churches in which the catechism is taught to children two days each week as well as on
Sundays" (Bucer, 1974, pp. 110-111).

John Calvin entrusted ministers with the catechetical teaching
of children and youth, subordinating roles of parents and schoolmasters. From 1541 parish churches were to offer catechetical
instruction every Sunday at midday; parents were to bring their
children, and later, academy masters were to attend to monitor
the attendance of their charges (Calvin, 1954, pp. 62 and 69;
Reid, 1955, p. 24; Calvin, 1863, XXXVIII, part 1, 20, 28, 71-72).
From 1548 the *Genevan Catechism* in French editions was divided
into 55 sections to facilitate its regular weekly use (Calvin, 1863,
XXXIV, pp. x and notes on pp. 8-134; 1954, pp. 84-87). From the
fourth 1563 edition the *Heidelberg Catechism* appeared divided
into 52 sections for exposition at afternoon services throughout
the year, with a final added summary including the Creed, Ten
Commandments, Lord's Prayer and selected scriptural verses
designed to be read verbatim at these services (Thompson, 1963,
pp. 81-82; Schaff, 1877, III, 355). The Second Helvetic Confession,
authored by Bullinger and widely accepted among Reformed
churches expresses a common understanding of pastoral responsibility for youth:

The pastors of the churches act most wisely when they early and
carefully catechize the youth, laying the first ground of faith, and
faithfully teaching the rudiments of our religion by expounding the
Ten Commandments, the Apostles' Creed, and Lord's Prayer, and
the doctrine of the sacraments, with such other principles and chief
heads of our religion (ch. 25; Cochrane, 1966, p. 294; Schaff, 1877,
III, 300).

Although these regular catechetical services were designated
for children, adolescents, and others judged ignorant, the reformers
wished to involve a wider swath of the adult congregation. Since
many attended two services on Sundays, where pastors offered

catechism at one of these, they reached a variety of parishioners. Luther urged pastors to preach on the catechetical topics quite apart from formal instruction, having little use for those who thought themselves above it:

> Our nobles and country-folk say, "Oh, our pastor cannot preach more than the Ten Commandments, the Creed, and the Our Father; he always sounds the same note." And so the preachers, according to the opinions of the hearers, apply themselves to higher things and leave the fundamentals neglected and ignored (1912, II, 522 #2554b; *see also* #2554a and #1002, I, 504).

Thompson has summed it up well:

> Neither Luther nor Calvin left the slightest doubt in their writings that they intended a lifelong discipleship to scripture, sermon *and* catechism; and it is mistaken to believe that catechetics in the sixteenth century was merely a theology for children (1963, p. 34).

In the Wittenberg church ordinance of 1533 preaching on the catechism was reserved for early matins (Richter, 1846, I, 220). The hour may have been chosen as a good time for servants, but insufficiently wide attendance at this early service may have led to the custom, developed in Wittenberg and copied elsewhere, for catechetical preaching to be held quarterly on fourteen consecutive days (Pauck, 1961, p. 129). The divisions in the *Heidelberg Catechism*, together with its theologically sophisticated character, suggest that the serial expositions reached many age and educational levels in the Palatinate congregations. But even if a Palatinate Christian never attended the afternoon lectures, he would hear the catechism read through every nine weeks, for in addition to the 55 sections for exposition, the fourth edition also indicated nine divisions for reading without commentary before the sermon on Sunday morning (Thompson, 1963, pp. 40 and 82). Ordained ministers, both by their authority and direct activity in leading catechetical instruction, were uniformly the supervising catechists in the churches of the continental Reformation.

The Ministry: Liturgical Preaching and Worship

Ministers exercised their authority and fulfilled their catechetical roles most obviously and frequently as they preached and led congregational worship. Liturgical worship can claim first place throughout Christian history as *the* locus for the nurture of the Christian community. The continental Reformation eminently illustrates this principle, for, determined to ensure that the regular gatherings of Christians include effective catechesis, in spite of differences in perspectives and methods, the reformers all insisted that (1) preaching be a principal, if not always *the* principal, activity of worship and (2) worship be in languages understood by the congregation. Scheduled catechetical lectures often fell within the category of liturgical action, ranging from catechetical discussion in a classroom-like setting to sermons within an ordered office of Matins, Vespers or newly devised liturgies of prayers and metrical psalms.

Preaching for the reformers was a special kind of teaching, not sharply distinguished from lecturing. Pauck has written that, except for Anabaptists, sixteenth-century ministers

> directed their sermons to the end of stimulating a right faith on the basis of a correct knowledge of evangelical doctrine. They did not try to arouse conversion experiences in their listeners nor did they cultivate religious emotions or sentiments. Early Protestant preaching was doctrinal and became more and more so (1961, pp. 129-130).

Reformers considered the sermon to be the Word of God spoken, opening for the congregation the Word of God written in the Scriptures. No longer was the sermon an optional accompaniment of the eucharist when convenient and a preacher available. Rather, the sermon became the *sine qua non* of not only the principal Sunday act of worship but of other Sunday services and, where feasible, of daily worship as well. In 1526 Luther designated "the preaching and teaching of God's Word" as the "most important and principal" part of worship. Sermons were preached at Matins, Mass, and Vespers on the epistle, the gospel, and an Old Testament lesson respectively. This being enough "preaching and teaching for the laity" in general, the catechism and assigned parts of the New Testament provided sermon topics at Matins on Monday through Friday and at Saturday Vespers for the clergy, theological students, or others specially motivated to attend. At other weekday Vespers, the Old Testament was read without exposition. Luther concluded that this was sufficient "to give the Word of God free course among us, not to mention the university lectures for scholars" (1883, XIX, 78-80; 1955, LIII, 68-69). The various Lutheran patterns of preaching all employed the traditional church calendar and lections to ensure a balance of scriptural topics. The instructions to the Saxon visitors explained:

> holy days have been instituted because it is not possible to instruct the people on all of the Scriptures in one day. So the different portions of the teaching are distributed over certain seasons, just as the schools might arrange to read Virgil on one day, Cicero on another (1955, XL, 309; 1883, XXVI, 232).

This balance in catechesis included concern for setting priorities:

> we have given these instructions to the pastors and explained to them that they should clearly and correctly present to the people these most important matters of the Christian life which we have here described, namely repentance, faith, and good works, while passing by many other things of which the poor masses understand little (1955, XL, 287; 1883, XXVI, 212).

These words of Melanchthon reflect Luther's description of the auditory to whom he aimed his preaching:

> When I preach [in Wittenberg] I adapt myself to the circumstances of the common people. I don't look at the doctors and masters, of whom scarcely forty are present, but at the hundred or the thousand young people and children. It's to them I preach, to them I devote myself, for they, too, need to understand. If the others don't want to listen, they can leave. . . . Take pains to be simple and direct, don't consider those who claim to be learned but be a preacher to unschooled youth and sucklings (1955, LIV, 236; 1912, III, 419-420 [#3573]).

The effectiveness of sermons for Christian nurture inevitably depended upon the ability and personality of the minister in a way which other parts of the liturgy did not; imagine the difference between Luther in the Wittenberg church and his theological students sent to surrounding villages! Many a Lutheran preacher memorized or read sermons from the published collections of Luther's own church and house postils or from one of the other popular collections by eminent preachers (Pauck, 1961, pp. 126-131).

Reformed churches emphasized the sermon in worship even more than the Lutherans, partly because they relegated the eucharist to a monthly or, more commonly, a quarterly celebration. This drastic alteration in Christian tradition, regretted by Calvin and Bucer, left the sermon in the climactic position whether in the

Zurich-type liturgies expressly designated as preaching services or
in the Genevan-type liturgies which were intended to include the
Lord's Supper. In outlining effective ways to dispense Christ's
teaching, Bucer describes four activities which ministers most
frequently undertook in the lection-sermon sequence during
worship:

> first, by the reading of Holy Scriptures; next by their interpretation;
> . . . then by the sound teaching of religion, i.e., by a lucid explana-
> tion and a sure confirmation of the dogmas of our faith; then by
> pious exhortations, admonitions, reproofs, and testimonials taken
> from the same Scriptures (Pauck, 1969, p. 233; Bucer, 1955, p. 62;
> note marginal numbering).

In commenting on read homilies, Bucer remarked:

> If there is no one who can properly expound the scriptures to the
> people in his own words, and so teach them in a holy and salutary
> way and admonish and exhort them, it is certainly better that godly
> and learned homilies compiled by others should be read than that no
> teaching or exhortation should be provided at the administration of
> the Lord's Supper. But since the Lord commended not only the
> reading of the gospel in his churches but also its preaching, and since
> the lively voice of the word of God is the more edifying, . . . for
> these reasons it will be necessary to see that . . . pastors . . . are found
> and appointed who are men so skilled in trustworthy modes of
> expression that are to be conveyed by teaching and also so resolute
> that they are able to give instruction in sound doctrine and refute
> those who contradict it (1974, pp. 44-47, translation altered).

A read homily could be tolerated temporarily, but Bucer was
unhappy with anything that compromised the sermon as a principal
means of nurture. Calvin left learners of the *Genevan Catechism*
in no doubt of the importance of the sermon: not only is it necessary
to hear pastors, but "to receive their exposition of the doctrine of
Christ from their lips with fear and reverence." As for the sufficiency
of a once-for-all instruction, the catechism continues:

> It is little to have begun unless you continue. For it behooves us to be
> disciples [*escoliers, discipulos*] of Christ up to the end, or rather
> without end. But he has committed this office to the ministers of the
> Church, that they teach us in his place and name (1954, pp. 130-131;
> 1863, XXXIV, 111).

The Genevan ordinances of 1541 established three Sunday

sermons, at daybreak, at "the accustomed hour" and in midafternoon in addition to the noon catechetical instruction, and a sermon on three weekdays as well (1863, XXXVIII, part 1, 20-21; 1954, p. 62). Preachers chose the biblical topics as the liturgical year lections were abandoned. Many Reformed preachers followed Zwingli's practice expounding whole books of the Bible section by section; others found the divisions of the catechisms helpful in organizing sermon topics.

Anabaptist liturgies, like those of Zurich, were expressly built around preaching. As self-contained communities, Anabaptists relied not on education but on direct inspiration of the Holy Spirit to identify and commission their preachers; sermons of early Anabaptists

> were certainly not expected to be rhetorical orations prepared and finished according to the practice of learned men. It was assumed that any member of the church could admonish the congregation out of his general knowledge of the Scriptures, his experience in life, and the help of the Holy Spirit (ME, 1965, IV, 503).

Friedmann's description of Hutterite preaching could be as well applied to other Anabaptists:

> The meaning of [the] sermon was and still is exhortation and instruction in the strictness of life as prescribed by the Scriptures. . . . Worship was never intended to promote "edification" of the mind, as in contemporary Pietism [or as among the magisterial reformers], but was rather understood as an occasion to reconfirm the strictness and sternness of a life in "obedience", a favorite idea with Anabaptists (1966, p. 10, *bracketed comment, mine*).

Although less doctrinal and not as central as in churches of the magisterial reformation, Anabaptists valued preaching for catechesis.

Sermons, unlike the university lectures to which many sixteenth-century reformers likened them, were preached within the framework of a liturgy, which was also shaped to serve catechesis. The Anabaptists provided a minimum of liturgical structure; the Reformed designed new structures based on biblical materials and principles; Lutherans preserved as much of the traditional elements in practice as they judged consistent with their theology and useful for catechesis.

The churches of the continental Reformation all introduced vernacular languages into the liturgies. Luther encouraged the continued use of Latin in appropriate situations and even wistfully suggested the occasional use of the biblical Greek and Hebrew, but he and his followers, like the Reformed and Anabaptists, embraced the principle of a language understood by the congregation. This touched an important social issue, for Latin was neither a "foreign" language in western Europe nor an exclusively ecclesiastical language. Latin was the language of the educated; its use in worship edified European peasants, servants, and small shopkeepers no more than it nurtured natives of the New World who dutifully learned the Latin formulas imposed upon them by Spanish friars. In addition to the educative value of vernacular lections, exhortations, and prayers, the use of the common tongue encouraged greater congregational participation in responses, canticles, hymns, or metrical psalms. Although reformation liturgies tended to be dominated by the minister and his assistants, as congregations became familiar with the new forms, their ability to follow with their voices as well as their ears increased the intensity of the learning experience in worship.

The Reformed liturgies broke sharply with the traditional western forms. The Reformed, regarding the human ear as the exclusive gate to the mind and heart, relied heavily upon verbal explanations for catechesis in worship. Zwingli was sparing with words in prescribed liturgies. His preaching service is starkly limited, and the Lord's Supper is brief, dramatizing the reenactment of the Last Supper and encouraging the congregation to meditate on Christ's passion and to realize their communion with one another (Thompson, 1961, pp. 147-155). He introduces no overlong explanations, concentrating his didactic efforts on the sermon and the symbolic actions of the occasionally celebrated Supper. Anabaptists followed the patterns laid down by Zwingli without, however, tying their rites to set forms of words. Reformed leaders who came after Zwingli adopted his white-washed churches cleansed of paintings, statues, and altars so that worshippers might concentrate on the Word spoken, but, unlike him, insisted upon rites designed to teach by the weight of their words. Lengthy and wordy exhortations and admonitions and seemingly interminable prayers characterize the work of Farel, Oecolampadius, Bucer, and Calvin (Thompson, 1961, pp. 216-224, 211-215, 167-179, and 197-208). Reformed worship of the sixteenth century was intensely cerebral, and the thrust of its preaching, written liturgies, and actions within a building bereft of visual distractions encouraged the faithful to attend to the words of Scripture and to meditate upon the Lord whom Scriptures revealed.

Lutheran liturgical reforms followed two principles which Luther stated in the prefaces to his Latin and German Masses:

> It is not now nor ever has been our intention to abolish the liturgical service of God completely, but rather to purify the one that is now in use from the wretched accretions which corrupt it and to point out an evangelical use (1955, LIII, 20; 1883, XII, 206).

> I do not propose that all of Germany should uniformly follow our Wittenberg order. . . . It would be well if the service in each principality would be held in the same manner and if the order observed in a given city would also be followed by the surrounding towns and villages; whether those in other principalities hold the same order or add to it ought to be a matter of free choice and not of constraint (1955, LIII, 62; 1883, XIX, 73).

Doctrinal purification of traditional forms and ordered freedom in liturgical matters provided the basis for changes in forms of worship.

Lutheran liturgies provided Christian nurture different from that of the Reformed. Whereas preaching and right teaching were serious concerns to Luther and his followers, they did not crowd out other traditional elements in Christian worship. Brilioth comments that

> the Lutheran rite preserved on the whole the order of the ancient mass, with an instinctive sense that its dignity and solemnity were a safeguard of the reverence due to the holy (1930, p. 141).

Although Lutherans insisted that crucifixes, statues, paintings, vestments, ceremonies, and incense became dangerous superstition when they were regarded as *necessary* to salvation, they were *adiaphora*, indifferent, and might be used where custom and usefulness dictated. Concerning the order for the German Mass, Luther wrote:

> Such orders are needed for those who are still becoming Christians or need to be strengthened. . . . They are essential especially for the immature and the young who must be trained and educated in the Scripture and God's Word daily. . . . For such, one must read, sing, preach, write, and compose. And if it would help matters along, I would have all the bells pealing, and all the organs playing, and have everything ring that can make a sound. For this is the damnable

thing about the popish services: that men made law, works, merits out of them—to the detriment of faith—and did not use them to train the youth and common people in the Scriptures and in the Word of God, but became so engrossed in them as to regard them inherently useful and necessary for salvation (1955, LIII, 62; 1883, XIX, 73).

Luther's sacramental understanding of the world and of the Word as *logos* makes it possible for him to stress the "Word" in the Bible as strongly as he does and still maintain the reality of God's outreach through beauty, art, music, and ceremony. The liturgical implications of the different theological perspectives of Luther and Zwingli are demonstrated in their attitudes towards music, an art for which both possessed appreciation and talent: Zwingli banished music from liturgy, and Luther embraced it. In a hymnal preface, Luther argued that hymns helped to win the young, "combining the good with the pleasing, as is proper for youth";

> nor am I of the opinion that the gospel should destroy and blight all the arts, as some of the pseudo-religious claim. But I would like to see all the arts, especially music, used in the service of Him who gave and made them (1955, LIII, 316; 1883, XXXV, 475).

The liturgical richness of Lutheran worship contributed to the nurture of its faithful.

The liturgies of the churches of the Reformation, with their common concern for preaching, for the vernacular languages, for the more frequent communions of all the laity, and in varying degrees, for congregational participation provided new emphases in nurture. Differing theological perspectives and applications of biblical and traditional materials made for contrasting styles of worship, but the catechetical goal was constant: that those baptized in Christ might mature in knowledge and commitment as they gathered to pray and to praise.

Sacramental Initiation into the Church

Unless born of Jewish parents, a western European in 1600 was baptized shortly after birth, shriven and communicated in early childhood, and usually confirmed before adulthood. Although local attempts occasionally provided some educational preparation for first communion, catechesis was related to the steps of sacramental initiation only by the individual requirements a confessor might ask of a young penitent at first confession. The Bohemian Brethren developed a discipline in which parents, godparents, or the clergy were to instruct a child of "years of discretion." Being brought to a bishop or priest, he would be questioned "with regard to the truths of the faith and the sacred precepts, and also with regard to his good will, his firm purpose and works of truth." Laying on hands, the minister would receive him into the fellowship of the church (Fisher, 1970, pp. 166-169). This Bohemian practice would seem to be the most serious attempt in the fifteenth century to insist upon instruction as an invariable part of Christian initiation.

Erasmus, commenting in 1522 on the number of ignorant Christians, proposed a series of sermons on Christian fundamentals to be offered "not unseasonably at the Paschal holy days." Baptized boys would be expected to attend these sermons when they reached puberty and subsequently be examined in private; if prepared adequately, they would ratify what had been promised for them at baptism, ideally in the presence of the bishop. Erasmus predicted that we then might have "more sincere Christians than we have" (Erasmus, 1706, VII, sig.** 3v; Mitchell, 1976, pp. 84-85; Fisher, 1970, pp. 169-170; Repp, 1964, p. 20).

The radical reformers made a clean break with traditional sacramental initiation, responding to their understanding of the church as a body separated from the world, to the scandal of baptized church people ignorant of Christian fundamentals, and to the New Testament pattern of baptism that followed profession of faith. Balthasar Hubmaier's order of baptism for his Nikolsburg congregation expressed the Anabaptist perception of the relation between catechesis and initiation:

> Whoever desires to receive water baptism should first present himself to his bishop [i.e. "pastor"] so that he may be tested as to whether he is sufficiently instructed in the articles of the law, Gospel, and faith, and in the doctrines which pertain to a new Christian life. Also he must give evidence that he can pray, and that he can intelligently explain the articles of the Christian faith. This must all be ascertained about the candidate before he can be permitted to be incorporated into the church of Christ [*die gemain der Christenheit*] through external baptism unto the foregiveness of his sins (Armour, 1966, p. 143; Hubmaier, 1962, p. 349).

The words "a new Christian life" reflect the conviction that Christian teaching, when appropriated, must issue in a changed life. Baptism, as Armour describes Pilgram Marpeck's views, is "a covenant or pledge by which one who already knows the forgiveness of God promises to lay aside the old life and take up the new in Christ" (1966, p. 118). Inner transformation and renewal were the keys.

Even in the sixteenth century, candidates for baptism tended more and more to grow up within the Anabaptist communities rather than to be converted from outside. Hubmaier devised a service for children in which they were commended to the Lord by the prayers of the church (ME, 1965, I, 699; Armour, 1966, pp. 23-24 and 132). Friedmann describes twentieth-century Hutterite baptismal practice that the conservative *Bruderhofs* probably have preserved from the sixteenth century. Young persons who would have received instruction in the community schools as children may request baptism only after reaching twenty-one. The elders may approve such a request or they may counsel the candidate to wait for further spiritual maturity. If approved, the minister conducts a "soul-searching" inquiry into the sincerity of the request, sets three days for instructions, gives three traditional baptismal talks which follow the pattern of topics in the Hutterite catechism, and baptizes the candidate into the community (Friedman, 1966, pp. 20-22). Serious catechesis precedes the formal commitment to dedicate oneself to the isolated community life of twentieth-century Hutterites; similarly, serious catechesis accompanied baptism in a century when Anabaptist membership carried the threat of torture and death.

Among magisterial reformers, Bucer most vigorously attempted to relate catechesis to sacramental initiation. Bucer knew Erasmus' writings; from his arrival in Strasbourg in 1523 he debated Anabaptists; and he may have been familiar with Bohemian practices through correspondence with Waldensians (Williams, 1962, p. 522). In response, perhaps, to the problems and proposals posed by Erasmus, Anabaptists, and the Brethren, Bucer sought to make confirmation an occasion at which a baptized person gave evidence of a knowledge of Christian fundamentals, made a profession of faith and commitment, and, by the laying-on-of-hands, was received into the full fellowship of the church and admitted to the eucharist. Bucer first urged such a practice in 1534; he first had an opportunity to put it into effect when he designed the Ziegenhain Order of Church Discipline for Philip of Hesse in 1538 (Repp, 1964, pp. 30-33; Sehling, 1902, VIII, 104).

Although Bucer never personally instituted confirmation of this type in Strasbourg, after his departure one city church adopted such a rite as he urged; the preface summarizes the historical setting and the biblical precedents to which Bucer appealed:

> Among other reasons why the Anabaptists reject infant baptism is this, that . . . as long as everyone is baptized in infancy but not everyone has faith, . . . voluntary submission to the obedience and discipline of the church is not practised, and no distinction can be drawn or preserved between true and genuine Christians who are such by a conscious act of their own will and false Christians who are Christians in name only. . . .

> But it is not the fault of precious infant baptism, . . . rather the fault lies in the fact that in the Popish church and among us supposed Evangelicals, . . . the catechism is neglected and not conducted with diligence, and that when children grow up and come to the age of reason they are not urged to make a public confession of their faith in the presence of the church and to submit themselves gladly to the discipline and admonitions of the church. . . . Now there is an old practice customary among God's people in the Old Testament, as also in the early Christian church, that children receiving circumcision and baptism in their infancy were afterwards instructed and taught . . . in the law by the Levites . . . and . . . by the catechists in the chief articles of Christian doctrine, which they then openly . . . confessed and recited, immediately after which as Jewish children by sacrifice and other ceremonies, so also Christian children with hand-laying and the Christian prayer of God's people . . . were received and confirmed.

In the rite itself, the pastor addressed the candidates:

> Dear children, you were born of Christian parents, who have made you, . . . members of the church and of . . . Christ through holy baptism, where they together with your godfathers and godmothers promised . . . to bring you up at home in the fear of God, and to teach you . . . the ten commandments, the articles of the Christian faith, the holy Our Father and all other things which every true Christian ought to believe and know, and further that when you had learned the same they would present you to the church again, so that you might confess your faith publicly and so submit yourselves willingly to the discipline and order of the church as devout children.

After questioning the children in the catechism, the pastor exhorted the candidates to continue to come to Sunday catechism "even more diligently than before," and to live up to their obligations to home and church. After the candidates affirmed their faith and

intentions, the pastor prayed for them with the laying-on-of-hands
(Fisher, 1970, pp. 174-178).

Bucer, in collaboration with Melanchthon, wrote a similar rite
for the abortive reform of Cologne in 1543 in which he explicitly
identified the service as a reformed version of medieval confirmation, restoring what he regarded as its primitive emphases on
catechesis, a profession of faith and obedience, and the laying-on-
of-hands in place of anointing (Fisher, 1970, pp. 194-203). Bucer
was stung by Anabaptist taunts that evangelical lives were not a
cut above those of papists, and he consistently insisted that true
catechesis involved character of life as well as intellectual understanding:

> It is evident that not a few children make a confession . . . with no
> more understanding of the faith than some parrot uttering his Hallo.
> So it would be far better to keep among the catechumens those
> children who as yet show no or only meager signs of the fear of God
> and faith in their lives and manners, and to instill into them the
> doctrine and knowledge of God, until not merely the works of the
> flesh but fruits of the spirit of regeneration appear in them (Fisher,
> 1970, p. 246; Bucer, 1974, pp. 104-105).

A personal profession of faith and of Christian obedience should
be required

> of adults, before they are baptized; and of those who are baptized as
> infants, when they have been catechized and instructed in the gospel
> of Christ; and if any do not permit themselves to be catechized and
> taught and refuse to follow all the precepts of Christ and to make a
> legitimate profession of faith and of the obedience to be rendered to
> Christ and his Church, they ought to be rejected from the company
> of the saints and the communion of the sacraments (Pauck, 1969, p.
> 229; Bucer, 1955, p. 59).

Although mistaken in his interpretation of confirmation in the
patristic church, Bucer provided an effective means for linking
catechesis organically to Christian initiation.

John Calvin, and the Reformed churches in general, followed
Bucer, except that they neither employed the name of confirmation
nor adopted the act of laying-on-of-hands. As early as the initial
1536 edition of the *Institutes*, Calvin wrote:

> Now I wish that we might have kept the custom which, as I have
> said, existed among the ancient Christians before this misborn

wraith of a sacrament came to birth! Not that it would be such a confirmation as they fancy, which cannot be named without doing injustice to baptism; *but a catechizing*, in which children or those near adolescence would give an account of their faith before the church. . . . A child of ten would present himself to the church to declare his confession of faith, would be examined in each article and answer to each. . . . If this discipline were in effect today, it would certainly arouse some slothful parents, . . . for then they could not overlook [instruction] without public disgrace. . . . In short, all would have some methodical instruction . . . in Christian doctrine (ch. 5 of 1536; 4.19.13 of 1559; Calvin, 1960, II, 1460-1461; 1863, XXIX, 147).

Whether or not he had been influenced by Bucer's earlier writing, Calvin while in Strasbourg introduced into his congregation Bucer's practice of not allowing children to receive holy communion until they had received catechetical instruction (Wendel, 1963, p. 61). On his return to Geneva, Calvin proposed similar requirements; the 1541 Ordinances required that a child, instructed in the catechism,

recite solemnly the sum of what it contains, and also to make profession of his Christianity in the presence of the Church. Before this is done, no child is to be admitted to receive the Supper; and parents are to be informed not to bring them before this time (1954, p. 69; 1863, XXXVIII, part 1, 28).

Peter notes that memorization of the vast *Genevan Catechism* is not required, but a resumé of its teaching; from 1553, the brief "Manner of questioning Children who wish to receive the Supper" was added to editions of the *Catechism* (Peter, 1965, p. 17; Calvin, 1863, XXXIV, 147-158). In the baptismal liturgy, Calvin linked this instruction to baptism by including an exhortation to parents or other sponsors:

You promise, when [this child] comes to the age of discretion, to instruct him in the doctrine received by the people of God as it is summarized in the [Creed]. . . . you will exhort him to live according to the rule which our Lord laid down in his law (1863, XXXIV, pp. 189-190, 189n5; 1849, II, 116-117).

A public profession of faith, without Bucer's explicit profession of obedience to the church's discipline, provided the link, in Geneva, the Palatinate, and other Reformed churches, between catechesis and initiation (Thompson, 1963, p. 40).

Lutheran practices for linking catechesis to initiation varied greatly. In an exhaustive study of Lutheran confirmation, Repp has identified four different strains prevalent in the sixteenth century (1964, p. 21). All four concern catechesis, and they divide into two main types: those in which a public or private examination in Christian doctrine preceded admission to communion and those that followed Bucer's pattern in providing, in addition, a ceremony entitled "confirmation" that usually included the laying-on-of-hands.

The type which Repp labels "catechetical" grew naturally out of the discipline required for all to be admitted to holy communion. The *Instructions* for the Saxon visitors required a pastor to examine communicants to see if they were prepared, and "whoever does not know why we should receive the sacrament is not to be admitted to it" (Luther, 1955, XL, 296, also 309; 1883, XXVI, 220 and 232). Increasingly, the "why" of receiving communion was tied to the catechism, and Repp has identified a long series of church orders from 1531 requiring communicants to be first examined in their catechetical knowledge. It was a short step to adapt such general requirements to the young seeking their first communion; the final step of full participation in the Christian community provided a convenient point for pastors to monitor the results of catechesis performed in family, school, and catechetical services. The Saxon Church Order of 1580 describes this common Lutheran practice:

> The pastors are diligently to examine in the catechism especially those who are going to the blessed Sacrament of the body and blood of Christ for the first time, to determine whether they have learned the catechism and to inform themselves whether they are in the position to partake of the Communion (Repp, 1964, p. 26; Sehling, 1902, I, part 1, 423-424).

These Lutherans, like Calvin, regarded true confirmation to be *catechizing*, but, unlike Calvin, they made no requirement that there be any public profession of faith before the congregation. Gradually, public ceremonies were introduced, but they were incidental to this manner of relating catechesis to initiation.

The other sixteenth-century types of confirmation, hierarchical, sacramental, and traditional, follow and were largely inspired by Bucer. Today all Lutheran bodies have adopted formal "confirmations," but such ceremonies were in a minority in Germany at the end of the sixteenth century and nonexistent in Scandinavia (Repp, 1964, p. 28; Wiencke, 1955, p. 103). Bucer's plan outlined in the Ziegenhain Order was implemented in the Hessian city of Cassel in 1539 and became the required order of all of Hesse by 1566 (Repp, 1964, pp. 32-35; Sehling, 1902, VIII, part 1, 124, 293-305, and 430-435).

Luther largely ignored confirmation, except for condemning its Roman form. In the *Babylonian Captivity*, he described confirmation "as a certain churchly rite or sacramental ceremony, similar to other ceremonies, such as the blessing of water and the like" (1955, XXXVI, 92; 1883, VI, 550). Regarding confirmation among the *adiaphora*, Luther never designed a rite for it, although he approved Melanchthon's use in the short-lived Wittenberg Reform of 1545 (Richter, 1846, II, 83 and 93; Repp, 1964, p. 47). Martin Chemnitz and Jacob Andreae, in a 1569 church order for Braunschweig-Wolfenbuttel, included an optional laying-on-of-hands by a visiting superintendent, to be used where it might not offend (Repp, 1964, pp. 38-43; Richter, 1846, II, 320-321). Some orders labeled "traditional" by Repp did not make confirmation an immediate prelude to first communion, but since they included requirements for instruction, they also served to link catechesis with initiation. The earliest of these, a 1535 order for Liegnitz, preceded Bucer's work in Hesse and may represent an original parallel development (Repp, 1964, pp. 44-55).

Lutheran churches developed different methods of relating catechesis with initiation. Confirmation, substantially as Bucer designed it, played an important part, but three centuries were to elapse before the rite won its way into all the Lutheran bodies. With the concern of the continental reformers for individual faith and knowledge of the Scriptures and their teachings, they devised ways of making sure that those who came to the Lord's Table and assumed responsibilities as adult Christians had been involved in some effective forms of catechesis.

Discipline: the Power of the Keys

Catechesis is a primary concern of discipline. *Disciplina* meant teaching or instruction, and a *discipulus* was first of all a student or a pupil, only derivatively a follower. The New Testament told of the apostles' authority to bind and to loose, and through the centuries the church exercised this "power of the keys" to censure deviant teachings and behavior (Matt. 16:18-20; 18:18-19). With

Constantine's conversion, the state began to use its coercive power to enforce some ecclesiastical decisions as church and civil authorities were blended in a variety of changing relationships. As discipline developed, the two principal purposes assigned to penalties both concerned catechesis: the correction of the person in doctrinal or moral error and the consequent restoration of the straying sheep to the flock (*poenae medicinales*); and the vindication of teaching and moral standards themselves (*poenae vindicativae*). The "greater excommunication" carried civil consequences, for the miscreant was effectively ostracized from society. The "lesser excommunication" deprived him of participation in the sacraments, but did not otherwise penalize him.

A growing complexity of canon law governed the exercise of this discipline. In theory, there were distinctions only in circumstances between the stipendary priest who refused to absolve an impenitent swearer, the archbishop who laid a ban on a duke who seized church properties, and the pope who excommunicated an emperor for controlling church appointments. Although the differences in political consequences were monumental, all three actions were justified as attempts to reform the sinner for his own salvation and to vindicate God's law for the benefit of all his people.

By the sixteenth century, an increasing number of voices questioned the misuses of discipline, the complexity and expense of its administration, and the apparent disparity between the working of the system and the religious gospel for which it had been established. Martin Luther's reforming zeal was fueled by the offence of penitential practices to his perception of the gospel. More than others, he remained profoundly suspicious of abuses in discipline, and he invoked it only in matters of the teaching and pastoral responsibilities of clergy without reference to the state. Although the Prince directed outward affairs of the church, he was not concerned with "the keys." As the 1537 Smalcald Articles declared, the greater excommunication is "merely a civil penalty which does not concern us ministers of the church"; pastors might exercise the lesser excommunication of "manifest and impenitent sinners" for their reformation, but "preachers should not mingle civil punishments with this spiritual penalty" (Tappert, 1959, p. 314; *Bekenntnisschriften*, 1959, pp. 456-457). Melanchthon echoed this view when he insisted that the pastoral punishment of excommunication "happens through the word and the sermon, not through physical coercion with fist and sword" (1965, p. 260; 1834, XXII, 521).

Luther urged pastors to invoke the lesser excommunication against those who refuse to learn the Christian basics. In the preface to the *Small Catechism* he advised pastors:

> If any refuse to receive your instructions, tell them that they deny Christ and are no Christians. They should not be admitted to the sacrament, be accepted as sponsors in Baptism, or be allowed to participate in any Christian privileges.

Although Luther suggested that parents and employers might "refuse to furnish them with food and drink and . . . notify them that the prince is disposed to banish such rude people," he was invoking social pressure rather than governmental authority; people ought to know community standards, but "we cannot and should not compel anyone to believe" (Tappert, 1959, p. 339; Luther, 1883, XXX, part 1, 270-273). Subsequent Lutheran regulations for examination before communion similarly enforced catechesis.

Luther counseled that auricular confession ought lead to "the comforting and strengthening" of conscience (Tappert, 1959, p. 457; Luther, 1883, XXX, part 1, 234). Confession provided priests with an unusual pastoral opportunity for effective catechesis, which Luther was concerned to preserve; the good news of God's forgiveness was brought to bear directly on the life of the penitents. As Melanchthon declared, "the ministry of absolution is in the area of blessing or grace, not of judgment or law" (Tappert, 1959, p. 197; *Bekenntnisschriften*, 1959, p. 273).

The Reformed churches were much more concerned with the proper exercise of discipline. Zurich was an exception. Zwingli and Bullinger left discipline in the hands of the city council, in which both exercised considerable influence. In the Second Helvetic Confession, the magistrate was to wield the sword of God against heretics and "all those whom God has commanded him to punish and even to execute," and ministers were to regulate discipline "for edification, according to the circumstances of the time, public state, and necessity" (Cochrane, 1966, pp. 300 and 276; Schaff, 1877, III, 306 and 284). Zurich never established the structures of church discipline that graced the church in Geneva.

The reformer of Basle, Oecolampadius, wrote in 1525 that "we shall never make satisfactory progress unless we retain excommunication" (Léonard, II, 157). Bucer, partly in response to Anabaptist taunts, argued for a discipline to shape lives that would reflect inner regeneration. He described three parts of discipline. The first, concerning "life and manners," called for mutual correction by ministers and "private Christians" of one another's lesser sins. This was, in effect, a pastoral substitute for a large portion of matters treated in private confession, a practice the Reformed churches uniformly repudiated. The second part of discipline comprised the juridical function or "penance" in which excommunication might be employed. The third reflected Bucer's liturgical interests, the reform and maintenance of "sacred ceremonies" (Pauck, 1969, p. 240; Bucer, 1955, p. 70). Juridical discipline would help to "distinguish between the undoubted people of God and those who in effect declare that they are not yet of his people":

> What a splendid thing it would be, . . . if the only people admitted to the Lord's table . . . were those who . . . were acknowledged as members of Christ because of the fruits of their life. . . . The rest should be kept among the catechumens until they will allow themselves to be instructed, and until the Lord directs them to receive fully the rebirth which he offered them in baptism and to make progress in their behaviour. By this means the lawful discipline and communion of Christ may be observed and the church of Christ may show its true face (1974, pp. 106-107).

Bucer identified *Kirchenpfleger* (church wardens) in Strasbourg with the lay elders he thought to have served in the primitive church. He worked without much success toward a system in which the lay elders and the pastors would jointly exercise discipline. In the church order of Ziegenhain, Bucer outlined such a system of discipline and required confirmands to pledge their obedience to it (Pauck, 1961, pp. 92-93; Repp, 1964, pp. 32-34; Sehling, 1902, VIII, part 1, 102-108).

John Calvin implemented discipline more successfully than any other Reformed church leader. Reflecting a long Christian tradition, he wrote that the "keys," or "jurisdiction," pertaining to "the discipline of morals" had three ends: first, that "they who lead a filthy and infamous life may not be called Christians, to the dishonor of God," the *poenae vindicativae*; second, that the "good may not be corrupted" by the wicked; and third, that "those overcome by shame for their baseness begin to repent," these last two the *poenae medicinales*, preventative and curative

(*Institutes*, 4.11.1, 4.12.5; 1960, II, 1211 and 1232-1233; 1863, XXX, 891 and 907-908).

To administer this dicipline, Calvin, like Bucer, insisted on ecclesiastical structures which he found in the New Testament alongside the juridical structures of the civil authorities. The key governing body was the "senate of presbyters," comprised of pastors and lay elders who were jointly charged with censure and correction of morals (4.4.1, 4.11.1, 6; 1960, II, 1068-1069, 1211-1213, and 1217-1218; 1863, XXX, 788, 891-893, and 896-897). Although Calvin carefully distinguished civil from ecclesiastical jurisdictions, stating that "the church does not have the right of the sword to punish or compel," he expected the magistrate, guided by the presbytery, to employ "punishment and physical restraint to cleanse the church of offenses." Like a medieval ecclesiastic, Calvin insisted that the magistrate himself submit to church discipline, for "if he is godly," he would not want "to exempt himself from the common subjection of God's children" (4.11.3, 4; 1960, II, 1215-1216; 1863, XXX, 895). The 1541 Ordinances prescribed that the weekly meetings of the church consistory ought to be concerned with those who dogmatize "against the received doctrine," are "negligent in coming to church," or are guilty of "notorious and public" vices (Calvin, 1954, pp. 70-71; 1863, XXXVIII, part 1, 29-30). Procedures called for secret and then open admonishments, excommunication from the Supper, and, finally, referral to the civil authorities. The goal was the edification, or catechesis, of the whole body of the church and its individual members. A Lutheran pastor, visiting Geneva in 1610, observed that:

> Not only is there in existence an absolutely free commonwealth, but as an especial object of pride (*ornamentum*), a censorship of morals (*disciplina*), in accordance with which investigations are made each week into the morals and even into the slighest transgressions of the citizens, first by the supervisors of the wards, then by the aldermen, and finally by the magistrate, according as the case demands. As a result, all cursing, gambling, luxury, quarreling, hatred, conceit, deceit, extravagance, and the like, to say nothing of greater sins, are prevented. What a glorious adornment—such purity of morals—for the Christian religion! With our bitterest tears we must lament that this is lacking and almost neglected with us (Eby, 1952, p. 119).

Reading between the lines, a twentieth-century Christian might be less enthusiastic about Genevan discipline, but that it produced an effective, if restrictive, form of nurture can hardly be denied. Other Reformed churches either adapted Genevan discipline to their own circumstances, or they followed Zurich, where the ordained ministers exercised an authority, juridically, much like that of Lutheran pastors.

The Anabaptist churches found in their strict voluntary discipline a principal means of catechesis. As a modern interpreter has written, for the Anabaptist understanding of discipleship the importance of discipline "can hardly be exaggerated" (Hershberger, 1957, p. 148). Community discipline taught the Anabaptist convert the meaning of discipleship. Children of Anabaptists grew up with the discipline, and, when they sought baptism, they had already learned what discipleship required. The Schleitheim Confession described the ban which underlay Anabaptist discipline:

> The ban shall be employed with all those who have given themselves to the Lord, to walk in his commandments, and with all those who are baptized into the one body of Christ and who are called brethren or sisters, and yet who slip sometimes and fall into error and sin, being inadvertently overtaken. The same shall be admonished twice in secret and the third time openly disciplined or banned according to the command of Christ (Wenger, 1950, p. 70; Köhler, 1908, pp. 307-308).

The faithful were to shun those who came under the ban; Menno Simons laid down guidelines:

> Paul says, . . . withdraw yourselves from every brother that walketh disorderly, and not after the tradition which ye received of us. . . . Inasmuch as the ban was so strictly commanded by the Lord, and practiced by the apostles (Matt. 18:17), therefore, we must also use it and obey it, since we are thus taught and enlightened by God, or else we should be shunned and avoided by the congregation of God. . . . Inasmuch as the rule of the ban is general, excepts none, and is no respecter of persons—therefore it is reasonable and necessary to hear and obey the Word of the Lord; . . . no matter whether it be husband or wife, parents or children (Williams, 1957, p. 264).

Even more extensive than Mennonite discipline, that of the communal Hutterites reached into every aspect of social, economic, and family life. The various Anabaptist groups developed their own internal structures of discipline, unrelated to any civil authority, as their most effective means of Christian nurture.

In all the churches of the continental Reformation, catechesis included some forms of discipline. Magisterial reformers related it in various ways to the civil authority; radical reformers rejected any such relationship. The moral authority of the pastor sufficed to undergird discipline in Lutheran and in some Reformed churches, and his use of authority in preaching, private admonishing, and occasional withholding of the sacrament was of a purely pastoral character. Bucer and Calvin, among other Reformed leaders, sought ecclesiastical structures which would enforce ministerial authority, with civil cooperation, when necessary. Discipline, like liturgy, reminds us that Christian catechesis is always personal and individual and, at the same time, social and communal.

Catechesis in the Churches of the Continental Reformation

The continental reformers undertook the task of reorienting and reeducating large populations of baptized Christians to that understanding of the Gospel which they believed to have been obscured for many centuries. They sought to kindle a personal apprehension of Christian faith, focused on the revelation in Holy Scriptures and nurtured either within the whole society or within a separated, spiritually self-sufficient community. Developing the written question-and-answer catechism as a distinctive genre, the reformers used various forms of catechisms for instructing children and adults, for grounding pastors and other catechists in the fundamentals of what they were to teach, and for maintaining their own standards of orthodoxy. Parents were expected to play key roles in the catechesis of their own children, and reorganized and newly formed schools shared catechetical responsibilities. Both were monitored by the ordained ministers who themselves taught children and adults directly and explicitly in catechetical lectures and indirectly, but perhaps more effectively, in preaching and liturgical rites. Changes introduced into Christian initiation all had catechetical aims, and disciplinary structures were designed for the edification, the building-up of the people of God. The successes and failures of the reformers' efforts in Christian nurture are written into the record. The scope and measure of those efforts are unquestionably among the greatest in two thousand years of Christian life and practice.

BIBLIOGRAPHY

In the case of sixteenth-century writings, I have usually given, where available to me, both the modern critical text and an English translation. Where the text is cited before the translation, I have chosen to translate the passage with some differences from the English work cited.

Armour, Rollin Stely, *Anabaptist Baptism: A Representative Study.* Scottdale, Pennsylvania: Herald Press, 1966.

Bender, Harold S., "A Hutterite School Discipline of 1578 and Peter Scherer's Address of 1568 to the Schoolmasters," *Mennonite Quarterly Review* 5 (1931), pp. 231-244.

Die Bekenntnisschriften der evangelisch-lutherischen Kirche, 4th revised edition. Gottingen: Vandenhoeck & Ruprecht, 1959.

Bolgar, R. R., "Education and Learning," *The New Cambridge Modern History*, vol. 3, pp. 427-452. Cambridge: The University Press, 1968.

Boyle, Marjorie O'Rourke, *Erasmus on Language and Method in Theology.* Toronto: University of Toronto Press, 1977.

Brilioth, Yngve, *Eucharistic Faith and Practice: Evangelical and Catholic.* London: SPCK, 1930.

Brouwer, Arie R., "Calvin's Doctrine of Children in the Covenant: Foundation for Christian Education," *The Reformed Review* 18.4 (May 1965), pp. 17-29.

Bromiley, G. W., *Zwingli and Bullinger.* Library of Christian Classics, vol. 24. Philadelphia: Westminster Press, 1953.

Bucer, Martin, *De Regno Christi*, Opera Latina, vol. 15. François Wendel, gen. ed. Paris: Presses Universitaires de France, 1955.

Martin Bucer and the Book of Common Prayer. Edited by E. C. Whitaker. Alcuin Club Collections, no. 55. Great Wakering, England: Mayhew-McCrimmon, 1974.

Calvin, John, *Commentaries*, 45 vols. Edinburgh: Calvin Translation Society, 1847-1855.

————, *Tracts*, 3 vols. Translated by Henry Beveridge. Edinburgh: Calvin Translation Society, 1849.

————, *Opera quae Supersunt Omnia*, Corpus Reformatorum, vols. 29-77, H. W. Baum, E. Cunitz, E. Reuss, P. Lobstein, A. Erichson, gen. eds. Brunswick: C. A. Schwetschke *et al.*, 1863-1900. Volume numbers are those of the whole Corpus.

————, *Instruction in Faith (1537)*. Translated by Paul T. Furhmann. Philadelphia: Westminster Press, 1949.

_____, *Institutes of the Christian Religion*, 1559 edition, 2 vols. Edited by John T. McNeill, translated by Ford Lewis Battle. Library of Christian Classics, vols. 20 and 21. Philadelphia: Westminster Press, 1960.

Letters of John Calvin, 4 vols. Compiled and edited by Jules Bonnet. Edinburgh: Constable, 1855-1858.

Calvin: Theological Treatises. Translated and edited by J. K. S. Reid. Library of Christian Classics, vol. 22. Philadelphia: Westminster Press, 1954.

Cochrane, Arthur C., ed., *Reformed Confessions of the 16th Century*. Philadelphia: Westminster Press, 1966.

Cohrs, Ferdinand, *Die Evangelischen Katechismusversuche vor Luthers Enchiridion*, Monumenta Germaniae Paedagogica, vols. 20-23 and 39. Berlin: A. Hofmann & Co., 1900-1907.

Dictionnaire de Théologie Catholique, (1903-1950), *s.v.* "Catéchisme." By E. Mangenot.

DeJong, Peter, "Calvin's Contributions to Christian Education," *Calvin Theological Journal* 2.2 (November 1967), pp. 162-201.

Eby, Frederick, *Early Protestant Educators: the Educational Writings of Martin Luther, John Calvin, and Other Leaders of Protestant Thought*. New York: McGraw-Hill, 1931.

_____, *The Development of Modern Education*, 2nd edition. New York: Prentice-Hall, 1952.

Eells, Hastings, *Martin Bucer*. New Haven: Yale University Press, 1931.

Desiderii Erasmi Roterodami Opera Omnia. Leiden: Vander Aa Petri, 1706 (republished London: Gregg Press, 1962).

Opera Omnia Desiderii Erasmi Roterodami. Amsterdam: North Holland Publishing Co., 1969.

Fisher, J. D. C., *Christian Initiation: the Reformation Period*. Alcuin Club Collections, no. 51. London: SPCK, 1970.

Friedmann, Robert, "Hutterite Worship and Preaching," *The Mennonite Quarterly Review* 40 (1966), pp. 5-26.

Gilbert, Allan H., "Martin Bucer on Education," *The Journal of English and Germanic Philology* 18 (1919), pp. 321-341.

Greenslade, L. S., ed., *The Cambridge History of the Bible: The West from the Reformation to the Present Day*. Cambridge: The University Press, 1963.

Grimm, Harold J., "Luther and Education." In *Luther and Culture.* Edited by G. W. Farrell, *et al.* Decorah, Iowa: Luther College Press, 1960.

Henkel, Julia S., "School Organization Patterns of the Brethren of the Common Life." In *Essays on the Northern Renaissance.* Edited by Kenneth A. Strald. Ann Arbor: University of Michigan Press, 1968.

Hershberger, Guy F., ed., *The Recovery of the Anabaptist Vision: A Sixtieth Anniversary Tribute to Harold S. Bender.* Scottdale, Pennsylvania: Herald Press, 1957.

Hubert, F., "Strassburger Katechismen aus den Tagen der Reformation (Capito, Butzer, Zell; die Laienbibel)," *Zeitschrift für Kirchengeschichte* 20 (1900), pp. 395-413.

Balthasar Hubmaier Schriften. Edited by Westin and Bergstied. Quellen zur Geschichteden Taüfer, vol. 9. Götersloh: Gerd Mohn, 1962.

Hudson, Elizabeth K., "The Colloquies of Maturin Cordier: Images of Calvinist School Life and Thought," *The Sixteenth Century Journal* 9 (1978), pp. 57-71.

Köhler, Walter, ed., "The Seven Articles of the Anabaptist Schleitheim Confession with an appended account of the martyrdom of Michael Sattler," as part 3 of *Flugschriften aus den ersten Jahren der Reformation*, vol. II, pp. 277-337. Leipzig: R. Haupt, 1908.

Koldewey, Friedrich, *Braunschweigische Schulordnungen von den ältesten Zeiten bis zum Jahre 1828*, Monumenta Germaniae Paedagogica, vol. 1. Berlin: A. Hofmann & Co., 1886.

Kohls, E. W., "M. Bucer und die Neuordnung des Strassburger Schulwesens," *Theologische Zeitschrift* 16 (1960), pp. 379-406.

Küther, W., "400 Jahre Heidelberger Katechismus," *Reformatio* 12 (1963), pp. 163-168 and 225-229.

Lang, A., *Der Heidelberger Katechismus*, Quellenschriften zur Geschichte des Protestantismus, vol. 3. Leipzig: G. Bohme, 1907.

Léonard, Emile G., *A History of Protestantism*, vols. 1. and 2. Edited by H. H. Rowley, translated by J. M. H. Kied. New York: Thomas Wilson, 1965-1966.

D. Martin Luthers Werke. Kritische Gesamtausgabe. Weimar: H. Böhlau, 1883.

D. Martin Luthers Werke. Kritische Gesamtausgabe. 3. Tischreden. Weimar: H. Böhlau, 1912-1921.

D. Martin Luthers Werke. Kritische Gesamtausgabe. 4. Briefwechs. Weimar: H. Böhlau, 1930.

Luther's Works, 55 vols., Jaroslav Pelikan and Helmut T. Lehmann, gen. eds. Philadelphia and St. Louis: Muhlenberg & Concordia Press, 1955-.

Works of Martin Luther, 5 vols. Edited and translated by C. M. Jacobs, *et al.* Philadelphia: A. J. Holman, 1915-1930.

Melanchthon, Philip, *Christian Doctrine.* Edited by Clyde L. Manschreck. New York: Oxford University Press, 1965.

_____, *Opera.* Edited by K. G. Bretschneider and E. Bindseil, Corpus Reformatorum, vols. 1-28. Brunswick: C. A. Schwetschke et filium, 1834-1860.

Meyer, Carl S., ed. and trans., "A Dialog or Conversation between a Father and his Son about Martin Luther's Doctrine (1523)," *Luther for an Ecumenical Age*, pp. 82-107. St. Louis: Concordia Press, 1967.

The Mennonite Encyclopedia, 4 vols. Scottdale, Pennsylvania: Mennonite Publishing House, 1955-1959.

Miller, Allen O. and Osterhaven, M. Eugene, "The Heidelberg Catechism, 1583-1963," *Theology Today* 19 (1963), pp. 536-550.

Mitchell, Leonel L., "The Reformation Period," *Made, Not Born: New Perspectives on Christian Initiation and the Catechumenate.* South Bend, Indiana: University of Notre Dame Press, 1976.

Müller, Joseph, *Die Deutschen Katechismen der Bohmischen Bruder*, Monumenta Germaniae Paedagogica, vol. 4. Berlin: A. Hofmann & Co., 1887.

Painter, F. V. N., *Luther on Education.* Philadelphia: Lutheran Publication Society, 1889.

Pauck, Wilhelm, *The Heritage of the Reformation.* Glencoe, Illinois: Free Press, 1961.

_____, ed., *Melanchthon and Bucer.* Library of Christian Classics, vol. 19. Philadelphia and London: Westminster Press, 1969.

Peter, R., "L'abécédaire genevois ou catechisme élémentaire de Calvin," *Revue d'Histoire et de Philosophie Religieuses* 45 (1965), pp. 11-25.

Reid, W. Stanford, "Calvin and the Founding of the Academy of Geneva," *Westminster Theological Journal* 18.1 (1955), pp. 1-33.

Repp, Arthur C., *Confirmation in the Lutheran Church.* St. Louis: Concordia Press, 1964.

Reu, Johann Michael, *Quellen zur Geschichte des Kirchlichen Unterrichts in der evangelischen Kirche Deutschlands zwischen 1530 und 1600*, 4 vols. in 9. Götersloh: C. Bertelsmann, 1904-1935(a).

————, "The Peculiar Characteristics of Luther's Catechism," *Lutheran Church Review* 24 (1904b), pp. 436-451.

————, "Religious Instruction of the Young in the Sixteenth Century," *The Lutheran Church Review* 34 (1915), pp. 566-585.

————, "Religious Instruction during the Sixteenth Century," *The Lutheran Church Review* 35 (1916), pp. 234-250.

Richter, Aemilius Ludwig, ed., *Die Evangelischen Kirchenordnungen des Sechszehnten Zahrhunderts*, 2 vols. Weimar: 1846 (reprinted Nieuwkoop: B. de Graaf, 1967). I wish to express thanks to my colleague Wolfgang M. W. Roth for help in the translation of passage cited from I, 120.

Schaff, Philip, *Creeds of Christendom*, 3 vols. New York: Harper, 1877.

Sehling, Emil, ed., *Die evangelischen Kirchenordnungen des XVI Jahrhunderts*. Leipzig and Tubingen: O. R. Reisland, 1902-.

Sodergren, Carl W., "Some Reflections on the Origins of Luther's Catechism," *The Augustana Quarterly* 25 (1946), pp. 132-141.

Staedtke, Joachin, ed., first part, a bibliography of *Heinrich Bullinger Werke*. Zurich: Theologischer Verleg, 1972.

Stupperich, Robert, *Bibliographia Bucerana*, Schriften des Vereins für Reformationsgeschichte, part 2 of #169, pp. 37-96. Götersloh: C. Bertelsmann, 1952.

The Book of Concord. Edited and translated by Theodore G. Tappert, *et al.* Philadelphia: Muhlenberg Press, 1959.

Thompson, Bard, ed., *Liturgies of the Western Church*. Cleveland: Meridian Books, 1961.

————, ed., *Essays on the Heidelberg Catechism*. Philadelphia and Boston: United Church Press, 1963.

Torrance, Thomas F., *The School of Faith: The Catechisms of the Reformed Church*. London: J. Clarke, 1959.

van Braght, Thielem J., *The Bloody Theatre of Martyrs Mirror of the Defenseless Christians who baptized only upon Confession of Faith*. Translated by Joseph F. Sohm. Elkhart, Indiana: Mennonite Publishing Company, 1886.

von Muralt, Leonhard and Schmid, Walter, eds., *Quellen zur Geschichte der Taufer in der Schweiz*. Zurich: S. Hirzel, 1952.

Wendel, François, *Calvin: the Origins and Development of his Religious Thought*. London: Harper & Row, 1963.

Wenger, John Christian, *The Doctrines of the Mennonites*. Scottdale, Pennsylvania: Mennonite Publishing House, 1950.

Wiencke, Gustav K., "Confirmation Instruction in Historical Perspective," *The Lutheran Quarterly* 7 (1955), pp. 99-113.

Williams, George Huntston and Mergal, Angel M., eds., *Spiritual and Anabaptist Writers*. Library of Christian Classics, vol. 25. Philadelphia: Westminster Press, 1957.

_____, *The Radical Reformation*. Philadelphia: Westminster Press, 1962.

Wills, Elbert Vaughan, "Johann Brenz's Catechism of 1535: A Translation," *Augustana Quarterly* 26 (1947), pp. 291-301.

_____, "Johann Brenz's Larger Catechism of 1528," *Lutheran Quarterly* 7 (1955), pp. 114-127.

Wiswedel, Wilhelm, "Das Schulwesen der Huterischen Brüder in Mahren," *Archiv für Reformationsgeschicht* 37 (1940), pp. 38-60.

Woodward, William Harrison, *Studies in Education in the Age of the Renaissance, 1400-1600*. Cambridge: The University Press, 1906.

Zwingli, Ulrich, *Hauptschriften*. Edited by Fritz Blanke, Oskar Earner, and Rudolf Pfister. Zurich: Zwingli-Verlag, 1940-.

The Reformation—II

Chapter 6
Godly Instruction in Reformation England: The Challenge of Religious Education in the Tudor Commonwealth

Fredrica Harris Thompsett

The imposition of massive religious change in a community is a phenomenon which has long fascinated and perplexed historians of Christianity. The Reformation in England provides a paradigm of abundant complexity. Historians continue to debate what critical factors were involved in shaping and nurturing reformed religion in Tudor society. Those events which marked the progress of the Reformation in sixteenth-century England were informed by and formed in an epoch of significant social, economic, political and educational, as well as religious, change. Chronologically the Reformation had its clearest beginnings in the reign of Henry VIII (1509-1547), developed into full expression in the reign of the child King Edward VI (1547-1553), and evolved into recognizable maturity under Elizabeth I (1559-1603). There were, however, aspects of religious life which were far from fully settled by the Elizabethans. Throughout this century religious reformers—politicians, clerics, scholars and popular polemicists—generally agreed that the central goal was to establish a right understanding of God's true religion in England. This was to be done in accord with biblical warrants, right reason, and the traditions of the primitive church. They understood their mission not as the formation of a new faith, but as the recovery and implantation of the true faith in the soil of a new Jerusalem, Tudor England.

Tudor attitudes toward, and provision for, religious education were central to the progress of the Reformation. As a distinct ordering, expression, and practice of the faith (which we today struggle to define as Anglicanism) evolved so too did the educational foundations for Anglicanism. The subject of this chapter is an analysis of these foundations. The focus is upon what was truly a revolutionary intent, the construction of a rigorous program designed to nurture each Tudor citizen—individually and corporately—in knowledge, discipline, and love of God. This analysis underscores the interrelation of educational goals and methods with the formation of reformation texts, doctrine, and legislation. It highlights the blunt, yet often overlooked, reality that the rooting and prosperous growth of the Reformation was in many ways dependent upon education. The efficacy of the church's teaching was critical to the overall success of the English Reformation.

This study begins by sketching basic dimensions and terminology for understanding Tudor society. Major topics for analysis include an appraisal of the state of religious education in the early days of the Reformation, noting both the debt to Christian humanism and the general Protestant inheritance; a description of educational ideals and goals held by English reformers; and an assessment of major components in the emerging educational program with special attention to methods and materials for instruction, including authorized and other popular, yet unofficial, texts. This study concludes with a brief discussion of the significance of religious education in the Tudor family. The apparent tidiness of these sections should not lead the reader to infer that the shaping of the church's teaching was part of a carefully planned or centrally directed program. Educational goals and methods evolved along with church doctrine and practice. The hallmarks of this evolution were a lively concern for educating clergy and laity in the fundamentals of the faith, increasing evidence of biblical literacy, and a pragmatic respect for various dimensions of Christian tradition. These and other elements of the church's life were summarized at the century's end by Richard Hooker (1553-1600) who provided both a philosophical foundation for Anglicanism and a distilled assessment of Tudor theological controversies and practices in his major work, *Of the Laws of Ecclesiastical Polity.*

In assessing Tudor thought and literature it is important to note that there was no distinct separation of secular from religious categories. Such categorization is a relatively modern invention. References about inflation, landholding patterns, domestic rebellions, foreign alliances and obedience to the Crown were all part of an eminently Christian world view. There also was no clear distinction between general education in letters and general education in knowledge and love of God. Education for Christian living and for societal reform were inseparable. The single objective was raising up saints and citizens for the Tudor commonwealth.

The term "commonwealth" or "commonweal" as a synonym for the body politic, the realm, reflected the prevailing political theory which viewed church and state not as identical powers but rather as coordinate dimensions of the common health of the realm. This essential linkage was not new to reformation society. The interdependence of church and state was, however, signaled in new and certain terms in the 1534 parliamentary Act of Supremacy which proclaimed the king, and his heirs, as "the only supreme head in earth of the Church of England called *Anglicana Ecclesia*" (Elton, 1962, p. 355). Commonwealth society was also based upon interdependent vocations. The anonymous author of the Edwardian Homily, "An Exhortation to Obedience," thus described the nature of the commonwealth:

> every degree of people in their vocation, calling, and office, hath appointed to them their duty and order: some are in high degree, some in low, some kings and princes, some inferiors, and subjects, priests and laymen, masters and servants, fathers and children, husbands and wives, rich and poor; and every one have need of other; so that in all things is to be lauded and praised the goodly order of God, without the which no house, no city, no commonwealth can continue and endure, or last (*Certain Sermons*, 1851 ed., pp. 109-110).

In application this meant, as Richard Hooker concluded, "there is not any man of the Church of England but the same man is also a member of the commonwealth; nor any man a member of the commonwealth, which is not also of the Church of England" (Hooker, 1888 ed., Book VIII, i, 2). The coherence of church and state within the commonwealth is the foundation for understanding that religious decrees enjoined by law were instruments both of religious reform and government policy.

One final cautionary note concerns the use of religious labels. Throughout most of the sixteenth century the designations "Protestant," "Puritan," "Anglican," and "Catholic" were more often blurred than distinct, and were frequently used as terms of derision. For the purposes of this essay the term "reformer" will be employed for those devoted to reforming the Church in England, and the term "papist" will be borrowed from Tudor thought to describe those whose primary religious loyalty was to the Church of Rome. With specific reference to educational goals, differences between Anglicans and Puritans were not of consequence in the sixteenth century, though there were significant contrasts in educational practices in the seventeenth century.

THE OLD FAITH AND THE NEW LEARNING ON THE EVE OF THE REFORMATION

Popular pamphleteers and polemicists writing in behalf of reformation policies occasionally referred in their texts to changes in the concept and practice of education. Some of these authors took particular care to demonstrate that the reformed faith was aided and based upon a new understanding of knowledge which was biblically centered. This emphasis was clear in a tract first printed in 1538 entitled, *The Olde learynge and the new, compared together whereby it may easily be knowen which of them is better and more agreeyng wyth the everlasting word of God* (Regius, 1548 ed.). The reformers maintained that the new learning was in sharp contrast to that of the papists whom, they said, had hidden the Gospel and promoted false doctrine and idolatry. Thomas Cranmer (1489-1556), central architect of the English Reformation and Archbishop of Canterbury, remarked in 1549 that the papists had depended upon religious images to be "lay-men's books" (Cranmer, 1844-46 ed., II, 179). William Turner, a skilled Tudor polemicist, personified the contrast between the old faith and the new learning in a dialogue drama telling how "Master Knowledge" led the successful persecution against "Mastres Missa" and her papist servants (1548?, sig. Ai, *passim*).* These and other authors believed that knowledge of the faith should be accessible to all God's people, and that good learning was a powerful aid to true religion. Knowledge of the Bible was thought

---

*The pagination of printed texts in Tudor England was irregular. Frequently a combination of letters, numbers and other symbols was employed by the printer at the foot of the first page of every section to guide the binding of the text in sequence. This was called a signature, and is abbreviated in this chapter as *sig*. The letters *r* and *v* are abbreviations for *recto* and *verso*, the right and left hand sides of a page.

to be a central ally in the progress of the Reformation, a weapon which would eventually banish superstition and idolatry from England.

In practice the educational principles of English reformers were greatly influenced by the ideals and innovations of humanism and Christian humanism. Generations of humanists since the four-teenth century had rigorously challenged scholastic thought, pursued new directions in literary, historical and philological studies, and revived study of biblical and classical languages. On the eve of the Reformation, Christian humanists, notably Desi-derius Erasmus and John Colet, were applying their scholarship to a search for deeper knowledge of the Scriptures. A Spanish student of Erasmus, Juan Luis Vives, devoted attention to detailing a philosophy and guide to educational practices. The educational principles of these and other reformers proved a rich legacy for English reformers. Attention was drawn to the connection between learning in and practice of the faith. Learning was no longer seen to be the sole preserve of schoolmen, but rather an avenue for the formation of Christian character. There was insistence upon studying the Bible and early church fathers. Humanists also emphasized the importance of the vernacular for general studies (Simon, 1966, pp. 69-72 and 102-123). These and other aims of Christian humanism were adapted by mid-sixteenth-century reformers and given new impetus in the service of the Reformation.

The most significant reason for the expansion of religious education in the sixteenth century was the value which reformers placed upon a biblically based faith and the consequent demand for a biblically literate populace. Reformation Protestantism on the Continent and in England was a religion of the book, the Bible. There had been a growing market from the fifteenth century onward for devotional books based wholly or in part upon the Bible. The progress of the Reformation strikingly expanded the market for biblical literature. Yet what enabled the reformers to provide materials for religious education was the epoch-making invention of printing. The Reformation was the first mass move-ment, on the Continent and later in England, to take advantage of a tremendous expansion of educational opportunities based on availability of inexpensive printed texts (Eisentein, 1969, p. 19). One reformer claimed that lack of books was what had enabled the Bishop of Rome to prevail and that with printing the word of God would be quickly spread abroad and the papists overthrown.

The Reformation generated pressure for the extension of literacy. Josiah Nichols wrote, in a manual on religious instruction in the family, that all persons should learn to read in that "God hath given a marveilous blessing of printing to further his Gospell: and we are very foolish, if we let slip any blessing or comfort" (1596, sig. G7ʳ). This same "blessing" assisted the rapid growth of the young printing industry which relied primarily on the production of religious literature. Bibles, psalters, sermons, devotional tracts, and a variety of other materials were produced which both spread the news and traced the course of the Reformation.

Despite the technological abilities of the printing industry, a gradual diffusion of education in Tudor society, and the enthusiasm of reformers, the challenge of educating the populace in the faith was immense. It is estimated that many, if not a majority, of clergy (and particularly those in rural parishes) were unlearned and some were illiterate. The sharp-penned Tudor polemicist John Bale (1495-1563) described in 1548 those clergy who still adhered to papist opinions as men whose "wyttes be drowsey, and their learnynge lowsye . . . scripturs they deprave" (1548, sig. A2). By all accounts the clergy in the early days of the English Reformation were at best casually educated. As late as 1551 the new Bishop of Gloucester, John Hooper (d. 1555), was dismayed when visitation records for his parish clergy indicated that out of 311 clergy: 168 were unable to repeat the Decalogue, 9 could not count the Commandments, and 33 were unable to locate them in Scripture; 10 clergy could not repeat the Lord's Prayer, 9 could not locate it in the Bible, and 34 were unable to name its author (Price, 1939, p. 101). Hugh Latimer (?1485-1555), a skilled preacher and zealous reformer, wryly noted that some laity were better learned in the Bible than clergy (Latimer, 1844-45 ed., I, 122). Another polemicist quipped, in a popular dialogue written in the 1530's, that if the common people became more learned in the Scriptures the clergy might find themselves without an occupation (Anon., *A goodly dyalogue*, 1550 ed., no pagin). These were rhetorical conclusions. Although literacy, provision for lay education, and standards for clerical learning perceptibly increased (Stone, 1964, pp. 41-80), there were abundant signs that ignorance, superstition and indifference remained powerful enemies of the Reformation. Even Hugh Latimer had to confess frankly that there were lots of people who preferred stories of Robin Hood to sermons (Latimer, 1844-45 ed., I, 208).

It is against this background that English reformers set their educational goals and methods. Despite the powerful incentives of a biblically-based religion, a thriving printing trade, and heightened expectations for learned clergy and laity, there were significant difficulties to be faced in effecting the policies and practices of the newly reformed church at the local level. The success of the Reformation depended, at least in part, upon educational strategies. Vital and accessible vehicles for nurturing Tudor citizens in the official faith of the realm had to be devised.

EDUCATIONAL GOALS OF TUDOR REFORMERS

The reformers' ambitions were revealed in their statements on education. Although there was neither a comprehensive, nor unified, program for religious education, Tudor reformers repeatedly expressed high expectations for the benefits of godly learning. In one of the most popular tracts on domestic education, *A Godly Form of Household Government*, first printed in 1598, the author challenged the social class structures of England and asserted his confidence in Christian education when he claimed, "We are changed and become good, not by birth, but by Education" (Cawdrey, 1630 ed., sig. R8). His sentiments reiterated the inheritance from Christian humanists that education was the primary means whereby the character of the individual Christian was formed. Hugh Latimer enunciated his educational goals in his 1537 injunctions for the diocese of Worcester. He urged his clergy to teach children to read English so that they may "better learn how to believe, how to pray, and how to live to God's pleasure" (Frere, 1910, II, 17). He echoed the plea from William Tyndale's (d. 1536) powerful tract of 1528, *The Obedience of a Christian Man*, that all children be brought up in "the nurture and information of the Lord" (Tyndale, 1849-50 ed., I, 233-34). Even ABC's, devices for teaching children letters, emphasized the riches of learning. Thomas Knell's *An ABC to the christen congregacion Or a patheway to the heavenly Habitation* illustrated this theme:

> Covet for learnynge, that maketh a man wyse
> Covet for knowledge, of gods preceptes
> Covet for wysedome, chiefe of pryce
>
> (Knell, 1550?, no pagin.).

For these reformers and others throughout the century, education provided a primary means whereby men, women and children in Tudor society were changed toward godly living informed by divine ordinances.

Reformers in the early days of the English Reformation faced a more specific two-fold agenda: raising up citizens to become zealous members of the newly reformed church also meant marshaling public opinion against policies and practices of the papists. As liturgical and other religious reforms progressed with increasing pace, energy was focused on weaning the English populace away from certain aspects of the worship, piety, and devotional expressions of late medieval and early sixteenth-century church life. The magnitude of this preparatory intent has often been overlooked by Reformation historians. An abundant corpus of popular literature provides testimony to the enormity of the educational task associated with religious change. From the 1520's on there was a steady stream of literature from official and unofficial propagandists decrying the evils of papist religion and rule. In one anonymous 1553 verse satire, *The Image of Hypocrisye*, the Pope was called "the father of foles and ignoraunce of scoless . . . Thou arte the devils vicar . . . O Lorde of Hypocrites." In this same text friars, cardinals, priests and other papist officers were described as men who "kepe your holy rules, As asses and mules" (Furnivall, 1868-72 ed., I, 181-266). Anticlerical attitudes, as any reader of Chaucer may note, were not new to Tudor thought. Nor is there any evidence that pre-Reformation clerics were more immoral than their late medieval predecessors. Tudor polemicists simply sharpened and intensified traditional anticlericalism to serve better their propaganda efforts in behalf of religious reform.

It was one agendum to attack the papists and quite another to enforce religious uniformity among Tudor citizens. In large measure calling public attention to the progress of religious reform and enjoining the nation to the reformed faith was carried out through legislation. Parliamentary statutes—notably the Acts of Uniformity which accompanied the Prayer Books—proclamations, royal and ecclesial injunctions, articles of Convocation and other texts were statements of religious policy and teaching devices. These documents often explained the rationale for change in policy. For example, the reason for further liturgical reform was explained in the second Act of Uniformity which accompanied the Prayer Book of 1552:

Where there hath been a very godly order [the 1549 Prayer Book] set

forth by authority of Parliament for common prayer and the administration of the sacraments, to be used in the mother tongue with the
Church of England, agreeable to the word of God and the primitive
Church, very comfortable to all good people desiring to live in
Christian conversation, and most profitable to the estate of this
realm, upon the which the mercy, favour, and blessing of Almighty
God is in no wise so readily and plenteously poured as by common
prayers, due using of the sacraments, and often preaching of gospel,
with the devotion of the hearers; and yet notwithstanding, a great
number of people in divers parts of this realm, following their own
sensuality and living either without knowledge or due fear of God,
do wilfully and damnably before Almighty God abstain and refuse
to come to their parish churches (Elton, 1962, p. 396).

This text and other official documents mandating observance of
the faith provide evidence of a century-long preoccupation by
government and ecclesial authorities to edify Tudor citizens while
enforcing religious uniformity.

The central educational intent of Tudor reformers was encouragement of biblical literacy. Scripture was the primary authority
for reformation doctrine and practice. Thomas Cranmer repeatedly emphasized the necessity for a biblically-informed faith.
His writings summarize crucial elements in reformed thought. In
the 1548 Homily on Holy Scripture Cranmer began by asserting
the authority of the Bible:

Unto a christian man there can be nothing either more necessary or
profitable, than the knowledge of holy Scripture, forasmuch as in it
is contained God's true word, setting forth his glory, and also man's
duty. And there is no truth nor doctrine necessary for our justification
and everlasting salvation, but that is, or may be, drawn out of that
fountain and well of truth. Therefore, as many as be desirous to
enter into the right and perfect way unto God, must apply their
minds to know holy Scripture; without the which, they can neither
sufficiently know God and his will, neither their office and duty.
And, as drink is pleasant to them that be dry, and meat to them that
be hungry; so is the reading, hearing, searching and studying of holy
Scripture, to them that be desirous to know God, or themselves, and
to do his will (*Certain Sermons*, 1851 ed., p. 1).

Cranmer was equally clear that the language of revelation was
accessible to ordinary citizens and not restricted to specialists, a
theme reiterated in his 1540 preface to the second edition of the
Great Bible:

> The Holy Ghost hath so ordered and attempered the scriptures, that in them as well publicans, fishers, and shepherds may find their edification, as great doctors their erudition: for those books were not made to vain-glory, like as were the writings of Gentile philosophers and rhetoricians, to the intent the makers should be had in admiration for their high styles and obscure manner of writing, whereof nothing can be understand without a master or an expositor. But the apostles and prophets wrote their books so that their special intent and purpose might be understanded and perceived of every reader, which was nothing but the edification or amendment of the life of them that readeth and heareth it (Cranmer, 1844-46 ed., II, 120).

For Cranmer the Bible was *the* handbook of Christian living:

> Here all manner of persons . . . of what estate or condition soever they be, may in this book learn all things what they ought to believe, what they ought to do, and what they should not do, as well concerning Almighty God, as also concerning themselves and all others (*Ibid.*, 121).

The emphasis in Cranmer's writings upon love of God and love of neighbor reflected the social dimensions of the Christian commonwealth. Personal godliness and corporate godliness were correlative goals. Tudor reformers maintained that education in the faith was sure grounding for stability in the commonwealth and obedience to the Crown. In the 1536 tract, *A Remedy for Sedition*, Richard Morrison explained that the cause of sedition and disobedience was evil education (pp. 173-4). This aspect of educational policy, the goal of producing loyal citizens, was affirmed in a 1599 letter to the burgesses of York:

> It is the duty of all Christian magistrates to have a care of the good education of all youths and children within their charge, that they may be instructed and seasoned at the first with the true knowledge of God and His religion, whereby they are liable to become good members of the Church and commonweal and dutiful subjects of her majesty and the state (quoted in Simon, 1966, p. 331).

Josiah Nichols reaffirmed this aspiration in a 1596 treatise on domestic education. He instructed parents that the central aim of religious nurture was "to bring forth holy generations to the Church, and a civill nation to the Commonwealth" (sig. B2).

The educational task claimed by Tudor reformers in the common service of church and state was ambitious. Their intention was to provide effective means, informed by biblical warrants, of converting and unifying religious life throughout the realm. They hoped thereby to lay a foundation for stabilizing the social order of the commonwealth. What was at stake was the well-being of the kingdom. Their aim was to raise up godly and obedient citizens who in their lives would follow the path to everlasting salvation.

MATERIALS AND METHODS FOR GODLY INSTRUCTION

The educational ideals of Tudor reformers evolved into three major and overlapping components: hearing, reading, and study of Holy Scripture; knowledge of the Creed, the Lord's Prayer and the Ten Commandments fulfilled largely by instruction in the Catechism; and communal participation in divine services which encompassed the whole of a person's life. A vast range of literature for religious instruction was available for private and corporate religious nurture. These materials—Bibles, Prayer Books, aids to biblical study, homilies, primers, catechisms—were generally published with official sanction, enforced by government and ecclesial legislation.*

The central educational materials of the English Reformation were written in the vernacular for ease of access to persons who might either read these texts, or hear them read. These documents were published and prescribed for use by clergy and laity. Texts for religious life were no longer set aside for the clerical estate. Materials for religious instruction were issued in forms that might conveniently be sold or otherwise easily distributed throughout the realm. For example, issuing a single Prayer Book of divine services at low cost, instead of the five texts required for worship in the late medieval church, was a decided advantage which Cranmer advertised in the preface to the 1549 *Book of Common Prayer*:

---

*In my analysis of the major texts of the English Reformation I am greatly indebted to insights from the forthcoming book, John E. Booty, ed., David Siegenthaler, John W. Wall, Jr., *The Godly Kingdom of Tudor England: Great Books of the English Reformation*, scheduled for publication by Morehouse-Barlow Co. in 1981.

by this order the curates shall need none other books for their public
service but this book and the Bible, by the means whereof the people
shall not be at so great charge for books as in time past they had
been.*

For larger and more expensive texts, such as Bibles and the *Paraphrases* of Erasmus, enabling legislation mandated purchase and
placement in each parish. These efforts demonstrate the reformers'
faith in the printed word.

Many of the educational tools of the Reformation, along with
standards and procedures for their enforcement, were devised
during the last ten years of Henry VIII's reign. The educational
foundations for the Reformation thus preceded the promulgation
of comprehensive statements on doctrine and worship which
preoccupied reformers during Edward VI's reign.

The design and implementation of the late Henrician educational program was directed by Thomas Cromwell (?1485-1540),
Henry's able and enthusiastic vice-regent. Cromwell, himself a
Christian humanist eager to promote a reformed and biblically-
based faith, directed his considerable energies to the preparation,
financing, and political machinations necessary to ensure authorization and distribution of Bibles in English. The story of Tudor
vernacular Bibles began with William Tyndale's 1526 edition of
an English New Testament. Cromwell's influence was clearly
evident as a patron for the unauthorized Coverdale Bible, printed
in 1535 probably in Zurich, and the Matthew Bible printed in
England in 1537. Cromwell's achievement as a foremost patron
of English Bibles culminated in 1539 with the publication of the
Great Bible, so called because it was the largest volume in English.
This text, Coverdale's revision of the Matthew Bible, was issued
with royal authority. The second edition of the Great Bible was
printed in 1540 with a preface by Cranmer and the addition of a
deceptively simple phrase on the titlepage, "This is the Byble
appoynted to the use of the churches" (Dickens, 1964, pp. 129-38).

---

*John E. Booty, ed., *The Book of Common Prayer, 1559* (Charlottesville:
University Press of Virginia, 1976), p. 16. Unless otherwise noted all
citations in this chapter from texts of the Tudor Prayer Books are from
Booty's edition of the 1559 Prayer Book. When the material cited is found
only in the 1549 or 1552 Prayer Books, the edition cited is Joseph Ketley,
ed., *The Two Liturgies, 1549 & 1552, in the Reign of Edward VI*, The
Parker Society (Cambridge: University Press, 1844).

Cromwell and Cranmer were also instrumental in shaping legislation to encourage the use of English Bibles. Royal and ecclesiastical injunctions, issued throughout the century, often defined procedures for religious instruction. In 1536 royal injunctions instructed parish clergy to place copies of the Bible, in Latin and in English, in church choirs "for every man that will to look and read thereon, and shall discourage no man from the reading of any part of the Bible . . . but rather exhort and admonish every man to read the same as the very word of God" (Frere, 1910, II, 9). Another set of royal injunctions, in 1538, required that the cost of the English Bible was to be born equally by the parson and his parishioners (*Ibid.*, 35-6). Hugh Latimer, always ready to keep pressure upon clerical leadership, directed his clergy in diocesan injunctions to read and study in Latin and English at least one chapter of the Bible a day (*Ibid.*, 15). Instructions for educating youth and others unschooled in the faith were explained in a lengthy and comprehensive section of the 1536 injunctions. The method for teaching the traditional instructional materials— the Lord's Prayer, the Articles of the Faith (i.e., the Apostles' Creed), and the Ten Commandments—was described:

> And to the intent that this may be more easily done, the said curates shall, in their sermons, deliberately and plainly recite of the said *Pater Noster*, the Articles of our Faith, and the Ten Commandments, one clause or article one day, and another another day, till the whole be taught and learned by little; and shall deliver the same in writing, or shew where printed books containing the same be to be sold, to them that can read or will desire the same (*Ibid.*, 7).

The 1538 injunctions added that the learning of sentences by rote should be led by the curate once every Sunday, or oftener if required, and that the clergy should also "expound and declare the understanding" of each phrase (*Ibid.*, 36).

Reference to printed materials in the 1536 injunctions was to biblical texts, devotional aids, and primers. Primers, vernacular books of prayer, were designed for laity. Since the middle ages they had played a prominent role in devotional life in England and on the Continent. With the advent of printing they came into more wide-spread use. A number of unofficial primers were printed in the first four decades of the sixteenth century. This activity culminated when Henry VIII authorized his own primer, *The Primer set forth by the King's Majesty and his clergy; to be taught, learned, and read, and none other to be used throughout all his dominions* (1545). Elements in this text included the Creed, Ten Commandments, and the Lord's Prayer, as well as the 1535 Litany, various prayers, psalms, Epistles and Gospels for Sundays and major holy days. The popularity of this official Primer was attested to by subsequent editions in Henry's reign and by its reissue, with further modifications, in the first year of Edward VI's reign. In 1553 Edward authorized a primer of his own, *A Primer or book of private prayer needful to be used of all faithful Christians, Which book is authorized and set forth by the King's Majesty, to be taught, learned, read, and used of all his loving subjects.*

During the final decade of Henry's reign work began on a translation of Erasmus' *Paraphrases*. With official sanction of this text early in Edward VI's reign, clergy and laity were provided an authorized, interpretative guide to the New Testament. The commitment of Henrician and Edwardian reformers, and especially that of Thomas Cranmer, to Erasmus' commentary is indicative of the seriousness with which Tudor reformers approached study of the Scriptures and of their expectation that humanistic exegesis would take place in Tudor parishes.

Work on a book of collected sermons by various authors for standard parish use was begun by Cranmer in 1539. The resultant Book of Homilies was completed and issued in the summer of 1547. The twelve sermons in this volume, four of which were certainly written by Cranmer, formed yet another piece in the standard teaching texts of the church. The preface to the Book of Homilies noted the worth of these sermons as means to enjoin loyalty to the Crown, end disruption in the commonwealth, and combat heresy. With provision of these Homilies and their use in Tudor parishes the reformers believed that even those curates who were unable to preach, popularly called "dumb dogs," and those clergy unlicensed to preach would be able to educate parishioners in the faith and promote social harmony.

Exhortation of the Word of God and emphasis on preaching as a primary means for religious instruction in the commonwealth were essential. Many reformers worried that England's parsons were ill-equipped for this ministry. With his usual sarcasm, John Bale proclaimed in a 1546 tract that there had been bad preaching in England since the time of Adam and estimated that not one English saint had been canonized for preaching God's word (sig. Aii). Hugh Latimer in his justly famous 1548 "Sermon on the Plough" proclaimed that the English people were spiritually starving for want of good preaching which was "meat" and not "strawberries" in feeding the soul. Salvation, Latimer insisted, was a preaching and not a "massing" matter (Latimer, 1844-45 ed., I, 62 and 178). So integral was the demand for godly preaching in the newly reformed church that the *Forty-Two Articles*, issued in 1553, defined the true Christian congregation as the place "in which the pure worde of God is preached, and the sacraments be duelie ministred" (cited in Davies, 1970, p. 27). Injunctions urged the provision of regular sermons. In the 1538 injunctions the parson was required to preach, or arrange to have preached, four sermons a year, "wherein ye shall purely and sincerely declare the very Gospel of Christ, and in the same exhort your hearers to the works of charity, mercy, and faith, specially prescribed and commanded in Scripture" (Frere, 1910, II, 37). This command was repeated in the 1547 royal injunctions along with requirements that because of "lack of preachers in many places of the King's realm," all clergy were to read each Sunday in their parish one of the sermons from the Book of Homilies (*Ibid.*, 115). The 1559 Prayer Book service of Holy Communion made provision for either a sermon or one of the authorized homilies (Booty, ed., 1976, p. 251). As the Reformation progressed, and certainly by the reign of Elizabeth, preaching became a major educational instrument, as well as a means of entertainment and an occasion for public pronouncements (Maclure, 1958, *passim*).

The reign of Edward VI provided opportunities for consolidating the achievements of Henrician reformers and for establishing the 1549 and 1552 Books of Common Prayer, the liturgical and educational foundations of public worship. Thomas Cranmer guided liturgical projects to completion and led the church toward more explicit expressions of Protestant theology and worship. Changes in ritual and doctrine proceeded, at first cautiously and then steadily, with official sanctions. An influx of Henrician exiles and Continental refugees began to swell the reformed ranks. Religious persecution of radical reformers was halted, and the cessation of censorship in the pulpit and press opened new opportunities for public extension of the Reformation.*

---

*The fullest description of the evolution of religious life and policy in Edward VI's reign is found in a two-volume history by Wallace K. Jordan, *Edward VI: The Young King, The Protectorship of the Duke of Somerset* (London: George Allen & Unwin Ltd., 1968); and *Edward VI: The Threshold of Power, The Dominance of the Duke of Northumberland* (Cambridge: Belknap Press of Harvard University Press. 1970).

The direction of the new government was signaled in the first injunctions (1547) of Edward's reign which required that every parish provide the Great Bible, the *Paraphrases* of Erasmus, and the newly authorized Book of Homilies as foundations for religious life (Frere, 1910, II, 117-18). The heart of the educational program —the Creed, the Lord's Prayer and the Ten Commandments— was reaffirmed in a semi-official catechism translated from the work of the Lutheran reformer Justas Jonas, *Catechismus. That is to say a short Instruction into Christian Religion for the synguler commoditie and profyte of children and yong people* (1548). This Catechism, dedicated to Edward VI, bore Cranmer's name as author and an introductory epistle in which he proclaimed that there was "nothinge more necessarie" for the furtherance of true religion begun under Henry VIII than the education of youth:

> Youth and tender age of youre louynge subiectes, maye be brought up and traded in the trewth of Goddes holy worde . . . such as have ben from childhode nouryshed and fed wyth the swete milke, and as it were the pappe of goddes holy word, and brydled and kept in awe wyth hys holy commaundementes. For as we are in youth brought up, so we continue in age, and saver longest of that thynge that we fyrst receave and taist of (Cranmer, 1548, sig. iii).

This Catechism, other legislation, and documents issued in the first three years of the new reign emphasized the need to nurture youth and elders in the faith. Additional legislation was directed toward the on-going task of purifying the church of papist superstitions and practices.

The essential instrument for the promotion of true religion and the perfection of the commonwealth was the Prayer Book. The Edwardian *Books of Common Prayer* of 1549 and 1552, and their Elizabethan successor of 1559, became centerpieces of religious life to which all other practices, including the educational life of the church, were directly correlated. The story of the origins, preparation, and authorization of the Tudor Prayer Books, and assessment of their liturgical and theological contributions has been told elsewhere.* From the vantage point of this chapter the

---

*The origins of the Prayer Book are treated in Frank Edward Brightman, *The English Rite: Being a Synopsis of the Sources and Revisions of the Book of Common Prayer*, 2 vols. (London: Rivingtons, 1915). The standard history of the Prayer Book is Francis Procter and W. H. Frere, *A New History of the Book of Common Prayer* (London: Macmillan and Co., 1902). For a general introduction to the history of the 1559 Prayer Book *see* Booty, ed., *The Book of Common Prayer, 1559*, pp. 327-82.

focus is upon these books as instruments of religious education; commentary is directed to the overall principles and educational assumptions in all three Prayer Books, rather than to distinctions among their texts.

The general educational principles of the Prayer Books were in accord with Christian humanist and early Protestant thought. These books were not only biblically based, they were intended to directly engage worshippers in study of the Bible. Cranmer, in the Preface of the 1549 *Book of Common Prayer*, emphasized the centrality of the Bible in worship:

> all the whole Bible (or the greatest part thereof) should be read over once in the year, intending thereby, that the Clergy, and especially such as were Ministers of the congregation, would (by often reading, and meditation of God's word) be stirred up to godliness themselves, and be more able to exhort others by wholesome doctrine, and to confute them that were adversaries to the truth. And further, that the people (by daily hearing of holy Scripture read in the Church) should continually profit more and more in the knowledge of God, and be the more inflamed with the love of his true religion (Ketley ed., 1845, p. 2).

In practice the Prayer Books provided daily reading of large segments, often entire chapters, from the Bible. Most of the Old Testament was to be read in the course of a year, the New Testament three times a year, and the Psalms every month. Orderly reading of Scripture, and study thereof, also presumed use of aids to biblical study such as the *Paraphrases*. The Prayer Book lectionary gave substance to the words of the Collect for the second Sunday in Advent:

> Blessed Lord, which has caused all Holy Scriptures to be written for our learning: Grant us that we may in such wise hear them, read, mark, learn, and inwardly digest them; that by patience and comfort of thy holy Word, we may embrace and ever hold fast the blessed hope of everlasting life, which thou hast given us in our Saviour Jesus Christ (Booty ed., 1976, p. 79).

It was equally clear that the Prayer Books were designed to be instruments for the public worship of the whole community of the faithful, lay and clerical. These were *common* prayers. Petitions in the Prayer Book Collects, for example, were addressed in behalf of: "all them that be admitted into the fellowship of Christ's religion," "thy Church and household," and "thy faithful people." In these and other prayers the intent was public edification, as well as amendment of life. This concern for public edification was invoked, after that of the primacy of Scripture, as one of the criteria for continuing certain traditional aspects of worship. In the introductory essay "Of Ceremonies, Why Some Be Abolished and Some Retained," printed in the 1549 and subsequent Tudor Prayer Books, Cranmer defended keeping ceremonies:

> which although they have been devised by man, yet it is thought good to reserve them still, as well for a decent order in the Church, for the which they were first devised, as because they pertain to *edification, whereunto all things done in the Church, as the Apostle teacheth, ought to be referred (Ibid.,* p. 18; *italics mine).*

Accordingly the language of the Prayer Books of 1549 and 1552 was designed to be clear and direct, "in such language and order as is most easy and plain for the understanding, both of the readers and hearers" *(Ibid.,* p. 16). This language for the most part was aural, written to be read aloud. The aim was to ensure that all participants in these services could be consistently involved in worship, rather than being observers or actors moving in and out of the liturgical drama. Even rubrics ordering the services were few in number and intended to be easily understood. The goal was to free worshippers to participate directly in a range of common services which encompassed the whole of their lives.

Specific instructions for parish education were included in the Prayer Book services for Baptism and Confirmation. Once more the traditional core for religious instruction—the Creed, Lord's Prayer, and Ten Commandments—was reaffirmed. The Prayer Books directed that baptism was normally to be administered in a public service, wherein all parishioners would receive the newly baptized and reaffirm their own baptismal vows. The service of Public Baptism concluded with a short exhortation to the God-parents which reemphasized the spiritual and educational implications of promises in behalf of the baptized:

> you must remember that it is your parts and duties to see that these infants be taught so soon as they shall be able to learn what a solemn vow, promise, and profession they have made by you. And that they may know these things the better, ye shall call upon them to hear sermons. And chiefly ye shall provide that they may learn the Creed, the Lord's Prayer, and the Ten Commandments in the English tongue, and all other things which a Christian man ought to know and believe to his soul's health; and that these children may be virtuously brought up to lead a godly and a Christian life, remembering alway that baptism doth represent unto us our profession, which is to follow the example of our Savior Christ *(Ibid.,* p. 276).

The Prayer Book service for Confirmation continued this emphasis and there was printed, in 1549 and later Prayer Books, an official Catechism for parish instruction. This Catechism was the instructional basis for carrying out promises made at baptism. It was to be learned before Confirmation, at which time the confirmand was publically examined by the minister. The rubric indicated that no one was to be admitted to Holy Communion "until such time as he can say the catechism, and be confirmed" (*Ibid.*, p. 289). The Catechism centered on learning the content and meaning of the Creed, Lord's Prayer, and Ten Commandments. In addition it underscored the reformers' belief that good learning was basic to inculcating social stability and morality. This was clear in the response to the question on one's duty to others:

> My duty toward my neighbor is, to love him as myself. And to do to all men as I would they should do unto me. To love, honor, and succor my father and mother. To honor and obey the king and his ministers. To submit myself to all my governors, teachers, spiritual pastors, and masters. To order myself lowly and reverently to all my betters. To hurt nobody by word nor deed. To be true and just in all my dealing. To bear no malice nor hatred in my heart. To keep my hands from picking and stealing, and my tongue from evil speaking, lying, and slandering. To keep my body in temperance, soberness, and chastity. Not to covet nor desire other men's goods. But learn and labor truly to get mine own living, and to do my duty in that state of life, unto which it shall please God to call me (*Ibid.*, p. 286).

Concern for instilling godly virtue and emphasis on nurturing loyal citizens found expression in Tudor catechetical instruction.

The procedure for teaching the Catechism was prescribed in a rubric at the conclusion of the Confirmation service and enforced by Edwardian and Elizabethan injunctions. The curate was to set time aside on Sundays and holy days, usually before Evening Prayer, to instruct and examine members of his parish. All "fathers and mothers, masters and dames" were to see that their "children, servants, and prentices" were present (*Ibid.*, p. 289). The time specified for instruction varied. Edmund Grindal (1519-83), when he was Archbishop of York, required his clergy to spend at least an hour every Sunday in this activity (Grindal, 1843 ed., pp. 124-25). Penalties were imposed on parents and others who did not send those under their charge for instruction, and parish clergy were required to keep a list of those between seven and twenty years of age who had yet to learn their catechism. The prescribed method of learning was memorizing sentences from the Catechism in rote dialogue between the curate and his pupils. Instructions also specified that students were to understand, as well as memorize, the Catechism. Memorization was considered essential, as Cranmer indicated in the Preface to the Great Bible:

> read the whole story, and that thou understandest keep it well in memory; that thou understandest not, read it again and again: if thou can neither so come by it, counsel with some other that is better learned (Cranmer, 1844-46 ed., II, 120-21)

From the reign of Edward VI onward the whitewashed east walls of many parishes bore in bold letters the text of the Creed, Lord's Prayer, and Ten Commandments. These texts, which frequently replaced religious statuary and other medieval iconography, were graphic reminders of the teaching foundations of the faith.

Other materials for religious education were keyed to the Prayer Books. Edward VI's official *Primer* of 1553 was unlike its royal predecessors in that it reprinted the Prayer Book Catechism, and its directions for private biblical study were based on the daily offices of the 1552 Prayer Book. For the first time an official order for private prayer was derived from forms of public worship. This practice and the authorizing of royal vernacular primers were continued with modest alterations by Mary I and Elizabeth I. The Prayer Book Catechism spawned publication of other popular catechetical texts. John Ponet's *A Short Catechisme* (1553), and Alexander Nowell's *A Catechisme or first instruction and learning of Christian religion* (1570), textbooks used in Elizabethan grammar schools, were based upon the Prayer Book Catechism with instructions for teaching young students Latin. These Catechisms were published under royal privilege, and linked the virtues of religious learning with those of loyalty to the Crown.

In these and other texts directly related to the Prayer Books, it is difficult to isolate elements of religious instruction from those of personal devotion. The same is true of the Tudor Prayer Books. Although in the services of Baptism and Confirmation specific attention was given to religious instruction, it is not an exaggeration to view the assembled Prayer Book texts as manuals for religious nurture as well as public worship. The repeated Prayer Book emphases of edification, exhortation, preparation, and discipline encouraged individual and corporate learning and a lively faith.

The schedule of daily offices, the yearly liturgical cycle of word and sacrament, and the flow of services marking major turning points throughout a person's life were all instruments for continuing growth in the Christian life.

In addition to the Great Books, the official texts of the English Reformation, Tudor presses throughout Edward VI's and Elizabeth I's reigns continued to produce a host of religious materials. Most of these texts were advertised under the common by-words of clarity, simplicity, brief instruction, necessary edification, and other such phrases. Abridgements, commentaries, and concordances of biblical materials proliferated. One popular volume was an anonymous text boldly entitled, *A bryefe summe of the whole byble. A christyan instruction for all parsons* (1548?). Robert Crowley (1518-88), an energetic printer and commonwealth reformer, underscored the worth and clarity of biblical materials in prefatory remarks to his 1549 metrical version of the Psalter:

> This have I done, to move thee to delyte in the readynge and hearynge of these Psalmes, wherin lyeth hyd the most preciouse treasures of the christian religion. And so far as my knowledge woulde serve me: I have made open and playne, that which in other translations is obscure & harde (Crowley, 1549, sig. ++ i—++ ii).

A similar theme was sounded in an anonymous aid to biblical study, *A Postill or Collection of moste Godly Doctrine through the year, as well for Holye dayes as Sondayes, dygested in suche order, as they bee appoynted and set forth in the booke of Common Prayer*. The remarkable preface to this text is worth citing at length for its appreciation of scriptural instruction:

> Truly it [this text] muste needes be a spurre unto the ydle, dul and negligent curates, bicause the doctrine hereof is so brief, simple and plaine, that a cyllye woman or poore prentyse occupyinge theimselves the whole weeke in their vocacion, onlye with the studynge and learnynge of this booke upon the sondaye and hollyedaye, shall within one yeare be better able to teach hereafter their own householdes, then many curats do now instructe their congregacion committed to their cure and charg. At whose hand, without fayl, the Lorde wyll requyre the bloude of everyone of their flock that perisheth for lack of godly teching (1550, no pagin.).

Yet another guide, typical of those printed by Tudor reformers, was a translation of Urbanus Regius' text on biblical themes. This lengthy document, *The righte foundation and principall comon places of the hole godly scripture*, was dedicated to Thomas Cranmer and advertised to be of use to all people (Regius, 1548 ed.).

Vernacular introductions to theology were also published. One of the simplest was by John Foxe (c. 1516-87), *A most breefe manner of Instruction to the principles of Christian Religion*. In his preface Foxe stated that he had attempted "to drawe out a few questions, with Aunsweres annexed and adjoined, verie fitte for the simpler sorte, both of youth and age, that are so long and harde to learne" (1550, sig. Aii^r). Foxe, like the author of *A Postill*, was concerned that injunctions urging parish education be better enforced. Robert Hutten translated an introductory theological textbook for curates, *The Sum of Divinity drawn out of the Holy Scriptures* (1548). This text was reprinted four times during Elizabeth's reign. There were also numerous tracts on popular theological issues. Many polemics printed in Edward VI's reign exposed differences between the doctrines and practices of the Protestant sacrament of the Lord's Supper and the papist mass. These tracts were designed for a general reading audience, as in Richard Tracy's text on the meaning of the eucharist, *A most godly enstruction and verie necessary lesson to be learned of all christen men and women* (1548). In Elizabeth's reign other issues of the day, for example, the debate over eucharistic vestments, were enthusiastically argued by popular pamphleteers. The Tudor appetite for religious controversy was vast. Popular polemical literature and the preaching of godly sermons were significant components in religious education.

The basic educational materials and methods of the newly reformed church were in place by the end of Edward's reign. These included the Prayer Books, English Bibles, the *Paraphrases* of Erasmus, the Book of Homilies, an official Catechism, royal primers, and other polemical and devotional materials. Elizabethans augmented, but did not change the character, of these primary resources. Instruction on the Catechism in the parish and at home provided the foundation upon which sermons, public debate, private and corporate study built. The processes for religious instruction permeated Tudor society for literate and illiterate, clergy and laity, rich and poor, young and old alike. The on-going task of nurturing citizens of the Tudor commonwealth in godly living commanded a variety of resources.

RELIGIOUS EDUCATION WITHIN THE TUDOR FAMILY

A survey of religious education in Tudor society would not be complete without a brief excursus into the role assigned to the family of nurturing youth and other household members in the faith. Emphatic provision for religious education in the Tudor household was, along with methods and materials designed for instructing men, women and children in the parish, a crucial component in generating fidelity to *Anglicana Ecclesia*. It was the household, not the schoolroom, which for many citizens became the center of daily religious nurture. Tudor reformers from the 1540's onward were adamant that the responsibilities of raising generations of godly children in large measure depended upon domestic instruction. The family provided the foundation for both public order and Christian virtue. As one author of a 1598 manual for household instruction asserted: "Well (we say) let there be never so good lawes in Cities, never so pure order in Churches, if there be no practice at home" (Cawdrey, 1630 ed., sig. T6ᵛ). Recent scholarship on the English family has illustrated the significance of the family, the basic societal unit, as the context in which social and religious change intersected.* The following analysis examines the educational responsibilities and methods which reformers delegated to parental instruction of youth. The literature upon which this study is based—sermons, tracts and domestic manuals printed in England between 1540 and 1610, and the few extant diaries of middle and upper-class families— indicates buoyant and insistent pressure to make Tudor households "seminaries of the commonwealth" (Perkins, 1616-18 ed., p. 671).

The importance of the family in religious life must be viewed within the context of reformation theology which signaled fundamental changes in the ways of looking at marriage and at the roles of parenthood. Reformers on the Continent and in England argued for the superiority of married life and, with prohibitions removed from clerical marriage, praised the role of marriage for providing a yoked or spiritual partnership in the faith. Reformers also viewed the family as a school of faith wherein both parents

---

*The most comprehensive history of the English family is Lawrence Stone, *The Family, Sex and Marriage in England, 1500-1800* (New York: Harper and Row, 1977). *See also* Jane Renner Hood, "The Impact of Protestantism on the Renaissance Ideal of Women in Tudor England" (unpublished Ph.D. dissertation, University of Nebraska-Lincoln, 1977).

shared a divine vocation to teach and instill godliness in children, apprentices, and servants (Douglas, 1974, pp. 292-318). While reformers stressed the common duties of parents in which the husband held final authority, the religious role of the wife was clearly asserted. Johann Heinrich Bullinger and Thomas Becon, authors of popular mid-century household manuals, argued that women needed to reclaim their responsibilities as domestic educators:

> It is not lawful for women to teach in the congregation openly . . . notwithstanding, women to preach and teach in their own houses, it is not only not forbidden, but also most straightly commanded. For who knoweth not that every man and every woman is a bishop in their own house, and ought to teach their family (Becon, 1844 ed., II, 376; cf. Bullinger, 1543, sig. BV^v).

Others suggested that the honor of the wife depended upon the quality of her religious nurture and commended a religious wife as "especially needful, both for instruction of her family and education of her children" (Heale, 1609, p. 35). It is not surprising that there is evidence for improved education of women in this period (Stone, 1964, p. 43). The responsibilities for bringing up children in knowledge and fear of God weighed heavily upon both parents.

The practical details and ideals for religious training were fully described in a plethora of treatises on domestic relations. John Hooper stated succinctly in a 1548 tract on the Ten Commandments that parents' duties included teaching their children the use and meaning of the Catechism, the virtue of prayer, the danger of sin, and the right use of the sacraments (Hooper, 1843 ed., p. 360). Work on this considerable agenda was to begin in infancy. "Even from the cradle" parents were instructed to bring up their children in "fear and nurture of the Lord" (Cawdrey, 1630 ed., sig. Q1^r). This timing was in accord with the exhortation in the Prayer Book service for Public Baptism that children be taught to lead a godly life "so soon as they shall be able to learn" (Booty ed., 1976, p. 276). The underlying assumption was that the early years, from birth to seven years of age, were most formative for inculcating godliness.

The reformers assumed that it was the responsibility of parents to teach children to read and write as they introduced them to the rudiments of the faith. Josiah Nichols in a 1596 guide to domestic life, *An Order of Household Instruction*, set forth a course of gradual instruction which was paralleled in other treatises. Children were first taught godly words and phrases, then short sentences and stories from Scripture, then the Commandments followed by the remainder of the Catechism. Major emphasis was appropriately given to teaching children to read the Bible, that (in Cranmer's words) "sweet milk" and "pappe of goddes holy word." Biblical literacy was the supreme treasure and blessing which parents could bestow upon their offspring. Besides, as Cranmer noted, parents would themselves benefit by hearing their children speak and learn of God (Cranmer, 1548, sig. iiii^r and vi^r). Finally parents were directed to enlighten their children in the doctrines and practices of the faith through a total program of family and public worship, daily study and meditation, and the ever-present instruction in the Catechism. The Prayer Book Catechism provided the most popular base for Christian education in the home as in the parish. Although there were no sixteenth-century storybooks specifically designed for children, the abundance of primers and catechisms tailored to assist children in discovering the biblical and theological foundations of their faith is testimony to the reformation commitment to early childhood education.

The reformers and authors of domestic guides were not unaware of the rigors implied in their scheme for early religious education. They cautioned parents to adapt the pace of training that suited each child best. Christian parenthood was to bear the marks of gentle, measured learning. John Jones, author of a 1579 tract on household casuistry, told parents that "children shall not be enforced to learn by too muche threatening, & over many strokes, for that may be daunting to infants . . . but that they shall rather with good examples, faire allurement, & fine behest" be enticed to master the principles of the faith (Jones, 1579, p. 63). The entire course for educational and spiritual formation was envisioned as filled with delights and comfort for diligent parents and children, and peril for those who neglected their duties:

> if thou despiseth these duties, the Lord will denie thee these blessings, and the curse of God will fall upon the childe, at home in thy house, abroad in the Church (Cawdrey, 1630 ed., sig. R7^v).

Apparently the energies which reformers directed toward elevating the educational responsibilities and theological significance of parenthood did, in some families, strengthen provision for domestic instruction. Elizabethan visitation records indicate the church's continuing concern for encouraging parents to present children for parish instruction. Funeral sermons and other memorial documents, in particular a genre of morality texts written by or about a dying mother, confirm the preoccupation many parents had with the religious education of their offspring. There are similar testimonies to the practices of domestic religious training in contemporary diaries. These journals record children's appreciation for their mother's role in religious nurture, as in Anne Halkett's description of her youth:

> My mother's greatest care, that for which I shall ever owne to her memory the highest gratitude, was the great care she tooke that, even from our infancy, wee were instructed never to neglect to begin and end the day with prayer, and orderly every morning to read the Bible, and ever to keepe the church as often as there was occasion to meet there, either for prayers or preaching (Nichols, ed., Halkett, p. 2).

These and other sources bespeak a lively concern for making the household a center of religious education and virtuous living. The energy and attention devoted by Tudor reformers to describing the ethics of household management are evidence of the prominence which the family, like the parish, held as a nursery and seminary for the Christian commonwealth.

In the final analysis, the challenge of setting the newly reformed Church of England on sound educational foundations, despite the medieval and humanist inheritance, was considerable. Major institutions and vocations in Tudor society contributed to this enterprise. Parliaments, ecclesiastical judicatories, monarchs and counselors, humanists and reformers, poets and pamphleteers, the family, and the printing trade all provided resources for religious training. The historical response to the question of how the church taught during the Reformation yields a rich collage of materials and methods, goals and directions. Bibles, Prayer Books, catechisms, primers, devotional and theological tracts, sermons, aids to scriptural study, ABC's, manuals for family and personal devotion were all part of the picture. Less tangible—yet at least as significant—were the energy, zeal, and discipline which many citizens devoted to the work of building the new Jerusalem in the Tudor commonwealth. The establishment of the Church of England, a faith both reformed and catholic, is in large measure testimony to the success of these efforts. The Tudor educational endowment for future generations of Anglicans was equally rich.

BIBLIOGRAPHY

Primary Sources

Bale, John, *The Actes of Englyshe Votaryes, comprehendynge their unchast practyses and examples of all ages.* Wesel?, 1546.

Becon, Thomas, *Works*, 2 vols. Edited by J. Ayre for The Parker Society. Cambridge: University Press, 1844.

Booty, John E., ed., *The Book of Common Prayer, 1559.* Charlottesville: University Press of Virginia, 1976.

A bryefe summe of the whole byble. A christyan instruction for all parsons. London, 1548?.

Bullinger, Juan Heinrich, *The godly boke of Christen matrimonye.* London, 1543.

Cawdrey, R., *A Godly Form of Household Government.* Amended and augmented by John Dod and Robert Cleaver. London, 1630 (first edition, 1598).

Certain Sermons or Homilies Appointed to be Read in Churches in the Time of Queen Elizabeth. London: S.P.C.K., 1851.

Cranmer, Thomas, *Catechismus. That is to say a shorte Instruction into Christian Religion for the synguler commoditie and profyte of children and young people.* London, 1548.

―――――, *The Works of Thomas Cranmer*, 2 vols. Edited by J. C. Cox for The Parker Society. Cambridge: University Press, 1844-46.

Crowley, Robert, *The Psalter of David newely translated into Englyshe metre.* London, 1549.

Foxe, John, *A most breefe manner of Instruction to the principles of Christian Religion.* London, 1550.

Frere, W. H. and Kennedy, W. M., eds., *Visitation Articles and Injunctions of the Period of the Reformation*, 3 vols. London: Longmans, Green & Co., 1910.

Furnivall, Frederick J., ed., *Ballads from Manuscripts*, 2 vols. Printed for the Ballad Society. London: Taylor and Co., 1868-72.

A goodly dyalogue between Pyers plowman, and a popyshe pryest. London, c. 1550.

Grindal, Edmund, *The Remains.* Edited by S. Carr for The Parker Society. Cambridge: University Press, 1843.

Heale, William, *An Apologie for Women.* Oxford, 1609.

Hooker, Richard. *Works*, 3 vols. Edited by John Keble, revised by R. W. Church and F. Paget. Oxford: Clarendon Press, 1888.

Hooper, John, *Early Writings*. Edited by S. Carr for The Parker Society. Cambridge: University Press, 1843.

Jones, John, *The Arte and Science of preserving Bodie and Soule in all Health, Wisdome, and Catholike Religion*. London, 1579.

Ketley, Joseph, ed., *The Two Liturgies, 1549 & 1552, in the Reign of Edward VI*. The Parker Society. Cambridge: University Press, 1844.

Knell, Thomas, *An ABC to the christen congregacion Or a patheway to the heavenly Habitation*. London, 1550?.

Latimer, Hugh, *The Works of Hugh Latimer*, 2 vols. Edited by G. E. Corrie for The Parker Society. Cambridge: University Press, 1844-45.

Morrison, Richard, *A Remedy for Sedition*. London, 1536.

Nichold, John G., ed., *The Autobiography of Anne Lady Halkett*. The Camden Society, new series, No. 13.

Nichols, Josiah, *An Order of Household Instruction*. London, 1596.

Nowell, Alexander, *A Catechism*. Edited by G. E. Corrie for The Parker Society. Cambridge: University Press, 1853.

Perkins, William, *Christian Oeconomie* in *Workes*, 3 vols. London, 1616-18 ed.

Ponet, John, *A Short Catechisme*. Edited by T. H. L. Parker in *English Reformers*, Vol. 26. The Library of Christian Classics. Philadelphia: Westminster Press, 1966.

A Postill or Collection of moste Godly Doctrine through the year, as well for Holye dayes as Sondayes, dygested in suche order, as they bee appoynted and set forth in the booke of Common Prayer. London, 1550.

A Primer or book of private prayer needful to be used of all faithful Christians, Which book is authorized and set forth by the King's Majesty, to be taught, learned, read, and used of all his loving subjects. London, 1553.

The Primer set forth by the King's Majesty and his clergy; to be taught, learned, and read and none other to be used throughout all his dominions. London, 1545.

Regius, Urbanus, *The Olde learynge and the new, compared together whereby it may easily be knowen which of them is better and more agreeing wyth the everlasting word of God*. London, 1548.

_____, *The righte foundation and principall comon places of the hole godly scripture*. London, 1548.

Spangenberg, Johann, *The Sum of Divinity drawn out of the Holy Scriptures*. Translated by R. Hutten. London, 1548.

Tracy, Richard, *A most godly enstruction and verie necessary lesson to be learned of all christen men and women.* London, 1548.

Turner, William, *A new Dialogue Wherin is conteyned the examination of the Messe: and of that kind of priesthode, which is ordeyned to say messe.* London, 1548?.

Tyndale, William, *Works*, 3 vols. Edited by H. Walter for The Parker Society. Cambridge: University Press, 1849-50.

V., R., *The olde fayth of greate Brittaygne and the newe learnynge of England.* London, 1549?.

Secondary Sources

Booty, John E., ed., Siegenthaler, David, and Wall, John W., *The Godly Kingdom of Tudor England: Great Books of the English Reformation.* Scheduled for publication in 1981 by Morehouse-Barlow Co., Wilton, CT.

Brightman, Frank Edward, *The English Rite: Being a Synopsis of the Sources and Revisions of the Book of Common Prayer*, 2 vols. London: Rivingtons, 1915.

Davies, Horton, *Worship and Theology in England, From Cranmer to Hooker, 1534-1603.* Princeton: University Press, 1970.

Dickens, A. G., *The English Reformation.* New York: Schocken Books, 1964.

Douglass, Jane Demsey, "Women and the Continental Reformation," *Religion and Sexism.* Edited by R. R. Ruether. New York: Simon and Schuster, 1974.

Eisenstein, Elizabeth L., "The Advent of Printing and the Problem of the Renaissance," *Past and Present*, No. 45 (1969), 19-89.

Elton, G. R., *The Tudor Constitution.* Cambridge: The University Press, 1962.

Hood, Jane Renner, "The Impact of Protestantism on the Renaissance Ideal of Women in Tudor England." Unpublished Ph.D. dissertation, University of Nebraska-Lincoln, 1977.

Jordan, Wallace K., *Edward VI: The Young King, The Protectorship of the Duke of Somerset.* London: George Allen & Unwin Ltd., 1968.

————, *Edward VI: The Threshold of Power, The Dominance of the Duke of Northumberland.* Cambridge: Belknap Press of Harvard University Press, 1970.

Maclure, Millar, *The Paul's Cross Sermons, 1534-1642.* Toronto: University of Toronto Press, 1958.

Price, Douglas F., "Gloucester Diocese under Bishop Hooper," *Transactions of the Bristol and Gloucestershire Archaeological Society*, LX (1939), 50-151.

Procter, Francis and Frere, W. H., *A New History of the Book of Common Prayer*. London: Macmillan and Co., 1902.

Simon, Joan, *Education and Society in Tudor England*. Cambridge: University Press, 1966.

Stone, Lawrence, "The Educational Revolution in England, 1560-1640." *Past and Present*, No. 28 (1964), 41-80.

_____, *The Family, Sex and Marriage in England, 1500-1800*. New York: Harper and Row, 1977.

Wood, Norman, *The Reformation and English Education*. London: George Routledge & Sons, 1931.

Roman Catholicism

Chapter 7
Evolution of Catechesis from the Catholic Reformation to the Present

Mary Charles Bryce, O.S.B.

INTRODUCTION

When, in 1551, the Catholic ruler of Austria, King Ferdinand, commissioned leading scholars of the Roman Church to produce a manual to counteract the growing popularity and spread of the reformers' doctrine and practice, he affirmed the trend already defined by Luther and imitated by numerous others, namely that of producing concise handbooks of instructions for the faithful, especially for children. Between the Protestants and Catholics the production of those compendiums of Christian doctrine, "catechisms," kept printing presses busy. On the part of Catholics it appeared to be a matter of fighting fire with fire—of attempting to stem the swelling tide of Protestant reform with the very instrument which some considered the principal vehicle for popularizing that reform. More significantly, however, the productions of those manuals set the pattern of catechizing in the Roman Church for the next four hundred years.

Dominant Characteristics

As one reviews the long sweep of history from the Reformation to the present, three characteristics emerge which dominated and ultimately defined the ministry of catechizing. First, catechesis became identified with a printed manual; secondly, catechesis was directed principally to children and youth; and finally, in relation to the first two, formal catechesis came to be associated with schooling—to the point that it was almost synonymous with textbooks and classrooms. It is necessary to examine these characteristics in some detail if one is to understand the strengths and weaknesses of the Roman Church's catechizing ministry in the period since the Reformation.

Catechesis: More Than a Catechism

The desire to capture Christian truths in a handbook dates back at least to Augustine's day, when his friend Laurentius asked him for a manual of Christian doctrine. Augustine responded with his famous treatise on faith, hope, and charity in the course of which he wisely counseled his friend that "the true way to obtain this instruction is not to have a short treatise put into one's hands, but to have great zeal kindled in one's heart" (ch. 6). In late medieval time manuals of devotions and small handbooks to prepare penitents for the Sacrament of Penance began to proliferate. They offered some instruction but were not intended to present concise and comprehensive summaries of Christian doctrine.

With the advent of the printing press, however, publishing catechisms offered the reformers, both Protestant and Catholic, an opportunity they could hardly resist. Nor should they have done so. A vast ignorance abounded regarding what it meant to be Christian, what were the principal doctrines of Christianity, and what the sacramental life was all about. Dispelling that ignorance was important, but to counter it with informational data alone and contain it within the binding of a small or even a large manual was expecting very much. Gradually, almost imperceptibly, an exaggerated responsibility descended on the catechism, a responsibility it neither could nor should have sustained.*

---

*The history of catechisms laces in and out of the present study and relies generally on the following works: Guy de Bretagne, "History of the Text-Book," *Lumen Vitae*, 5 (1950), 470-76; Jean Claude D'hotel, *Les Origines du Catéchisme Moderne* (Paris: Aubier, 1966); Michael Gatterer, S. J. and Franz Krus, S. J., *The Theory and Practice of the Catechism*, Trans. J. B. Culemans (New York: Frederick Pustet & Co., 1919); Chanoine Hezard, *Histoire de Catéchisme* (Paris: Librairie Victor-Retaux, 1900); Christoph Moufang, *Katholische Katechismen des sechszehnten Jahrhunderts in deutscher Sprache* (Mainz: Franz Kirchheim, 1881). Specific references will be noted in the corpus.

Catechesis: Not Just for Children

In the oldest tradition catechesis was almost exclusively associated with the enculturation of adults into the Christian community. By nature, however, catechesis is life-long. It is for all Christians, though the approaches and emphases may vary according to the individuals involved—their ages, the cultural, economic, and societal circumstances in which they live, etc. The almost exclusive concentration on children's catechesis which steadily developed in the Catholic Reformation era was in sharp contrast to earlier times.

New Setting for Catechesis

The call for education for the children of the poor, the lower and middle classes as well as those from society's upper and wealthy strata was one that had been sounded for some time. The proliferation of catechisms in dioceses and regions, along with the strong movement to provide schooling for all, collaborated in allocating catechesis into an educational setting. As universal schooling and compulsory education* became realities with school textbooks integral to classroom learning, catechisms became part and parcel of formal education. That fact applied to state schools as well as to those under church auspices.

In the sixteenth-century schools of western Germany the curriculum comprised reading, writing, catechism, and music. Even John Sturm (1507-1589), no great devotee of religion, insisted on the memorization of Luther's catechism. His motive may indeed have been to develop pupils' skills in memorizing, or it may

---

*Compulsory education in the post-Reformation period was eventually mandated. The Synod of Nijmegen in Holland legislated it in 1606. In 1619 children ages six to twelve in Germany were to attend school regularly. Gotha ordered it in 1642, Denmark in 1712, England in 1802, and France in 1882. A law of Massachusetts in 1642 asserted the commonwealth's right to train children to read and write and be versed in the principles of religion but it made no mention of schools as such. In 1852 Massachusetts required all children between eight and fourteen to attend school seven and a half months a year. From that time on until 1918 the other states in the Union enacted similar legislation. Cf. Frederick Eby and C. F. Arrowood, *The Development of Modern Education* (New York: Prentice-Hall, 1934), pp. 131, 557-59, 616, 378, 881-82; S. E. Frost, Jr., *Historical and Philosophical Foundations of Western Education* (Columbus: Charles Merrill Books, 1966), pp. 254-58, 306, 311, 433-34.

have been a diplomatically wise requirement on his part; but for whatever reason it was included on the regular program. It was the patterned procedure in Catholic schools, as well. "Teaching the catechism," and "learning the catechism," became the accepted description for religion classes in schools during the last half of the sixteenth century and down to recent times.

In subsequent centuries both the schools and the catechisms were held responsible for catechesis. They were complemented at least up through the eighteenth century by a stable Christian environment. Both the family and church-going congregations gave credence in the home, in the parish, and in the broader Christian community to the message memorized in the classroom. Thus catechesis was not limited to four walls, rows of desks, and a question-answer manual. Consciously or not, the Church continued to rely on the living witness of a faithful and practicing community in "handing on" the living Christian message.

I INITIAL SIXTEENTH-CENTURY MOVES

One major result of the sixteenth-century Reformation was to effect the reform movement in the Roman Catholic Church, a movement that had early champions but seemed to require a crisis to gain the needed thrust for sustained renewal.

The Council of Trent became the focus and force for the reform effort in the church. Meeting sporadically for eighteen years (1545-1563), it aimed at ordering and clarifying Catholic doctrine and legislating church reform. It was in that context that Trent addressed the matter of catechesis both directly and indirectly.

Indirectly, Trent confronted the existing state of intellectual ignorance by urging the opening, and in some cases, the reopening of parish schools. It mandated the establishment of seminaries in dioceses where none existed and prescribed the curriculum for them. The objective was to produce a pastoral and well-educated clergy, a matter easier to legislate than to implement. In time the reform, long needed and called for slowly but steadily, became effective.

Trent's Catechism

Facing the issue of catechesis directly, the Council, in its fourth session in April 1546, decreed that a catechism be written. The original plan was to provide a catechism for children and unedu-

cated adults. In the course of events, little was done on the matter.
In 1562, after the catechism issue had lain dormant for some
time, it came before the Council again. The assembly acted by
recruiting a new committee of theologians under Cardinal Charles
Borromeo's leadership. After considerable discussion the committee
proposed a new plan. That plan specified that the catechism
would be a source book for the use of parish priests in their preaching to and instruction of the faithful.* In December 1566, three
years after the Council's last session, the volume appeared. Its
official title was *Catechismus ex decretis Concilii Tridentini
ad parochos* ("The Catechism of the Council of Trent for the
Clergy"), but it became known popularly as the "Roman Catechism." Written in expository prose with no questions and answers,
it was more like Calvin's *Institutes* than Luther's catechism. It
treated the Creed first, then the sacraments, the commandments,
and, finally, the "Our Father" as the model for prayer. In adopting
that sequence Trent's catechism indicated how integral sacraments
are to Christian doctrine and life.

The work was avowedly apologetic though it contained only
one general reference to "poisonous doctrines" ("Introduction,"
p. 15) and refrained from naming particular points. The ends of
catechizing were cited in the introduction: knowledge of Christ,
love of God, and observance of commandments. Those introductory pages also insisted that instruction should be accommodated
to the circumstances and capacity of the catechized; hence age,
ability, environment, particular status, etc., were to be taken
into account by the instructor or catechist.

A notable lacuna in the Trent catechism was the treatment of
Scripture. Gone was the biblical narrative of saving events extolled
by Augustine in *De catechizandis rudibus* and carried on by
Boniface (672-754), Alcuin (735-804), Pirmin of Reichenau (d.
754), and other medieval missionaries in central Europe. The
sixteenth century was a time of defining theological doctrines and
transmitting them as clearly as possible to the faithful. Biblical
references were sought and cited to prove the veracity of the

---

*In the introduction to their translation of Trent's catechism McHugh and
Callen provide a brief history of the Council's deliberations and decisions
regarding the manual. *See* John A. McHugh and Charles J. Callan,
Catechism of the Council of Trent for Parish Priests (New York: Joseph F.
Wagner, Inc., 1923) pp. xxiii-xxv. *See also Dictionnaire Théologie Catho-
lique*, II, 2, pp. 1917ff.

formulae but no concentration on the Bible as a whole was included. Thus Scripture became a "theological source book" instead of the center of catechesis. The contention was that the Bible required authentic interpretation; indiscriminate reading of the Bible in the vernacular was therefore viewed as dangerous.

Trent's original text, which is not extant, appeared in a continuous, monotonous form without paragraph, chapter, or sectional divisions. At the insistence of Pope Pius V it was eventually divided and sub-divided into a more appealing and readable format. Written in Latin, the volume was later translated into German, French, and Italian. The first English version came out in 1675 and included only the first two parts. Fifteen years later a complete English translation appeared.

Despite the catechism's slow start it gained in popularity and came to enjoy enormous universal appeal. The clergy used it as a guide for homilies as well as for catechizing. Pope Gregory XIII (1572-1585) called it the norm of Catholic teaching and discipline. Leo XIII (1878-1903) recommended it and the *Summa* of Thomas Aquinas as the two works with which seminarians should be thoroughly acquainted. Numerous diocesan and provincial synods made its use obligatory for convert classes and instruction courses. Attesting to the volume's popularity are the one hundred different editions of the catechism among the holdings of Catholic University in Washington, D. C.

Canisius, Innovator and Model

While Trent was working its way through the labyrinth of proposals, recommendations, debates, and the like, life went on. It was in that period that Ferdinand called for assistance for the people in his kingdom. His call did not go unheeded. Dutch-born Peter Canisius (1521-1597) responded. A man of great kindness and generosity, he had as his dearest ambition, according to one biographer, "the religious instruction and formation of youth" (Brodrick, 1950, p. 22). Canisius wrote three catechisms. His first, *Summa Doctrinae Christianae*, earned Ferdinand's praise and commendation when it appeared in 1555. That volume, first published anonymously, was written in Latin and directed to undergraduates and pupils in classes comparable to our advanced high school years. Canisius intentionally addressed students capable of following an easy theological inquiry. The questions were direct and brief, the answers, deliberately lucid and logical, varied in length from a half to four pages. Obviously they were for thoughtful assimilation, not for parrot memorization.

The corpus of his *Summa* was simple but comprehensive. As an overall theme Canisius relied on an admonition from Sirach: "If you desire wisdom, keep the commandments, and the Lord will bestow her upon you" (Sir. 1:23). Thus he divided his volume into two parts: doctrine of wisdom and doctrine of justice. Following Augustine, he held that wisdom has for its object the three theological virtues: faith, hope, and charity. His manual treated faith in the articles of the Apostles' Creed on the basis that what the Christian believes is summarized there. What one hopes and prays for is found in the Our Father, while true charity is expressed in observing the Ten Commandments. The "justice" part dealt with avoiding evil and doing good—on which depends God's bestowal of wisdom. The two sections were linked by a treatise on the sacraments, described as necessary both for the "keeping" of justice and the acceptance of wisdom. Actually, as the title indicates, the book was more a compendium of theology than a catechism as one has come to identify the latter today.

In assessing his "God's word-humankind's response" approach, one cannot, at the outset, fail to suspect a faint Pelagian strain in the work. A deeper study, however, discloses the emphasis on God's initiative in the total salvation experience. Canisius consistently kept sight of the gift-character of Christian life and faith. For example, he perceived wisdom as more than a characteristic of human cognition.

> Wisdom is concerned, according to Augustine, with the theological virtues: faith, hope, and charity which are infused by God, and when they are especially cherished in this life, they render one happy and God-like. (Canisius, 1842, p. 5).

The *Summa* received an enthusiastic welcome. That is somewhat surprising considering its style and size, 202 pages. It sold well and within a year's time was translated into German and circulated even more widely.

Canisius was not content with addressing the inquiries and needs of those on the threshold of adulthood. In the following year, 1556, he published his so-called "Shortest Catechism" for small children. Written as an appendix to a Latin grammar, that catechism differed from his *Summa* in at least two ways: its fifty-nine questions and most of their answers were terse and memorizable and it included a series of prayers for all occasions—morning, evening, at meal-time, when the clock strikes, prayers for the needs of all Christians. When one considers that prayer was the very breath of life for Canisius, the inclusion of specific prayers in that "shortest" of his catechisms should cause no surprise. Furthermore, it demonstrated his belief that catechesis was not limited to the imparting of doctrinal information.

One youthful group still had no catechism addressed to them— children in the middle years. So Canisius began work on what became his most widely acclaimed manual. In it, questions-answers, illustrations, and prayers combined to form an appealing volume of information and instruction. It came out in 1558.

The genius of Canisius is that he was able to communicate the doctrine and spirit of what it meant to be Christian in a way that was neither defensive nor "armed to the teeth against assailants" (Chadwick, 1970, p. 264). His manuals conveyed an unction that few, if any, later catechisms were able to capture. At the same time his works were informative and doctrinally sound, all of which may account for their perduring popularity which extended well into the nineteenth century.

To focus on this man whose great preoccupation in life was to provide manuals "suited to the needs of Germans,"* as he had written to a friend in March, 1550, is also to perceive the form and direction of catechesis within Roman Catholicism for approximately four centuries.

Schools and Religious Communities

In the sixteenth century religious orders assumed fresh vigor in response to the acute spiritual and social needs of the day. As older communities shifted their efforts and attention to meet the demands of the period, there also sprang up new orders and congregations whose emphasis on apostolic activity and style of life distinguished them from existing groups. Two of the new communities, the Ursulines and the Jesuits, are especially important in the history of catechesis.

The Company of St. Ursula, named after the legendary patroness of education, was founded in 1535 in Brescia by Angela de Merici

---

*Cited in Brodrick, 1950, p.222. The passage came from a letter written to John Polanco, S.J. (1516-1577) who was the Jesuit Secretary-General in Rome at the time. Polanco, with whom he corresponded frequently, was one of Canisius' closest friends.

(1474-1540). Some years earlier she had begun to organize a small group of women to help with the catechetical effort she had undertaken on behalf of young girls. Angela's intention was to combat the teachings of the Protestant reformers and the ignorance which exposed women to all kinds of exploitation.

For the first thirty years of their existence the Ursulines lived with families, gathering girls in homes and the parish church to instruct them in virtue and to impart knowledge of Christian doctrine. In the wake of the Council of Trent and at the insistence of Charles Borromeo, archbishop of Milan, however, they began to live in formal communities. In the seventeenth century most Ursuline communities were given the status of monasteries and thus fell under strict rules that required them to live a cloistered life. It meant that they could no longer go freely among the people to carry on their catechetical ministry. Instead they started schools and girls came to them, some as day-students, others as boarders (Cf. Ledochowska, 1968, II, 107ff).

The number of Ursuline foundations increased rapidly, especially in France. In the seventeenth century other congregations of women committed to education in their own and parish schools came into existence. The Congregation of Notre Dame (1597), the Order of the Visitation (1610), the Sisters of Charity (1633), the Good Shepherd Sisters (1641), the Daughters of Providence (1643), the Sisters of St. Joseph (1650), and the Sisters of Notre Dame de Montreal (1657) are but a few. Like the Ursulines, most of those new congregations were forced to live a cloistered or semi-cloistered life. About the only form of ministry open to them was the schooling of girls and young women.

Jesuits: Educators, Catechists

The sixteenth century also saw the birth of new men's communities, but it is the Society of Jesus that is generally credited with being the most effective force in the Catholic Reformation. They did the most to inaugurate new catechetical approaches and to promote the cause of Catholic education among the upper classes.

Early in the 1520's Ignatius of Loyola (1491-1556), convalescing from a war-wound, underwent a conversion experience. During this crucial period in his life Ignatius began to compose a small book called the *Spiritual Exercises* which perhaps more than any other single work shaped the Catholic mind in the post-Reformation period. It was not just a book to be read; it was a program of action. The *Spiritual Exercises* consisted of a carefully orchestrated series of detailed instructions on methods of prayer, ways to examine one's conscience, and activities to discern God's will. The thirty-day program was designed to lead the exercitant to make a significant decision about the Christian way of life.

The *Spiritual Exercises* played a major role in recruiting young men to join the Jesuits, but Catholics who never made the Exercises were also influenced by it. At the end of the small volume Ignatius had appended "Rules for Thinking with the Church." They were in fact practical guidelines which affirmed many of the Catholic practices which had been challenged by the Protestant reformers —sacramental confession, frequent communion, veneration of the saints, indulgences, fasts and abstinences, scholastic theology, etc. Ignatius' basic principle was obedience to the church, even to the point of stating, "I will believe the white that I see is black, if the hierarchical Church so defines it" (Rule 13). The Rules for Thinking with the Church, widely disseminated because of their association with the *Spiritual Exercises*, provided both the contents and inspiration for much of the basic catechesis among Roman Catholics into the twentieth century (Bangert, 1972, pp. 8-11, 435-39).

About the time that the Society of Jesus was formally established in 1540, the Jesuits had to face the problem of training the men who had enlisted in their ranks. They began by setting up residences near universities where the scholastics followed courses. In 1545 Francis Borgia founded a training college in Spain at Gandia, to which secular students were later admitted. This marked the beginning of Jesuit schools, and a few years later at Messina they opened their first school in Europe primarily for secular students. Between the time the college in Messina opened in 1548 until his death in 1556, Ignatius had authorized the establishment of thirty-nine schools in Europe alone (Bangert, p. 3-46). The Jesuits were very much aware that their schools were a major force in the Catholic reform. *Puerilis institutio renovatio mundi* ("education of youth, renewal of the world") was both a slogan and a program of action. With the code of studies *ratio studiorum* as a guide, Ignatius' followers sought to instill in their students along with humanistic ideals and basic skills "habits worthy of Christians" (Meyer, 1975, p. 99). Integral to Christian doctrine classes was the catechism and the Jesuits were prolific in the publication of those manuals.

Peter Canisius' work in Germany has already been reviewed. Edmund Auger, S.J. (1515-1591), sometimes dubbed the "Canisius of France," wrote a large manual in 1563 and a smaller one five years later. The two volumes addressed certain Calvinistic positions but avoided a polemical tone (D'Hotel, 1972, p. 57). Written as dialogues instead of as series of concise questions and answers, both books were popular, being reprinted and even translated several times, but they were not known widely outside of France. The catechisms most used in Spain also came from the pens of Jesuits: Jerome Ripalda (1535-1618) published his small catechism in Saragossa two years before his death. It went through at least seven editions, the last of which was recorded in 1890. (The 1892 diocesan synod of the Apostolic Vicariate of Arizona, U.S.A., recommended its use for Spanish-speaking Catholics there.) Gaspar Astete (1537-1601) published a catechism in Salamanca in 1593. It too appeared in numerous editions, the most recent of which was in 1887 (cf. Sommervogel, 1890, Vol. I, Col. 603-608; Vol. VI, Col. 1864-1873).

Bellarmine and his catechisms

The Italian Jesuit, Robert Bellarmine (1542-1621), probably has the distinctive honor of writing the catechism that became universally the most popular of all for Roman Catholics. Two years after Bellarmine's *Dottrina christiana breve* appeared it had been translated into sixty different tongues and dialects. Its enthusiastic acceptance was due in part, no doubt, to the clarity and directness of the questions and answers. They in turn were the results of Bellarmine's own experience as a catechist. He earned an enviable reputation long before he wrote a catechism. His weekly instructions on Christian doctrine given to Jesuit brothers became so popular that laymen began to attend them regularly. He could address inquirers in clear and winning rhetoric and keep them returning for more. Pope Clement VIII (1592-1605) learned of those once-a-week sessions and entreated Bellarmine to put on paper the corpus of his teaching so that it could be promulgated more widely.

Two catechisms were his response to that entreaty. Bellarmine's first manual, *Dottrina christiana breve* (1597), comprised memorizable questions and answers and was meant for children and uneducated adults. The large one, similar to a contemporary teacher's manual, was a complement to the first. It appeared one year after the shorter work. Both volumes treated the Creed, Our Father, Commandments, and Sacraments in that order. A cursory comparison of the two indicates their differences. In the first the teacher was expected to ask the question, the learner to recite the memorized answer. That process was reversed in the larger one. The student questioned and the teacher responded, clarifying and explaining the matter under consideration. Material in each was intended to engage, to make understandable, and to induce reflection. The first inquiry in *Dottrina christiana breve* was: "Are you a Christian?" The response: "By the grace of God, I am."

Bellarmine centered the whole Christian religion on the theological virtues—faith, hope, and charity—and pointed to the sacraments as "tools," or "means of grace," as they came to be called. It was a long way in time and ideal from the early church when the mysteries (sacraments) were understood as participatory events in the saving acts of Christ's passion, death, and resurrection. Bellarmine laid out clearly the accepted theological views of his time and promulgated a pattern which endured for subsequent centuries (Brodrick, 1928, I, 380-90). Furthermore, he sought no acclaim for himself, willingly acknowledging the achievements of others. In fact, some time after his own catechisms were published he discovered those of Peter Canisius and declared that had he known of them, especially the *Summa*, he would have translated them into Italian and promulgated them instead of writing his own (*Ibid.*, p. 250, n. 2).

Confraternity of Christian Doctrine

A movement which became particularly effective in Counter-Reformation catechesis was initiated by an Italian priest in Milan in 1536. Castellino da Castelli (1476-1566) founded the first school especially organized for instructing children in Christian doctrine. That and others like it were not the elementary or secondary schools which were increasing in numbers across the land. Castelli's objective was to acquaint children with the truths of Christianity systematically and thoroughly. He formed *compagnia*, groups of dedicated teachers, for the project. The movement became popular and grew steadily. Trent approved it in 1546 and in 1566 Charles Borromeo (1538-1584) widely implemented the theory and practice throughout his archdiocese under the title of "Confraternity of Christian Doctrine." Associated with catechizing outside the regular school setting, the Confraternity has retained its effectiveness even to the present time. In the United States the CCD has been particularly useful in rural areas and in those places where Catholic schools are few or do not exist.

By the end of the sixteenth century the Roman church was clearly defined in its Tridentine image—compact, strengthened, with a somewhat defensive and static ecclesiology. Catechesis of the period reflected that church. Catechisms relied heavily on theological formulae. Emphasis was on summaries of Christian doctrine in relatively simple, understandable language. The manuals satisfied a critical need and served in preserving a certain purity of doctrine. Gradually they came to be regarded as the sole form of catechizing, with the three major catechisms of Canisius, Trent, and Bellarmine serving as models and sources.

In historical perspective one recognizes the fragmentary character which they presented in contrast to an integrated whole in which the biblical-narrative approach (well-known in the early church and in medieval times), the full experience of the church's sacramental life, and societal witness and testimony were combined with defined doctrinal truths to provide a total on-going catechesis for Christians of every age.

II   THE PATTERN CONFIRMED AND EXTENDED

By the early seventeenth century the catechism mold constructed by the theologian-architects who, consciously or unconsciously, shaped the post-Reformation church, was pretty firmly set. There were those who wished to "color" or "fashion" the product in different ways, but the essential form remained. Schooling was the shape; books, the instrument; and catechized children, the product. Innovators and opportunists tampered with and endeavored to alter the style—sometimes for the better, sometimes not, occasionally as propagators of a particular point of view—but in the end the form remained fixed.

Injection of Historical Narrative

There were those who recognized the inadequacies of the catechism and sought to supply missing elements. Outstanding among them was the great church historian Claude Fleury (1640-

1723). Fleury grew increasingly appalled at the catechisms he saw coming off the presses all around him. Deciding that he himself was knowledgeable in matters of Christian doctrine and that he had a more comprehensive perspective than many writers of his day, he composed a manual of his own. He published it in 1683 and called it, not surprisingly, *Catéchisme Historique*. The first part of Fleury's work was an abridgement of sacred history from Adam to Constantine; the second half a condensation of sacred doctrine, a kind of theological construction of the first portion of the work. The catechism enjoyed phenomenal success in France until 1728 when it was censured for Gallican tendencies.* A corrected edition published at Avignon earned an imprimatur of approval in 1859. To this day Fleury's forty-page introduction on the role of catechesis and especially the catechism is still considered valuable. He indicted the form and content of existing catechisms and stressed the need for doctrinal information rooted in Scripture, the value of the bible story and biblical imagery, significance of liturgy, criticism of scholastic language in catechetics, methods of teaching, the respect due to pupils, the ideal manner of catechists, and a list of notable supplementary texts (cf. Fleury, trans. 1753, pp. i-xi).

The great court preacher, Jacques B. Bossuet (1627-1704) also composed a manual with an historical base. In his work as tutor to the dauphin he wrote *Discours sur l'histoire universelle* (1681) in which he illustrated his conviction that the whole of history is directed by Providence. He confirmed that point in *Le Second Catéchisme* (1687). François Aime Pouget (1666-1723), an Oratorian, was commissioned by the bishop of Montpellier to write a catechism which could be used throughout his diocese. Pouget's work is unique in that not only was it biblico-historically oriented, as were the works of Bossuet and Fleury, but it was written for adults. The book had a seven-line title but was commonly referred to as "The Montpellier Catechism." Pouget justified the elongated caption as a kind of protest to the label "catechism" because the common association of that word identified it with children. The

---

*J. S. Marron reported that Fleury's catechism was used beyond the boundaries of France. In 1753 it was selected for use in the Standon School in England. That school was founded by the zealous bishop Richard Challoner who is responsible for the most widely used catechism in England. *See* Marron, "History of the Penny Catechism," *The Sower*, #125 (1937) p. 201.

work did not enjoy long life or acclaim because of its link with the Jansenist bishop of Montpellier.

None of the historically-oriented volumes of the seventeenth and eighteenth centuries changed the direction or influenced the content of catechisms. The question-answer handbook had become a firmly accepted instrument in catechesis. Nevertheless there were creative approaches to catechesis.

Facing the challenge of social reform in his own way, John Baptist de LaSalle (1651-1719), a French priest, discerned the crying need of the poor for education and set up schools where the less affluent could learn basic skills and the elements of Christian doctrine. He recruited helpers whom he trained as teachers and with them he formed a congregation, the Brothers of the Christian Schools ("Christian Brothers"), in 1684. His followers increased, spreading throughout France and gradually into the whole world. In a way LaSalle was a kindred spirit to the English founder of Sunday Schools, Robert Raikes (1735-1811), whose concerns, like his, were for the poor, especially for the children who worked from dawn to dark in sweat shops, mines, factories, and chimneys. Raikes organized schools for them on Sundays where they could learn the basics—reading, writing, and the catechism.

Catechesis among English-Speaking Roman Catholics

Catechesis in the British Isles centered on catechisms just as it did on the continent. The first known Roman Catholic catechism in the English language was written by Laurence Vaux (1519-1585) who, with a Bachelor of Divinity degree from Oxford, was warden (pastor) of a parish church in the region of Manchester College. Summoned by the ecclesiastical commissioners of Elizabeth I, Vaux fled from his parish and after a period of hiding found refuge in Louvain, Belgium. There he opened a school for children of English exiles. Perceiving the pupils' need for an instructional manual he compiled *A Catechism, or Christian Doctrine necessarie For Children and Ignorante People* (1567). The volume was based in part on the works of Peter Canisius and explained the Apostles' Creed, the Our Father, the Ten Commandments (an extensive treatment), the sacraments, and Christian justice. Vaux returned to England in 1580 at the urging of Roman Catholic authorities to resume "perilous missionary work" there. Accosted at one point by an inimical challenger, he was asked, "What relation are you to that Vaux who wrote a popish catechism in English?" Vaux replied that he was the author. He was immediately imprisoned and five years later died a lingering death. Vaux probably has the distinction of being the first if not the only person specifically martyred for writing a catechism.

The Vaux account points up the role Belgium and France played in the survival and revival of Roman Catholic life and thought in England. The city of Douai (Doway) in northern France became the site of an English college/seminary from which most of England's early bishops and many priests came. St. Omer's and Louvain in Belgium earned similar recognition for their contributions.

The second of the three principal catechisms in England was called the *Doway Catechism*. It was written by Henry Turberville (ca. 1609-1678), a priest of Douai, who was originally from Staffordshire, England. The small manual appeared sometime before 1649 under the title of *Abridgement of Christian Doctrine*. Turberville followed Bellarmine's order of presentation but injected enough additional material and variation of treatment to earn his title as author validly. It was not a simple translation of the Italian Jesuit's work.

The Catholic Christian Instructed, published in 1737, became the most perduring and influential manual among English Catholics. It was written by Richard Challoner (1691-1781), who wrote out of a rich practical experience. Challoner was a catechist who both as priest and later as bishop of London talked with and taught people in the places where they lived, worked, and recreated. For him catechesis had a more expansive connotation than it had for most of his contemporaries. J. D. Crichton described him as one who "sought to provide for the entire religious needs of the people . . . summed up in the Bible, history, doctrine, spiritual reading, meditation, the liturgy (in however narrow a sense), and catechism" (Crichton, 1958, p. 81). Thus the name Challoner is often associated with the best concept of catechesis. Challoner relied on but was not tied to the work of Vaux and Turberville. He is perhaps best known for his revision of the whole Bible—the Douay-Challoner version (1750)—which was the sole Roman Catholic version in use in England and America for nearly 200 years. (*See* Pickering, 1980, pp. 6-15).

The catechism of James Butler (1742-1791), archbishop of Cashel, is almost synonymous with catechesis in Ireland even to the present day. Shortly after he became archbishop in 1774, Butler began visiting all the parishes in his diocese. In the course of that experience he came to realize that the people were in need of more doctrinal bases for their faith. Since a gradual relaxation of the anti-Catholic penal code was in effect, he felt that publication of a catechism was feasible. In 1775 his *Catechism for the Instruction of Children* appeared. It carried no by-line but existing evidence in public records establishes beyond doubt the authorship of Cashel's archbishop (cf. Wallace, 1975, pp. 96-104). The small manual was heartily welcomed by nearby dioceses as well as his own and it soon gained widespread acceptance throughout Ireland. Eventually and with small modifications a revised form of Butler's manual was adopted as the national catechism for Australia.

Meanwhile schooling steadily established itself as the unchallenged setting for catechesis. Religious orders of women and men increased in numbers and the dedication and generosity of those bodies provided testimony to the validity and veracity of their life and teaching. In some ways their institutions were untouched by the movements of the times but in others they could not but be affected. Increased stress on individualism and utilitarian measurement of human actions placed special emphasis on each child, each person, often at the cost of community focus. Rationalism and the Enlightenment steered attention to the relationship of faith to reason. On the whole, however, there was no redirection of the course or form of catechizing, nor any re-writing of the catechism.

III   QUEST FOR UNIFORMITY

At the beginning of the nineteenth century another catechism appeared from an unlikely source. Napoleon Bonaparte, in his campaign to leave his imprint on every aspect of French life, published a catechism. As with the Napoleonic Code, it was part of his design to impose uniformity on the whole country. The *Catéchisme a l'usage de toutes les Églises de l'Empire français* appeared May 1, 1806. The chapter on the Fourth Commandment ("Honor thy father and mother") included statements calling for respect and affection due to authority and pointedly named Napoleon's person and dynasty (cf. Latrielle, 1935). Bishops throughout the country managed to avoid using the volume, and Louis XVIII suppressed the Imperial Catechism in 1814 after

Napoleon's person and dynasty (cf. Latrielle, 1935). Bishops throughout the country managed to avoid using the volume, and

The Catechism of Vatican I

It is a little known fact that the Conciliar Fathers at Vatican I spent more time debating the need for a uniform catechism than they did on infallibility. The proposal was initiated by a Spanish archbishop who suggested that just as Trent had prepared a catechism for the clergy so the 1869-70 Council should prepare one for the faithful. A special commission was assigned to prepare and draw up a proposal to present to the entire assembly. They were instructed to include the recommendations that the universal catechism be modeled on that of Robert Bellarmine and that the catechism, once approved, be mandatory world-wide. The proposal was brought to the floor of the Council and animated debates ensued. Almost all of February 1870 was given to the issue.

A number of bishops opposed the project on the ground of its impracticality, difficulty of implementation, and the complications involved in adapting the proposed manual to regional situations. Felix Dupanloup (1802-1878), bishop of Orleans, spoke powerfully against it, facing the body with the question: "What does this Council want? Unity of doctrine or uniformity of teaching methods?" If the former, unity of doctrine is already provided in the Creed, the Our Father, and the Commandments. If the latter, that is an impossibility considering the differences of ages and circumstances" (cf. Donnellan, 1972, p. 54).

Augustin Verot (1805-1876), bishop of Savannah, was the only bishop from the United States to address the Council on the matter. He vigorously supported the catechism, appealing to the need for a single manual to serve the numerous immigrants in the new country. Debate continued. On May 4, the schema was placed before the Council for a vote; 491 favored it, 56 voted against it, and 44 approved it with certain reservations (Mansi, 1923, LI, 501-512). Other matters diverted the prelates' attention both at the Council and after they returned to their dioceses. Thus no implementation of the project followed and the issue did not rise again until some ninety years later when preparations for Vatican II began.

The idea of uniformity was not dead, however. It surfaced in different parts of the Roman Catholic world in terms of hopes and plans for "national" catechisms. In the United States episcopal reaction against the multiplicity of catechisms had expressed itself from time to time. The First Plenary Council of Baltimore in 1852 named a committee of three bishops to settle the "vexed question" of a uniform catechism. Nothing came of it. Evidently the time was not right. The fact, too, that many earlier U.S. bishops had already written or adopted catechisms for their own dioceses must have played a part in the failure to produce a single manual for the church in the United States.

There was precedent for a certain independence. John Carroll (1735-1815), first Roman Catholic bishop in America, had a catechism which bore his name. In 1808 Boston's first bishop, Jean L. Cheverus (1768-1836), translated Claude Fleury's *Caté-chisme Historique* for the people in his diocese. Henry Conwell (1745-1842), Philadelphia's Irish-born second bishop, borrowed from Butler's manual for the 1827 catechism he composed for Catholics in that city of brotherly love. John England (1786-1842), Charleston's first bishop, was more imaginative and less dependent on existent manuals and wrote his own in 1821. John Baptist David (1761-1841), Auxiliary bishop of Bardstown, wrote a catechism in 1825 which served that Kentucky area for over fifty years. There were many others. Few if any of those works were totally original. Various versions of Canisius' manuals appeared in German-speaking settlements. Several bishops translated catechisms into the tribal languages of Indian people in their dioceses. Chief among them were Frederic Barraga (1797-1868), who authored a catechism for the Ottowa Indians in 1832, and Francis N. Blanchet (1795-1883), who wrote a Chinook Dictionary and catechism in 1838.

One of the most interesting catechisms was that of the English historian John Lingard (1771-1851), whose catechism had come to this country with the immigrants. An 1841 copy carried these questions:

Q. What is the meaning of the word Roman Catholic?

A. It means a Catholic in communion with the see of Rome.

Q. Do you adopt this name?

A. We glory in our communion with the see of Rome, but call ourselves American Catholics.*

*These questions and answers and those following them in the text reveal Lingard's sensitivity to prejudice as it existed in England and in the U.S. His work originally appeared in England in 1836. It was widely used there and evidently enjoyed some popularity in the U.S. inasmuch as two

Periodically the plurality so characteristic of this nation was felt within the church and the desire for uniformity would precipitate a new call for a common catechism. After Vatican I sanctioned the "ideal" of a universal catechism, the idea for a national manual took on fresh vigor. The idea gained adherents and the Third Plenary Council of Baltimore approved the project in 1864. Under the leadership and pen of John L. Spalding (1840-1916), bishop of Peoria, the so-called "Baltimore Catechism" came into existence in 1885. It followed the subject-matter sequence of Trent's manual, but differed very little in quality or content from any of its predecessors (Bryce, 1971, pp. 239-40). Neither did it halt the composition of other catechisms or religious texts.

In retrospect one perceives the rationale behind the quest for a common catechism as a matter of mistaking uniformity for unity, "a single faith, a single catechism" (Donnellan, 1973, p. 123).

IV   OTHER NINETEENTH-CENTURY DEVELOPMENTS

There were healthy signs of church renewal going on simultaneously with the elusive quest for uniformity. These were more like hearty seedlings than full-grown living plants. In the long run, however, they played their part in bringing about a renewal of the church in general, particularly within the area of catechesis because of the integral relation between catechesis and the church-as-experienced. At least six of these signs of renewal need to be identified and commented on briefly.

1. A revised recognition of the liturgy and sacramental life as the heart of the Christian reality. Because of the work and conviction of a Benedictine monk, Prosper Gueranger (1805-75), the church's attention was gradually turned back to the altar, to the Body's worship life of ritual and celebration, as the center and source of the true Christian spirit. The renascence of the spirit of liturgical life that Gueranger initiated at Solesmes Abbey in France from 1833 onward steadily spread throughout the world.

2. The emergence of new vigor in ecclesiastical thought and life. In Germany, especially at Tübingen, an ecclesiology was developed

---

editions were published here. The title reveals a struggle in itself, a struggle for accurate terminology in the area of catechesis. John Lingard, *Catechistical Instructions on the Doctrines and Worship of the Catholic Church*, (New York: P.S. Casserly and Sons, 1841, 2nd ed.) pp. 48-49.

that emphasized the integration of the church's visible structure, the community, with the mystery of interior life. Johann Adam Möhler (1796-1838) is regarded as the great light in seeing the church in that new way, but he did not stand alone. A group of thinkers led by Klemens Shrader (1820-1875) drew up a proposed schema for Vatican I that described and defined the church as the Mystical Body of Christ. The schema was rejected by the majority of the Council Fathers but the concept did not die. Seventy-three years after the close of Vatican I, Pope Pius XII wrote his great encyclical, *Mystici Corporis Christi* (*Acta Apostolicae Sedis*, vol. 35 [1943], 193-248).

   3. *A fresh interest in the development of pastoral theology.* One might argue that the church has an unbroken tradition of pastoral theology, but it must be acknowledged at the same time that a poorly trained clergy and neglect of pastoral duties have played their part in undermining the pastoral emphasis of the church's life. Johann M. Sailer (1751-1832) is regarded by many as the founder of the science of pastoral theology. He and his colleagues rejected the notion that education—seminary or otherwise—was just a matter of intellectual formation. Instead they stressed the formation of the whole person in its psychic, moral, affective, and physical aspects instead of the training of the intellect alone.

   In this renewal of pastoral theology the term "catechetics" appeared for the first time in Christian literature. It was used to designate the characteristics, theory, practice, and history of that branch of pastoral theology that deals with catechesis. In short, catechetics became the name of the discipline of catechizing. At least two periodicals were founded at that time to treat issues and theories related to catechetics. *Katechetische Blätter*, founded in Munich, published its first number in 1875 and continues its monthly publication today. Austria's *Christliche Pädagogische* began its publication in 1887. A bi-monthly, this journal also enjoys unbroken publication to this day.

   4. *New recognition of the value of patristic studies and of their meaning for the church in all ages.* Jacques Paul Migne (1800-1875) began to examine the church's early history in order to "discover his own roots." He sensed that the church fathers could not have perceived doctrine in isolation from experience, that orthodoxy was to be found in a study of orthopraxy. He wanted the vitality

of the Christian past to be available to every Christian. For him it was necessary "to look backward" in order to be able "to go forward." Thus he began carefully and painstakingly to collect and publish the patristic texts, his corpus eventually extending to 221 volumes of the Latin fathers and 162 of the Greek. Reference to his edition is still the standard means of citing patristic texts. The "return to the fathers" began with his work.

5. *A call for a return to the historical narrative of Scripture.* "We live in troubled times; but it is the Gospel, not the works of scholasticism, which has been promised unerring validity from on high," observed Johannes B. Hirscher (1788-1826), professor of moral and pastoral theology at Tübingen, thus advocating the presentation of the doctrine of salvation in biblical, historical form. He illustrated his convictions in his *Katechismus*(1842) and joined ranks with other scholars and catechists who held the same view. Bernard Heinrich Overburg (1754-1826), a parish priest and practicing catechist, also emphasized the merits of narrative in presenting Christian truth to children and wrote a manual describing his method, *Biblische Geschichte des alten und neuen Testamentes . . .*, published in 1799. He followed in 1804 with a catechism illustrating his methods. Bernard Galura (1764-1856), proponent of the same theories, was the "guiding light of the catechetical movement" in Austria (Jungmann, 1959, p. 31).

6. *Advances in the human sciences, especially in psychology and sociology, that illuminated the process of growth, development, and learning in children.* Johann H. Pestalozzi (1746-1827) was among the most influential educational thinkers of his day. Although his theories and philosophy are nearly impossible to state definitively, it can be said that he insisted that the nature of the child must determine all details of his education and that work—involvement—is more important than words. He further maintained that "education must be essentially religious" (Kinloch, 1969, p. 90). Johannes F. Herbart (1776-1841), though dependent on Pestalozzi to a certain extent, was much clearer and more definite. He delineated the stages of children's learning and outlined five formal teaching steps that corresponded to those stages: preparation, presentation, comparison, generalization, and application. Inasmuch as catechesis was considered to be the responsibility of the school, such psychological insights were valued highly by catechists.

Other currents were also distinctly present during this period, even if they were less defined. One was the halting but genuine effort toward ecumenical understanding. No great strides forward resulted from those endeavors, but at least noteworthy beginnings were made (Daniel-Rops, 1967, pp. 385-94).

V CATECHESIS IN THE TWENTIETH CENTURY

The state of catechesis among Roman Catholics at the beginning of the twentieth century may be described as "promising." A sharpening of pastoral concerns combined with developments in professional education served to advance the cause of catechesis in fresh and unexpected ways. Movements, congresses, and study weeks; emphasis on adult learning; new genres of catechetical writings, notably, sophisticated text-series and catechetical directories; and the use of electronic media came together to transform catechetical programs. Early in the century interest focused on *methods*, then it shifted to the *message*, while in the present decades late in the century, interest seems to be more concerned with the *milieu* that shapes catechesis.

International Developments

About 1900 parallel catechetical movements emerged almost simultaneously in Munich and Vienna. The nucleus of the former was a group of serious minded catechists who formed the "Munich Catechetical Society."* Meeting regularly, they aimed at improved methods of catechizing though the "subject matter should not only be imprinted on the child's memory but also be grasped by the understanding" (Jungmann, 1955, pp. 32-33). Basically the movement employed principles borrowed from Herbart and his followers. Relying on those principles and their progressive learning theories, catechists endeavored to address children in ways that related to the youngsters' process of acquiring knowledge and understanding. The Munich group collaborated with leaders in other countries of Europe and in 1903 they gathered in Vienna for a Catechetical Congress—the first such gathering of its kind in history. Two years later they convened in Munich and the practice

---

*See F. L. Kerze, "A Catechetical Movement," *Ecclesiastical Review*, 37 (1908), 202-208. The aims and progress of the Munich Society are recorded in numerous articles in *Katechetische Blätter*, Volumes 22-29, 1896-1903.

was set. From that time until 1971, congresses (sometimes referred to as "weeks") were held periodically in Munich, Vienna, Salzburg, Lucerne, Milan, Rome, and elsewhere. At those gatherings scientific and practical lectures were given; the best literature, both Catholic and Protestant, was on display; and formal and informal discussions were held. During most of the first three decades of the Movement methodology held center-stage, but in time it became clear that method was only part of the problem. Insightful thinkers were uneasy with prevailing practices, admitting that something had to be done with the content—questions and answers. Theological formulae isolated from the context of Christian history and experience were grossly inadequate.

In the 1930's an Austrian Jesuit, Josef A. Jungmann (1890-1975), charged that seminary theology and catechesis as then practiced were incapable of communicating the gospel message in all its richness, simplicity, and directness. His 1936 work *Die Frohbotschaft und unsere Glaubensverkundigung*, called for a renewal of the *kerygma* to nurture faith in place of the speculative, polemical and defensive catechesis that prevailed.

Jungmann insisted that to be a true herald of the gospel one needed more than orthodoxy of doctrine. If catechists, whether clerical or lay, were to become effective witnesses to God's love, they needed above all to have a clear concept of the very core of the Christian message, the *kerygma*, along with a comprehension of Scripture's relation to liturgy, and that of liturgy to doctrine and the totality to Christian life. Jungmann knew the organic unity of the whole and strove tirelessly to share his understanding of it (Hofinger, 1976, pp. 356-57).

The monumental work of the Austrian Jesuit was not translated into English until twenty-six years after he wrote it.* Nevertheless the catechetical movement continued to gain momentum. It did not always move as a single phalanx nor at a rapid pace. Sometimes in spurts and thrusts, isolated and far-reaching on world-wide fronts, it gained ground. It was aided by such unrelated occurrences as improved communications and advanced technology and progress in scriptural, theological, and liturgical studies. It was impeded by equally unexpected events, especially by war. The

---

The Good News Yesterday and Today translated, abridged and edited by William A. Huesman, S.J. (New York: W.H. Sadlier, Inc., 1962). The literal translation of *Die Frohbotschaft* . . . is "The Good News and Our Proclamation of the Faith."

movement progressed out of the conviction, zeal, and dedication of individuals and groups who recognized its importance and relied on the Holy Spirit.

In 1935 the Jesuit faculty at Louvain, Belgium, opened a Catechetical Documentary Centre, an international library and documentary service for those interested in catechetics. Eleven years later they moved the center to Brussels, retitled it "Lumen Vitae," opened their doors to students from all over the world for academic programs, and launched a new international review which bore the center's new name (Pelissier, 1960, pp. 217-230). The center's activities were intensified in several directions but in the main the concentration was on the inter-penetration of religion and life. Eventually the four-sources theory emerged from studies at Lumen Vitae. Scripture, liturgy, doctrine, and Christian life, are, according to that theory, the four elements which comprise the basic ingredients for an ideal and true catechesis. This was a move toward integration and comprehension. Through Lumen Vitae's international student body the theories fanned out across the globe.

Catechists, theorists, and other church leaders continued to gather in congresses. The 1960 congress, meeting in Eichstatt, Bavaria, was a kind of watershed for the "kerygma" apostolate in catechetics. "Kerygma," the "Paschal Mystery," and "salvation history" were common currency there. However, a new star was rising in the catechetical sky: anthropology. In 1962 at Bangkok (Thailand), 1964 at Katigondo (Africa), 1967 at Manila (Philippines), and especially at Medellin (Colombia, South America) in 1968, the focus shifted to cultural, social, economic, and environmental realities that affect the way in which people interpret and live their Christian faith (Erdozain, 1970, pp. 7-31). Those aspects affected both the method and the message. Trent and modern pedagogy had insisted on the principle of adaptation in view of cultural diversity. In keeping with that principle the new dimension injected by the four congresses was at the level of *praxis*.

In a significant way Medellin achieved a high-water mark in the rising flood of recognition of modern catechetics. Its emphasis on the role that environment and culture play on the formation of the Christian community and individuals in the community gained global attention. No longer could *message* be separated from *method* and neither could be effective outside the context of the *milieu*. "Catechesis is the means by which any section of human society interprets its own situation, sees it, and expresses it in the light of the Gospel," Jacques Audinet had observed at the Medellin Congress (Audinet, 1968, p. 62). Several years later Audinet observed further that catechesis is the church building the church in a given culture.*

Catechesis in the United States

While the concern for restructuring catechesis was fermenting in central Europe, vital movements with similar interests were forming in the United States. At the 1931 meeting of the National Catholic Rural Life Conference in Wichita, Kansas, an entire day was given over to catechists and leaders in the Confraternity of Christian Doctrine to discuss ways and means, successes and failures, the "how-to" and the "what" of catechetics. Largely the result of one man's apostolate among rural Catholics, the one-day-a-year conference became a custom until 1935 when the Confraternity began holding its own annual conferences. Edwin V. O'Hara (1881-1956), bishop of Portland, Oregon, had initiated the organization of the NCRLC and had given the necessary impulse also to organizing the Confraternity on a national scale. It was through his efforts that summer vacation schools came into existence in places where Catholic schooling was unavailable during the academic year. It was through his insistence, too, that the Bible was eventually translated into more easily understood English for people's everyday reading. The *New American Bible*, which appeared in 1970, is the posthumous fruit of that insistence.

A contemporary of O'Hara was likewise involved in the cate-chetical scene but in a different way. Virgil Michel (1890-1938), a Benedictine monk who had recently completed post-doctoral studies in Europe where he found a vibrant, revived liturgical life, was determined to spread the good news about the centrality of the church's worship life. In 1926 he published the first issue of *Orate Fratres*, a journal intended to herald and sustain the apostolate of the liturgy. That journal continues its publication under the name *Worship*. Enthused and convinced about the

---

*"Catechesis: the church building the church within a given culture," *Our Apostolate*, 24(1976), 132-156. This article also appeared in *Catéchèse*, 16 (1976) entitled "Catéchèse, action d'église et culture," pp. 53-83. It was originally presented to the French bishops in preparation for their participation in the Synod on "Catechesis in our time," September-October, 1977.

indispensable role of the liturgy to Christian life, Michel won
followers and supporters. But that was not enough for him. He
noted the neglect of liturgy in religious instruction and so planned
summer schools at St. John's University in Collegeville, Minnesota,
to prepare teachers in that sphere of the church's life. Still not
content, he planned a series of textbooks which would center on
the liturgy as the heart and source that "permeates and leavens
the entire curriculum" in the school and becomes the wellspring
of Christian living. Between 1929 and 1935 he published the
Christ-Life Series for grade schools in order to "unlock the treasures
of the doctrine and practice enshrined in the liturgy." Because of
lack of teacher-readiness for that "new" thrust the volumes enjoyed
only limited success (Bryce, 1978, pp. 47-55).

The move to interrelate catechesis and liturgy did not end
there, however. The liturgical revival, already in full vigor in
Europe, was in the beginning stages in the United States. It became
identified in 1940 with a volunteer body of people known as the
Liturgical Conference. Convinced of the integral essence of liturgy
to Christian life, they held annual "rally-like" gatherings in cities
throughout the country. In almost every one of those gatherings
special sessions addressed matters of liturgical catechesis, education
in or about the liturgy, etc. At least twice the major theme of the
annual assemblies (Collegeville, MN, 1957; Philadelphia, PA,
1964) addressed the issue of liturgy as the integrating principle in
Christian education. The Conference retains its concern for
catechesis at the present writing.

Vatican II

It was Vatican II (1962-1965) which brought all of those forces
into clear perspective for catechesis and provided future directions
as well as a confirmation of the steps already taken. After a considerable struggle in the antepreparatory stages, the project of a single
or uniform catechism held over from Vatican I was abandoned.

It is impossible fully and accurately to measure the merits of
Vatican Council II for the church. It is possible to identify the
two major directives which are significant for catechesis. They
are: (1) the mandate for a general catechetical directory and for
national directories, and (2) the re-introduction of the catechumenate.

The *General Catechetical Directory* appeared in the Spring of
1971. Among other things, it delineated the purpose of catechesis:

"To make peoples' faith become living, conscious, and active" (#17).* Catechesis was understood as "that form of ecclesial action which leads both communities and individual members of the faithful to maturity of faith." Furthermore, the Directory called on the community as a whole to be conscious of its duty as catechist and witness (#101, 107, 130), cited adult catechesis as normative (#20), reiterated Trent's insistence on the principle of adaptation (#6, 8, 13, 34), and, in relation to that principle, urged that national or regional catechetical directories be written which would provide specific norms and guidelines in accord with local sociocultural circumstances (#77, 117). In the main it reaffirmed and validated the recognition of the ministry of catechizing.

In 1972 the Congregation for Divine Worship, in keeping with the provision of Council's decree on the Liturgy that the catechumenate be restored (#68), promulgated the revision of the *Rite of Christian Initiation of Adults.* That revision, with its emphasis on the importance of the Christian community (#41, 135, 138, 142), its progressive stages of admission into the body of believers, its reliance on catechesis adapted to each of those stages, and its concentration on the initiation sacraments (baptism, confirmation, and eucharist) offered promise of a second spring in the life of the ecclesial community.

In 1977 an international synod on "Catechesis in our Time" took place. That synod, comprised of bishops from all over the world, began in Rome on September 30 and lasted until October 29, 1977. It served to strengthen the positions of many catechetical leaders and theorists and to confirm approaches and gains already made. Pope John Paul II, then Cardinal Wojtyla of Poland, was a participant in the synod. On November 1, 1979, Pope John Paul disseminated a document affirming "the happy results of the synod" in his apostolic exhortation, *Catechesi Tradendae*, "Handing on the Teaching." He observed that the synod "saw in catechetical renewal a precious gift from the Holy Spirit to the Church of today, a gift to which the Christian communities at all levels throughout the world are responding with a generosity and inventive dedication that win admiration" (CT, #3).

In an impressive manner the synod emphasized the significance of culture in catechesis. That struck a sensitive and receptive vein in the national directory being composed by the church in the United States. When *Sharing the Light of Faith*, this country's

---

*Numbers refer to paragraph-passages in the Directory.

national catechetical directory, appeared in 1979, awareness of the uniqueness of the church in this country was clearly manifested. Special recognition of cultural diversity, the vast range of pluralistic and environmental circumstances that mark this nation's population, stood out (cf. #13-16,/#39, 72c, 137-139,/#159, 192-196). That 182-page book represents not only seven years of preparation involving the collective efforts of countless people as it went through massive consultations on each of its three preliminary drafts, it represents also a kind of new identifiable self-awareness of the church in the United States.

CONCLUSION

In the last quarter of the twentieth century Roman Catholics have a broader and more positive view of the task of catechesis than they had in the period immediately before and after the Council of Trent. Catechesis is not restricted to the mastery of a book (or books). It is directed at a broader audience than children. And the church rather than the classroom is its focus.

The symbiotic relationship between church and culture, which had begun to disintegrate about the time of the French Revolution, all but collapsed as the twentieth century progressed. Early in the century there was a great concern about the adequacy of catechetical methods. As the decades passed, however, the concern shifted to the message—the *what*, not just the *how*—of catechesis. And, as if coming full circle, leaders in the field now recognize that catechesis must once more address the questions of culture.

The Christian world, splintered by the Reformation, now faces common needs, the first of which is healing and bridging divisions. As evident in *Sharing the Light of Faith*, (#75, 76, 95, 239) and the *General Catechetical Directory* (#27, 66, 129), Roman Catholics have come to recognize that catechesis has, in addition to the tasks that have surfaced in the modern movement and congresses, the responsibility to promote ecumenism. Catholic catechists are called upon to make common cause with Christian educators everywhere. Unwilling to accept the so-called post-Christian world passively, catechesis today recognizes the important function of recreating *The Church* in the midst of that world. Responsive to that mission, catechesis is a benevolent agitator that is not content with *being* Christian, it is restlessly earnest in ever *becoming* Christian.

ANNOTATED BIBLIOGRAPHY

Alberigo, Giuseppe, "The Council of Trent." *Concilium*, Vol. 7. New York: Paulist, 1965, pp. 69-87.

Bangert, William V., S.J., *A History of the Society of Jesus*. St. Louis: The Institute of Jesuit Sources, 1972.

Brodrick, James, *The Life and Work of Blessed Robert Bellarmine*, 2 Vols. London: Burns and Oates, 1928.

_____, *Robert Bellarmine, Saint and Scholar*. Westminster, MD: Newman Press, 1961.

_____, *Saint Peter Canisius, S.J.* Baltimore: Carroll Press, 1950.

Bryce, Mary Charles, *The Influence of the Catechism of the Third Plenary Council of Baltimore on . . . Elementary Religion Text Books*. Ann Arbor: University Microfilms, 1972. This work includes a well-documented history of the origins of the "Baltimore Catechism."

_____, "Four Decades of Roman Catholic Innovators." *Religious Education*, 73 (1978), pp. S36-S57.

Canisius, Peter, *Summa Doctrinae Christianae*. 4 Vols. Landishuti: Josephus Thomas, 1842. (A critical study.)

Chadwick, Owen, *The Reformation*. Middlesex: Penguin, 1970.

Crichton, J. D., "Religious Education in England in the Penal Days (1559-1778)," in Gerard S. Sloyan, ed., *Shaping the Christian Message*. New York: Macmillan, 1958, pp. 63-90. Chrichton's keen historical knowledge offers a rare view of that period in England.

Cunningham, Agnes, "The Migne Centennial: Survival or Revival of Patristic Studies?" *American Benedictine Review*, 28 (1977), pp. 67-76. A timely reminder of the worth of the Fathers to any historical study.

Daniel-Rops, H., *Our Brothers in Christ*. Translated by J. M. Orpen and John Warrington. New York: E. P. Dutton & Co., 1967. From the title one discerns the nature of this volume. The brief treatment of ecumenism in the 19th century is especially good, pp. 385-394.

D'Hotel, Jean Claude, "French Catechisms and Consensus of Faith." *Concilium*, 71. New York: Herder & Herder, 1972, pp. 135-141.

Donnellan, Michael T., *Rationale for a Universal Catechism, Vatican I to Vatican II*. Ann Arbor: University Microfilms, 1973. This is a detailed report of the reasoning, the development, and the people involved in the issue of a common catechism for the Catholic world.

Dupanloup, Felix, *The Ministry of Catechizing.* Translated by E. A. Ellacombe. London: Griffith Farrar and Co., 1890. The content of this volume was originally a series of lectures. As bishop of Orleans he had published a catechism for his diocese in 1865 and was a well-known catechist. He considered catechesis an art as well as a science.

Erdozain, Luis, "The Evolution of Catechetics." *Lumen Vitae,* 25 (1970), 7-31. Erdozain traces the development in modern catechetics through the International Congresses, especially since 1960. Excellent assessment.

Fleury, Claude, *An Historical Catechism,* 2 Vols. Dublin: Booksellers, 1765. Though the translator is not identified, this is a translation of Fleury's well-known catechism. His philosophy and theory of catechesis is found in the extensive introduction.

General Catechetical Directory. Washington, D. C.: United States Catholic Conference, 1971. This is a translation of the *Directorium Catechisticum Generale* approved by the Sacred Congregation of the Clergy, Rome, 1971. The English text appears with excellent commentary and background history of the Directory in a paragraph by paragraph explanation in Berard L. Marthaler's *Catechetics in Context,* Huntington, Ind: Our Sunday Visitor Press, 1973.

Jungmann, Josef A., *The Good News Yesterday and Today.* New York: W. H. Sadlier, 1962.

————, *Handing on the Faith.* New York: Herder and Herder, 1959. This is a kind of vintage Jungmann inasmuch as it is "the result of lectures which . . . I gave at the University of Innsbruck from 1934 onward" (Preface, p. ix). The work is addressed to catechists for whom the writer has, he says, deliberately placed emphasis on essentials.

Kerze, F. L. "A Catechetical Movement." *Ecclesiastical Review,* 37 (1908), 202-208. A pastor in this country gives an early recognition of the movement in Europe.

Latrielle, Andre, *Le Catéchisme imperial de 1806.* Paris: Société d'édition les Belles Lettres, 1935.

Ledochowska, Teresa, *Angela Merici and the Company of St. Ursula,* 2 Vols. This is considered by contemporary Ursulines to be the best biography and study of Angela Merici and her sisters.

Mansi, Joannis Dominicis, *Sacrorum Conciliorum Nova et Amplissima Collectio.* Paris. A set of volumes which covers all the acts of the Church councils through 1870, including Vatican I.

Marthaler, Berard L., "Socialization as a Model for Catechetics," in Padriac O'Hare, ed., *Foundations of Religious Education.* New York: Paulist, 1978, pp. 64-92. An important and discerning study which points out the catechetical responsibility of the Christian community to impress its meanings and values powerfully and unforgettably on its members (p. 77).

Marx, Paul, *Virgil Michel and the Liturgical Movement*. Collegeville, MN: Liturgical Press, 1957. A biography and assessment of Michel and his ideals.

Pelissier, Jean, "The International Centre—'Lumen Vitae'." *Lumen Vitae*, 15 (1960), 217-230.

Pickering, Bernard, "Bishop Challoner and Teaching the Faith." *The Clergy Review*, 65 (1980), 6-15.

Schroeder, H. J., *Canons and Decrees of the Council of Trent*. St. Louis: Herder, 1955.

Sharing the Light of Faith. Washington: National Conference of Catholic Bishops, 1979. This is the national catechetical directory of the United States Church.

Sloyan, Gerard S., *Modern Catechetics*. New York: Macmillan, 1962. Sloyan's chapter four, "The Relation of the Catechism to the Work of Religious Formation," is particularly valuable. In the course of it he assesses the works of Canisius and Bellarmine.

Sommervogel, Carlos, S.J., *Bibliotheque de la Campagne de Jesus*. Paris: Alphonse Picard, 1884. An encyclopedic "Who's Who" of notable Jesuits and their recorded accomplishments.

Wallace, Patrick, *Irish Catechesis: The Heritage from James Butler*. Ann Arbor: University Microfilms, 1975. This makes available the little known history of the Butler catechism.

Eastern Orthodoxy

Chapter 8
The Orthodox Experience

Constance J. Tarasar

In the Orthodox experience, Christian catechesis is comprehensible and truly possible only within the context of worship, i.e., within the living experience and expression of the faith. Worship encompasses the whole of Christian life, for worship is "liturgy" (Greek: *leitourgia*) in the widest possible sense, meaning both liturgical celebration in the gathered community and witness and service to Christ in the world:

> You will be enriched in every way for great generosity, which through us will produce thanksgiving (*eucharistian*) to God; for the rendering of this service (*leitourgias*) not only supplies the wants of the saints but also overflows in many thanksgivings to God. Under the task of this service, you will glorify God by your obedience in acknowledging the gospel of Christ (2 Cor. 9:11-13).

Therefore, as we examine the nature of Christian catechesis from the Orthodox perspective, we must keep in mind this relationship of teaching and learning with worship as both liturgical celebration and witness or action in the world. As catechesis is inextricably related to the vitality of the corporate life of the church, it will become evident that the periods in the history of the church in which catechesis is weakest are also the periods in which the church herself is weak. When church life is vital, active, liturgically and spiritually enriching, we discover that education also enjoys an active role in that life; when church life is stagnant, self-centered, and reduced to ritualistic forms, education also becomes mired in static forms or, for all practical purposes, is non-existent. The historical conditions of church life thus become necessary and important lenses through which we view the nature and form of catechesis through the centuries.

I ORTHODOX EDUCATION IN HISTORICAL PERSPECTIVE

From an Orthodox perspective, the history of church life and education can be viewed in terms of five periods or types of experiences, each of which emerges from and overlaps the preceding stage and continues to influence successive stages. Each experience has contributed a view or form of education which—for better or worse—has become part of our present heritage, a heritage that must now be sorted out in order to determine our understanding of Orthodox catechesis and its direction for the future.

The Conversion Experience

The growth and life of the apostolic and early Christian church is directly linked to the centrality of the conversion experience. The proclamation of the gospel (*kerygma*) was greeted by a willingness and sense of urgency that was reminiscent of the wholehearted and eager response of the prophet Isaiah or the disciples to the call of God (cf. Isaiah 6:8; Mark 1:14-20; Acts 2:37-42, 4:4). The call to repentance resulted in a true conversion or *metanoia*, an actual "turning around" or change of mind, will, and action—a complete and total change which affected one's entire being—directing one's life entirely to the kingdom of God and the "way" or path leading to that ultimate goal.

In the context of that conversion experience, education was part of a continuing way of life.

> They devoted themselves to the apostles' teaching and fellowship, to the breaking of bread and the prayers . . . all who believed were together and had all things in common; and they sold their possessions and goods and distributed them to all, as any had need. And day by day, attending the temple together and breaking bread in their homes, they partook of food with glad and generous hearts, praising God and having favor with all the people (Acts 2:42-47).

A threefold pattern emerges from this description of the early Christian community. The Christian life is a life of *teaching* and *learning*, a life of *eucharistic fellowship* and *prayer*, and a life of active *witness* and *sharing*—concrete answers to the calls to "repent," "believe in the Gospel," and "be baptized" (Mark 1:15; Acts 2:37). Such a life was both the context and the content of the catechesis which nurtured those "households" of believers of which the Acts and Epistles speak. In such a context, even the departures from the "way," as expressed in the incidents involving Ananias and Sapphira, or Simon the magician (Acts 5:1-11, 8:18-24), become important pedagogical notes, for one learns by them that a Christian "cannot serve God and mammon" (Matthew 6:24). The "way" demands a single vision of life, a total giving of oneself to the life in Christ and the community of faith (cf. also *The Didache*).

Not surprising, then, is the effect of martyrdom on the strengthening and growth of the Christian community. The early Christians were nurtured as much by the blood of the martyrs as by their teaching and fellowship. The witness of the martyrs was the supreme act of faith in and service to the gospel of the kingdom. The message of the gospel was inseparable from these new bearers of the message, who, through their very lives and deaths, conveyed the victory, power, and joy of the resurrection. Whether children or adults, these witnesses became teachers and proclaimers of the faith through their calm, self-assured presence and confession of Christ before their accusers and executioners. Throughout history, even centuries later to our own day, the witness of Christ through the blood of the martyrs continues to be a source of enlightenment and sustenance to the church. The Orthodox churches, particularly, have not only suffered but have experienced the continuing revivification of church life through persecution and martyrdom, at times when more direct or more formal methods of preaching and teaching have not been possible.

The conversion experience, whether realized as a result of preaching and baptism or martyrdom, was in essence based upon an eschatological vision of life. The kingdom of God was the goal and the meaning of life; life in the kingdom could already be tasted *now*, but the realization of its fullness was eagerly anticipated when "this perishable nature must put on the imperishable, and this mortal nature must put on immortality" (1 Cor. 15:53). Until that time, all of life was lived in the context of that end and thus, sacrifice, witness, *metanoia* were the chief characteristics of the life lived in anticipation of the kingdom.

If we examine our church life and catechesis today, we find too little of that conversion experience—sacrifice, witness, holistic Christian vision, true *metanoia*—permeating our lives. The absence of such experience can only guarantee a shallowness or superficiality in whatever we do attempt in the area of Christian catechesis.

The Catechetical Experience

The growing numbers of Christians towards the end of the second and the beginning of the third centuries necessitated a more formal preparation for entrance into the life of the church as well as a means for strengthening and furthering the development of the members of the community. Montanism, Gnosticism, and other heresies posed another kind of threat to the church; the gospel message was being distorted by deviations from the "way." The growth in numbers of Christians resulted in the expansion of the church beyond the existence of small, tightly-knit communities of house churches. Repeated persecutions caused the weakening of some of the church's members who recanted not so much by reason of weakness of faith as much as by weakness of body and spirit. The church was thus confronted with a totally new situation which required new strategies for maintaining both the purity of the faith and the discipline of its life and witness.

The catechumenate, the process by which a catechumen or "hearer of the Word" was prepared for baptism and reception into the community of the faithful, rapidly became the means for screening and educating prospective members of the church. It also (as is still evidenced today during the Divine Liturgy and the services of Great Lent) provided a means of edifying and strengthening the faithful (Schmemann, 1974a, pp. 9ff.). Documents such as the *Didache*, the *Apostolic Tradition* of Hippolytus, the *Didascalia*, and other collections of this period which define and elaborate on church order provide us with information on both the form and content of the instruction that was given, as well as some insight into the education of children by parents (cf. also Laistner, 1951, pp. 30ff.). More importantly, they provide us with a further insight into the life of the community and the interrelationship of teaching with liturgical experience and Christian life and action.

The liturgical assembly provided the context and the content for the instruction of the catechumen and his integration into the life of the church. The enrollment took place before the bishop who presided over the assembly and the candidate was vouched for by a member of the community, i.e., the sponsor. Sponsorship was not limited, however, to a verbal statement concerning the moral life of the candidate, but involved a continuous participation in the preparation of the candidate for admission into the community through baptism. As the *Pilgrimage of Egeria* relates, the godfathers and godmothers are present, as well as other members of the faithful who wish to listen, when the bishop gives the daily instruction in the law to the catechumens during the forty days of Lent (*Egeria*, 46). The entire community also fasts and prays with the catechumens during this period. For those catechumens who were "preparing for illumination," i.e., for baptism during the coming Paschal celebration, special instruction was given which included readings from the Gospel and presentation of the Creed (other catechumens being dismissed from the assembly before this part of the catechesis). That the catechesis was also related to Christian moral life and action is evidenced by the several categories of catechumens. As Hippolytus testifies, "They who are to be set apart for baptism shall be chosen after their lives have been examined: whether they have lived soberly, whether they have honored the widows, whether they have visited the sick, whether they have been active in well-doing. When their sponsors have testified that they have done these things, then let them hear the Gospel" (*Apostolic Tradition*, 20). Even those who have been set apart may still be put aside and not admitted to baptism if, after the exorcisms, the bishop is still not personally assured of their purity. Thus, the threefold character of Christian life as expressed in the apostolic church is maintained and reinforced throughout the period of the catechetical experience.

It should also be noted that the catechesis of the newly-baptized did not cease in its intensity after baptism. The church took particular care that the mysteries into which they had just been initiated were clearly understood by providing a special period of instruction during the week following baptism and the Paschal celebration. During this week, the bishop explained what had taken place during their baptism, the meaning of the water, the oil, etc., and expounded also to them the meaning of the eucharist (cf. Cyril of Jerusalem's *Lectures on the Christian Sacraments* and John Chrysostom's *Baptismal Instructions*).

Much of the catechetical experience of the earlier Christian centuries remains as a living part of the tradition of the Orthodox Church and can be vividly experienced in the lenten and Paschal liturgical cycles. It is only recently, however, that the baptismal meaning of the services of this season, as well as those of Christmas, Epiphany, and Pentecost, has been brought again to light (Schmemann, 1980, 1974a, 1974b, 1966). Consequently, it is only in the past few decades that this work in liturgical theology has been able to provide the basis for any reflection in the field of Christian education. This reflection, both on the baptismal character of Christian catechesis and the interrelationship of teaching with liturgical experience and Christian life and action, has led to a rediscovery of the basic principles of Orthodox catechesis, which will be elaborated upon in later sections of this chapter.

The Monastic/Ascetical Experience

With the rapid growth of church life in the new "Christian society" of the Byzantine State, Christian life was "normalized" and thus posed new problems and new spiritual dangers to the faith. The form of baptismal catechesis used to prepare individual converts was then inadequate for the Christianization of the masses (Schmemann, 1966, p. 87). New heresies provoked doctrinal controversies that penetrated the entire Empire; at times, it was the majority of church members who accepted the beliefs of those who distorted the true teachings. Such doctrinal controversies were eventually settled in Councils and defined in Canons, and the adherents of false teachings were expelled from the church. The necessary and increasing institutionalization of the church, due to sheer numbers, resulted in two differing tendencies: one was the imposition on the church, by the masses of formerly pagan people, of a liturgical piety rooted in a sacred/profane dichotomy, focusing on the sanctification or sacralization of "holy" places and the symbolizing of ritual acts; the other was a "drawing back from" the masses and the growing nominalism of the church's membership, in order to recover the eschatological dimensions of Christian life (Schmemann, 1966, pp. 102ff.). This latter tendency, of monks and ascetics, focused on spiritual warfare against the devil—a fight of the personal will, whose main weapon against evil was prayer. Both tendencies obscured the experience of church as "assembly," and resulted in a piety that was more individual than corporate. An educational outgrowth of this piety was the highly personal form of teaching expressed in the disciple/ elder relationship; the elder was the personal spiritual guide to whom one turned for guidance in matters of Christian living and, in particular, for instruction in the way of prayer as a means of combatting the passions. The complex interweaving of all these developments—doctrinal, liturgical, monastic—within the context of a church that was, for all practical purposes, coextensive with society contributed to a much more formalized system of beliefs and a highly elaborated liturgical life. It is futile to try to place any value judgments on the results, but we must examine, for the purposes of this study, the effects on the content and form of catechesis in the life of the church.

The construction of large churches had a most profound effect on the development of liturgical forms which were to play a major role in the form of catechesis used to educate the masses. As Father John Meyendorff elaborates (on the "cathedral rite" of Hagia Sophia):

> Devoting comparatively little time to scriptural reading, or psalmody, this rite had favored the mushrooming of hymnography and the development of the liturgy as a "mystery," or "drama." It was indeed difficult to preserve the communal concept of Christian worship, or the notion that the Eucharist is a communion *meal*, when the liturgy began to be celebrated in huge basilicas holding several thousand worshippers. But since the early Christian community was now transformed into a crowd of nominal Christians (a transformation described as a real tragedy by Chrysostom in his famous sermons at Constantinople), it was necessary for the church to emphasize the *sacred* character of the Christian sacraments, to protect them from secular profanation, and to surround them with veils and barriers, thus practically excluding the mass of the laity from active participation in the celebration, except through the singing of hymns (Meyendorff, 1979, p. 118).

In spite of the obvious negative aspects of this transition, these new developments led to a tremendous growth in all forms of Christian art—music, poetry and hymnography, iconography, architecture—which, by their very nature, provided a new means of catechesis. Education then took place largely through sermons (which were often faithfully transcribed for wider use, e.g., the sermons of Chrysostom), liturgical hymnography (which contained doctrinal and scriptural themes), Christian art (frescoes, mosaics, and icons which told in imagery the story of salvation), liturgical commemorations (the cycles of feasts and fasts, the sanctoral), liturgical processions, and pilgrimages to holy places and monasteries (especially for confession and spiritual counsel with holy fathers or *startsi*). Monastic centers and famous monk-theologians not only produced much of this liturgical and doctrinal content in its varied forms of expression, but also a rich treasury of spiritual (largely penitential) literature: collections of sayings from the counsel of holy men, commentaries on Scripture, and a whole literature on devotional rules and prayer. Commenting on the struggle with iconoclasm, which challenged the use of church art, Meyendorff asserts:

> If the goal pursued by Constantine V to "purify" Byzantine Christianity, not only of the image cult, but also of monasticism, had been achieved, the entire character of Eastern Christian piety and its ethos would have evolved differently. The victory of Orthodoxy meant, for example, that religious faith could be expressed, not only in propositions, in books, or in personal experience, but also through man's power over matter, through aesthetic experience, and through gestures and bodily attitudes before holy images. All this implied a philosophy of religion and an anthropology; worship, the liturgy, religious consciousness involved the whole man, without despising any functions of the soul or of the body, and without leaving any of them to the realm of the secular (Meyendorff, 1979, p. 52).

Much of what forms both the content and the context of Orthodox education today is derived from the heritage of the Byzantine period. Discretion, however, is needed in order to "sort out" what is not only relevant and helpful for church life today, but what is essential. The whole question of the shape of a liturgical Ordo for our time and place (cf. Schmemann, 1966), i.e., an Ordo for parish (and not monastic) usage, is problematic also for the future shape of programs in Christian education. The problem of church education is not unlike the problem faced by secular education today: What, of the tremendous wealth of accumulated information and experience that forms our heritage, should be selected for transmission to future generations? What kinds of understandings, experiences, and methodologies are essential for grasping the spirit of Christian life in order that the revelation of Christ and the experience of his church may illumine the children and adults of ages to come?

The Scholastic/Pietistic Experience

With few exceptions, the fall of Byzantium in 1453 signaled an end to creative development in the Orthodox East and led to what some scholars describe as the "Western captivity" of the church (Florovsky, 1975, p. 172; Schmemann, 1979). For a few centuries, a form of Russian Byzantinism carried on the patristic tradition; but with increasing contacts with the West and political attempts at unifying the Christian East with the Christian West, as well as a certain "fascination" of things "western," Orthodoxy gradually began to take on the forms as well as the tone and content of Western theology. Specifically, this meant the introduction of scholasticism into theological schools, the use of Latin in teaching, and the adoption of juridical forms and methods, e.g., the *Orthodox Confession* or "Catechism" of Peter Mogila. Whether Roman Catholic or Reformed in outlook, these scholastic influences forced a "*pseudomorphosis* of Orthodox thought. The Orthodox were forced to think in essentially alien categories and to express themselves in foreign concepts" (Florovsky, 1975, p. 170). Later, the pietistic reforms directed to the inner, spiritual life and the interest in "mysticism" led to a moralism which was more individualistic than corporate. As Florovsky comments: "The 'Latin Captivity' could easily be replaced by a German or English 'captivity,' only in the place of scholasticism there arose the danger of vague mysticism and German Theosophy" (1975, p. 172). The real danger of these influences lay in the separation of theological "thought" from the living faith of the masses, though, to be sure, that faith was not entirely immune to the influence of what was happening in theological schools. Nevertheless, the liturgical continuity (at least in form and language) and the monastic experience (especially in its missionary outreach) continued to maintain among the people the basic expressions of Orthodox life and teaching.

This theological "schizophrenia" did not contribute to the positive development of Orthodox catechesis. The reduction of theological concepts to the "catechism" form meant a reduction of the wholeness of faith and life to a system of juridical questions and answers that had little to do with Christian life. On the other hand, the pietistic and "mystical" influences stemming from the Reform tradition led to a certain dualism in worship—the individual's immersion into the praying of "private" prayers during the corporate celebration of the eucharist, as well as the development of a piety totally divorced from the faith of the church. That remnants of both tendencies can still be found among clergy and laity alike further complicates the problem today of creating a specifically Orthodox catechesis in the midst of a modern, Western, and totally secular society, as we shall see in the next section.

The Secular/Sectarian Experience

The present situation of the Orthodox is no different, in terms of context, from that of all Christian churches, for secularism has engulfed us all regardless of the cultural situations in which we live. For those in the West, the church is at least free to function and to try to develop her life, educational programs, and forms of Christian witness and charity. For those in the geographical East, where most of the Orthodox still reside, such freedom is non-existent; there is no real opportunity for education, let alone a Christian witness in society. In spite of the differences in political climate, however, the problems faced by the church in a secular society—Eastern or Western—are only too similar.

The most pervasive element of secular society is that of separation, the tendency to compartmentalize life into its various "aspects," be they religious, economic, political, social, leisure, or what have you. Church life is but one aspect among many, to which we apportion a certain amount of our time, efforts, and resources; it is not, unfortunately, the foundation and context which gives life, purpose, vision, and meaning to all that we do. This desire for compartmentalization or fragmentation permeates also the very life of the church; the hesitancy (or even refusal) to relate theology to finances, mission, charitable activities, or education is but one example. Instead of seeing the church or the kingdom as the norm by which society is measured, we find the church being measured by the norms, however changeable they may be, of society.

If this is true for Christianity generally in our society, there is then a further difficulty for Orthodox Christians within that context, for however we describe them or try to differentiate between them—even those societies in the Communist world, and those in the so-called "Third" world—most (if not all) of the social contexts in which the Orthodox faithful may be found are "Western." The secular society *is* a Western society, whether located in Chicago, New York, Moscow, or Athens. Despite all of their weaknesses, what the traditional "Orthodox" societies or nations of the past had in common was a holistic understanding of life, an eschatological vision whereby all of life was judged by God and no "aspect" of life could escape that judgment. That understanding and that vision still reside (or lie buried) in the Orthodox consciousness, and it is precisely this which creates the greatest agony for Orthodoxy—in society generally, and within Christendom particularly. The analytical, scientific method, empiricism, and dialecticism are all methodologies foreign to the spirit that underlies Orthodox life and thought. Though one may be born in the West, trained in the West, and competent in the methodologies of the West, the committed Orthodox Christian—be he convert or "native-born"—is at heart an "Easterner" in the way he or she views and approaches life in the world.

Consequently, the Orthodox Christian who has difficulty in reconciling these two radically different approaches to life generally submits to one of two options: to acquiesce or surrender to the ways of society (even within one's church life), or to withdraw from the society in order to preserve what remains of the "truth." It should not be surprising, therefore, to discover many Orthodox communities clinging to their almost "ghetto" situations or re-treating into a sectarian mentality. A third option, which is actually a combination of the first two, is the submission to societal norms while preserving secondary mores or customs (generally national or ethnic) that are associated with church life. Either way, the church is not challenged by the society nor does it fulfill its role in challenging the society; instead, it seeks some degree of "co-existence."

It is within this context that we can begin to examine the more recent history of Orthodox Christian education in the Western world, and particularly in North America. Except for the original Russian mission to Alaska, the Orthodox church on this continent was founded by small groups of immigrants—generally peasants—who came to the "new world" during the period of the "new immigration" (i.e., after 1850). The establishment of a church in the midst of the new settlement was a priority for most of the newcomers. As soon as a priest could be obtained from the "old country," some semblance of normality was restored to the community, which was accustomed to centering its life around the rhythm of the church's life. Education, usually in the foreign language, accompanied the establishment of church life. This pattern was the norm for those of the first, and even for some of the second generation Orthodox in America.

As with nearly all immigrant groups that arrived around the turn of the century, the real crisis began to appear with the second and third generation Americans. The old culture which was inseparable from the religious life of the immigrants was no longer the culture of their children and grandchildren. The "tripartite" (Protestant, Catholic, Jew) formula described by Herberg (1960, p. 31), by which religious association became the primary context of self-identification and social location for the third generation, only proved to be a further source of frustration for Orthodox Christians. Unless one associated with one of the three main religious groups, one was a "nothing," had no name or label by which he could be identified (Herberg, 1960, p. 40). The pressure to conform and to become a member of one of the above groups in order to have such an identity was indeed great, and many second and third generation Orthodox did just that.

The major change in this attitude comes with the events of World War II. In spite of the identity problem, participation in the armed forces and the war effort "legitimized" and confirmed (at least in their own minds) the Orthodox populations' sense of belonging to America. Through the war Greek-Americans also met Russian-Americans, Syrians, Serbs, and others, and discovered their common bond as Orthodox Christians. The return of servicemen from the war brought a breath of new life to the churches; while abroad, they had discovered the church, and now—as Americans—they returned home and brought the church into their lives. The primary concerns now dominating church life were the use of English in services and educational programs for adults and, particularly, for their children.

Although some Orthodox parochial schools and Sunday Schools (or "afternoon" or "evening" schools) had existed in nearly every parish prior to this period, the post-war "baby boom" together with the new attitude towards the church resulted in a wave of interest in the establishment of Sunday Schools. But after several centuries of minimal education for the masses, and the instructional forms that had resulted from Western influence, the criteria for what should constitute an Orthodox program of Christian Education were non-existent, as were curricula or materials for such programs. What did exist were small, abbreviated catechisms, and, if one looked about, a wealth of slick-looking Bible-study programs packaged by non-denominational and Protestant publishing houses. Not only were the latter readily adopted, if only for the lack of anything else, but the very organization of the schools became an imitation of the Protestant form of Sunday School—even the "normal time" for such programs became the time during the celebration of the eucharist.

Thus, an amalgam of elements from both the scholastic/pietistic and secular/sectarian experiences became an accepted part of Orthodox life in the West, until, that is, even that superficial and essentially non-Orthodox educational experience led its very subjects to "hunger and thirst" for something deeper in their Orthodox subconsciousness. It was in that search for "something more" that the seeds were planted for a tremendous renewal of Orthodox faith and life.

II MISSION, EDUCATION, RENEWAL

As indicated earlier, there existed some few exceptions to the scholastic/pietistic experience that so dominated the life of the official church from the late medieval period. Among these were the tremendous missionary efforts of predominantly Russian missionaries, which continued the Orthodox missionary pattern established by the great "Evangelizers of the Slavs"—Cyril and Methodius. At the heart of this effort was the conviction that the gospel must be proclaimed to peoples of different lands in their own tongue and with an understanding of their customs, beliefs, and daily life.

New Missionary Efforts

Notable among the later evangelizers were Stephen of Perm, Nicholas of Japan, and Innocent of Alaska. Stephen, a fourteenth-century bishop, spent thirteen years, while a novice monk, preparing to preach to the native Permian (Zyrian) tribe which resided in an area just west of the Ural mountains. He created a written language for the Permians, translated the services and the gospels, and founded two monasteries (Bolshakoff, 1943, p. 30; Smirnoff, 1903, pp. 4-5). The fruits of the efforts of Nicholas (Kasatkin), a young Russian who went to Japan in the nineteenth century as an embassy priest, are visible today in the active and growing native Japanese Orthodox Church. Being encouraged by his older contemporary, Innocent (Veniaminov), to do more than just minister to the needs of the small Russian community, Nicholas undertook to learn the Japanese language and translate the services and the Scriptures for his flock. Innocent, who arrived in Alaska in 1824 as a young priest with his family, began by studying the ethnography of the region (later published in a three-volume work) and learning the Aleut language, for which he created an alphabet from the Cyrillic. He then proceeded to translate parts of the gospel, the services, and a catechism; he also wrote a dictionary, a grammar, and a primer. Later, he repeated these efforts among the Kolosh

(Tlinget) Indians of Southeastern Alaska and still later among the Siberian tribes in Kamchatka. Education was a primary interest of Innocent; he not only established schools in every village where there was a church and a seminary in Sitka for the training of clergy and readers, but also prepared elaborate instructions for those who were sent out to preach and teach among the native peoples—an excellent model, even for our time (*American Orthodox Messenger*, Oct.-Nov., 1899).

Nor were these isolated examples; within the vast Russian territory, missionary efforts were conducted over a period of several centuries—often by monks (eight monks were the first missionaries to arrive in Alaska in 1794), and later by graduates of the famous Kazan Academy, which focused on languages and the preparation of scholarly persons for missionary work in Asia (Bolshakoff, 1943, pp. 38ff.). The Kazan Academy was responsible not only for the translation of the sacred books into dozens of languages and dialects, but also for the establishment of schools throughout the vast Russian territories (Smirnoff, 1903).

Continuation of the Monastic Tradition

Closely related to the missionary effort in its impact on education and the maintenance of the Orthodox spirit was the continuing monastic impact on the life of the church. Existing as "spiritual islands" in the midst of both cities and forests, the monasteries were centers of scholarship (the revival of the patristic tradition was stimulated by the translations of the writings of the Fathers and the study made possible by these works), the development of music and art (the evolution of several forms of monastic chants, the iconographic schools of Theophan the Greek, Andrei Rublev, and others), and the development of a rich spiritual tradition through such figures as SS. Theodosius of the Caves in Kiev, Sergius of Radonezh, Seraphim of Sarov, and the spiritual fathers of the Monastery of Optino who carried on the tradition of the venerable Paissy Velichkovsky (translator of the *Philokalia*). The tradition of seeking out the wisdom of such holy men, by prince and peasant alike, served as a major source of Christian nurture and education in the Orthodox lands (cf. Ware, 1963, pp. 129-135).

Theological Renewal

The present century has witnessed a renewal of Orthodox church life throughout the world, expressed in three main forms:

theological (patristic), eucharistic, and spiritual. Education has
been intrinsically tied to the development of each. The theological
renewal, which had its beginnings in the development of Russian
theology in the last century, found its primary expression in the
Russian emigré community in Western Europe, particularly in
France and the St. Sergius Theological Institute in Paris (Ware,
1963, p. 186). Not only did this center have an impact on Orthodox
theology, but it also led to the creation of a student movement
(the Russian Student Christian Association) that became responsible
for a variety of educational programs for adults and children in
the community. It is interesting to note that of the young men and
women trained at St. Sergius in the decade of the 40's, a good
number are now bishops (including one Patriarch), internationally-
known theologians, and leaders of the church in the Middle East,
Western Europe, and America, and are largely responsible for the
renewal efforts in those areas. Today, the major theological center
of the Orthodox world, which is especially noted for the Orthodox
publications issued by its SVS Press, is St. Vladimir's Orthodox
Theological Seminary in New York. There is literally no area of
church life—missions, education of youth and adults, continuing
education of pastors and church workers, administration, spiritual
life, liturgical music, church art, etc.—in which faculty members
and students alike have not been involved. The Orthodox Christian
Education Commission (the major publisher of Orthodox curriculum materials), as well as other "pan-Orthodox" agencies and
commissions, owe much of their formation and development to
the members of this faculty.

Stimulated by the Russian Student Movement in France and
the ZOE Movement in Greece, a small group of young men in
Lebanon and Syria (some of whom were studying at St. Sergius)
inaugurated a similar movement within the parishes of the Patri-
archate of Antioch. Regular communion, Bible-study classes, and
educational programs for children, youth, university students,
workers, and professionals, formed the basis of the Movement's
activities. These study programs were complemented by regular
gatherings for prayer and the celebration of Vespers (often preceded
by instruction in liturgical chant) in the Movement "Centers."
The Centers also served as a community base for rather wide-
spread social work among the poor, and as a location for medical
clinics for the poor. During the civil war in Lebanon, this social
activity was expanded to include assistance to refugees who were

forced out of their homes. Although once looked upon with some suspicion by officials of the church, the Movement's work has become increasingly integrated into the structures of church life, especially as its "graduates" now fill the ranks of the clergy, and even the episcopacy. A renewed interest in monastic vocations has also been stimulated by the efforts of the Movement, and two monasteries—one for men and another for women—have been established in Lebanon.

Eucharistic Renewal

This renewal in theology led naturally to a recovery of the baptismal and eucharistic understanding of church life. In America, the Sunday School programs became a major instrument in the renewal of the sacramental life of the parish. Teachers and children were led to an understanding of the importance and meaning of the eucharistic celebration and encouraged to participate in the reception of the sacraments on a more regular basis. As classes of children approached the chalice with greater frequency, parents were also encouraged. Supported by the combined effects of preaching, teacher-training, retreats for youth, adult classes, and educational materials stressing the importance and meaning of sacramental life, this eucharistic renewal led to a new awareness of Christian responsibility and church life. Official documents endorsed by the hierarchy allowed for the reintroduction of the practice of general confession along with private confession, restored the evening celebration of the Liturgy of the Presanctified Gifts during Lent, and, in one diocese, instituted the evening celebration of feast-day liturgies, all of which encouraged greater participation in the eucharist. This eucharistic reawakening has led to a renewed interest in the support of missions; the establishment of dozens, if not hundreds, of new parishes throughout the United States; involvement in mission work in Alaska, Japan, and Africa; increase in the support of charities; and an interest in stewardship and lay ministries.

As Orthodox faithful from widely differing cultures in different parts of the world meet in ecumenical gatherings and international conferences, it becomes increasingly evident that such renewal efforts are not isolated manifestations. It is with great joy that these persons recognize in each other an absolute unity of mind, purpose, and spirit that is immediately identified as "Orthodox." After years of separation, persecution, Western influence, and spiritual stagnation, something has come alive, been resurrected from the depths of the Orthodox consciousness.

Spiritual-Monastic Renewal

Finally, there is the spiritual renewal (though certainly each of the previous forms must also be deemed "spiritual"), particularly in the sense of monastic renewal and its related forms. Paralleling the other youth movements mentioned previously and, in some cases, originating before them, was the establishment in Greece of a semi-monastic movement known as *ZOE* ("life"). Composed originally of single professional men and some monks, this movement was the forerunner of several related movements (*SOTIR*, the *Orthodox Christian Unions*, and Orthodox professional societies) which focused on the spiritual life and its relationship to service and witness in the world. Though in some respects, the movements are heavily moralistic and bear the marks of pietistic expressions, they have contributed to a renewed interest in church life (at times, even militant) among their members. Alongside the efforts of *Apostoliki Diakonia*, the official "home missionary" unit of the church, the movements each produce a variety of magazines for all ages and interests—children, families, young adults, and professionals. A separate missionary movement, *Porefthendes (Go Ye)*, stimulated an international interest among young Orthodox in missions, and particularly in the support of groups of Orthodox Christians in Africa (cf. *Orthodoxy 1964*, pp. 136ff.). With the increased difficulties of working within the changing political and ecclesiastical situations during the past decade, many of the members of these movements have chosen to leave their professional careers for the monastic life. In one case alone, ninety young men —all intellectuals and professionals (doctors, lawyers, teachers, theologians)—left the cities to take up residence in a nearly-abandoned monastery on Mt. Athos. Efforts such as this have given a great boost to the revival of monastic life and interest in monasticism in Greece and elsewhere.

In nearly all parts of the Orthodox world, especially where monasticism is weak or non-existent, there is a growing recognition of the need—even a "longing"—for a monastic presence. In the old Orthodox societies, especially those in communist countries, the few monastic centers that exist are popular spiritual havens. One notable exception to the decreasing numbers of monks and nuns is Romania, where monasteries abound and are utilized for education and personal visits of pilgrimage, in addition to functioning as a major tourist attraction in the country. Whether the monastic life will ever again become a source of judgment for the church in this world—an eschatological sign and presence—as well as a source of creative spiritual and theological development, is a major question for the future of the Orthodox Church.

Having examined in a very brief and sketchy synopsis the particular events and experiences that have had an effect on the educational situation in the Orthodox Church through the centuries, it is now our task to reflect upon that history and draw some conclusions about the nature and shape of Orthodox Christian education, especially in the light of the issues we face today.

III ASSESSMENT AND REFLECTION: OUR NEEDS FOR THE FUTURE

Orthodox Christian education today might best be summarized: "We know where we come from. We can observe where we are. We know where we want to go. But, the 'way' still eludes us." Insofar as the Orthodox tradition is a living tradition, the heritage and the spirit of the past is still with us; we know whence we come. It is not sufficient, however, to know the past, for the accumulation of experiences of the past that we have inherited must be critically evaluated. This process of discerning between "The Tradition" of the church and "traditions," i.e., practices and customs that are not essential, is a difficult but essential one if Orthodoxy is to preserve her integrity and wholeness (cf. Meyendorff, 1962, pp. 121, 125). It is because of the past, also, that we know where we want to go, i.e., we know the goal of our existence: the kingdom of God. The basic message of the gospel is the kingdom, and it is this message and this eschatological vision that has always guided Orthodox faith and life. But, if we observe where we are today, we can see that something of that vision has been lost or obscured by the secularism of our lives. In order to recover that vision and to find the "way" to communicate it to others, we must assess the sum total of our experience and reflect upon the elements in our life and in our understanding or approach to catechesis that are presently lacking.

Christians in Need of Conversion

One of the most difficult lessons of the past and of the present is the recognition that education has failed. In spite of our efforts, and regardless of the numbers of educational programs we offer or the numbers of persons who enroll in these programs, nothing really seems to change. People ask for adult education, faithfully attend classes, read books, and even become more "active" in the life of the church, but they are not "converted." There is always an invisible line which is drawn between "activity" and "commitment"—the kind of commitment that determines one's vision of life, orders one's priorities, and is based on the willingness to sacrifice our individual, and often petty, desires for "the one thing needful" (Luke 10:42). What is lacking in our present understanding of catechesis is the recognition of the power of the "will" and the power of evil. Freedom of choice does not always result in the choice of the good. The secular experience of life is, in spite of the practical social and economic problems we face today, a rather comfortable way of life. It is easier to put religion aside when it interferes with other interests and desires. Compartmentalization is convenient, for it avoids a basic conflict of interests. One can be an active, regular "church-going" Christian "in good standing" without having to impose Christian faith and principles on all of life; that is "expecting too much."

For the committed Christian, for the one who is truly "converted," there is no possibility for an easy co-existence of the secular and the sacred. As we have already seen, true conversion involves *metanoia*—i.e., change, the will to "turn around," to direct the totality of one's life to life in Christ. This does not mean that the converted Christian will cease to sin—no!—but that person will begin to judge his thoughts, his actions, his beliefs and values in terms of sin, i.e., in terms of what separates him from God and from life in the kingdom. What the Christian educator must realize is that whatever method, approach, technique, or content, is used for communicating the Christian message, that message can still be rejected (and often rejected in subtle or nearly indiscernible ways) because the person does not *want* to change, does not *want* to sacrifice, does not *want* to make that total commitment that is required as the result of the true understanding and reception of the gospel of the kingdom. For the educator, this means that all of our understandings of psychological development—cognitive, moral, emotional, etc.—though helpful, are not sufficient; recognition of the power of God, prayer and humble submission to the Spirit of God, intercession on behalf of those we hope to bring to God—this is the understanding and the activity that is essential if we hope to have any chance of succeeding in our task. If we have learned anything from the past, from that first Christian community or from the martyrs, monks and ascetics, it is that "the gate is narrow, and the way is hard that leads to life, and those who find it are few" (Matthew 7:14). Conversion and commitment demand asceticism—training, practice, exercise, i.e., spiritual effort, discipline, and sacrifice—for asceticism is the way to the kingdom. Joy, peace, love, faithfulness (the fruits of the kingdom) are given only to those who "have crucified the flesh with its passions and desires" (Galatians 5:22-23). Asceticism is not an ideal in our secular society, in spite of the numerous "fasts" for losing weight or for social causes, for the true ascetic has the wholeness of vision which gives life and direction to all of his efforts. The ascetic is the "spiritual athlete," the one whose whole life is dedicated to finishing the race and winning the "crown of righteousness" which is laid up for him in the kingdom of heaven (2 Tim. 4:7-8). Our task as Christian educators is not simply to turn out greater numbers of nominal Christians who have some understanding of the faith and some degree of participation in the life of the church, but to encourage more of those numbers to commit themselves to running and finishing the course of the race, to help them to train and discipline themselves for the fight, that they may win their crowns. To do this, we must recognize that our struggle is a struggle of the will in its fight against evil; the first step toward winning the battle is in recognizing the true enemy against whom we are fighting.

Catechesis in Need of Integration

The second lesson that we can derive from the history of catechesis is that catechesis cannot be divorced from the life of the church, from the sacramental life of the community. Liturgical catechesis, according to Schmemann, understands the aim of religious education as that of bringing the individual into the life of the church; "it is not merely the communication of 'religious knowledge,' not training the human being to become a 'good person,' but the 'edification'—the 'building up'—of a new member of the Body of Christ, a member of that new 'chosen race' and 'holy nation' whose mysterious life in this world began on the day of Pentecost" (Schmemann, 1974a, p. 11). In the Orthodox experience, this edification begins in infancy with the "Churching," Baptism, Chrismation, and participation of the child in the

Eucharist as a full member of the gathered community. From the first moment of participation in the Body of Christ, the child is being nurtured into the community of faith. "Taste and see how good is the Lord" (Ps. 34:8)—*experience* and then *understand*—this is the form of catechesis that has been given to us by the church. From the moment of their baptism (and during the period of the catechumenate, even before baptism), persons who desired to enter into the church were immediately integrated into the fellowship of the community; further instruction took place within that fellowship, the mysteries were explained as soon as they were experienced, life was a reflection of that experience and that teaching. Worship, doctrine, and action were inextricably linked in the fellowship of the church, but it was worship that served as the key. It was in the "breaking of bread" that the disciples recognized Christ at Emmaus, and it was in the eucharistic fellowship that Christians recognized one another as members of his body—the church.

Today it is in that eucharistic gathering, as well as in other liturgical and sacramental acts, that the church is "made present." It is in that gathering that all that we are and do as persons living in "this world" is brought together, lifted up, offered, and transformed into the life of the kingdom. And, finally, it is from that gathering that we as Christians are sent back to illumine, transform, and re-activate—as God's own—the world of which we are his stewards.

The real lesson of the scholastic/pietistic experience is that this eucharistic "key" was lost. Doctrine and teaching became divorced from liturgy and life; doctrine, sacraments, and Christian witness and action were reduced to legalisms, ritual, and pietistic expressions. The essential integration of all of these elements was destroyed and catechesis was reduced to empty formulas and prescriptions. The reintegration of worship with teaching and action is essential if we are to recover the holistic vision and experience of life in the church. In order to accomplish this task, several things must first be changed.

First of all, worship must recover its eschatological dimension; the liturgy as the sign and presence of the kingdom of God cannot be experienced if liturgy is reduced to either ritualistic or, at the other extreme, "experimental" forms. The eschatological dimension necessitates that worship be God- and kingdom-oriented. The purpose of the liturgical gathering is not to dwell on our own needs and concerns ("let us lay aside all earthly cares," *Liturgy of St. John Chrysostom*) but to "lift up our hearts" and our minds as we enter into God's presence. The eucharist as the "lifting up" of all of life enables us to "hear with our ears" and "see with our eyes" the glory of the kingdom; it enables us as well to look at this world with a new vision—to see it as God's world and to see ourselves as his stewards entrusted with the vocation of filling it with his love, his care, and his peace, i.e., of making it the means of communion with him. The recovery of the eschatological dimension means the recovery of the scriptural content of worship in both its kerygmatic and didactic expressions, the proclamation and teaching of the kingdom that is both a reminder (in the sense of "remembrance") and a judgment, a reminder of the death and resurrection of Christ, and our response to his gift of salvation.

Secondly, the home and parish community must reinforce and reflect the life of the church. Our daily life and work cannot be separated from church life but must be a witness of it. Consistency is the key, especially in the nurture of children but important as well for adults. Somehow, during Lent, we are all able to make an effort at the practice of Christian life, be it only for a few days or a few weeks. The liturgical cycles of the Church Year are exactly the means for helping us to maintain that effort, to see all of life in shorter segments of *preparation* and *fulfillment*, to look forward to certain feasts and seasons and to fulfill them, to experience both the effort and discipline of preparation or waiting and the joy of celebration. The meaning of these special days and seasons is a continual reminder that our lives are "hid with Christ in God" (Col. 3:3). To go to church as a family on a weekday evening for the celebration of a feast or saint's day, while the neighbors are busy cutting the lawn, going to a baseball game or entertaining guests, can be both a painful and a joyful reminder that "someone else" is the standard by which our lives are lived.

Finally, the church school must present the vision of the Christian life and the foundations of the Christian message in their wholeness. Scripture, liturgy, ethics, and doctrine must be integrally related and not presented as separate content areas. Only in this way can liturgy be understood as the unifying element of belief and action. The concept of church as community should be able to be experienced as well as taught in the classroom. The role of the teacher as he or she relates to the students is critical; inexperienced teachers who find their security in being an authority figure do not present the proper role model. The teacher who can create an open, warm, caring climate in which students are shown how to care for and be mutually responsible for one another is a more appropriate model. The literature of the holy fathers and saints of the church may help us to understand the nature of the loving, yet serious, disciple/elder relationship of which discipline is still a part. The implications for the classroom are many, but these few examples should suffice as a starting point for asking the right questions about the content and method of catechesis in the church school.

The proper understanding of how catechesis should be practiced in each time and place is dependent upon a continuing reflection of our present situations in the light of our heritage and our goals. There is no single answer that is appropriate to every age or every place; at every moment we must discern the situation and also discern the Spirit, asking God to guide us in our task. In the process we need also to assess our own spiritual journey on the road to the kingdom; whether we be teachers, administrators, pastors, or bishops, the degree to which we can make a contribution to the understanding and practice of catechesis is dependent upon our own spiritual development. In this way we can join our prayer to that of the celebrant in the Liturgy of St. Basil and say:

> The mystery of Thy dispensation, O Christ our God, has been accomplished and perfected as far as it was in our power; for we have had the memorial of Thy death; we have seen the type of Thy Resurrection; we have been filled with Thine unending life; we have enjoyed Thine inexhaustible food; which in the world to come be well-pleased to vouchsafe to us all, through the grace of Thine holy and good and life-creating Spirit, now and ever and unto ages of ages. Amen (Schmemann, 1974a, p. 73).

BIBLIOGRAPHY

American Orthodox Messenger, "Instruction of Metropolitan Innocentius to the Hieromonk Theophanes." October, November, No. 20-21, pp. 234-43; 564-74. 1899.

Apostolic Tradition of Hippolytus. Translated by Burton Scott Easton. Archon Books. Cambridge: University Press (U.S.A.) 1962.

Bolshakoff, Serge, *The Foreign Mission of the Russian Orthodox Church*. London: SPCK, 1943.

Cyril of Jerusalem: *Lectures on the Christian Sacraments*. Edited by F. L. Cross. Crestwood, NY: St. Vladimir's Seminary Press, 1977.

Didache. Library of Christian Classics, Vol. I. Edited by Cyril C. Richardson. Philadelphia: Westminster Press, 1953.

Didascalia Apostolorum. Translated by R. Hugh Connolly. Oxford: Clarendon Press, 1929.

Egeria: Diary of a Pilgrimage. Translated by George E. Gingras. New York: Newman Press, 1970.

Florovsky, Georges, "Western Influences in Russian Theology," *Aspects of Church History*. Belmont, MA: Nordland Publishing Company, 1975.

Garrett, Paul D., *St. Innocent: Apostle to America*. Crestwood, NY: St. Vladimir's Seminary Press, 1979.

Herberg, Will. *Protestant, Catholic, Jew*, Anchor Books. Garden City, NY: Doubleday and Company, Inc., 1960.

John Chrysostom: *Baptismal Instructions*. Translated by Paul W. Harkins. Westminster, MD: Newman Press, 1963.

Laistner, Max Ludwig Wolfram, *Christianity and Pagan Culture in the Later Roman Empire*. Ithaca, NY: Cornell University Press, 1951.

Matsagouras, Elias G., *The Early Church Fathers as Educators*, Minneapolis, MN: Light and Life Publishing Co., 1977.

Meyendorff, John, *Byzantine Theology: Historical Trends and Doctrinal Themes*. New York: Fordham University Press, 1979.

_____, "Tradition and Traditions," *St. Vladimir's Seminary Quarterly*, Vol. VI, No. 3, 1962, pp. 118-127.

Orthodoxy 1964: A Pan-Orthodox Symposium. Edited by The Brotherhood of Theologians "ZOE." Athens, Greece: 1964.

Schmemann, Alexander, *Church, World, Mission: Reflections on Orthodoxy in the West*. Crestwood, NY: St. Vladimir's Seminary Press, 1979.

_____, *For the Life of the World: Sacraments and Orthodoxy*. Crestwood, NY: St. Vladimir's Seminary Press, 1973.

_____, *Great Lent: Journey to Pascha*. Crestwood, NY: St. Vladimir's Seminary Press, 1980.

_____, *Introduction to Liturgical Theology*. Translated by Asheleigh E. Moorhouse. London: The Faith Press Ltd., 1966. Reprinted by St. Vladimir's Seminary Press, Crestwood, NY: 1975.

_____, *Liturgy and Life: Christian Development through Liturgical Experience*. Department of Religious Education, Orthodox Church in America, New York: 1974a.

_____, *Of Water and the Spirit: A Liturgical Study of Baptism*. Crestwood, NY: St. Vladimir's Seminary Press, 1974b.

Smirnoff, Eugene, *Russian Orthodox Missions*. London: Livingtons, 1903.

Ware, Archimandrite Kallistos, *The Orthodox Way*. Crestwood, NY: St. Vladimir's Seminary Press, 1979.

Ware, Timothy, *The Orthodox Church*. Baltimore, MD: Penguin Books, 1963.

The American Church

Chapter 9
Since the Reformation:
An Emphasis on the American Experience

John E. Booty

Robert Ulrich rightly states that "in a secular age we are inclined to underestimate the role of religion in the history of education. All early education was religious, and all early religion was educational" (Ulrich, 1968, p. v). Before the eighteenth century, when in Old and New England it was assumed that every Christian was a citizen and every citizen a Christian, it was expected that what we call religious education would not be limited to an hour on Sunday morning, but would involve the totality of life in home, school, church, and community. Narrowly considered, catechesis might be aimed toward a specific event such as baptism, confirmation, or some other rite of initiation into full membership in the local congregation and the wider church, but in reality it was expected among Protestants that learning, involving both belief and practice, was a lifelong adventure. At the end of the sixteenth century Richard Hooker, the Anglican theologian, wrote of the great challenge involved in establishing and maintaining a constant relation of mutuality between mind and will, faith and practice: "That the minde . . . maie abide in the light of faith, there must abide in the will as constant a resolution to have no fellowship at all with vanities and workes of darkenes" (*Lawes*, V.63.2). The achievement of such a resolution was the aim of baptism, confirmation, and of catechesis which was lifelong.

The aim of catechesis, thus, was the development and nurturing of Christian piety, or lifestyle, directing both mind and will in the way of righteousness. Preaching and sacraments, prayer and praise, intellectual enrichment and bodily discipline all contributed to the perfection of the saints in the body of Christ. Serious attention was, of course, given to catechesis in relation to the rites of initiation. Generally speaking, initiation consisted of infant baptism, confirmation or some similar rite at about the age of twelve, and admission to the Lord's Supper, or to communion at the Eucharist. The process was not adhered to by all and not all parts of it were uniformly observed at the beginning of the seventeenth century. The successors of the early Anabaptists, such as the English Baptists, practiced believer's baptism and dispensed with confirmation as a separate rite. Among Anglicans confirmation was often neglected. The difficulties involved in the travel necessary for bishops to reach all confirmands and the carelessness of those bishops who seldom if ever visited the parishes of their dioceses contributed to the neglect. In the American colonies, where there were no bishops, the devout either returned to England for confirmation or were unconfirmed. In instances where confirmation was deemed impossible, people were admitted to communion on the strength of their preparation and their intent to be confirmed. Joseph Hall, bishop of Exeter in the seventeenth century, bemoaned the neglect of confirmation, but he was also critical of the excessive evaluation of it as a sacrament (Moore and Cross, 1935, pp. 445-449). There was an inclination to argue that in baptism the infant is incorporated into Christ and the church and that in confirmation the infant receives the Holy Spirit, as though the Spirit were not involved in baptism.

The process of initiation as generally observed was based upon the understanding that baptism is complete, involving entry into Christ and the church and reception of the Holy Spirit. It properly belongs to infants because through baptism persons are initiated into God's covenant of grace. Confirmation is the individual's ratification of his or her baptismal vows, vows made on the infant's behalf, and thus of the terms and conditions of the covenant established by God. It was also generally held that confirmation involved additional gifts of the Spirit such as were deemed necessary for adulthood and that the once confirmed Christian could now participate fully in the Lord's Supper. Catechesis involved the preparation of young people for confirmation and first communion.

Such preparation was strongly influenced by the conviction expressed by various Anglican theologians and formularies that the participant in the Supper of the Lord must have "a right and worthy estimation of this mystery," "a sure faith, not only that the death of Christ is available for the redemption of the world, for the remission of sins, and reconciliation with God and Father; but also that he hath made upon his cross a full and sufficient sacrifice for thee; a perfect cleansing of thy sins," and "newness of life and godliness of conversation" (*Certaine Sermons*, 1850, pp. 446, 448, 451). That was John Jewel's way of stating the common understanding in the *Second Book of Homilies* (1563), and it was generally accepted by Anglicans from the sixteenth century through the eighteenth. In the 1604 *Book of Common Prayer* and in subsequent Prayer Books, the child is asked: "What is required of those who come to the Lord's Supper?" "*Answer*. To examine themselves, whether they repent them truly of their former sins, stedfastly purposing to lead a new life; have a lively faith in God's mercy through Christ, with a thankful remembrance of his death; and be in charity with all men."

The young Christian was expected not only to learn the Ten Commandments, the Apostles' Creed, and the Lord's Prayer as the 1559 Prayer Book Catechism demanded, but also to achieve an acceptable understanding of the Lord's Supper and exhibit a sufficient degree of personal purity, as the addition to the Prayer Book in 1604 indicated. It was the totality of one's life that was to be nurtured through catechesis. Furthermore, it was obvious that what was begun in baptism, nurtured through instruction of mind and will, and ratified through confirmation was but the beginning of a lifelong process. The extension of the initiation events was indicated for Anglicans by the way in which the Holy Communion was reserved for worthy receivers whose worthiness was cultivated by preparation for communion as well as by the working of the Holy Spirit in the sacrament and at all times. Consequently, catechesis was to be viewed broadly and not narrowly in terms of confirmation and first communion.

To promote the perfection of the saints in the body of Christ there were handbooks of piety written for literate but otherwise ordinary people. Such books illustrate the fundamental goals of Christian catechesis in the broad sense during the seventeenth century. In Colonial America three of the most influential were Lewis Bayly's *The Practice of Piety*, Richard Allestree's *The Whole Duty of Man*, and Richard Baxter's *The Poor Man's Family Book*. All seem to rely, at least to some extent, on William Perkins, the great sixteenth century English Puritan, and his teaching that cases of conscience divide into three categories: the self considered in and of itself, the self in relation to God, and the self in relation to other humans, that is, the self as belonging to and participating in family, church, and commonwealth. On this basis Bayly concluded that the "practice of piety consists of (1) knowing the essence of God, (2) knowing one's own self, (3) glorifying God by dedicating one's life to his service, and (4) glorifying God by dying in and for the Lord" (Cremin, 1970, p. 46).

The cultivation of Christian piety in Colonial America was focused on the Scripture: learning it, studying it, and hearing it read and preached. The Assembly in Virginia stressed the importance of preaching and in 1661 provided for the revival of the office of lay reader in the congregation, that services might be conducted and children catechized in parishes devoid of pastors. In New England an effort was made to provide two ministers for every congregation, a pastor to provide exhortation and inspiration, and a teacher who preached instructive, informative sermons, explained the Scripture, and catechized the children. The teacher's concern was thus for all of the people and not for children alone. In Virginia the Assembly required that "upon every Sunday the ministers shall half an hour or more before evening prayer examine, catechize, and instruct the youth and ignorant persons" of the parish in accordance with the Prayer Book Catechism, penalties being levied upon those who failed to abide by the rule. In New England it was at first believed that the family had the chief, if not the sole, responsibility for leading its members toward righteousness, but in time, due to apparent laxity on the part of the heads of the households, the task of oversight in spiritual development was assumed by the parish church and principally by the teacher. The Governor and Council of Massachusetts in 1669 asked the clergy "to catechize and instruct all the people (especially youth) under your charge in the orthodox principles of the Christian religion, and that not only in public, but privately from house to house." Such instruction was usually conducted in a routine and barely inspiring fashion, repetition constituting the primary pedagogical technique. But we should not be misled. Catechizing was but a part of the large catechesis involving the formation of Christian character through the development of Christian piety. We should also note that formal catechizing formed a part of the general education provided at the time. The pastors sometimes served as schoolmasters to the children of their congregations, passing beyond catechism and Scripture to instruction in the arts and in ancient languages.

In sum, catechesis involved the nurturing of all citizens in Christian piety, in home, school, church, and in and through all of the communities to which people belonged, in which they located their own identities. But even in New England there were indications that the old assumptions concerning church and commonwealth as an organic whole were eroding away. The Half-Way Covenant is a symbol of the decline of Christian piety. Formerly in New England church membership involved the union of mind and will to which Hooker referred. Now a synod of 1662 declared that the formal rite of baptism alone was "sufficiently constitutive of church membership to allow its recipients to bring their children also within the baptismal covenant, although an experience of regeneration was still required of full communicant members" (Ahlstrom, 1972, p. 159).

The old ways of catechesis, inherited from the sixteenth century and the Middle Ages, persisted into the modern era, but changes were occuring which would radically alter everything related to the initiation and nurturing of people in the church. At the heart of the change there was the gradual desacralization or secularization of the West, a process assessed as disastrous or glorious according to one's predilections and understanding. The geographical expansion of the West contributed to the change, Lacey Baldwin Smith rightly commenting that "within two generations after Columbus, the medieval earth was smashed beyond recognition" (Smith, 1960, p. 234). The Copernican revolution was also far reaching: the earth was displaced by the sun as the center of the universe, heaven was removed to some unknown location, and human certainty concerning ultimate truth was severely challenged. From Copernicus' *De Revolutionibus* (1543), to the condemnation of Galileo by the church in 1633, to Newton's *Principia* (1685), the church was shaken, provoked to irrational reaction, and Christian dogma was brought under direct attack, shifting the basis of reality from revelation to plausibility. In addition, Christianity was seemingly divided with no possibility of reunion.

In England, following the civil war and the bloodless revolution, religious pluralism was officially acknowledged, although the Church of England remained the state church. Where there had been but one profession of the Christian faith and one gathering of Christians in each locality, there were now numerous bodies competing with one another and displaying to the sceptical world their various disagreements. In an effort to maintain a viable Christian faith under the circumstances, there were those intellectuals who sought to isolate the few essential tenets of Christianity and of religion in general from the host of dogmas and superstitions. It seemed possible to reduce the creed to a simple assertion of God as Creator assuring to believers immortality. In the process a religiously neutral civilization came into being. John Donne, the poet Dean of St. Paul's Cathedral, London, lamented:

> . . . new Philosophy calls all in doubt,
> The Element of fire is quite put out;
> The Sun is lost, and th'earth, and no mans wit
> Can well direct him where to look for it.
> When in the Planets, and the Firmament
> They seeke so many new; then see that this
> Is crumbled out againe to his Atomies.
> 'Tis all in peeces, all cohaerence gone;
> All just supply, and all Relation:
> Princes, Subject, Father, Sonne, are things forgot,
> For every man alone thinkes he hath got
> To be a Phoenix and that there can bee
> None of that kinde of which he is, but hee
>
> (*First Anniversary*, 11. 205-218).

The development of such a situation, in which all that was dependable and trustworthy seemed to be crumbling and destroyed, involved the dissolution of the ties binding church and state in an organic union. The appearance of religious toleration as a state policy in the seventeenth century was one result of the breakdown of religious and cultural coherence. The state gradually withdrew from alliance with the church and in the aftermath not only proclaimed toleration but in America asserted the separation of church and state as a positive principle. Christianity was relegated to the private sphere, becoming a matter for personal enrichment but with no direct bearing on the affairs of state. Not that the state was irreligious; Thomas Jefferson believed that there was a universal religion beyond all denominational expressions of it, a common faith such as was witnessed to in the Declaration of Independence and the Constitution of the United States. As a result of this separation of church and state, general education, formerly the responsibility of churches and churchmen, was taken over by the state. In its just concern for the liberty of its people and the promotion of responsible citizenship, the process was begun in the national period following the Revolutionary War in America which would lead to compulsory public education supported by means of property taxes. How much religious content should be involved in such education has been debated from the beginning until now and may never be settled. But the main point here is that the secularization of the West challenged the authority and universality of Christianity, promoted the erroneous belief that Christian piety concerned only an isolated portion of life, and made it more and more imperative for the local churches and other ecclesiastical societies to provide catechesis in whatever remnants of time the faithful could devote to pious exercises, principally on Sundays.

There were, however, those who observed the birth of the modern era without descending into despair, agnosticism, or atheism. Writing of Elizabeth Drury, John Donne said:

> Shee, shee is dead, shee's dead: when thou knowest this
> Thou knowest how poore a trifling thing man is
> And learn'st thus much by our Anatomie,
> The heart being perish'd no part can be free.
> And thou, except thou feed (not banquet) on
> The supernatural food, Religion,
> Thy better Growth growes withered, and scant;
> Be more than man, or Thou'rt lesse than an Ant
> *(First Anniversary*, 11. 183-190).

In the face of growing secularism, the erosion of belief, and the distortion or dissipation of Christian piety, there were various reactions, some defensive, some aggressive, all determined to do battle with the evil forces of atheistic rationalism and blatant immorality. In England the Evangelical revival began somewhere around 1714. There were evidences of spiritual revival in Wales and in other localities of Great Britain. This revival spread, eventually counting John Wesley and George Whitfield as its most prominent leaders. By means of ardent, itinerant preaching directed more to the heart than to the mind, the English Evangelicals sought for conversion, involving conviction of sin, sudden awareness of divine mercy, and a subsequent, dramatic, and continually expanding alteration in lifestyle.

Among Anglican Evangelicals, such as Charles Simeon of Trinity Church, Cambridge, the revival involved taking the Prayer Book and its sacraments seriously. Baptism, confirmation, and first communion were all too often performed with minimal concern for their meaning and the demands that they made. Simeon reminded his congregation and others of the solemnity with which they were dedicated to God through baptism and the seriousness with which sponsors are made to pledge that the person baptized shall be brought up "in the true faith and fear of God" with the expectation that there shall be a "progressive, total, and permanent renovation of our souls." He then says:

> No sooner are we capable of receiving instruction, than she [the church] provides for us, and expressly requires that we be well instructed in, a Catechism, so short that it burthens the memory of none, and so comprehensive that it contains all that is necessary for our information at that early period of our life. When once we are taught by that to know the nature and extent of our baptismal vows, the Church calls upon us to renew in our own person the vows that were formerly made for us in our name; and, in a service specially prepared for that purpose, leads us to consecrate ourselves to God; thus endeavouring to *confirm* us in our holy resolutions, and to establish us in the faith of Christ (Simeon, 1813, p. 81).

There was a certain tension among Anglican Evangelicals between those who followed Simeon in promoting "progressive renovation" and those who sought for a dramatic conversion. But even the latter were forced to admit that although they placed priority on a singular, dramatic conversion experience, a gradual turning away from sin towards God with evidence of regeneration was equally valid.

William Wilberforce, the great lay Evangelical and Parliamentarian, wrote to his son Samuel, later the bishop of Oxford, on his ninth birthday, telling the boy, who had been baptized, how much he hoped that he would "see decisive marks of your having begun to undergo the great change." Those marks would indicate the occurrence of the hoped-for conversion, although under the circumstances there might not be any singular, dramatic conversion experience to relate. Whether sudden or gradual and progressive, conversion was the goal.

Preparation for conversion involved exposure to biblical preaching, to the examples of those who had been converted, and to the Bible directly through the study of it in a systematic fashion. In some ways just as important for such preparation, and certainly important for growth in regeneration, was the discipline of self examination. To promote such discipline many Evangelicals kept diaries in which they daily recorded their sins of omission and commission with reference to the interior state of the soul and to the daily performance of Christian duties. Henry Thornton, the economist and philanthropist identified with the Evangelicals of the Clapham Sect, wrote on one occasion, accusing himself:

"First I lie idly in bed often and generally longer than I need. 2. I am not steady and punctual enough in reading the Scriptures. 3. In my prayers I am idle. 4. In my secret thoughts and imaginations I am far from having learnt self-denial. 5. I am not self-denying in my business" (Bradley, 1976, p. 23).

Such discipline was necessary if one was to conquer the secular, immoral world and not be conquered by it. And thus, while such a staunch Anglican Evangelical as Charles Simeon recognized the importance of corporate worship, the emphasis among Evangelicals in general fell upon individual conversion and the performance of recognizable fruits of such conversion. Those fruits would include promotion of Christian family life, devotion to the affairs of the congregation, and the pursuit of those not yet converted, the heathen in foreign lands, the dissolute rich at home, and the immoral, ignorant poor. Whether conversion was sudden and dramatic or gradual, it was expected that one could know who was converted and who not by means of their actions. As with the Puritans and others like them in the seventeenth and eighteenth centuries, the Evangelicals cultivated Christian piety. As Hannah More put it in her *Estate of the Religion of the Fashionable World*: "Piety is not only necessary as a means, but is itself a most important end. It is not only the best principle of moral conduct, but is an indispensable and absolute duty in itself" (More, 1809, pp. 262-63).

Among Evangelicals catechesis was first of all a family matter. Family prayers were the rule. Henry Thornton provided a book of *Family Prayers*, first published in 1834, followed by thirty-one editions in two years. In the Hey family the head of the household began morning devotions by reading a section from Doddridge's *Family Expositor*. The family then sang a psalm or hymn. Mr. Hey prayed, sometimes in his own words, sometimes from a book such as Thornton's. In the evening the family gathered again for the reading of a psalm or a portion of the Old Testament, ending with prayers and a song. Occasionally as he read, Mr. Hey commented on what he read, delivering a kind of homily. At church, in addition to the regular services with preaching, there would be prayer groups and Bible study. All was designed to bring about conversion and the cultivation of the piety of the Real Christian, the Christian who pursued the Christian gospel with the utmost seriousness in every aspect of daily life.

The Evangelicals, doing battle with the evil world, were concerned for others, outside the boundaries of family life. It was in 1789 that Wilberforce visited Hannah More at her home in Cowslip Green and observing the depressed state of the poor living nearby urged her to action. She then started a school which at first met only on Sundays to study the Prayer Book catechism and to read the New Testament. Soon the school was meeting daily, with children learning to sew and knit and spin as well as receiving basic instruction in Christian belief. For twenty years Hannah More went about founding schools and caring for them by means of regular visitations. What she did was not unrelated to the Sunday School movement begun in 1780 by Robert Raikes, leading to the founding of the Sunday School Society in 1785. By 1788 there were 333 schools with 21,000 students affiliated with the society. By the next year there were 590 schools with 39,298 students. From the beginning such schools were created by Raikes in order that poor, unruly children might be taught to read and learn the church catechism. As with Hannah More's schools, these schools combined attention to the rudiments of learning in general with instruction in the Christian faith. Sarah Trimmer was the theorist and publicist of the Sunday School movement. In 1787 she published *The Oeconomy of Charity*, a book designed to explain the movement and induce women to teach in the schools. In it she makes it clear that the Sunday Schools were aimed at a reformation of manners, the uniting of divided countrymen, the training of servants, laborers, and mechanics "to religion and virtue" which would lead inevitably to there being fewer highwaymen and more efficient and dedicated servants (Pickering). The aim thus, in addition to securing the conversion of otherwise lost souls, was to assure the stability of society, especially in the face of Jacobinism and other evils associated with the troubles in France.

In America during the eighteenth and nineteenth centuries (and, indeed, into the last quarter of the twentieth century), the history of Protestantism has been dominated by a series of Evangelical revivals. These revivals, beginning with the first Great Awakening in the eighteenth century and extending through a series of revivals through the next century, began, as did the revivals in Wales and England, in various places, including the

Middle Colonies and New England, as reactions to the spiritual decline and growing immorality. There was a firm conviction that, unless the tide were turned back, utter ruin awaited the colonies. The revivals aimed at the conversion of sinners and the development of Christian piety. Many, such as Gilbert Tennant, were inclined toward extreme emotionalism and even fanaticism. Others, such as Jonathan Edwards, were learned clerics. Edwards, on the basis of his understanding of Lockian psychology, preached to the mind as well as to the heart, but with a vital understanding of the importance of the affections in religious development. Revivalism in America encompassed a wide variety of experiences, from sedate preaching in sedate churches on the Eastern seaboard to the highly-charged camp meetings of the burnt-over districts on the American frontier.

Catechesis on the American frontier had less to do with learning than with emotion and with the cultivation of that atmosphere of doom leading to conversion, but there was learning. One of the results of the second Great Awakening at the beginning of the nineteenth century was the founding of numerous voluntary societies or associations. There had been such societies in the past, including Anglican ones such as the Society for Promoting Christian Knowledge for educational purposes and the Society for the Propagation of the Gospel for missions, but now a flood of societies emerged, benevolent and philanthropic, including ones dedicated to Christian education. In some ways these societies, many non-denominational, engaged in out of the zeal overflowing from conversion experiences, were as important as the churches for the dedicated members.

In 1791, under the leadership of William White, the first bishop of Pennsylvania, the First Day or Sunday School Society was founded at Philadelphia to educate "the rising generation" in reading and writing, using as textbooks the Bible and other religious and moral books. The movement grew and, as it did, emphasis fell more and more on religious matters to the eventual exclusion of general education. In 1824 the American Sunday School Union was organized and two years later the General Protestant Episcopal Sunday School Union came into being to promote the establishment of Sunday Schools throughout the church. According to the recommended scheme,

> children met at eight o'clock on Sunday mornings, and again at half-past one in the afternoon. After the morning opening exercises,

which lasted fifteen minutes, there were six five-minute periods of reciting Catechism and prayer in unison, and four lesson periods of fifteen minutes each. The last quarter of an hour, until 10 o'clock, was used for the closing exercises, during which a missionary box was passed. The afternoon session was fifteen minutes shorter; its activities were much like those of the morning, even to the passing of the missionary box again (Brewer, 1924, pp. 152-53).

The Sunday School movement proceeded in time to spread through the entire land, such schools becoming a familiar American institution, an important instrument for reaching out to new members, and a means of cultivating Christian piety. In some places Sunday Schools and Bible Classes overshadowed the accustomed weekly worship of the congregation. This was so in part because they provided much desired fellowship as well as instruction and allowed for greater participation by individuals than did the formal worship services of the church.

During the urban revivals of 1857-58 the Sunday School movement experienced a major spurt of new growth. After the Civil War, under the influence of Dwight L. Moody, B. F. Jacobs, a wealthy Chicagoan, reinvigorated the Sunday School Union, bringing into being a new lesson plan, with the same lesson graded for different ages, taught each Sunday in all of the churches that adopted it. Interdenominational, mirroring the tone and temper of American Protestantism and the values of middle class America, the Sunday Schools of the later nineteenth century exercised very great influence in the development of a knowledgeable, pious laity prepared to do good works for the sake of mankind.

The Sunday Schools were not without their critics. Some during the nineteenth century found them inadequate and preferred to emphasize either education in the home or the establishment of parochial schools and colleges. During the latter part of the century private boarding schools such as St. Marks and Groton were founded, influenced by Thomas Arnold's Rugby, imparting "muscular Christianity" to a privileged few. The General Convention of the Episcopal Church listened to the reports of its Committee on Christian Education every three years and in 1880 proclaimed that the church "must surround and guard her children in all their training with the instruction and influence of religion." Clearly, the Sunday Schools were not capable of performing such a task. It was asserted at the same time that the church must protect its children from the evils of secular education, the implication being that whatever the church might do on Sunday was negated during the week.

In 1865 the Committee on Christian Education of the Episcopal Church deplored the lack of trained teachers and added the suggestion that Protestant clergy should arrange with school authorities for the release of children for one or two hours a week to receive Christian education from their pastors. In 1884 the American Church Sunday School Institute was formed to inspire a higher quality of education in Sunday Schools and published *The American Church Sunday School Magazine* to further its cause. Most of the efforts to improve the quality of catechetical instruction were local, however. In 1898 Bishop Henry C. Potter of New York appointed a diocesan Sunday School Commission which insisted that Sunday Schools are primarily schools. "To train teachers was the commission's first and most valuable undertaking. Courses of lectures for them were offered not only in such subjects as the Bible and the Prayer Book, but also in child study and pedagogy. In the course of the next few years, by means of extension courses in various churches, as many as three hundred teachers were equipped with new ideals and new methods. A standard curriculum was composed and more than twenty manuals were prepared to implement it" (Addison, 1951, p. 220). Such planning and training was undertaken in various churches in different parts of the country. The age of the modern, institutional Sunday School was beginning.

With this development we arrive at evidence of important change. The aim of church catechesis was no longer dominated by the Evangelical concern for conversion. Now the emphasis fell on nurture. The beginnings of what might be called the second strand of development in religious education involved, first of all, the Romantic Movement on the continent of Europe and in England. Jean Jacques Rousseau was the father of the movement. His views of humanity and of the world were positive and optimistic. Education he regarded in terms of "natural" development. Standing in stark contrast to the views of the Evangelicals, Rousseau's disciple Johann Heinrich Pestalozzi taught that "when the child is still young, nature asks us to continue consciously that which so far it has done instinctively." Pestalozzi recognized the vital psychological relation between religion and education: "The unifying vitality of the human race is impossible without a common spirit which motivates us from within and binds the various forces in our nature one to another" (Ulich, 1968, pp. 231-32). Friedrich Schleiermacher, the theologian, emphasized that religion is inherent in all worthwhile human activities. Religion is a peculiar matter, but it is at the same time a reflection upon the whole of which we are a part.

> In order that you may understand what I mean by this unity and difference of religion, science, and art, we shall endeavor to descend into the inmost sanctuary of life. There, perhaps, we may find ourselves agreed. There alone you discover the original relation of intuition and feeling from which alone this identity and difference is to be understood (*Ibid.*, p. 238).

The teachings of the Romantics influenced the development of Anglo-Catholicism, liberalism, and the Broad Church Movement in England. Anglo-Catholicism, which developed out of the Oxford Movement of Pusey, Newman, and Keble, placed renewed emphasis on the importance of the church, its hierarchy and its sacraments, in the process of catechesis. Participation in the eucharist was infinitely more important than attendance at Sunday School or Bible class. Newman taught at Oxford that the visible church which we know when the faithful gather on Sundays is dependent upon an invisible world. The church is that portion of the invisible world that encroaches upon the world we see. We can go further and assert that the avenue through which the power of the invisible encroaches on the visible world is the sacraments administered by those who stand in apostolic succession. It is enough, therefore, that the Christian of whatever age be present at the holy mysteries, and not just present but in a state of preparation to receive grace. Sunday School classes could aid in that preparation as could sacramental confession. Their understanding of the sacredness of the church and its sacraments led Anglo-Catholics to become serious, morally rigorous, utterly devoted Christians, dead to the world and alive to God. As Pusey put it:

> By Baptism we were made partakers of Christ's Death, that we might henceforth share His Life. We were deadened that we might remain dead, and His imparted Life absorb into Itself our whole selves, and quicken us in every part, that we might live to Him, be dead to all out of Him. Since that hour each act of sin . . . has been a revival of that which was dead, a minishing of our life. Self-indulgence of every sort, following our own wills, love of pre-eminence, of man's praise, covetousness, self-display, self-applause, deadens our inward life (Chadwick, 1967, p. 211).

Pusey and others of the Tractarians were convinced that the Prayer Book taught the doctrine of baptismal regeneration. Those who are baptized are regenerate, receiving nothing less than new life in Christ.

This is it which makes possible a real and not merely an imputed holiness and provides the incentive as well as the means of a progressive sanctification. The baptized has more and more to become what in spiritual *status* he already is, learning to contemplate himself, so Newman explains, not as he is in himself, but as he is 'in the Eternal God'. . . . All the necessary exactness of obedience, the anxiety about failing, the pain of self-denial, the watchfulness and zeal and self-chastisement, do not interfere with this vision of faith. Moreover, the baptized does not stand alone, even though fortified by the resources of grace within. For by the sacrament he becomes a member of the Church, Christ's Body. He is now as by right a citizen of a new realm of faith, hope, and love (Reardon, 1971, p. 119).

Confirmation, involving preparation for making the first communion, was emphasized by the Tractarians, not only because it enhanced the office of bishop for which they were concerned, but because it provided strengthening to the baptized. Robert Isaac Wilberforce, an impressive Tractarian theologian, knew that confirmation was widely regarded as a useful rite affording the candidate the opportunity "at a critical period of life, for confirming the promises of childhood." He did not doubt that such a view had merit, but he knew it to be altogether inadequate. According to what he called the rationalistic view of confirmation, the candidates come to the bishop to confirm themselves, not to be confirmed. He then writes:

What converts this act of natural religion into a Christian rite is, that through the instrumentality of His minister, the new Head of man's race receives his younger members into closer union, and *confirms* those graces which at baptism have already flowed into them from Himself. This is a natural mode of converse with God exalted into a means of supernatural union. Unless this truth be admitted, unless Christ be discerned to be truly present through the agency of His servants, to bless in the laying on of hands, and to communicate through external means that supernatural life, of which His humanity is the source, wherein does this act differ from any other, whereby responsible agents pledge themselves to serve God, and what especial benefit is there in Christian confirmation? (Wilberforce, 1849, pp. 256-257).

Catechesis as preparation for confirmation and first communion must of necessity have been taken quite seriously where Tractarian teaching was dominant. The Prayer Book catechism provided the core of learning and was supplemented by numerous books intended to guide the instructors and pupils. Preparation would be heightened in importance to the degree that the bishop made confirmation into a solemn festival occasion. A. R. Ashwell tells of Samuel Wilberforce, bishop of Oxford, speaking directly, forcefully, and eloquently to the young people in words and with images that they could understand, moving everyone present to tears, calling on everyone present "to kneel in silent intercession for those about to be confirmed for a few moments before the laying on of hands" (Ashwell, 1880, I, 394). Confirmation, and the instruction leading up to it, was indeed vitally important to the Tractarians and to the Anglo-Catholics who came after them.

In some respects, at least in the early stages of development, the Anglo-Catholics seemed to be in tune with the Evangelicals, combining High Church devotion to the church, her ministry and sacraments. They often seemed to be other-worldly, viewing the transcendent, righteous God as being altogether in opposition to this sinful world. This is, however, not altogether true. Partially influenced by sixteenth- and seventeenth-century Anglican theology and partially by continental and English Romanticism, they taught a doctrine of the Incarnation that was world affirming and not world denying. Robert Isaac Wilberforce taught, indeed, that the world is crumbling and cannot of itself be saved, but that is because it has become divorced from the natural law of its being. Its salvation depends upon its acceptance of that law as revealed in Christ. That law is love, not force. Through the Incarnation that law of human being has been operative in humanity, and collective humanity is the perpetual manifestation of the Incarnate Lord.

This understanding was further developed in *Lux Mundi* (1889) where J. K. Illingsworth wrote (p. 176):

The Incarnation opened heaven, for it was the revelation of the Word; but it also re-consecrated earth, for the Word was made Flesh and dwelt among us. And it is impossible to read history without feeling how profoundly the religion of the Incarnation has been a religion of humanity. The human body itself, which heathendom had so degraded that noble minds could only view it as the enemy and prison of the soul, acquired new meaning, exhibited new

graces, shone with a new lustre in the light of the Word made Flesh;
and thence, in widening circles, the family, society, the state itself
felt in their turn the impulse of the Christian spirit with its
"Touches of things common,
Till they rose to touch the spheres."

In some ways akin to the teaching of F. D. Maurice who, although
not a part of the Oxford Movement and its successors, exercised
some influence on later Anglo-Catholicism, this view implied that
the task of catechesis was not that of causing a dramatic conversion
but rather that of assisting the baptized Christian in various ways
to recognize and live by that which has been from the moment of
birth the very law of its being. Nurture, primarily through the
sacraments, was the vital matter.

On the other hand, also influenced by Romanticism, there
were the theological liberals and Broad Churchmen. Thomas
Arnold, headmaster of Rugby School and author of *The Principles
of Church Reform*, believed in the progressive revelation of goodness. "The revelations of God to man," he said, "were gradual
and adapted to his state at the several periods where they were
successively made." With this in mind Arnold combed the Scriptures
for moral lessons and regarded the church as the conscience of the
nation, designed to nurture individuals and communities towards
the fullest realization of goodness.

F. D. Maurice, the inspirer and prophet of the Christian Socialist
Movement in the middle of the nineteenth century, asked the
question, "What is the true nature of humanity?" and answered
by saying that, contrary to the opinions of many, human beings
are not fundamentally evil. Beneath the evil there is righteousness
and such righteousness as every human must in time acknowledge
to be the deepest truth about himself or herself (Maurice, 1853,
pp. 44, 47, 80). He taught, too, that Christ died for everyone and
that becoming a Christian involves acknowledging the truth of
that fact. But to acknowledge this as true also involves commitment
to that which Christ revealed by his death: that the fundamental
law of the universe is sacrifice and that societies were created for
cooperation and not competition. With these convictions, Maurice
was a zealous advocate of education in the broadest sense. "For
education was nothing less than the search after truth, and that
was manifestly of God." Religious education narrowly defined by
Evangelicals and others was but a truncated form of that education
that was needed to cultivate Christian character. Furthermore,

with its negative attitude toward human nature, Evangelicalism neglected the true basis upon which to build a sound Christian education program. It must be recognized that Christ died for all and that all are on their way to redemption. Therefore, it is not separation from the world that matters but involvement in the world wherein Christ lives and works by the Spirit. To Maurice the separation of the sacred from the secular was false; at the Workingmen's College in London the Bible was taught alongside art and literature. In such all-inclusive education persons were nurtured into their full humanity in Christ.

In the context of these views Maurice regarded baptism as the sacrament of constant union. To him the Gospel bids Christians to go forth calling all people, whoever they are, wherever they may be, into the fellowship of God's love. He wrote, commenting on the Prayer Book service,

> We shall invite these men, when they have understood our message, to receive the seal of God's new Covenant, the filial baptism; the witness that they are adopted into the Divine family. We shall bid them claim a portion in it for their children also; for God has not made them fathers and mothers that they should bring up sons for the evil spirit, but for Him. We shall tell them that they are the Sons of God, and therefore members of another, and that they have God's good Spirit to enable them to act out both these characters (Maurice, 1880, p. 230).

This was, to Maurice, the Gospel. Through baptism people are brought into an everlasting communion with God and with one another, the bond of which is the body and blood of Christ, the manifestation of divine love. In this communion they receive nourishment from God, bread and wine, the body and blood of his Son, in "the Sacrament of His continual presence with His universal family" (*Ibid.*, pp. 230-231). As to confirmation, it adds nothing to baptism, which is of itself complete, and yet it is important, for through this rite the person consciously and voluntarily recognizes that Christ died for all and that the confirmand is indeed a member of the church, the body of Christ. The child possesses all spiritual powers necessary to life in Christ; through catechesis and by means of confirmation the child consciously owns these powers as a feeling, thinking person. Maurice believes that there is a time, "a wonderful crisis in education," when the child not only feels and thinks but knows that he or she feels and thinks.

Now the church seizes this time of consciousness—this awful moment, when the mystery of our own personality first begins to scare and confound us—when there is a dim perception of responsibilities, and a struggling of the sinful nature . . . then, I say, does the church meet us with her service of confirmation, tells us that these responsibilities are really ours, that these struggles of the sinful nature must be overcome, and that the duties may be discharged, the victory may be won; because the hope is no dream—because the Spirit who took charge of us in childhood, who has been himself educating us to behold the light which now seems to rush in upon us with such blinding power, will be with us—not as heretofore the watchful nurse over thoughts yet unborn . . . but henceforth as the awful friend, and companion, and fellow-worker, the witness with our spirits that we are the sons of God (quoted in Vidler, 1966, p. 107).

What Maurice was saying may be put in terms of an analogy. A person is born an American citizen and nothing more is necessary to establish that fact. But there comes a time when the state decrees that the person is of sufficient age (a feeling, thinking individual conscious of feeling and thinking) to assume the rights and duties of citizenship. The confirmation rite is simple, involving registration to vote. The first communion comes when the persons cast their first votes in an election. Catechesis concerns bringing the individual to conscious understanding of all that citizenship means and thus in schools across the nation children study the history of the nation, the governmental structures, and all else that seems pertinent to good citizenship.

In America, Horace Bushnell, the "American Schleiermacher" and minister of North Church in Hartford, Connecticut, was influenced by Maurice, as well as by Kant and Emerson, and published his first and most famous book in 1847, *Christian Nurture.* Here he dealt "with the problem of Original Sin, provided an escape from revivalism, and . . . the foundation stone for new approaches to religious education. Accepting the view . . . that 'sin is in the sinning,' he denied that children were lost in sin until visited by the Spirit in conversion; a person need never know a time when he had not been a Christian. Bushnell's intensely organic view of family, church, and nation led him to view nurture as the means of evoking the goodness of human nature" (Ahlstrom, 1972, p. 611). Asking, "What is the true idea of Christian education?" Bushnell answered that it is:

> *That the child is to grow into a Christian and never know himself as being otherwise.* In other words, the aim, the effort, and expectation

should be, not, as is commonly assumed, that the child is to grow up in sin, to be converted after he comes to a mature age, but that he is open to the world as one spiritually renewed, not remembering the time when he went through a technical experience, but seeming rather to have loved what is good from his earliest years (Bushnell, 1916, p. 4).

In the seventh chapter of his book, Bushnell deals in detail with the Christian teaching of children, affirming that it should be focused on Scripture, that it should interpret the truth to the child's feelings by living example, and that it should always take into account the child's capacity for learning at any given stage of development. The teaching he has in mind is that

which feeds growth, not that which stirs a revolution. It is to be nurture, presuming on a grace already and always given, and, for just that reason, jealously careful to raise no thought of some high climax to be passed. For precisely here is the special advantage of a true sacramental nurture in the promise, that it does not put the child on passing a crisis, where he is thrown out of balance not unlikely, and becomes artificially conscious of himself, but it leaves him to be always increasing his faith, and reaching forward, in the simplest and most dutiful manner, to become what God is helping him to be (*Ibid.*, p. 328).

Bushnell tended to emphasize the catechesis of the individual in the context of the family, assisted by the insights of psychology and the general understanding of human nature and human development. Toward the end of the century there was increasing concern with the Christian in the larger dimensions of society. The Social Gospel, relying heavily upon the new science of sociology, revealed the relevance of the teachings of Jesus to the crises of modern society. Various efforts were made to explore the social implications inherent in catechesis. The most important began in 1908. Josiah Strong and Rudolf Binder of the American Institute of Social Service published *The Gospel of the Kingdom*, "a course of study on living social problems in the light of the gospel of Jesus Christ." Largely written by W. D. P. Bliss, these studies, intended for use in Sunday Schools and elsewhere, sought to make known the social implications of the Bible passages provided in the International Sunday School lessons.

A more or less obvious development was followed in these studies, wherein Scripture was quoted and Christian teaching elaborated on the problem at point. Topics were recommended for study and discussion and references to useful sociological materials cited. A notable feature of the lessons was the printing of extensive bibliographies from time to time. The topics for the first year were representative: child labor, women in industry, wealth and capital, the organization of labor, housing, civic corruption, public utilities, socialism, immigration, foreign relations, the race question, and labor conditions. In 1910 the magazine was expanded to include a program of "What to Do" to make the lessons effective in actual reform (Hopkins, 1940, pp. 262-65).

Liberalism and the Social Gospel stood in contrast to the Evangelicalism of the nineteenth century. Where the latter was pessimistic concerning human nature and argued the necessity of radical conversion with subsequent development in Christian piety, the former regarded human nature as essentially good, was optimistic about the possibility of the kingdom of God coming on earth, and focused attention upon the duties of Christians as participants in the wider society in America. The liberal Broad Churchmen and the Social Gospelers were open to the influence of all truth and all science, and absorbed what they could of the insights of modern pedagogues and psychologists. Thus they tended to view catechesis as the nurture of that good already present in everyone, individually and in society.

Bushnell's educational philosophy was not fully appreciated and thus did not exercise very great influence until the end of the nineteenth century. The Social Gospel Sunday School lessons came and went, *The Gospel of the Kingdom* being no longer published after 1916. In spite of the growing knowledge of human psychology, Christian education continued to be ungraded, Bible-centered, and with little or no concern for the learning capacities of the children and adults who were its recipients. This is not to say that nothing was happening. Certainly in churches staffed by persons such as Bushnell, Bliss, and others, much attention was paid to catechesis in terms of nurture rather than conversion.

A major turning point came in 1903 with the founding of the Religious Education Association in this country. The birth of the association marked the beginning of a "new" discipline and a new seriousness concerning the educational responsibilities and opportunities of the churches. The association, and its journal, begun in 1906 and called *Religious Education*, was dominated by liberals, both theologically and socially, who were white, male, Protestant intellectuals. George Albert Coe was its most prominent early theorist. Building on Bushnell's insights, he taught that religion is not something external or extraneous to human nature, but a normal capacity of the human mind. This being so, general education ignores religion to its own, and to its students' detriment. In addition, he adopted the claim of general education, that the child is

> a determining factor in the whole educational scheme. The child is a living organism, a being that grows from within by assimilation, not from without by accretion. Therefore the laws of the child-mind yield laws for educating the child, laws as to method, and laws as to material. Education is not to press the child into any pre-arranged mold, but to bring out his normal powers in their natural order (quoted in Westerhoff, 1978, pp. 15-16).

That which is true for general education is true for religious education. After castigating those teachers who seek to "attach" religion to a barren mind, Coe passionately asserted:

> Religion has come up out of the mind of man as a natural response to universal experience. There is debate as to the content, the utility, and the significance of this response, but none as to its naturalness. The psychology of the day finds that religion is as deeply rooted in *human* nature as any of the higher instincts or impulses that distinguish man from the lower orders of life (*Ibid.*, p. 16).

From the beginning of the twentieth century on, catechesis in America was widely viewed in relation to the conviction that religion belongs to the natural order of human development, that growth in religious awareness and expression is progressive, and that it possesses pragmatic importance for both individual and society. At times it would seem that prominent religious educators were altogether dependent upon the dominant progressive view of education and the social pragmatism of John Dewey. And yet the older Evangelical methods, involving the rote learning of the contents of the catechism, did not altogether disappear. Rather, a more intense competitiveness and a greater tension was building between those whom John Westerhoff has called the immanentists and the transcendentists. To the transcendentists the immanentists seemed to lack sufficient concern for theological content and dogmatic orthodoxy. To the immanentists the transcendentists seemed to be rigid and seriously ignorant of the realities of human nature and in particular of the growth-learning process.

While struggling with one another, both parties suffered reverses. The old Evangelicals lost the battle with biblical criticism and either retrenched, moving backward into biblical and moral fundamentalism, or acknowledged defeat and participated in the emergence of liberal Evangelicalism. The liberals and Social Gospelers were dealt blow after blow as two World Wars and a worldwide economic depression challenged the veracity of their progressive and optimistic views of persons and societies. A new orthodoxy was born claiming the attention of the world and led by men of prominence, such as Karl Barth in Europe and Reinhold Niebuhr in the United States. This neo-orthodoxy tended to be harshly realistic regarding humans and societies—all were deeply flawed by sin and evil. The Christian Gospel stood over against the world in judgment, engaged in a dialectical struggle characterized by perpetual tension. There was no possibility of resolution this side of the eschaton. And yet, having said this, it must also be said that the neo-orthodox viewed the Gospel as the hope of the world, its only hope. This Gospel must be preached and Christians, marred as they are and will be, must seek to live hopefully in the midst of the tension, seeking to realize justice with humility.

The implications of neo-orthodoxy for catechesis were persuasively outlined by Randolph Crump Miller of Yale in 1953. He began with criticism of those who preceded him.

> Progressive education began its influential career among the leaders of secular education after the turn of the twentieth century, and Church educators followed the lead of John Dewey and his cohorts. Mixed with sound educational theory was a secular metaphysics or a simple naturalism among the secularists, and a type of liberal Christianity among the Church leaders, which lacked much of the profundity and depth of biblical Christianity. These leaders knew their educational theory, and they made use of all the findings of science in biblical study and theology as well as in educational processes, but their system crashed against the rocks of resurgent orthodoxy (*Ibid.*, pp. 111-112).

Miller's educational theory was grounded in theology. Psychological and sociological insights concerning human nature and societies occupied important but subservient positions in his theory. With Martin Buber's "I-Thou" relationship in mind, and similar ideas expressed by theologians such as Paul Tillich and psychiatrists such as the colorful Harry Stack Sullivan, Miller treated *relationship* as the key concept, a concept which he finds deeply rooted in Scripture. Thus he wrote: "Christian nurture takes place when the believer trusts in God and in turn God's gracious favor comes to him, because that grace was there all the time awaiting the act of faith. Therefore, the application of theology to education leads to a dynamic personal relationship of faith and grace, and the ideas of theology arising from the relationship of men to God are the guides to a greater and deeper experience of God" (*Ibid.*, p. 114).

The *relevance* of this theology is apparent for there are redemptive experiences occurring all around us every day. Miller would have the child, or any catechumen, encounter theology experientially, identifying redemption in the rhythm between rejection and acceptance in the home and elsewhere. The task of the teacher is to assist the learner in experiencing theological truth as relevant. This is a far different matter from the mere memorization of a creed. Thus it would seem that over against simplistic and naive liberals, Miller emphasized biblical theology. Over against rigid and unimaginative Evangelicals, he emphasized the experiential dimensions of learning, illuminated by psychology and sociology. The theology to which Miller refers is finally that of the creed, the Lord's Prayer, and the Ten Commandments—in effect the inherited catechism—with a modern thrust:

> Theology begins with the assertion that every man is the creature of God and becomes a child of God through Baptism (or its equivalent experience in communions without infant Baptism), and then grows in grace in the life and fellowship of the Church. It says that man's destiny is to live in harmony with God and that after death there will be resurrection. But man is also a sinner. He is so disobedient, so selfish, so profoundly traitorous to the nature which God implanted, that he crucifies the best that God can do in sending his own Son. Thus man is capable of crucifying the best man that God has made, and at the same time he is capable of being the Christ. One historic incident reveals to the full the glory and misery of man.
>
> But Christian theology never stops with analysis. It turns to the cure immediately. The *reconciliation* which comes through Christ is the central issue. God has acted so that man will be saved if he turns in faith to the Father. It is the relationship of faith and grace which is the heart of Christian nurture (*Ibid.*, pp. 115-16).

In churches where this understanding of catechesis is dominant, there may still be requirements which call for little more than formal observances, but the heart of the matter, the chief means by which a person is brought into the company of the faithful, is in understanding and appropriating experientially the Gospel of reconciliation as preserved in formal creeds and in such summaries as that provided by Miller. And it is this theological viewpoint which neo-orthodoxy insists must prevail over modern child psychology and liberal social and theological views, no matter how much it may benefit from them.

Following the second World War various churches strove to create new educational programs. Among the most important were those of the Presbyterians (U.S.A.), the United Church of Canada, and the Episcopal Church in the United States. All were influenced by the new insights derived from the neo-orthodox critiques of Evangelicalism and liberalism. The Episcopal Church provides a striking example. Sunday School enrollment in this church had been gradually and inexorably declining. "In 1901 the Church had 750,000 communicants, and a Sunday School enrollment of 440,000; in 1941, while the number of communicants had jumped to 1,500,000, only 470,000 pupils were in Sunday School" (DeMille, 1955, p. 125). The situation was considered to be grave and was at least partially the result of a mixture of uninspired lesson plans and lassitude on the part of clergy and lay leaders. In 1947 Presiding Bishop Henry Knox Sherrill appointed as director of the Department of Christian Education of the Episcopal Church's National Council, John Heuss, a vigorous administrator who proceeded to convince the church of the importance of education. Heuss persuaded the church on the national level to increase its allotment for Christian education from $50,000 in 1946 to over $300,000 a year by 1949.

As consultants Heuss called on Theodore Wedel, theologian and Warden of the College of Preachers, Ruel Howe of Virginia Seminary, David Hunter, and Dora Chaplin. Professor Howe developed a theological framework in his book *Man's Need and God's Answer*, a work which reflected the influence of Barth, Tillich, Niebuhr, Buber, and the New Testament theologian A. T. Mollegen. With a broad theological base provided, Heuss and the rest insisted that Christian education is not simply a matter of setting up and running Sunday Schools. It is, rather, the sum and total of all redemptive activity in which Christians are engaged, in the family, in the parish, and in the secular society. This activity, they concluded, is fundamentally theological and liturgical. Howe conducted his own teaching in terms of the sacraments of

Baptism and Holy Communion, seeking to identify the redemptive activity mediated by these sacraments in ordinary life.

Furthermore, as the first step towards the achievement of a more theological and relevant education, a series of books entitled "The Church's Teaching" was published. They summarized the church's understanding of Scripture, history, doctrine, worship, ethics and canon law, and provided a common basis of learning for those who would become leaders in the new educational program. The Seabury Series of graded lesson plans was then published. These lesson plans attempted to make use of theological content in creative, relevant ways. To this end experts in group dynamics were employed as the curriculum evolved. Because the students were considered to be central in this curriculum, and were not to be forced or otherwise manipulated into the circle of faith, but rather find their own ways with expert assistance and group support, the series made very heavy demands upon teachers, observers, and students. When the lesson plans failed it seemed that the lack of ability to teach and learn in the way the curriculum demanded was at the heart of the matter.

Whether it succeeded or failed, however, this educational adventure had important ramifications for the church in the 1950s and 60s. From then on it was firmly believed that whatever the shape of catechesis might be in the future, it must be firmly rooted in the Gospel as informed by biblical theology, and not subservient to any secular insights or methodologies. It was equally believed that pedagogical method must be, on the one hand, congruent with the Christian Gospel and, on the other hand, sensitive to the students, taking into consideration who they are and where they are, always encouraging their growth in faith. In fact, as is apparent, the methodology itself is rooted in and informed by the Christian Gospel which commands respect for all people.

Then too, the experiments of the 1950s and 60s were related to other events of great importance: parish life conferences for renewal, liturgical reform, reconsideration of the family as an institution in modern life, and much else. Indeed, one of the major insights of this era has been to understand that catechesis involves the whole life of the Christian community into which people are initiated and in relation to which they live and grow in faith.

A vital part of the modern adjustment concerns rethinking the process of initiation. Questions have arisen concerning infant baptism, the place and the meaning of confirmation, and the issue of first communion as tied to confirmation. In a society dominated by religious pluralism and a growing indifference towards religion, infant baptism seemingly cannot help but add to the number of nominal Christians. Some propose a rite similar to the Anabaptist service for the dedication of infants while baptism is postponsed until adulthood. Others have defended infant baptism as signifying God's love working in the life of the child, hopefully through parents who provide the necessary and gracious nurturing. Through those around him the child will know God before being able to name God. And there is the Lutheran who argues: "Since infant baptism inevitably ties the church more closely to the culture, while adult baptism establishes a break with the culture, the Church should baptize infants when it is attempting to penetrate a culture in the post-missionary situation, and become more reluctant to do so when it is attempting to re-establish its transcendence of culture after capitulating to it" (Stevick, 1973, p. 45).

Modern theologians and liturgiologists have argued against confirmation as known in Anglican tradition and elsewhere on the basis of their objection to it as a separate rite. They contend that what we know as confirmation is properly speaking the post-baptismal blessing inseparable from baptism. It was separated during the Middle Ages and viewed as a second stage in the initiatory process and subsequently has been viewed by various persons either as a separate although related sacrament or as a supplementary rite not properly named a sacrament. Among Anglicans Dom Gregory Dix argued in 1946 that baptism in water and baptism with the Spirit are distinct and separate parts of the total initiatory process. Baptism is a rite of cleansing, regeneration, and participation in Christ, while confirmation with unction by a bishop is equated with the 'seal' of the Spirit. Both are necessary but it must be noted that the latter must follow the former or else the baptism by water is of no effect (Dix, 1946, pp. 36-42; Cully, 1962, pp. 76-77). Another view regards confirmation as the rite ratifying baptism. As G. W. H. Lampe has put the case:

> Confirmation must . . . be what its name signified. It is a ratification of Baptism, just as Holy Communion is a maintenance and continual renewal, in another mode, of the baptismal gift of union with Christ. As *confirmation* it is related historically to the development of infant baptism as the universal rule, being regarded in the medieval Church as the sacramental bestowal of grace, that is, gifts of the Spirit or the presence of the Spirit in a special mode, for the equipping

of the already enlisted Christian soldier with the weapons of his warfare, and by the Reformers as the Godward ratification of baptismal vows after a course of Christian education, to which there was a divine counterpart in the manward ratification of baptismal grace (Cully, 1962, p. 81).

Daniel Stevick in the Episcopal Church has pointed to historical diversity and theological confusion through the ages and at the present time concerning confirmation. Most disturbing, in a sense, is the supposition that a person is confirmed at a certain age, supposedly when entering into adulthood. Endless arguments have taken place concerning the proper age in contemporary society. Stevick comments: "In the conditions of modern society, no single point can represent the meaning of growing into adulthood. Growth is a process—long and complex. Confirmation, insofar as it is part of Christian initiation, in an unrepeatable event." And he asks whether these two things are compatible. The answer must be negative. Stevick then asks: "Might not the dynamics of coming-of-age be met better by a flexible response— a rite corresponding with moments of need or recognition and repeated as such moments recur? And most important of all, if the spoken ratification of baptismal vows is an important action of a person of faith, why must that action be associated normally with childhood? We never stop in our encounter with developmental stages and their tasks. We make a lifelong response to the baptismal reality. The privilege of bearing witness to that response ought not to end as though it were a childish thing to be put away" (Stevick, 1973, pp. 68-70). Answers to such questions suggest that baptism should be regarded as complete in itself, with water and the Spirit, and that the old rite of confirmation should be replaced with a service or form for the affirmation of baptismal vows to be used when needed. There have been objections made to this line of thought, especially by those who see the bishop being denied an office which has come to be viewed as peculiarly episcopal.

There has also been a movement to separate confirmation from admission to communion, or, having combined baptism with confirmation (the post-baptismal blessing), to admit infants to communion immediately, thus demonstrating the intimate connection between the two dominical sacraments. The arguments for infant communion are various but Daniel Stevick touches upon some of the chief issues when he states:

It is true that a baptized person who is not yet admitted to Communion is a member of the Body of Christ and is not cut off from the Holy Spirit or the redemptive life of the Church. But the question seems now to be: why, if Baptism is full Christian initiation, does it not admit one into the full sacramental practice of the Christian life? If the Eucharist is a meal of a caring, supporting community—a meal which speaks of Jesus sharing himself in the life of his people—its reality can impart itself to a child before he can think out its meaning or reduce it to words. When he does begin to think, his experience will have given him something to think about (Stevick, 1973, p. 76).

Philip Edgcumbe Hughes is especially concerned with the implications involved in the latter part of Stevick's statement, although he is not directly addressing that particular statement. Thus Hughes writes that since Christian faith is verbal, being response to the Word, it is rational, God's Word addressing humans as rational beings. Remove the word from the sacrament and we are left with a bare element. This statement includes both Holy Communion and Baptism. Hughes concludes:

The child, as he grows and matures, must be instructed in *the meaning* of his baptism as a sacrament *of the Gospel*, which demands the response of his trust and commitment. If the child is denied this instruction and this challenge, then he is as one who has not been baptized, because in his experience the word has not been added to the element (Hughes, 1973, p. 43).

There is no unanimity on these matters, but rather diversity and liturgical variety in both structure and practice. Close to the heart of all of these discussions, however, there is the mutual concern for catechesis, such catechesis as extends through all of Christian life.

It should now be clear that in the course of historical development during the nineteenth and twentieth centuries, catechesis involved much, much more than Sunday Schools or Christian education narrowly defined. Catechesis involves the whole of Christian life in the localities where Christians live together under God's judgment as recipients of God's grace in the midst of a world in constant danger of self-destruction. Viewing thus, then, what do we see? Ideally, we find people, young and old, growing in fellowship with God and with one another. This growth involves much, including a deepening acquaintance with God's Word in Scripture, in sacraments, and in the ordinary occasions of daily life. Such acquaintance is not confined to abstract intellectual learning, but involves decision-making in the midst of the ambiguities and tensions of this modern world. Because we are who we are, redeemed sinners, growth in faith involves the never-ending contrapuntal rhythm of contrition and thanksgiving, whereby we become more and more available to the Other and to others through whom forgiveness and strength for living in this age come. And, imperfect as it is, the community of Christians called the church is the classroom in which we learn, learning to live with God through Christ and Christ's living body. Here in the church we learn to live together in ways which are redemptive for us as individuals and for the wider world. Christians can and do become, as they grow in grace together, examples, teachers, leaders, role models for all who struggle for meaning in this nuclear age of shrinking resources, over-population, cut-throat competition, wars, and all the rest.

Finally, in reviewing what has gone before in the modern era, we may rightly perceive that catechesis involves a tension between transcendence and immanence, conversion and nurture, theology and the social sciences, the individual and the group, and similar polar realities. Catechesis is thus dynamic and not static. There is no one way, but there are ways better than others in widely differing circumstances. The important thing to remember, so it seems to me, is that attention must always be given to God's judgment and grace and to human capacities and responsibilities in relation to judgment and grace.

BIBLIOGRAPHY

Addison, James Thayer, *The Episcopal Church in the United States, 1789-1931*. New York: Charles Scribner's Sons, 1951.

Ahlstrom, Sidney, *A Religious History of the American People*. New Haven: Yale University Press, 1972.

Anglicanism: The Thought and Practice of the Church of England, Illustrated from the Religious Literature of the Seventeenth Century. Compiled and edited by Paul Elmer More and Frank Leslie Cross. Milwaukee, Wis.: Morehouse Publishing Co., 1935.

Ashwell, A. R., *Life of . . . Samuel Wilberforce*, 3 Vols. London: John Murray, 1880.

Bradley, Ian, *The Call to Seriousness*. London: Jonathan Cape, 1976.

Brewer, C. H., *A History of Religious Education in the Episcopal Church to 1835*. New Haven: Yale University Press, 1924.

Bushnell, Horace, *Christian Nurture*. Introduction by Luther A. Weigle. New Haven: Yale University Press, 1967.

Certaine Sermons appointed by the Queen's Majesty. [The Two Books of Homilies.] Edited by G. E. Corrie. Cambridge: The University Press, 1850.

Chadwick, Owen, ed., *The Mind of the Oxford Movement*. Stanford, California: Stanford University Press, 1967.

Cremin, Lawrence A., *American Education: The Colonial Experience*. New York: Harper and Row, 1970.

Cully, Kendig Brubaker, ed., *Confirmation: History, Doctrine, and Practice*. Greenwich, Conn.: The Seabury Press, 1962.

DeMille, G., *The Episcopal Church Since 1900*. New York: Morehouse-Gorham, 1955.

Dix, Dom Gregory, *The Theology of Confirmation in relation to Baptism*. Westminster: Dacre Press; Adam and Charles Black, 1946.

Hopkins, C. H., *The Rise of the Social Gospel*. New Haven: Yale University Press, 1940.

Hughes, Philip Edgcumbe, *Confirmation in the Church Today*. Grand Rapids, Mich.: William B. Eerdmans Publishing Company, 1973.

Maurice, F. D., *The Prayer-Book considered especially in reference to the Romish System, Nineteen Sermons preached in the Chapel of Lincoln's Inn; and The Lord's Prayer*. London, 1880.

More, Hannah, *Estate of the Religion of the Fashionable World*. London, 1809.

Pickering, Samuel, Jr., "The First Years of the Sunday School Movement in Great Britain," unpublished paper.

Reardon, Bernard M. G., *From Coleridge to Gore: A Century of Religious Thought in Britain*. London: Longmans Group Ltd., 1971.

Simeon, Charles, *The Excellency of the Liturgy*. New York: Eastburn, 1813.

Smith, Lacey Baldwin, *The Elizabethan Epic*. London: Jonathan Cape, 1960.

Stevick, Daniel B., *Holy Baptism together with A Form for the Affirmation of Baptismal Vows with the Laying-On-of-Hands by the Bishop also called Confirmation*. Supplement to Prayer Book Studies 26. Prepared for the Standing Liturgical Commission. New York: Church Hymnal Corporation, 1973.

Ulich, Robert, *A History of Religious Education*. New York: New York University Press, 1968.

Vidler, Alec R., *F. D. Maurice and Company: Nineteenth Century Studies*. [Formerly *Witness to the Light*] London: SCM Press Ltd., 1966.

Westerhoff, John H. III, ed., *Who Are We? The Quest for a Religious Education*. Birmingham, Ala.: Religious Education Press, 1978.

Wilberforce, Robert Isaac, *The Doctrine of the Incarnation of our Lord Jesus Christ in its Relation to Mankind and to the Church*. First American, from the Second London Edition. Philadelphia: H. Hooker, 1849.

The Future

Chapter 10
Framing an Alternative
for the Future of Catechesis

John H. Westerhoff III

The fascinating and complex history of catechesis now greatly illumined remains a somewhat blurred picture. There is both too much to explore and too much we can never recover. The fact that the church has survived twenty centuries and indeed that there are Christians today is a witness to both the effectiveness and the mystery of catechesis. All we can determine for sure is that the church has attempted to be faithful in its pastoral ministry of the Word within various historical-social-cultural contexts. Our task is to be as faithful in the present as our foreparents strove to be in the past.

In the most recent past Protestants developed a Sunday Church School as an act of faithfulness while Roman Catholics depended upon either parochial schools or CCD programs which often resembled Protestant Sunday Schools. Both focused on catechesis in terms of instruction in a school setting. Because the Sunday School is indigenous to the history of the United States, it is important to say a few words about this institution and its future in the church's pastoral ministry of catechesis.

It is difficult to birth an institution. Institutions emerge slowly out of vital movements to give them shape, form, and permanence. Institutions survive because they embody certain enduring characteristics: they are largely independent of the individuals and groups through which and by which they function; they serve to conserve established cultural values and lifestyles; they provide acceptable, familiar means to address basic human needs and concerns; they offer both universality and variability; they become intricately interrelated with other institutions so that a change in one brings about dis-ease and necessitates change in all the others; and they provide people with contexts and roles necessary for meaningful corporate life.

A Sunday School may die or suffer from terminal illness but the Sunday School lives on, conserving the memory and dreams of the people, especially the most conserving ones who tend also to be most loyal institutionally. The Sunday School has met various human needs and concerns, such as nurturing the well being of children, perpetuating the institutional church and its faith, and providing a context for the experience of community in an impersonal world. The Sunday School, while a world-wide phenomenon, has had its unique shape and character in every land, denomination, and congregation; to see one you have not seen them all. The Sunday School has been so much an aspect of national life on this continent that new persons in a community are reluctant to associate with a church which does not have one, and churches which have eliminated them are faced with the difficult task of envisioning, planning, and developing an alternative—which is typically more difficult than maintaining that which is familiar. Further, the Sunday School has provided many lay persons with a place of significant influence and ministry in a clerically-dominated church. Is it any wonder that it survives no matter what its health and vitality or lack thereof? Is it any wonder that attacks on its continuing viability are ineffective?

Of course, the future of even this enduring institution could change radically; institutions do die. For example: if new, more enticing lay ministries were to emerge there would be fewer adults available for and interested in the Sunday School as a place of service; if worship were to change and children made both more welcome and more at home, there would be less need for children to be separated from adults during Sunday morning; if activities at times other than Sundays were to become more vital to family life, there would be a diminished interest in age-graded schooling activities on Sunday; if the public school were to provide quality religious education within its curriculum, there would be less of a demand for Sunday School classes; if churches were to become smaller and more communal, there would be less need for the Sunday School class as a place of caring fellowship.

Institutions can also change radically to meet new situations; institutions are reformable. For example: in an age when there is a growing number of persons who are outside the church and unfamiliar with the gospel, the Sunday School might return to its original missionary purpose. In that regard it is well for us within mainline Protestantism to realize that the Sunday School among Southern Baptists and the Evangelical sects continues to be understood as an agency of evangelism more than nurture.

Further, the Sunday School might become an instrument of the ecumenical movement, existing alongside the boundaries of the parish church and its denominational prejudices. The Sunday School might also be given new birth by the emergence of a new core of committed laypersons who could attract, excite, and lead large numbers of people in the joy of shared teaching and learning. Smaller parishes might, for economic reasons, begin to unify into larger parishes where the Sunday School could provide them with small, intimate communities of nurture and pastoral care. If the culture and its public schools should become increasingly secularized, the church might transform the Sunday School into a Christian day school to preserve the faith and identity of Christians. Or, if our society refuses to meet the needs of families and children, the Sunday School might become transformed into child care centers.

Of course one last option remains. We might simply blunder along providing the Sunday School with a series of drugs, operations, and support systems to keep it alive, though acknowledgedly terminally ill, because we lack the imagination or will to frame an alternative.

All of this is pure conjecture. There are, however, two trends which could influence the future. First, it appears that we are reaching the end of a secular age. A longing and hunger for a new spirituality is emerging. Increasingly, adults are seeking a context for their own growth in faith and a means to share their faith journey with their children and each other. In many congregations reformed Sunday Schools are providing a convenient and useful context for the birth of a new spirituality as they once did during the birth of Methodism.

If this trend continues and becomes dominant, however, it could also result in a renewed pietism (a traditional heresy on this continent) with an excessive concern for feelings and right experience and the neglect of both reason and faithful social, political, economic action. We appear to be emerging from a reign of the secular; a return of the sacred is an event in our time. As always, the issue is how we will respond. My own commitment is to stress the contingent and dependent existence of the universe and ourselves on the will and activity of God; to integrate the eschatological and historical so that there is no disjuncture between our passion for social justice and personal fulfillment; to be open to secular thought and reason so that a return to the sacred does not inevitably mean a return to the inner world of religious experience; to integrate piety (personal religious experience) and politics (prophetic personal and social action); to develop a healthy, intrinsic religion of involvement rather than a sick, extrinsic religion of escape; and to affirm both a material physical reality known indirectly through sense experience and reason and a nonmaterial spiritual reality known directly through participation and encounter. I fear that the Sunday School will have difficulty addressing these commitments; its history is antithetical to such concerns and it is a questionable context for their actualization, no matter what occurs within them.

Second, the liturgical renewal movement is taking hold. With the reform of the Sunday liturgy into a family-oriented, participating, communal celebration of word and sacrament, there is a renewed interest in the relationship of learning and liturgy. In many churches the Sunday School is being transformed into an intergenerational preparation for the Sunday Eucharist based upon an experience of and reflection upon the lectionary texts. If this trend continues and becomes dominant I fear it could result in a community of nurture without a prophetic transforming word or evangelistic outreach. The history of liturgical life in mainline churches is a history dominated by a concern for nurture, interpretation, formation, and growing-up.

Indeed, the emphasis of both worship and church schooling has tended to neglect proclamation, conversions, transformations, and new beginnings. As a result, many mainline churches have a basic understanding of evangelism as institutional incorporation and of ministry as service and care of their members. Faced by our pressing contemporary needs for community, identity, nurture, and institutional growth/survival, the church could easily ignore social, political, economic action in the world, openness, and the need for continuous institutional reform and personal conversions. While a renewed, vibrant community that offers the world a sign of God's kingdom could emerge, it is likely to be insular and to be unable to make an adequate witness on behalf of God's kindgom in the political and economic contexts of society. My own commitment is to the integration of these polarities: conversion-nurture; identity-openness; and piety-politics. Yet typically the church has emphasized one or the other. I fear that the Sunday School, no matter how it understands its purpose functionally, cannot address these necessary polarities adequately.

While these possible trends need to be acknowledged, I suggest that we need to face the fact that we are in the midst of a change period in history as significant as those of the first, fourth, eleventh, and sixteenth centuries. We have come, I contend, to the end of a period in our history when there has been a basic trend in spite of many fluctuations. We are facing a period of radical foundational change. Our recent understandings of the church's educational ministry and the Sunday School itself have been directly related to a historical period that is ending.

Like most folk caught in such a time, it is extremely difficult for us to imagine or plan for the future. It seems as if we have all we can do merely to respond. Neither a doomsday nor a utopian mentality is reasonable in such a day. Daniel Bell once quoted Augustine as saying, "Time is a three-fold present: the present as we experience it, the past as a present memory, and the future as a present expectation." By that criterion, Bell continued, the year 2000 has already arrived, for in the decisions we make now, the future is committed. Well, yes and no. I still contend it is God's future and that God, in the mystery of things, is still acting on behalf of that future. Hope is born at the moment we begin to turn our attention to God's vision and realize that we are not finished but have an infinite number of tasks to be accomplished. In just such a time as this we might best spend our time and energy on renewing the gospel vision of life and our lives, deepening our experience of God, and preparing ourselves to act faithfully in the political, social, economic world; that is, we ought to live under the merciful judgment of God to the end that God's will is done and God's kingdom comes. We could easily deny that calling by worrying too much about the Sunday School and its future.

Personally, in spite of all evidence to the contrary, I do not envision a place of significance for the Sunday School in the future. I believe it is too bound to the past to meet the needs of a new age. I do not believe I am being melodramatic when I say that we are entering a new period in church history. I can, however, hear my conservative friends, especially my historian mentors, saying that I have let my emotions overwhelm my reason. Still I remain committed to framing an alternative and would prefer failing at that effort to succeeding in reforming old, worn ways. I hope that this position does not make me appear either arrogant to those who are struggling for survival in the confusion of the present or judgmental to those who are striving responsibly to reconstruct our present understandings. I am aware that it is likely to frustrate those who desire simple, immediate, practical anwers to the pressing needs of the day. I am also aware that the best way to achieve recognition and popularity is to offer simple, practical, pragmatic resources for the maintenance of familiar understandings and ways. Nevertheless, I contend that the history of catechesis and the call to faithfulness defends and demands an imaginative alternative. To that I turn.

Catechesis, I have suggested, is a pastoral ministry of the Word, the energy or activity of God which continuously converts and nurtures those whom God has chosen to witness to the Gospel of Salvation. The aim of catechesis is to make God's saving activity or liberating/reconciling Word known, living, conscious, and active in the personal and corporate lives of God's baptized people. Catechesis, therefore, is a process, a course to be run (which is the original Latin meaning of *curriculum*).

Insofar as catechesis has functioned in our most recent past within the confines of a schooling-instructional paradigm, it had adopted the language of general education. Within the framework of education and the social sciences there has typically been a division of instruction or curriculum and teaching. Correspondingly, curriculum has been described by either a classist or romanticist metaphor.

The classist metaphor expressed in the philosophy of Locke and Hume and advocated by the behaviorists is *production*. The curriculum is like an assembly line, the teacher a skilled technician, and the student a valuable piece of raw material. The process is one of shaping this valuable raw material into a pre-determined design established in the mind of the designer. In this case the church, its clergy, and adult teachers do something to children and youth to make them into persons of faith and responsible members of the institutional church.

The romanticist metaphor expressed in the philosophy of Kant and Rousseau and advocated by the humanists and developmentalists is *growth*. The curriculum is a greenhouse, the teacher a gardener, the student a seed, and the process is one of caring for each individual seed so that it might grow naturally into a pre-selected plant which is known to the gardener and established by nature. In this case the church, its clergy, and adult teachers do things for children and youth that will help them become what these adults know they can and therefore should become.

While vastly different theoretically, these two metaphors look much alike functionally, for both are concerned with environmental design and technique and, like most traditional understandings of curriculum in modern general education, operate according to four assumed tasks: (1) the formulation of educational objectives, (2) the selection of learning experience which will best aid the achievement of these objectives, (3) the organization of learning experiences to achieve the objectives, and (4) the evaluation of whether or not these educational objectives were reached.

It is this accepted curriculum construct and language and the metaphors upon which it is based that need to be questioned. Regretfully, curricular language is borrowed from the symbol systems of the social sciences, especially psychology. As such it tends to turn mysteries into problems, doubts into errors, the unknowable into the yet to be discovered. It assumes that all human behavior is caused or has purpose and, consequently, that the activity of teaching must be goal-oriented. Now there is just sufficient value and truth in this language to warrant its use, but we must never forget that to be in the presence of another is to be faced with mystery, doubt, and the unknowable. To accept curricular language without question can easily lead to ignoring the fullness of the eternal mysteries present and to opting for the sterility of a predictable future.

Aware of the limits of current curricular thought, Dorothy Soelle, the German theologian, writes, "In a time when learning theories are reduced to a technical model within the framework of which the conditions under which we can learn and experience are researched and put into operation, the idea of a journey becomes a counter model."

Thus, I have chosen as a more adequate metaphor for curriculum the image of pilgrimage used by the spiritual writers throughout the history of the church. In this case, the "curriculum" is like a route over which we travel, the "student" a pilgrim, the "teacher" a pilgrim, companion, and guide who has experience in journeying. The process is a shared journey in community in which all share both experiences and reflections upon them. In this case, the church, its clergy, and people do things with each other in a posture of mutuality. Each pilgrim is affected differently by the pilgrimage since its effect is as much a function of what each pilgrim brings along as it is of the contour of the route. With only a vague longing to go on a pilgrimage, no effort is made to anticipate the exact nature of the effect of the pilgrimage on the pilgrim. An effort is made by the guide though to help the pilgrim plan a route that will be rich, fascinating, and memorable to them both. The pilgrimage we share is to individual and corporate salvation. Begun at our baptism, it is a journey to fulfillment, to sanctification, to the actualization of our new being and the actualization of a new heaven and new earth. It is a journey toward maturity or integration, that is, the establishment existentially of what is essentially true for humanity and society as a result of God's radical action in Jesus Christ. It is more a process of actualizing our true being than a process of becoming something we are not yet. God has acted and made all creation new; the government of God has begun. Baptism announces and celebrates that fact, the gift of faith gives us the "eyes" to perceive this truth symbolically enacted at this ceremony of death and rebirth. When we baptize a child we make clear our conviction that children are to be valued for what they are and not for what they can become. We each have something valuable to contribute as we share in a pilgrimage of co-equal souls.

The biographies of the saints give us some clues as to the nature of the pilgrimage, which appears to express itself stylistically in these ways.

The beginning of the pilgrimage is *affiliative* in character. It is communal (a matter of belonging through participation in a community), fiducial (that is, it focuses on significant relationships and experiences in which the affections, the nonrational, dominate), heteronomous (persons are non-productive and dependent; authority rests in a community with its understandings and ways, stories and visions), conserving (looks to the past, seeking order, stability and a sense of tradition), and concrete (understandings are imaginative and literal).

The next mode in the pilgrimage is *searching* in character. It is ideological (a matter of experimenting with alternatives so as to achieve commitment to "right" beliefs and actions), intellectual (that is, it focuses on foundational issues and reflection in which the intellect, the rational, is dominant), autonomous (persons become productive, independent, critical of their inherited understandings and ways; authority rests in internal conviction and a person's own story and vision), transforming (looks to the future, seeking through critical judgment to reshape and re-tradition), and abstract (understandings are logical and conceptual).

The final mode in the pilgrimage is *integrating* in character. It is mystical (a matter of wholeness and health in which the paradox of polar opposition is integrated and unity of God, self, and community achieved), performative (that is, it unites the intuitive and the intellectual, and the contemplative and the active), theonomous (persons achieve interdependence in a world of mystery and mastery; authority now rests in unity with God's will), unifying (seeks to affirm polar opposites; past and future, dependence and independence, reason and emotion, productivity and nonproductivity), and mythic (understandings are symbolic). Thus, insofar as maturity combines and integrates the styles of life lived by persons at two earlier times in their pilgrimage, everyone can contribute to and aid everyone else in a journey of actualizing our true essential being. Catechesis is the process by which persons are aided in their pilgrimage of being, that is, becoming what they already are by living into their baptism, working out their salvation, achieving perfection or sanctification.

Now this process of catechesis necessarily takes place within an intergenerational community of faith. The community which is at the heart of catechesis is a gift, a miracle, a grace. In that sense, we can only engage in a prayerful yearning which opens us to receive and recognize it when it comes. Just as the experience of God's Holy Spirit at Pentecost transformed a fragmented, diverse mob of people into a community of faith empowered and stimulated to love and serve the Lord, so it comes to those who are open to God's working in their lives and who have the "eyes of faith" to see it coming.

While community is a gift, institution can be created. Often community and institutions are confused. Both are important, for community without organization results in chaos; and organization without community becomes a self-serving bureaucracy. Organization gives enduring shape to the future, and life experienced within an organization provides people with a structure for expressing the consequences of community. Still community is essential for catechesis and when we forget that fact we begin to worry more about institutional survival, maintenance, and incorporation than about faith, revelation, and vocation.

Nevertheless, we can describe the characteristics of a community of faith. Insofar as we strive to realize these characteristics we can both contribute to a healthy institutional church and provide a context for receiving the gift of the Spirit in community.

A community of faith has a strong sense of identity and openness to the world; a common memory or sharing story; a common vision of goals (ends) and means (norms) for which and by which it lives; a common authority or principle for resolving conflicts between the community's understandings and ways and the situations confronting individuals; and shared life together similar to that of a "family." Such life (a) has a common acknowledged purpose, (b) shares interaction and affective bonds between at least three generations, (c) necessitates total involvement of the whole personality and belonging participation of its members, (d) focuses its concerns on every aspect of life: political, social, economic and religious, (e) encourages emotional sharing in depth, (f) regulates behavior implicitly by custom while tolerating diversity of opinion, (g) obligates its members to give whatever is necessary to meet the needs of others, and (h) establishes the worth of persons by their membership in the community rather than by their contribution or performance. Since catechesis takes place best with such a community of faith, it is necessary for us to work for the realization of these characteristics.

Further, our pilgrimage in community requires pilgrims who are guides, more than teachers who are technicians. A catechist needs to be a sacramental person, one who brings God to people. As such the catechist is a person whose identity is hidden in God, a person who prays and meditates day and night on the love and activity of God. Without this single-minded devotion to God the catechist will rarely hear anything worth repeating, will rarely catch a vision of anything worth pointing to, will rarely live a life that can illumine anything of importance. The catechist is a person converted and nurtured within the Christian community who has had experience in listening to the essential word of God as found in Scripture and tradition and in listening to the existential word of God in present experience, who has had experience in discerning and doing the will of God. While a catechist is a unique personality willing to make his or her life and experience available to others as a resource for their pilgrimage, a catechist is not one who has arrived or who has all the answers. The catechist has no difficulty saying I have no solution, but I will not leave you alone in your quest; I am as lost as you are, but together perhaps we can find the way; I do not know, but I will aid you in your search. A catechist is a compassionate person, respectful of others as unique personalities with much to contribute. The catechist can therefore easily affirm others in their search, encourage others in their struggles, without a need to answer their question or solve their problems. A catechist is one who says either: Where do you want to go? Would you like me to join you? You'll have to find your own way, of course; *or* I am going toward _____. Would you like to join me? You'll have to find your own way, of course. A catechist is one who has a perception of others as redeemed persons living in and by grace while being aware of one's own incompleteness and brokenness and yet expecting change and growth in oneself. But most of all a catechist is one who knows that no new insight comes unless it comes from a source that transcends both the pilgrim and the guide, namely God. Therefore the catechist strives to help others to realize that the Lord is always the source of all knowing and the giver of life.

Thus far we have discerned the pilgrimage process of intentional socialization or catechesis in community. We now turn to the two foci of catechesis and their integration. The two foci can best be designated as evangelization and assimilation.

Evangelization refers to encounters through deeds and words which aid conversions or human transformations in the realms of thought, feeling, and behavior. Its concern is new beginnings or births. As such it aims to introduce persons to Christian understandings and ways through experience and to summon persons and the community to Christian understanding and ways through consciousness raising.

Assimilation refers to incorporation through deeds and words which aid nurture or growing up in the realms of thought, feeling, and behavior. Its concern is actualization and maturing. As such it aims to aid persons in the adoption or internalization of Christian understanding and ways through participation in community life and to encourage persons to interpret and apply Christian understandings and ways through reflective action.

While evangelization and assimilation are both essential aspects of intentional socialization or catechesis, their integration is also necessary to aid faith to become living, conscious, and active.

This integrating process has four steps: (1) critical awareness, (2) significant experience, (3) reflection and resolve, (4) assimilation. It is a process that has two manifestations: the first aids personal individual life and the second personal corporate life.

The four steps for personal individual life are as follows: (1) experience of being treated as a person of worth, as a healthy, whole, saved person, (2) an awareness of one's brokenness and incompleteness, (3) reflection on this dissonance, and the act of accepting the grace of health, wholeness, and completion, (4) practice in living with the aid of the community in one's new grace.

The four steps for personal social life are as follows: (1) naming one's present action and understanding the why (the story) of that action and its implications (vision) for the future, (2) becoming aware of the Christian story and vision, (3) engaging in a dialectical hermeneutic between one's own story and vision and the Christian story and vision so as to resolve the dissonance, (4) deciding to act in response to this resolution.

Catechesis must also be concerned with various ways of knowing, modes of thinking, or dimensions of human consciousness. Insofar as catechesis is concerned about faith as perception, revelation as experience, and values as goals and norms for life, it must concern itself with the intuitive, the affective, the responsive dimension of human life.

The intuitive way of knowing, the affective mode of thinking, the responsive dimension of consciousness focuses on experience and non-verbal images. It is the world of chaos (abyss), surrender, mystery, imagination, surprise, and passion nurtured by the arts and expressed through symbols, myths, and rituals. The intellectual way of knowing, the rational mode of thinking, the active dimension of consciousness focuses on reflection and verbal signs. It is the world of order (structure), prediction, logic, analysis, control, and disinterest nurtured by the sciences and expressed through signs, concepts, and reflective actions.

It is important to recognize that the intuitive, affective, responsive mode is typical of children. The intellectual, rational, active mode begins to take shape during adolescence or early adulthood. Obviously, it is the integration of the two that is to be sought. We need to acknowledge, however, that just as most mainline Protestant and Roman Catholic churches have tended to ignore evangelization, they have also emphasized the intellectual and rational to the exclusion of the intuitive and affective. At the same time, conservative Evangelical churches have tended to ignore assimilation and a concern for social justice. They have emphasized the intuitive and affective to the exclusion of the intellectual and rational. Worse, the integration of the two ways of knowing has tended to be ignored by almost everyone.

In the light of this analysis of catechesis we can turn to planning. Typically, planning and designing education in the church has begun with organization—the Sunday School, Vacation Church School, Youth Fellowship, Women's and Men's Fellowships, and so forth—with programs contained in denominational curriculum resources, youth program aids, adult study aids, and with age- and sex-classes or groups arranged by grades in public school or by age for boys and girls, men and women, couples and so forth. Characteristically, if a church of 100 persons has a church school to which 25 come, it will develop an advertising campaign to attract the other 75 persons. A few might be lured into the school, but within a year a significant number of these will drop out again, having discovered what they thought all along—it wasn't for them. Just as foolish are those congregations who eliminate their church school because only a few children attend.

We seem to forget that catechesis is a lifelong process and that any place the church touches the life of a person can be a setting for catechesis. We also seem to forget that in terms of catechesis, quality is more important than quantity. A three-day youth retreat or conference may offer better time for catechesis than one hour each week of the year. Further, significant experiences of catechesis are like a rich dessert, they cannot be a steady diet. We forget that space and rest between such occasions can be valuable and necessary. Similarly, when we place persons in a group and assign them a teacher and the teacher a teaching resource we are establishing a condition in which some persons will not learn and may become discipline problems, and in which some teachers will experience failure and frustration. We seem to forget that if pilgrims choose their guide and together they choose aids to help them on their journey we might eliminate all such problems.

The key to meaningful catechesis is found in a planning process that is different from that used in general education. Planning for catechesis is a matter of intersecting four components. First, we need to consider the historical-social-cultural reality in which our people live. Catechesis cannot be planned in a vacuum. The church is in the world; we need to understand our historical situation, our contemporary society, and the culture of our people. We, individually and corporately, are to be prepared for a vocation which is a call to join God in the transformation of the world into the kingdom of our Lord and Savior Jesus Christ. It is for mission and ministry that we engage in catechesis. Without a critical analysis of our historical-social-cultural condition we cannot plan for a faithful catechesis.

Second, we need to be aware of the human needs of our people, that is, the physical, emotional, mental, and spiritual needs, both those which are general to all people and those which are particular to each person. Third, we need to be concerned about the needs our heritage brings to us. That is, we each need to have our faith enhanced and enlivened, divine revelation made known, and our vocation realized. Another way to say it is that we need to know the story and vision of our people, we need to make our community's story our personal story, and we need to learn to live in word and deed, individually and corporately, that story and for that vision. And last, we need to be aware of the places the church touches the lives of people and the quality of that touching in terms of the other three components. In this regard we need to explore those places of touching or settings which may best contribute to catechesis. For the sake of planning, I have identified three major settings: a liturgical-communal setting, a retreat-devotional setting, and a moral-societal setting.

Planning for catechesis is a process of intersecting the needs of persons and the heritage within a particular historical-social-cultural context and in one or more of the settings mentioned. Those who can best and most naturally contribute to catechesis in these settings need to become catechists, and persons need to choose freely which experiences they need to participate in to aid them in their pilgrimage. Persons should choose experiences and guides rather than be placed in a group by age or sex, assigned a teacher and expected to use a particular curriculum resource. While some groups may be persons of a particular age or sex, none will be restricted.

In the light of this description of the planning process for catechesis we can turn to those settings within a community of faith through which catechesis can best be accomplished. While each setting contributes to every aspect of catechesis, some settings are better than others for aiding particular aspects of our pilgrimage.

The liturgical context best aids us to know the story and vision of the community or to acquire, enhance, and enliven faith; the pastoral setting best aids us to internalize the story and vision of the community or make divine revelation known; and the moral setting best aids us to live the story and vision of the community or realize our vocation.

While each of the settings can contribute to the various dimensions and foci of catechesis and to their integration, particular settings are more appropriate for some. For example the liturgical setting is dominated by the intuitive, affective/responsive dimension of consciousness. The retreat setting is similar, but the moral setting is dominated by the intellectual/rational/active dimension of consciousness and serves best to integrate the evangelization and assimilation foci.

Further, catechesis takes place in two distinct but related ways in each setting. Catechesis serves to prepare persons for meaningful participation in the communal, devotional, or societal setting just as it also is found within the experience itself. For example, as people prepare the celebration of a Saints Day, a Sunday ritual, or baptism, they are engaged in catechesis. They are also engaged in catechesis as they participate in each of these events or experiences. The church needs to be mindful and faithful about all its communal experiences and all its celebrations so that each person's pilgrimage in terms of faith, revelation, and vocation may be meaningful and purposeful.

In order to make clear the possibilities of catechesis in each of these contexts I will share a few concrete examples. These are obviously only for illustration and therefore will be brief and sketchy. None are intended to be copied. Each congregation needs to design its own unique plan for catechesis.

Liturgical: During Lent intergenerational groups prepared dramatizations, dances, songs, and the like for each of the tales in the story of Salvation, including the story of creation, the flood, Abraham's sacrifice of Isaac, Israel's deliverance at the Red Sea, Isaiah's song of salvation, the valley of dry bones, the gathering of God's people, and the birth, passion and death of Jesus. On Holy Saturday, a camp fire was lit on the church lawn and on Easter Eve the congregation gathered to sit as families around the camp fire and to experience the story of Salvation interspaced with psalms, songs, and prayers. Then the paschal candle was kindled from the fire and the congregation processed into the church singing. Pausing at the entrance to celebrate baptism and the renewal of their baptism vows, the congregation then continued into the nave for the announcement of Easter and the celebration of the Eucharist. Both preparation for and participation in this event offered opportunities for catechesis.

Increasingly, congregations are using the hour before the liturgy on Sunday to "study" the lectionary texts and prepare for the liturgy. Others are using the Service of the Word more imaginatively for catechesis. Catechesis for initiation rites and the pastoral offices is growing. The church year, festivals, and saints days provide exciting opportunities for catechesis. Indeed any time the congregation gathers as a family, whether for business or pleasure, there is the possibility of catechesis.

Numerous other examples come to mind. What is important, however, is an awareness of the crucial role that ritual plays in transforming and forming our lives. Learning related to the significant movements in our lives and to the celebrations we hold provide what is perhaps our most significant catechesis.

Retreat: On the first weekend in Lent an intergenerational group went to a retreat house an hour's drive from the church. After they settled in, they divided into fourteen groups, one for each of the stations on the Way of the Cross. Members of each group were to make a symbolic representation of their station, a play to dramatize its scriptural foundation, and to identify some situation in their community where their station was being experienced in the lives of people today (for example, where injustice or suffering could be experienced). The next day they went on a car trip to observe and experience each place in their community where the Way of the Cross was being relived. When they returned, they went on their pilgrimage. At each station they dramatized the biblical account and were taken on a guided meditation about their morning experience and encouraged to pray for discernment. That evening all persons picked the station where they believed God was calling them to act. In these groups they discerned the ministry to which God was calling them. At the Sunday Eucharist they made these commitments to service and action their Lenten offering and spent the rest of the day in prayer and meditation that God might empower them for ministry. Both the presentation and participation in this event offered opportunities for catechesis.

Increasingly, congregations are holding daily morning prayer (with a free nursery) followed by catechesis on spirituality: meditation-contemplation, the praying of the Scriptures, discernment and the examination of consciousness. Noontime lunches, organ concerts, guided meditations, or short three-hour evening retreats on topics such as the Lord's Prayer or marriage provide opportunities for catechesis.

Other examples are legion, but it is important to acknowledge the importance of using the leisure moments in life and retreat environments for catechesis, remembering that people are significantly affected when they are away from familiar settings and engaged in concentrated learning activities.

Moral: Every morning from six to seven a group of farmers met for coffee and conversation before picking up their supplies and heading back to the farm. They began by discussing their present actions, why they acted the way they did, and what the future would look like if they continued in the same course. The picture was bleak. The small family farm was in trouble and their lives of independence threatened. Then they turned to Scripture and explored passages about the lives of Christians, such as Acts 2:42-47 in which they read about how in the early church everyone held everything in common and made a general distribution as the need of each required. They reflected on their lives as Christians and those of the early church. They prayed through the relationship between the gospel and their lives as farmers today. As a result they formed a Christian farmers cooperative. This process involved them in catechesis.

Increasingly, physicians, lawyers, business men and women, community leaders, officers of voluntary associations, parents, teachers, and students are meeting together to reflect on the relationship between their lives and the Gospel. Even church vestry (official board) meetings are being used to explore the church's actions in the community in terms of the Gospel as a means of engaging in catechesis.

The examples can multiply. What is important is to acknowledge that catechesis for individual and corporate daily life in mission and ministry is best conducted in the places where people live and work. Transfer of learning on global issues from study groups in church buildings to daily life issues where people make their decisions is difficult.

But perhaps the major issue of catechesis remains Christian initiation; once again this issue is being addressed anew. New questions are being asked about baptism, first communion, and confirmation. A faithful church needs to address such questions in ever changing and radical ways, for Christians are made and not born. Of course, initiation cannot be separated from other catechetical concerns. Christians are always initiated into a community of faith and within the life of such communities they grow and mature.

Baptism establishes a person as a Christian and incorporates that person into the church. The burden of baptismal work, therefore, is upon the church, the baptizers. That is why arguments over infant versus adult baptism are often misplaced, for they tend to forget that the principle actor in baptism is God, not the recipient, and that God working through the church is the principle means by which a person is enabled to make a free response to God's free gift. It is the depth of faith, the character of revelation, and the quality of vocation held and expressed by the church that is essential for faithful baptisms, for it is a community into which we initiate persons and within which they come to ever-deepening consciousness.

Still, Christian initiation requires a responding person. For this reason the norm for Christian initiation is an adult catechumenate who knows something of the cost of discipleship and is willing to pay the price. Only if we maintain this norm will the church remain faithful in a secular, pluralistic world; only if we maintain this norm will the church be able to defend the baptism of children as a desirable exception for the children of faithful Christian parents within a faithful community.

Concerned that baptism be the focus of Christian initiation and catechesis, the Episcopal Church in the 1979 *Book of Common Prayer* has recommended that Baptism and/or the renewal of baptismal vows take place at the Easter Vigil, Pentecost, All Saint's Day, the feast of Jesus' baptism, or the visitation of the Bishop. The first date helps the community to recall that in baptism we are killed and reborn a new person, the second that at our baptism we receive the gift of the Holy Spirit and are once again united with God's Spirit, the third that we are made perfect—saints—with the potential for wholeness of life, the fourth that we are called to minister in Christ's name so that others might know what is true for them also, and the last that we are now adopted into the family of God, the community of faith, welcome to eat with the family and participate fully in its life, and are called to mission and ministry in the world.

The Episcopal Church has further placed a new emphasis on adult baptism and on the preparation of adults for Holy Baptism in the supplement to the *Book of Common Prayer*, the 1979 *Book of Occasional Services*. In this book the catechumenate, or period of preparation for Christian understandings about God, human relationships, and the meaning of life, is described in detail and marked by three stages.

Stage one is a pre-catechumenal period characterized by inquirer's classes to enable persons to determine that they wish to become Christians. It is described as a time to examine and test persons' motives so that they may freely commit themselves to pursue a disciplined explanation of Christian living.

In stage two, the catechumenate, a person is accompanied by a sponsor—a faithful member of the community. This stage includes regular participation in the liturgical life of the community, the practice of Christian life with special emphasis on Christian service and action, encouragement and instruction in the life of prayer, and basic instruction in the history of salvation as revealed in the Old and New Testaments.

Stage three, the candidacy for baptism, takes place after the community affirms that a person is ready. It continues for a number of weeks before baptism and involves private disciplines of fasting, examination of conscience, and prayer in order that the candidate is spiritually prepared. At the baptism the candidates renounce cosmic, social, and personal evil, turn to Jesus Christ, and place their trust in his grace. Promising to follow and obey Christ, the candidates make their baptismal covenant, which includes an affirmation of faith in God as Creator, Saviour, and Sanctifier, and they promise to participate in the liturgical life of the community, to resist evil, to repent and return to the Lord when they fall into sin, to proclaim the Gospel by word and example, to seek and serve Christ in all others, loving their neighbor as themselves, and to strive for justice and peace among all peoples. The candidates making their vows are accompanied by the other members of the congregation who are renewing theirs.

A fourth period immediately follows baptism. It is a period devoted to informal and formal activities to assist the newly baptized to experience the fullness of the corporate life of the church in the world and to gain a deeper understanding of the meaning of the sacraments.

Thus the church has once again re-affirmed the importance of the catechumenate and of adult baptism and returned to the practices of the early church. At the same time, the church is searching for new, appropriate, and faithful ways to initiate the children of the faithful into the church so that they and the church may make a faithful witness to the Gospel in the world. With that purpose in mind, numerous recommendations have been made. To their number I simply add my own plan for a life-long pilgrimage characterized by seven stages, each with a catechetical and a liturgical component.

1. A Rite at the Time of the Birth or Adoption of a Child

As soon as convenient a new child is to be brought by his or her parents to the church for a rite of thanksgiving. At this time the church appoints Godparents for the child and the parents promise to prepare for their child's baptism. The parents may for personal reasons also choose other Godparents, but to the Godparents appointed by the church falls the responsibility of preparing the parents for their child's baptism. This preparation should include an investigation of the baptismal covenant so that the parents can renew the vows for themselves and make them on behalf of their child; an examination of the parents' spiritual life of prayer in terms of piety and social witness and aid to them in deepening their own spirituality; and an exploration of the care and Christian nurture of children in Christian faith.

2. Holy Baptism and First Communion

It is my contention that children should receive their first communion at their baptism and be encouraged to participate in this Eucharistic meal every Sunday thereafter.

3. Reflection on Communion

On the seventh anniversary of a child's baptism, perhaps during Eastertide, the parents should conduct a series of events for their children on the meaning of communion. During Lent, all the parents who have had children baptized in the same year could prepare for these catechetical events; included might be the following points: the church is a family to which the child belongs (perhaps films of their Baptism and first communion could be shared); signs point to something beyond themselves (banners could be made expressing the children's understanding of communion); love means being accepted for nothing (biblical stories could be dramatized); Jesus Christ is a sign of God's love (hymns and songs could be learned); the Eucharist is a thanksgiving meal (bread could be baked, wine made, and the table set); and, last, when we eat we receive nourishment so we can love others (the children and their parents after each communion could perform an act of Christian service in the community). At a Pentecost party the children could be given a copy of the *Book of Common Prayer* or *Praying With the Family of God*.

4. Life in Christian Community

During the season of Epiphany, between the ages of twelve and thirteen children are gathered together to explore the nature of the church year, the biblical story of salvation, Christian symbols, the liturgy, the lives of the saints (they could also pick a saint they would like to emulate), and the nature of Christian life and service. At this time they also could be prepared to serve as acolytes, ushers, choir members, and so forth, and on the Sunday before Lent receive their saint's medal.

5. A Rite of Reponsibility

Somewhere between the ninth and tenth grades, persons, by their own choice, might begin a period of Lenten preparation for this new and yet to be developed rite of discipleship. It might include the acquisition of skills for critical Bible study and the ability to engage in theological reflection, an exploration of the nature of the church (vision and reality) along with skills for the reform of the church, an exploration of vocation and responsible corporate life and witness in the world, and an exploration of self-identity, sexuality and marriage, spirituality, and the meaning of sin, confession and the rite of reconciliation. On Palm Sunday they and their parents might participate in a rite establishing them as adults in the church and passing on to them the responsibility for their conduct and faith. The gift of a Bible and a biblical commentary might be appropriate.

6. Confirmation

Sometime during adulthood, after twenty-one, a person might choose to prepare for confirmation understood as an "ordination" of the laity to their ministry.

Over a period of at least a year such persons, with the aid of a sponsor, might examine their vocation and discern the ministry or ministries to which God is calling them. They would be aided further in exploring that ministry as a believer in Jesus Christ and a member of his church. At their confirmation they would renew their commitment to God, be strengthened with the Holy Spirit, and empowered for service or ministry in the church and the world.

7. Commitment of Christian Service

At other times during life the church might provide opportunities for persons to reflect on their baptism and confirmation so that they might renew their baptism covenant more faithfully and commit themselves to new or recommit themselves to already established ministries.

Through such a process the church could provide a catechetical and liturgical means for aiding persons in their pilgrimage of faith. Combined with an adult catechumenate and an ongoing program of catechesis, as already described, the church could take seriously its educational ministry and contribute to the creation of a more faithful church.

That brings us to the close of this chapter on the future. The insights discussed resulted from our exploration of catechesis throughout the history of the church. The proposals offered, while not specific, attempt to describe future responses to our present historical context in the light of the church's mission. In every age the issue is the same: how do we maintain a faithful church and prepare it for faithful life in the world. The catechetical task is central to this pastoral ministry. Our day requires radical new means and modes of catechesis if the church is to be reformed for life in-but-not-of the world. We are called in our day to be as faithful as our foreparents. As a small contribution to that ever-present responsibility we have presented an incomplete and vague outline of a vision for catechesis in the next decade. Perhaps it will die in our imaginations or abort if it was ever impregnated. That is not important. Our conviction is that together we need to imagine, experiment, and share alternative understandings and ways even as we maintain and continue adoptions of our known understandings and ways. The future is, as always, with those who do. Our hope is that, if nothing else, this book will have stimulated and aided in this important task.